TM

...FOR DUMMIES™

BESTSELLING BOOK SERIES

References for the Rest of Us!®

Are you intimidated and confused by computers? Do you find that traditional manuals are overloaded with technical details you'll never use? Do your friends and family always call you to fix simple problems on their PCs? Then the For Dummies® computer book series from Wiley Publishing, Inc. is for you.

For Dummies books are written for those frustrated computer users who know they aren't really dumb but find that PC hardware, software, and indeed the unique vocabulary of computing make them feel helpless. For Dummies books use a lighthearted approach, a down-to-earth style, and even cartoons and humorous icons to dispel computer novices' fears and build their confidence. Lighthearted but not lightweight, these books are a perfect survival guide for anyone forced to use a computer.

Already, millions of satisfied readers agree. They have made For Dummies books the #1 introductory level computer book series and have written asking for more. So, if you're looking for the most fun and easy way to learn about computers, look to For Dummies books to give you a helping hand.

Wiley Publishing, Inc.

Deke McClelland and Galen Fott

Wiley Publishing, Inc.

Photoshop® Elements 2 For Dummies®

Published by
Wiley Publishing, Inc.
909 Third Avenue
New York, NY 10022

www.wiley.com

Copyright © 2002 by Wiley Publishing, Inc., Indianapolis, Indiana

Published by Wiley Publishing, Inc., Indianapolis, Indiana

Published simultaneously in Canada

For general information on our other products and services or to obtain technical support, please contact our Customer Care Department within the U.S. at 800-762-2974, outside the U.S. at 317-572-3993, or fax 317-572-4002.

Wiley also publishes its books in a variety of electronic formats. Some content that appears in print may not be available in electronic books.

Library of Congress Control Number: 2002108104

ISBN: 0-7645-1675-2

Manufactured in the United States of America

10 9 8 7 6 5 4 3 2

1B/RZ/QY/QS/IN

Ⓦ Wiley Publishing, Inc. is a trademark of Wiley Publishing, Inc.

About the Authors

Deke McClelland: Pioneering electronic publishing expert Deke is the author of *Photoshop 7 Bible* (John Wiley & Sons, Inc.), which is the best-selling guide of any kind on digital imaging. Having written more than 60 titles in 20 languages with 3 million copies in print, Deke is one of the most award-winning writers in the business, including a total of seven honors from the Computer Press Association. In addition to designing and editing a new visual learning series called *Look & Learn* (John Wiley & Sons, Inc.), Deke hosts the in-depth training videos *Total Photoshop, Total Illustrator,* and *Total GoLive* (all Total Training Inc). He is a contributing editor for *Macworld* and *Photoshop User* magazines, and a member of the PhotoshopWorld Instructor Dream Team.

Galen Fott: Galen is a regular reviewer and writer for *Macworld* magazine, and a contributor to the best-selling *Photoshop 7 Bible*. He created and hosted the tutorial CD *Total Training for Mac OS X,* and co-hosted the DVD series *Total Training for Adobe Premiere 6*. Galen has presented more than two hours of Photoshop training for the Apple Computer Web site, and he has also been a presenter for Adobe Systems. In his theoretical spare time, Galen is involved in a number of other pursuits. As an animator, he has worked for clients such as AT&T and Paramount. As an actor and singer, he has played leading roles in musicals across the country. And as a puppeteer, he has performed with the Jim Henson Company. Those with piqued interest can visit his Web site at www.grundoon.com.

Dedication

To Max, Sam, and Burton: The future of digital imaging is in good (if grubby) hands.

And to Elle and Laura: Whose good hands we're glad to be in.

Author's Acknowledgments

The authors would like to thank Matt Wagner at Waterside Productions, Susan Christophersen, Brian Maffitt, the Corbis Corporation, Barbara Obermeier, Linda Bigbee, and especially Laura Bigbee-Fott for many wonderful photos.

Publisher's Acknowledgments

We're proud of this book; please send us your comments through our online registration form located at www.dummies.com/register/.

Some of the people who helped bring this book to market include the following:

Acquisitions, Editorial, and Media Development

Project Editor: Susan Christophersen

(Previous Edition: Colleen Williams Esterline)

Acquisitions Editor: Bob Woerner

Technical Editor: Allen Wyatt

Editorial Managers: Constance Carlisle, Carol Sheehan

Editorial Assistant: Amanda Foxworth

Production

Project Coordinator: Nancee Reeves

Layout and Graphics: Scott Bristol, Sean Decker, Joyce Haughey, LeAndra Johnson, Stephanie D. Jumper, Jackie Nicholas, Betty Schulte, Jeremey Unger, Erin Zeltner

Proofreaders: TECHBOOKS Production Services, Laura Albert, John Bitter, Andy Hollandbeck, Linda Quigley, Charles Spencer

Indexer: TECHBOOKS Production Services

Publishing and Editorial for Technology Dummies

Richard Swadley, Vice President and Executive Group Publisher

Mary C. Corder, Editorial Director

Andy Cummings, Vice President and Publisher

Publishing for Consumer Dummies

Diane Graves Steele, Vice President and Publisher

Joyce Pepple, Acquisitions Director

Composition Services

Gerry Fahey, Vice President of Production Services

Debbie Stailey, Director of Composition Services

Contents at a Glance

Cartoons at a Glance

By Rich Tennant

"Why don't you try blurring the brimstone and then putting a nice glow effect around the hellfire."

page 353

"THAT'S A LOVELY SCANNED IMAGE OF YOUR SISTER'S PORTRAIT. NOW TAKE IT OFF THE BODY OF THAT PIT VIPER BEFORE SHE COMES IN THE ROOM."

page 9

"I THINK YOU'VE MADE A MISTAKE. WE DO PHOTO RETOUCHING, NOT FAMILY PORTRAI... OOOH, WAIT A MINUTE-I THINK I GET IT!"

page 251

"...and here's me with Cindy Crawford...And this is me with Madonna and Celine Dion..."

page 101

"I'VE GOT SOME IMAGE EDITING SOFTWARE, SO I TOOK THE LIBERTY OF ERASING SOME OF THE SMUDGES THAT KEPT SHOWING UP AROUND THE CLOUDS. NO NEED TO THANK ME."

page 185

Cartoon Information:
Fax: 978-546-7747
E-Mail: richtennant@the5thwave.com
World Wide Web: www.the5thwave.com

Table of Contents

Introduction

· ·

*I*n showbiz terms, the first version of Adobe Photoshop Elements did boffo box office. What's not to love? Adobe took Photoshop — that venerated classic — stripped a few high-end features from it, stuck on some friendly, helpful new features, and sold the result at a fraction of the original ticket price. People were practically camping out in sleeping bags in front of their local computer stores to get a copy. Adobe missed out on a fortune in T-shirt sales and action figure tie-ins.

And now, just one year later, along comes the sequel: Adobe Photoshop Elements 2.0. Happily, the latest version of Elements belongs in the ranks of *The Godfather: Part II* and *Toy Story 2*: sequels that improve on the original. (Drive all thoughts of *Jaws: The Revenge* and *Grease II* from your mind.) In truth, what made the first release of Elements so impressive wasn't that it was especially easy to use; it was how much of Photoshop's power you could get for such a low price. Elements 2.0, however, takes big steps forward in both power and ease of use. Here's a brief rundown of the new highlights:

- ✔ A Quick Fix command that lets you apply a range of fast improvements to your images from within one dialog box.

- ✔ The Selection Brush, which for the first time gives Elements users a chance to really *see* their selections.

- ✔ A hugely improved File Browser, giving you unparalleled ability to preview, organize, and open your images.

- ✔ A reworked, comprehensive, cross-referenced Help system, explaining complex terms and offering helpful tips.

- ✔ A totally revamped painting engine, packing the Brush tool with enough power and control to realize your artistic vision.

- ✔ Compatibility with Windows XP and Mac OS X, letting you run Elements on the most up-to-date version of your operating system.

That's just a few of the major changes in Elements 2.0, and there are innumerable smaller ones as well.

However, as with version 1.0, all this power comes at a price. Elements is hands-down the best midrange image editor around, but it's also the most complex. As we mentioned earlier, Adobe Photoshop Elements is an easier-to-use, scaled-down version of Adobe Photoshop, a program legendary for its power and complexity. There are some distinct differences between the two applications: Photoshop Elements is missing some of Photoshop's high-end features, and it has some exclusive tools of its own. However — we said it in the last edition of this book, and we'll say it again:

Photoshop Elements Is Photoshop

What exactly do we mean by that? Well, we don't mean that Elements isn't *any* easier to use than Photoshop; as we said, Elements' help-related features have even been substantially improved for version 2.0. And we also don't mean that Elements doesn't need its own *For Dummies* book. (Perish the thought!) Here's what we mean: To get the most out of Photoshop Elements 2.0, you still have to come to grips with the same complex concepts and tools that Photoshop uses. And if you've ever experimented with Photoshop, you know that isn't easy.

You want examples? We've got examples. First, take a gander at this Exceedingly Cute Cat photo:

Exceedingly cute, huh? Maybe the photo's a little dark, but it can be fixed. Now, if you wanted to fix this somewhat dark photo with an image-editing application, and you saw a command called Brightness/Contrast, you'd be tempted to use it, wouldn't you? Heck, your TV's got brightness and contrast controls! And so do both Elements and Photoshop. Brightness/Contrast it is!

Terrible move. Brightness/Contrast is actually among the worst commands that Photoshop or Elements has to offer. Sure, it's easy to use, but correcting photos on the computer is like many things in life: You get out of it what you put into it. Instead of Brightness/Contrast, what you should use to correct brightness — in Photoshop or Photoshop Elements — is the Levels command. And here's the Levels dialog box when applied to the Exceedingly Cute Cat photo above:

Yikes! What the heck is that scary mountain-range-looking thing? What do all those sliders and buttons do? And what does this monstrosity have to do with that Exceedingly Cute Cat?

Well, in truth, Levels isn't really that difficult once you understand the concept it's based on, but we show it to you here to prove a point: Levels is a splendid tool for brightening up images, but it's hardly intuitive. And Levels is exactly the same in Elements as it is in Photoshop. If you think you would need help in mastering Photoshop (and you would), you'll need help using Elements, too.

And that's where this book comes in.

About This Book

Before we tell you why you should buy this book, let's talk for a second about something you've already purchased: Photoshop Elements 2.0. (Incidentally, if by some twist of fate this book has ended up in your hands and you *don't* have Photoshop Elements 2.0, there's a free tryout version available for downloading from the Adobe Web site at www.adobe.com. As we said before, Elements boasts the majority of Photoshop's power — plus a couple of features that inspire Elements-envy in Photoshop users — for a fraction of Photoshop's price. Elements can give you professional results that are virtually identical to Photoshop — if you take the time to find out the fundamentals of how to use the program.

And because Elements' roots are in Photoshop, we hope you'll forgive us for feeling that we're particularly well suited to guide you through Elements. Deke has been using Photoshop since version 1.0 of the program was introduced and has gone on to become the best-selling author of *Photoshop For Dummies, Photoshop Bible,* and a bevy of other books on digital imaging. Galen, slacker that he is, didn't get with Photoshop until version 2.0 came out in 1991, but since then he's used it almost daily. It's the benchmark against which he's judged many other image-editing applications as a reviewer for *Macworld* magazine.

In this book, we set out to explain Photoshop Elements 2.0 from the ground up, assuming that you know absolutely nothing about the program or even about image editing in general. (That, incidentally, is what's meant by the word *Dummies* in the title; we know you're not a Dummy about every topic. But the title *Photoshop Elements 2 For Dummies About Photoshop Elements 2* was deemed to be lacking in elegance.) After a general introduction to image editing in Chapter 1, Chapter 2 digs in without much of an assumption that you've ever even used a computer before. Step by step, concept by concept, tool by tool, we gradually work through a thorough examination of Photoshop Elements 2.0 and the incredible things it can do for your images.

Just as one CD contains both the Windows and Mac versions of Elements, so this one book tells both Windows and Mac users everything they need to know to use Elements on their system of choice. And because Elements 2.0 runs on both Windows XP and Mac OS X, we've also updated the figures in this book to show off the spiffy look of these two new operating systems.

What's in This Book

We've tried our best to organize the material in this book in logical order, with the lofty idea that you'd read it straight through from cover to but you don't have to. The first two parts in particular contain a whole lot of important stuff you ultimately need to know about how digital images on a computer "work" and how Elements 2.0 works with them. But feel free to skip ahead or skip around if you get restless. All that info will still be there in the front of the book when you need it (and you will). The contents of this book are 100 percent guaranteed not to shift around from page to page or chapter to chapter for the lifetime of the book, or double your money back. There are even 16 color pages stuck in the book — double the amount of them in the previous edition — to show things about color that can't be explained in black and white.

To give you an overview of the kind of information you're likely to find in these pages, here's a quick rundown of the five parts.

Part 1: Element-ary School

We begin at the beginning, by answering the question "What exactly *is* image editing, anyway?" From there we get face to interface with Elements 2.0, exploring the array of tools and palettes it places on your screen. We talk about opening images and then do a profile on the pixel, without which digital images wouldn't be. And although the last chapter is an examination of color, we hope it will be free of any purple prose.

Part 11: Be Prepared

This is the part you'll skip because you're too eager to start cleaning up your photos, but you'll come back when you can't figure out what the heck is going on. It's perhaps not the most exciting stuff in the book, but it's vitally important. Chapter 6 tells you about how to save your files in the proper format. Chapter 7 tells you how to fix your mistakes and also how to print your images when there are no more mistakes to fix. Chapter 8 focuses on isolating parts of your pictures with selections, and Chapter 9 introduces the multileveled concept of layers.

Part 111: Realer Than Life

This part of the book details how to take a bad image and make it better, or how to take a good image and make it great. In Chapter 10, we get down and dirty with the topic of cleaning up your images. In Chapter 11, we check out

Elements 2.0's editing tools. Chapter 12 looks at the powerful tools for brightening up your images — including that eagerly anticipated Levels command.

Part IV: The Inspiration/Perspiration Equation

The previous part was all about making images look better; this part begins with a chapter on how to make them look weirder, using Elements 2.0's many distorting capabilities. From there we start with a clean canvas and explore the subject of painting and coloring. From painting pictures, we move on to how to create a thousand words (or fewer) with the type tools. And we wrap up this part with a bang as we reveal some extraordinary tricks that Elements 2.0 can do all on its own.

Part V: The Part of Tens

The Part of Tens is a ...*For Dummies* tradition. You don't want to follow traditions? Don't read this part. But then you'll miss a couple of really neat Top Ten lists: Ten important techniques to remember that utilize the keyboard, and ten reasons you might possibly want to upgrade from Elements 2.0 to Photoshop someday.

Icons Used in This Book

These ...*For Dummies* books have always gone out of their way to make learning easy for you. After the release of the very first ...*For Dummies* books, a scientific study revealed that although most people were indeed learning great amounts from ...*For Dummies* books, a few were distracted by a compulsive need to doodle in the margins. The publishers decided there was only one solution: Do the margin doodling themselves. And so the *For Dummies* icon system was born. Over the years, the icons have taken on specific meanings, alerting you to the type of information the text may contain. Here are a few icons and their meanings:

 This icon lets you know that we're talking about a new feature in Photoshop Elements 2.0 or a change that the program has undergone since the first version. This means that you experienced Elements 1.0 users can just rifle through the book in search of this icon, culling all the juicy new bits and ignoring the rest of our deathless prose. (Sniff.)

You can pretty much bet there are going to be some eight- and nine-letter words in these sections. Technical Stuff is information that maybe isn't completely vital for you to know, but that can help enrich your understanding if you take a few minutes to wrap your brain around it.

This is the really good stuff. Generally, a Tip is a less-than-obvious technique for accomplishing the task at hand. Here's where you get to reap the benefits of our years of image-editing experience. Don't bother to thank us. It's our job. Oh, okay, you can go ahead and thank us.

Not that you should forget everything else, but these "Remember" sections contain particularly important points.

Okay, the worst thing that can happen to you when using Elements 2.0 is that you'll lose a few hours of work. You're not going to find any warnings in this book that say "Clicking this command will make your laptop suddenly snap shut and break your fingers" or anything like that. But hey, lost work is no fun, either.

Well, this is the stuff that's not really technical, or a tip, or particularly worth remembering, or a warning about anything. And yet it seemed somehow icon-worthy. So . . . it's gossip. So there.

Feedback, Please

Want to send us congratulations, compliments, or complaints? If so, you can visit Deke's Web site at www.dekemc.com and drop him a line, or stop by Galen's Web site at www.grundoon.com and e-mail him as well. We get a ton of e-mail, but we definitely read it all, and respond to a fair amount of it as well. We'd especially appreciate suggestions for improving this book in its next edition.

You can also contact the publisher or authors of other *For Dummies* books by visiting the publisher's Web site at http://dummies.com or sending paper mail to Wiley Publishing, Inc., 10475 Crosspoint Boulevard, Indianapolis, IN 46256.

Part I
Element-ary School

The 5th Wave   By Rich Tennant

"THAT'S A LOVELY SCANNED IMAGE OF YOUR SISTER'S PORTRAIT. NOW TAKE IT OFF THE BODY OF THAT PIT VIPER BEFORE SHE COMES IN THE ROOM."

In this part . . .

*I*f just thinking about the name *Photoshop Elements* makes you feel as though you're about to drown in a sea of confusing concepts and terminology, consider this part of the book a life preserver thrown overboard with your name on it. (Yeah, life preservers usually have the name of the ship on them, but whatever.) Taking in anything new can be intimidating, but we've set out to make the process just as painless as possible, starting with the very first chapter.

Speaking of that very first chapter, it seeks to answer the timeless question: "Just what exactly *is* Photoshop Elements, anyway?" We very slowly pick up steam in the next chapter; even if you're only vaguely acquainted with your own computer, you'll be fine. From there we look at the all-important topic of opening images and how to view them from different perspectives. Next, we take a penetrating look at that teeny tiny giant, the pixel. And finally, we teach you just enough about color theory to make you dangerous, yet to keep your colors Web-safe.

By the end of Chapter 5, you won't know everything there is to know about Elements — otherwise, we could have dispensed with the chapters that follow it — but you'll know enough to phrase a few intelligent questions. And please remember that as you read these chapters, there's no shame in being as yet uninformed. Millions of *For Dummies* readers would agree.

Chapter 1

Braving the Elements

*A*s you know if you bothered to read the introduction to this book, Photoshop Elements is based on another Adobe application called simply "Photoshop." But you still may not be aware that Photoshop is the most comprehensive and popular image editor around. In fact, there's probably not a single computer artist who doesn't use Photoshop almost daily, regardless of what other programs he or she may use. As an Elements user, you've got most of that professional power coiled up inside your computer, waiting for you to discover how to harness it.

If you haven't yet used Elements or Photoshop, you probably at least have a vague idea of what they're all about. But just so that we're all clear on the subject, the primary purpose of these applications is to make changes to photographic images that you've managed to get on disk, whether from a digital camera, a scanner, or other means.

If you've used Elements for only a week or so, you may have mistaken it for a fairly straightforward package. Certainly, on the surface of the program, Elements comes off as quite friendly. But lurking a few fathoms deep is another, darker program, one that is distinctly unfriendly for the uninitiated but wildly capable for the stout of heart. Sigmund Freud would no doubt declare Elements a classic case of a split personality. It's half man, half monster; half mild-mannered shoeshine boy, half blonde-grabbing, airplane-swatting King Kong; half kindly old gent with white whiskers chewing on a pipe, half green-gilled invader from another planet chewing on your . . . well, perhaps you don't want to know. In short, Elements has a Dr. Jekyll-and-Mr. Hyde thing going — only it's way scarier.

As you may recall from the last time you saw *Abbott and Costello Meet Dr. Jekyll and Mr. Hyde* — indisputably the foremost resource of information on this famous tale — this Jekyll character (not to be confused with the similarly named cartoon magpie) is normally your everyday, average, nice-guy scientist. Then one day, he drinks some potion or gets cut off in traffic or something and changes into his ornery alter ego, known at every dive bar in town by the surname Hyde. Elements behaves just the same way, except that no magical transformation is required to shift between the program's two halves. Both personalities — both "elements," if you will — coexist simultaneously in what you might call a symbiotic harmony.

This chapter explores in turn both sides of the Elements brain. (We'll leave the exploration of Abbott's and Costello's brains for another book.) We'll also take a look at Elements' built-in Help features, which are the chief means of distinguishing Elements from its not-so-friendly big brother, Photoshop.

The Bland but Benevolent Dr. Jekyll

To discover the benevolent Dr. Jekyll half of Photoshop Elements, you need look no further than the standard painting and editing tools. Shown in Figure 1-1, these tools are so simple they're practically pastoral, like the kind of household appliances your great-grandmother would have been comfortable with. The Eraser erases, the Pencil draws hard-edged lines, the Brush paints, and so on. These incredibly straightforward tools attract new users just as surely as a light attracts miller moths.

Figure 1-1: Many of Elements' tools have an old-world, rustic charm that's sure to warm the cockles of the most timid technophobe.

But you quickly discover that, on their own, these tools aren't super-duper exciting, just like the boring Dr. Jekyll. They don't work much like their traditional counterparts — a line drawn with the Pencil tool, for example, doesn't look much like a line drawn with a real pencil — and they don't seem to be particularly applicable to the job of editing images. Generally speaking, you have to be blessed with pretty strong hand-eye coordination to achieve good results using these tools.

The Dynamic but Dastardly Mr. Hyde

When the standard paint and editing tools don't fit the bill, you try to adjust the performance of the tools and experiment with the other image controls of Elements. Unfortunately, that's when you discover the Mr. Hyde half of the program. You encounter options that have meaningless names such as Dissolve, Multiply, and Difference. Commands such as Image Size and Brightness/Contrast — both of which sound harmless enough — can easily damage your image. It's enough to drive a reticent computer artist stark raving insane.

The net result is that many folks return broken and frustrated to the under-equipped and boring, but nonthreatening, painting and editing tools that they've come to know. It's sad, really. Especially when you consider all the wonderful things that the more complex Photoshop Elements controls can do. Oh sure, the controls have weird names, and they may not respond as you think they should at first. But after you come to terms with these slick puppies, they perform in ways you wouldn't believe.

In fact, the dreaded Mr. Hyde side of Elements represents the core of this powerful program. Without its sinister half, Elements is just another rinky-dink piece of painting software whose most remarkable capability is keeping the kids out of mischief on a rainy day.

The Two Elements of Photoshop Elements

Generally speaking, the two halves of Photoshop Elements serve different purposes. The straightforward Jekyll tools concentrate mostly on *painting,* and the more complex Hyde capabilities are devoted to *image editing.* Therefore, to tackle this great program, you may find it helpful to understand the difference between the two terms.

Painting without the mess

Painting is just what it sounds like: You take a brush loaded with color and smear it all over your on-screen image. You can paint from scratch on a blank canvas, or you can paint directly on top of a photograph. The first option requires lots of talent, planning, and a few dashes of artistic genius; the second option requires an opposable thumb. Okay, that's a slight exaggeration — some lemures have been known to have problems with the second option — but most people find painting on an existing image much easier than creating an image from scratch.

Notice in Figure 1-2 the charming young lady, possibly in costume to portray Glinda the Good Witch in her high school play. We introduce this lovely person solely to demonstrate the amazing functions of Elements.

Were you to paint on our unsuspecting fairy queen, you might arrive at something on the order of the image shown in Figure 1-3. All these changes were invoked using a single tool — the Brush — and just two colors — black and white. Clearly, the artistic work here is a little, shall we say, unsophisticated. It's about on the order of what you can do with a ballpoint pen in a magazine. However, it's worth pointing out that the image isn't permanently damaged, as it would have been with a real-life paintbrush. Because the original image is saved to disk (as explained in Chapter 6), we can restore details from the original at whim.

Editing existing image detail

The lady in Figure 1-3 may be entertaining to look at, but she's nothing compared to what she could be with the aid of some image editing. When you edit an image, you distort and enhance its existing details. So rather than paint with color, you paint with the image itself.

Figure 1-4 demonstrates what we mean. To arrive at this bizarre image, we started by doing a little plastic surgery on our subject, using the Liquify filter as a substitute for the traditional ugly stick. Liquify was also used to create her stylish hairdo. We selected her crown with the Lasso tool and placed it back on her head at a mischievous tilt. Her skirt was turned into a sort of seahorse tail by the Twirl filter. We replaced her pitiful little fairy wings with a pair of eagle wings from another picture, then cut the whole thing out and placed it on a new background. And finally, we used the Custom Shape tool to draw the yin/yang symbol at the end of her wand, and applied a couple of layer styles to give it dimensionality and a nice glow. We're not sure exactly what it all means, but she certainly has a little more credibility as an authentic magical fairy-type creature than she did in Figure 1-2, huh?

Figure 1-2:
Are you a
good witch
or a bad
witch?

Figure 1-3:
A few
strokes and
clicks of the
Brush tool
alter the
image,
albeit in
rather crude
fashion.

Figure 1-4:
If you see
this in the
skies, be
afraid. Be
very afraid.

Mind you, you don't have to go quite so hog wild with the image editing. If you're a photographer, for example, you may not care to mess with your work to the point that it becomes completely unrecognizable. Call you weird, but you like reality the way you see it. Figure 1-5 shows a few subtle adjustments that affect neither the form nor composition of the original image. These changes merely accentuate details or downplay defects in the image.

Just for the record, here are a few common ways to edit photographs in Elements:

- ✔ You can *sharpen* an image to make it appear in better focus, as in the first image in Figure 1-5. Generally, sharpening is used to account for focus problems in the scanning process, but you can sometimes sharpen a photograph that was shot out of focus.

- ✔ If you want to accentuate a foreground image, you can blur the focus of the background. The image on the right side of Figure 1-5 is an example.

- ✔ If a photograph is too light or too dark, you can fix it in a flash through the miracle of color correction. You can change the contrast, brighten or dim colors, and actually replace one color with another. Both of the images in Figure 1-5 have been color-corrected.

- ✔ Using Photoshop Elements' selection and move tools, you can grab a chunk of your image and physically move it around. You can also clone the selection, stretch it, rotate it, or copy it to a different image.

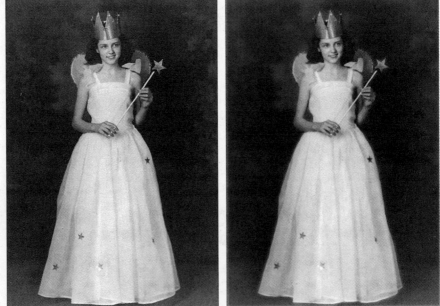

Figure 1-5:
You can apply more moderate edits to your image.

And that's only the tip of the iceberg. The book's remaining chapters explore Photoshop Elements as both a painting program and an image editor. Some chapters contain a little bit of information on both topics, with Part III pertaining to image editing in particular. But you'll find both aspects of Photoshop Elements' split personality flourishing inside this book, making it an ideal candidate for some big shot movie producer to come along and turn it into a fascinating psychological drama. Or maybe just a cheapie horror flick.

Psychiatric Help (The Doctor Is Built-In)

Poor Dr. Jekyll. He spent all his time trying in vain to mix together a drinkable antidote for that split personality problem of his, when all he needed was to seek help from another doctor — one of the *psychiatric* kind. Luckily, Photoshop Elements has seen the light, and the many built-in Help features that it puts at your disposal ensure that you'll never suffer by association with its split personality. What's more, version 2 of Elements has woven the various aspects of its Help system together in such a way that help is always just a click away.

The Welcome screen

Let's start with first things first — and the Welcome screen is literally the very first thing you'll see once you've fired up Photoshop Elements. (Don't worry if you don't know how to start Photoshop Elements yet — we'll cover that thoroughly in the next chapter. If you feel lost, just smile and nod as you read and come back to this section later. We'll understand.) As Figure 1-6 makes clear, the Welcome screen gives you six options:

- ✔ **New File:** Click here to start out with a pristine new canvas, just waiting for you to express yourself all over it. You'll be asked to specify some properties of the new canvas, but we'll get to those in the next few chapters.

- ✔ **Browse for File:** Click here to open the File Browser palette, which lets you search for images on your hard drive, giving you image thumbnails to help you find exactly the file you're looking for. We cover the File Browser palette thoroughly in Chapter 3.

- ✔ **Connect to Camera or Scanner:** Click here to start the process of bringing an image into your computer from a scanner, digital still camera, or digital video camera. You'll be taken to the Select Import Source window, where you can choose a source from the Import menu. Frankly, there are so many different scanners and cameras out there, each with its own quirks and oddities, that we can't possibly begin to thoroughly explain this process for each and every device. But if you have a scanner or digital camera (and there's a good chance that your copy of Photoshop Elements came bundled with just such a device), it's of primary importance that you've correctly installed the software that came with your digital device. For instance, if you've installed your scanner software properly, you should see that option listed in the Import menu. Some Windows users will be able to take advantage of Windows Image Acquisition (WIA), a technology that facilitates importing digital images from cameras and scanners. If your digital camera shows up as its own little hard drive when you connect it to your computer, you may have better luck using the Open command to import images from that camera instead (see Chapter 3 for the skinny on opening files.)

You can also choose Frame From Video from the Import menu to be taken to the VCR-style controls, which let you import a frame from pre-captured video. Just use the controls to locate your frame, click the Grab Frame button, and you've got it. Note that the video already has to be on your hard drive; the command can't pull the video in directly from your camcorder.

No question about it, making electronic devices talk to each other can be fraught with peril. The Web site for the company that made your device can be a great place to turn for help as well as an easy source for downloading updated software for your device. And the Photoshop Elements manual that came with the program has a surprising amount of helpful information.

✔ **Common Issues:** When you click here, the most dramatic thing that happens is that the Welcome screen goes away. However, upon closer inspection you should notice that the menu at the top of the How To palette (see Chapter 2 to find out about palettes) has automatically set itself to Common Issues, and the palette itself is displaying a sort of Frequently Asked Questions-type list of everyday concerns that Elements users might have. If you're starting your Elements session wondering how to accomplish a given task, you may find the answer here.

✔ **Tutorial:** Click here and Photoshop Elements will fire up a Web browser and direct you to interactive tutorials for working with Elements. Another place to look for Photoshop Elements tips and tutorials is, naturally, on the Adobe Web site at www.adobe.com/products/tips/photoshopel.html. Tell them we sent you.

✔ **Exit Welcome Screen:** If every Elements option were this easy to understand, we'd never sell any books. But don't forget you can always bring back the Welcome screen by choosing Window➪Welcome.

Okay, actually there is one more button in this window, though technically it's a check box. Click the check mark for Show This Screen at Startup to deactivate the Welcome screen feature, and you'll receive a thoughtful reminder that this screen can be turned on again by choosing Welcome under the Window menu. That's the great thing about Elements' Help features: They're there when you need them, but they happily stay just out of sight when you don't need them.

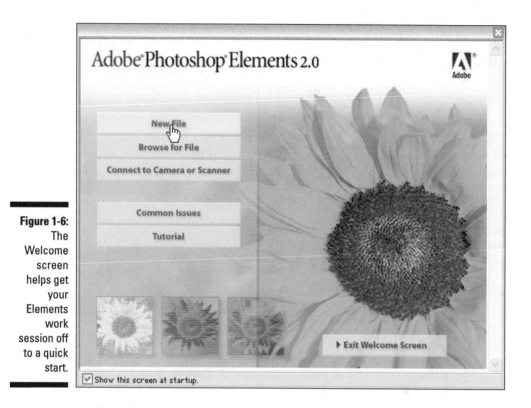

Figure 1-6:
The Welcome screen helps get your Elements work session off to a quick start.

The Glossary

If you've been following along with the home game, you may have noticed something about that little message you just got when you deactivated the Show This Screen at Startup check box in the Welcome Screen. The message said `You can show the Welcome screen again by selecting 'Welcome' from the Window menu`, and the first word `Welcome` was colored blue and underlined like a link on a Web page. Sure enough, clicking this link takes you to a new Elements feature called the Glossary. Part of Elements' browser-based built-in help system, the Glossary provides you with definitions of obscure words and phrases that you may find confusing. If you want to peruse the Glossary at your leisure, there's a direct link to it on the left pane of Elements built-in Help.

The Hints palette

So you launch Elements and click the Exit Welcome Screen button. One of the windows already open by default is the Hints palette, captured in all its splendor in Figure 1-7. And what is this supposedly helpful Hints palette doing? It's giving hints about *itself,* bragging about how it can provide "helpful descriptions of tools and palettes, and links to related Help documentation." Just what we needed — a self-referential tool. Next thing you know, the Pencil tool will start drawing little pencils, and the Hand tool will start making shadow puppets on your desktop.

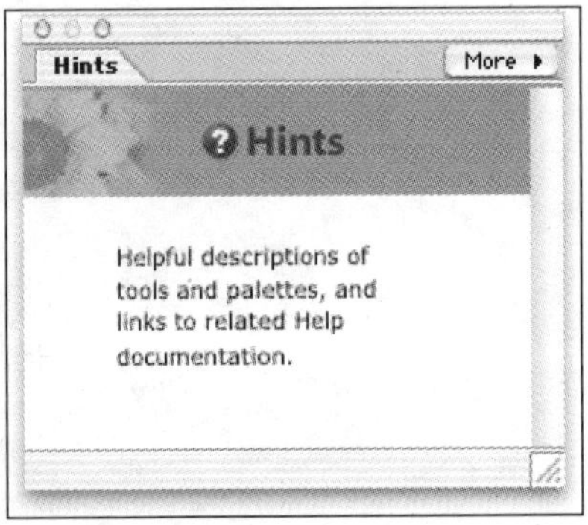

Figure 1-7: You can visit the Hints palette anytime you need a clue about a tool or palette.

But speaking of that Hand tool, move your cursor over to the Hand tool at the bottom left of the Toolbox. And now take a look at that Hints palette: It's telling you about the Hand tool! And that's the beauty of the Hints palette, folks. It gives you an instant and concise description of Elements' many tools and palettes.

But what if your thirst for knowledge is only whetted, not quenched? Scroll down to the bottom of the Hints palette and you'll find links to related topics, proving that — as usual with Elements — help is only a click away.

The How To palette

The How To palette, pictured in Figure 1-8, is the place to turn in Elements for the latest and greatest recipes. Now, if the thought of recipes makes you hungry, then put down this book, make yourself a sandwich, eat it, and then come back to us when you're finished (but please wipe your hands first). These recipes can't help you remember how to make your great-aunt Naomi's famous porcupine meatloaf, but they are a big help where Photoshop Elements is concerned.

In the How To palette, you'll find an assortment of image-editing recipes divided into several different categories. Say, for instance, you want to remove the redeye from a cherished photo of your great-aunt Naomi with a face full of porcupine quills. Under the Select a Recipe menu, choose Retouch Photos, and then click Remove Redeye. All you have to do now is follow along with the step-by-step instructions — but Elements makes it easier yet.

Figure 1-8:
The How To palette presents you with finger-lickin'-good recipes for image editing.

Throughout the recipes Elements puts at your disposal, you'll see numerous hot links. Clicking these will automatically perform the described task for you, whether it be selecting a tool, opening a palette, or creating a new document. You can also use the browser-style Home, Back, and Forward buttons to navigate your way through the How To palette.

But wait — there's more. At the bottom of the Select a Recipe menu, there's a lone command called Download New Adobe Recipes. Choose that command and, sure enough, Elements will go online (provided that you have an Internet connection, of course) and fire up the Online Services Assistant. Here you'll be presented with a list of new recipes that are currently available. Select the ones that sound useful to you and click Download. And don't forget to check back frequently for updates. Those folks in the Adobe kitchens never rest.

There are two other ways of summoning the Online Services Assistant: There's a handy button in the Shortcuts bar (the one with the globe and wrench) and an almost-as-handy Online Services command in the File menu.

The Search Results palette

Perhaps, upon reading the above heading, you've started your own search for the hard-to-find Search Results palette. After all, it's not on-screen by default as the Hints and How To palettes are; nor is it lurking at the top of the screen in the palette well. Although you can command its presence merely by choosing Window⇨Search Results, the real key to accessing the Search Results palette lies in the text field located in the Shortcuts bar. By default it reads "Enter search criteria," but you can always click in the field and type in the name of whichever Elements feature is troubling you at the moment. Then click the Search button, and the Search Results palette appears on your screen, loaded with information about the topic you requested. Elements scours its intensive built-in Help, the Glossary, and the How To palette for relevant assistance.

The menu at the top of the palette is set to All Search Results by default, as shown in Figure 1-9. However, you can choose Results for Recipes to see only the recipes that pertain to your search request, or choose Results for Help to see just the Help and Glossary entries that match your request.

You know, there's another way you can apply the whole Jekyll/Hyde analogy to Photoshop Elements. Although Elements definitely has its wild and woolly Hyde side, full of intimidating tools and forbidding commands, the Dr. Jekyll side of Elements — represented by all the Help features — is dedicated to making sure you understand the darker half of the program. Doctors are generally helpful that way. So with this much help at your fingertips, why have we decided to write this book? Well, we thought you might want a second opinion.

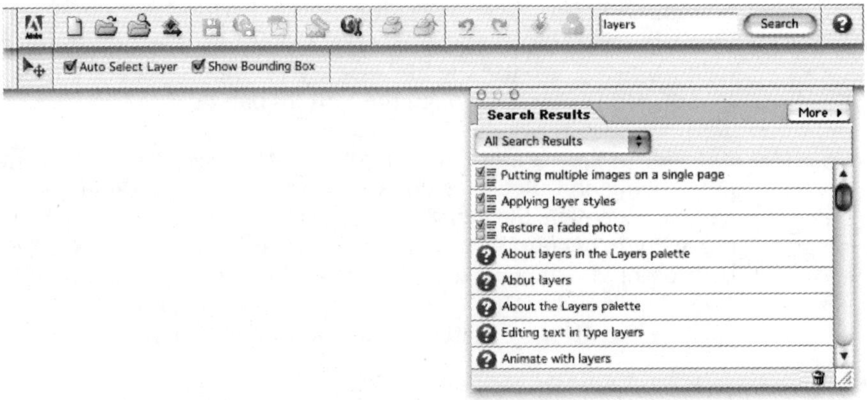

Figure 1-9:
Type a term in the Shortcuts bar's text field, click Search, and the Search Results palette arrives on the scene.

Chapter 2

Dissecting Your Desktop

. . . .

In This Chapter

▶ Launching Elements

▶ Taking some first, tentative looks at the Elements interface

▶ Dealing with mouse terminology

▶ Working with the program window

▶ Switching between Elements and other programs

▶ Choosing commands

▶ Using dialog boxes and palettes

▶ Picking up tools from the Toolbox

. . . .

*I*f you're brand new to Photoshop Elements — or to computers in general — this is the chapter for you. You get the basic stuff you need to know before you can begin using the program to distort the faces of all your family members.

Even if you're already familiar with the basic interface of Elements, you may want to give this chapter a once-over to make sure we're all speaking the same language. Here, we can calibrate brains, so to speak.

Giving Elements the Electronic Breath of Life

Before you can use Elements, you have to start up — or launch — the program. Here's how:

1. **Start your computer.**

   Mac users: After you reach the Finder, proceed to Step 3.

2. **PC users: Click the Windows Start button.**

3. **PC users: Choose Adobe Photoshop Elements 2.0 in the Start menu.**

   Depending on which flavor of Windows you're using, it's possible you won't immediately see Elements sitting in the Start menu, just waiting to be clicked. If you're using Windows XP, click All Programs and you should see it in the submenu. If you're using a system prior to XP, you may need to look in the Programs submenu and then possibly in an Adobe submenu.

   If you can't seem to locate Elements on your system, choose Search or Find⇨ Files or Folders in the Start menu. (This command may vary slightly depending on which flavor of Windows you're using.) Type Photoshop Elements in the relevant field, and click the button to begin your search. A list should appear with all files and folders whose names contain the words *Photoshop Elements.* Locate the program icon and double-click to launch the program directly from this list.

4. **Mac users: Locate and activate the Adobe Photoshop Elements folder.**

   Double-click your hard drive icon on the desktop (it's probably the one in the upper-right corner). If you're using OS X, Elements is probably located in the Applications folder. If you're using an earlier Mac system, Elements is probably in the Applications (Mac OS 9) folder. Either way, open that folder and you'll see another folder inside labeled Adobe Photoshop Elements 2. Open that folder and double-click the Photoshop Elements 2.0 icon.

   If you're not sure where Elements is located on your hard drive, choose File⇨Find from the menu bar (or press ⌘+F). Sherlock will open. Then type the words **Photoshop Elements**, make sure there's a check mark next to the hard drive you want to search, and press the Return key. A list appears with all files containing the words *Photoshop Elements.* Locate the program icon and double-click to launch the program directly from this list. If you still can't find the program, cry in anguish and beat your monitor with something soft and squishy. If you have a new iMac, be careful: It may hit back.

5. **Hope it works.**

   If you see the Elements splash screen, you're in business. If your computer complains that it doesn't have enough memory to open Elements, check out the sidebar, "Why does Elements give your computer amnesia?" later in this chapter. If you see some equally discouraging message, scream loudly and hope that the resident computer expert is in close proximity. You need help. Check out the Elements manual or Adobe's Web site, or phone technical support.

After your computer stops making little shicka-shicka noises and your screen settles down, you'll see the Elements Welcome screen, which we covered in the last chapter. Go ahead and click the Close button for now, and you'll see the basic Elements interface, as shown in Figures 2-1 and 2-2. We cover the various elements of the interface later in this chapter.

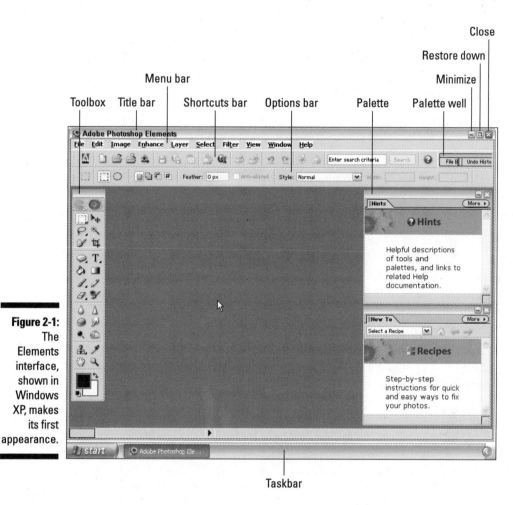

Figure 2-1:
The
Elements
interface,
shown in
Windows
XP, makes
its first
appearance.

Taskbar

Don't freak out and start running around the room in a frenzy if you're a little fuzzy on the meaning of *menu, dialog box,* and a few other terms. We cover all this stuff in fairly hefty detail in this very same chapter.

Note: As you read, you'll see that you can also use the keyboard and mouse in tandem. For example, in Elements, you can draw a perfectly horizontal line by pressing the Shift key while dragging with the Pencil tool. Or you can press Alt (Option on a Mac) and click the Rectangular Marquee tool in the upper-left corner of the Toolbox to switch to the Elliptical Marquee tool. Such actions are so common that you often see key and mouse combinations joined into compound verbs, such as Shift+drag or Control-click.

Toolbox　Menu bar　Shortcuts bar　Options bar　　　　Palette　Palette well

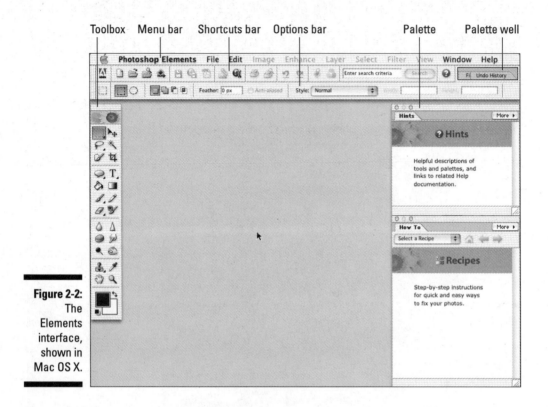

Figure 2-2:
The
Elements
interface,
shown in
Mac OS X.

Working with Windows

This section is relevant to PC users only. Mac people skip down to the "Switching between Elements and the Macintosh Finder" section below. In Elements, as in most other Windows programs, you have two kinds of windows: the program window, which contains the main Elements work area, and image windows, which contain any images that you create or edit. To see the program window, refer to Figure 2-1; for a look at image windows, see Chapter 3.

Elements windows — both program and image — contain the same basic items as those in other Windows programs. But just in case you need a refresher or you're new to this whole computing business, here's how the Elements program window works with Windows:

TECHNICAL STUFF

Why does Elements give your computer amnesia?

If your computer says it's out of memory, it just means that a part of the machine is filled to capacity. Memory — known in computer dweeb circles as *RAM* (random-access memory, pronounced *ram,* like the sheep) — allows your computer to run programs. Elements needs lots of RAM — this version requires you to have a minimum of 128MB in your computer and prefers that you have even more. If you can't launch Elements because of a memory error, you have three options:

✔ Free up RAM by quitting all other programs that are currently running.

✔ PC users: Windows XP users, restart your computer by choosing Turn Off Computer from the Start menu and then click Restart.

Other Windows users, restart your computer by choosing the Shut Down command from the Windows Start menu and then choosing the Restart the Computer option. After your computer restarts, try to launch Elements again.

Mac users: OS X users, restart the computer by choosing Restart from the Apple menu. OS 9 users, restart the computer by choosing Special⇨Restart at the Finder and try to launch Elements after the Finder reappears.

✔ Buy and install more RAM.

If you've never tried to upgrade the RAM in your machine, seek out expert advice from your local computer guru.

✔ Windows users can click the Close button in the upper-right corner of the window to shut down Elements. If you have open images that haven't been saved, the program prompts you to save them. (For details on saving images, see Chapter 6.) The quickest way to close your program window (and Elements) is to press the keyboard shortcut for the Exit command, Ctrl+Q (as in Quit).

✔ Click the Minimize button (refer to Figure 2-1) to reduce the program window to a button on the Windows taskbar. To redisplay the program window, just click the taskbar button.

✔ You can also use the taskbar buttons to switch between Elements and other running programs. In the taskbar, just click the button of the program you want to use.

✔ The appearance of the Maximize/Restore Down (or just Restore) button changes, depending on the current status of the window. If you see two boxes on the button, the button is the Restore Down button. Click this button to shrink the window so that you can see other open program windows. You can then resize the window by placing your mouse cursor over a corner of the window until you see a double-headed arrow. When you see the arrow, drag the window to resize it. To move the window around, drag its title bar.

✔ After you click the Restore Down button, it changes to the Maximize button, which looks like a single box. Click the button to zoom the program window so that it consumes your entire screen. After the window zooms, the button changes back to the Restore Down button. Click the button to restore your screen to its former size.

Switching between Elements and the Macintosh Finder

In back of the myriad components of the Elements interface, you Mac users can probably see the icons and open windows from the Finder. (These are hidden in Figure 2-2 just to make the picture less confusing.) If you click a Finder window or on the desktop, you're taken back to the Finder, and the Elements Toolbox and palettes disappear. If you have an image open, however, the image window remains visible. Here are some tips to help you manage working between the Finder and Elements:

✔ If you're using OS X and you inadvertently click yourself out of Elements, go to the Dock (located at the bottom of the screen by default) and click the Elements icon. If you're using OS 9, choose Adobe Photoshop Elements from the list of running programs in the Applications menu, which is on the far-right side of the menu bar. Or, no matter which version of the Mac OS you're using, you can just click the Elements image window. The Toolbox and palettes return to the screen to show you that Elements is back in the game.

✔ You may be wondering why this program switching happens. The Finder is a piece of software, just like Elements. The only difference is that the Finder is running the entire time you use your Mac. This means that all the time you're using Elements, the Finder is working away in the background. When you click the desktop or some other component of the Finder, the Finder comes to the foreground, and Elements goes to the background. But both programs continue to operate until you quit Elements or shut down your computer.

✔ If the clutter from the Finder gets too distracting when you're using Elements, choose the Hide Others command to hide every Finder element except the icons. In OS X, this is located in the Photoshop Elements menu; in OS 9, it's in the Applications menu.

✔ If you're using OS 9, you can hide the icons by choosing Apple⇨Control Panels⇨General Controls. (If you don't know how to choose things from menus, see the section, "Maneuvering through Menus," later in this chapter.) Inside the General Controls dialog box, click the Show Desktop When in Background check box to deselect it. Then close the dialog box. Bye-bye go the icons. (Note that you can't click the background to switch to the Finder if you choose this option; you have to use the Applications menu to switch between programs.)

✔ Remember that you can always tell where you are just by looking at the menu bar. If you see the words Photoshop Elements anywhere in the menu bar — or in OS 9, if you just see the Elements icon in the far-right corner of the menu bar — you're in business.

Maneuvering through Menus

As do all Windows and Macintosh programs, Elements sports a menu bar (refer to Figures 2-1 and 2-2) at the top of its window desktop. Beneath that menu bar, though, are two things many other programs don't have: a Shortcuts bar and an Options bar. The Shortcuts bar is a handy way to perform many common functions with just a single click of the mouse. It also features the palette well, a convenient place for placing palettes you don't need at the moment. The Options bar gives you control over the tool you currently have selected. Both of these bars can be repositioned by clicking the handle on the left side and dragging to another location And if you ever want to reset the options in the Options bar, click the tool icon on the far left of the bar and choose Reset Tool to reset the options for that particular tool, or Reset All Tools to return them all to their default settings. We'll make frequent visits to both the Options bar and the Shortcuts bar when appropriate in the book; for now, let's belly up to that menu bar.

Each word in the menu bar — File, Edit, Image, and so on — represents a menu. A *menu* is simply a list of commands that you can use to open and close images, manipulate selected portions of a photograph, hide and display palettes, and initiate all kinds of mind-boggling, sophisticated procedures.

We explain the most essential Photoshop Elements commands throughout this book. But before we send you off to cope with a single one of them, here's a bit of background information on how to work with menus:

✔ To choose a command from a menu, click the menu name and then click the command name. Or you can press and hold the menu name, drag down to the command name, and release the mouse button at the desired command.

✔ Some commands bring up additional menus called *submenus*. For example, if you choose File➪Import, you display a submenu offering still more commands. If we ask you to choose File➪Import➪PDF Image, you choose the Import command under the File menu to display the submenu and then choose the PDF Image command from the submenu, all in one beautiful continuous movement. When you do it just right, it's like something out of Swan Lake.

✔ Did you notice those underlined letters in some of the commands in the preceding paragraph? Those letters are called *hot keys*. If you prefer using the keyboard rather than the mouse, and you're using a PC, you can press hot keys in combination with the Alt key to choose a command. (You may need to press the Alt key to see the hot keys, depending on which version of Windows you're using.) For example, to display the File menu, press Alt+F. Then to choose the Import command from the File menu, press M — no Alt key needed this time. You can also use hot keys to access options inside dialog boxes (we explain dialog boxes later in the section, "Talking Back to Dialog Boxes"). Macintosh OS X users wanting to navigate their computer exclusively from the keyboard can activate Full Keyboard Access in the Keyboard System Preferences; for details, check the Mac Help in the Help menu of the Finder.

In addition to using hot keys, you can access some commands by pressing keyboard shortcuts. For example, to initiate the File⇨Open command, you can press the keyboard shortcut Ctrl+O (⌘+O on a Mac) — that is, press and hold the Ctrl key (⌘ key on a Mac), press the O key, and then release both keys.

There are certain Elements keyboard shortcuts that conflict with keyboard shortcuts built into Macintosh OS X. The principal conflict is over the ⌘+H shortcut. As a rule in OS X, this shortcut hides the currently active application, be it Elements, Microsoft Word, or what have you. But (happily,) Elements 2.0 now observes its grandpappy Photoshop's longstanding tradition of using ⌘+H to hide the "marching ants" indicating an active selection (for details on making selections, see Chapter 8). So by default, Elements appropriates ⌘+H for its own ant-hiding purposes and uses ⌘+Control+H to hide itself. However, you can change this behavior by visiting Photoshop Elements⇨Preferences⇨General and selecting the Use System Shortcut Keys check box. Activating this preference makes Elements play Hide along with the other applications in OS X, and assigns ⌘+Control+H to its exclusive ant-hiding needs.

✔ Some keyboard equivalents select tools, and some perform other functions. Either way, we keep you apprised of them throughout this book. If you take the time to memorize a few keyboard shortcuts here and there, you can save yourself a heck of a lot of time and effort. (For the most essential shortcuts, read Chapter 18. Also, tear out the Cheat Sheet at the front of this book and tape it up somewhere within easy ogling distance.)

✔ Elements offers you yet another way to access some commands. If you right-click (Control-click on a Mac) inside an image window, you display a context-sensitive menu. In nongeek-speak, a context-sensitive menu, also known as a shortcut menu, is a minimenu that contains commands that are related to the current tool, palette, or image, as shown in Figure 2-3.

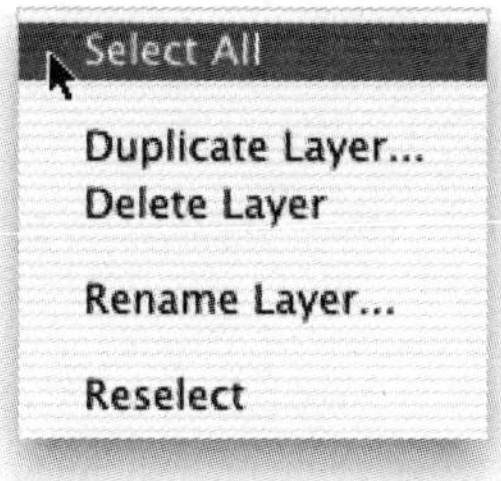

Figure 2-3:
Right-click
(Control-
click on a
Mac) inside
the image
window to
access
context-
sensitive
menus.

Select All

Duplicate Layer...
Delete Layer

Rename Layer...

Reselect

Talking Back to Dialog Boxes

Elements reacts immediately to some menu commands. But for other commands, the program requires you to fill out a few forms before it processes your request. If you see an ellipsis (three dots, like so . . .) next to a command name, that's your clue that you're about to see such a form, known in computer clubs everywhere as a *dialog box.*

Figure 2-4 shows a sample dialog box. As the figure demonstrates, dialog boxes can contain several basic kinds of options. The options work as follows:

✔ A box in which you can enter numbers or text is called an *option box.* Double-click or click and drag in an option box to highlight its contents and then replace the contents by entering new stuff from the keyboard.

✔ Some option boxes come with *slider bars.* Drag the triangular slider to the left or right to lower or raise the associated numerical value. (All without hydraulics, mind you.)

✔ You can select only one circular *radio button* (not shown in Figure 2-4) from any gang of radio buttons. To select a radio button, click the button or on the option name that follows it. A black dot fills the selected radio button; all deselected radio buttons are hollow.

✔ Although you can select only one radio button at a time, you can usually select as many *check boxes* as you want. Really, go nuts. To select a check box, click the box or on the option name that follows it. A check fills the box to show that it's selected. Clicking on a selected check box turns off the option.

✔ To conserve space, some multiple-choice options appear as *drop-down menus.* Click the menu to display the option choices. Then click the desired option in the menu to choose it, just as if you were choosing a command from a standard menu. As with radio buttons, you can select only one option at a time from a drop-down menu.

✔ Not to be confused with the radio button, the normal, everyday variety of *button* enables you to close the current dialog box or display others. For example, click the Cancel button to close the dialog box and cancel the command. Click OK to close the dialog box and execute the command according to the current settings. Clicking on a button with an ellipsis (such as Load. . . or Save. . .) displays yet another dialog box.

As you can with menus, you can select options and perform other feats of magic inside dialog boxes from the keyboard. The following shortcuts work in most dialog boxes:

✔ To advance from one option box to the next, press the Tab key. To back up, press Shift+Tab.

✔ PC users can also move from option to option by using the hot keys (those underlined letters in the option names). Press Alt+an option's hot key to move to that option.

✔ Press Enter (Return on a Mac) to select the button surrounded by a heavy outline (such as the OK button in Figure 2-4). Press Esc to select the Cancel button.

✔ Press ↑ to raise a selected option box value by one; press ↓ to decrease the value by one. Pressing Shift+↑ and Shift+↓ raise and lower the value by ten, respectively.

✔ If you change your mind about choices you make in a dialog box, you can quickly return things to the settings that were in force when you opened the dialog box. In most dialog boxes, pressing the Alt key (Option key on a Mac) magically changes the Cancel button to a Reset button. Click the Reset button to bring back the original values.

If a dialog box gets in the way of your view of an image, you can reposition the box by dragging its title bar.

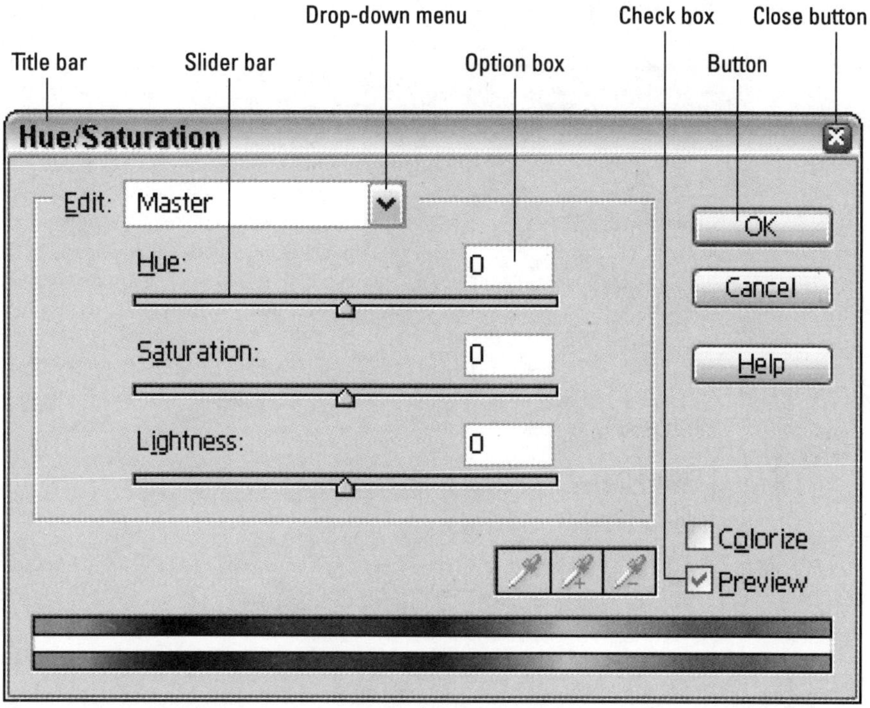
Drop-down menu
Check box
Close button
Title bar
Slider bar
Option box
Button
Hue/Saturation
Edit: Master
Hue: 0
Saturation: 0
Lightness: 0
OK
Cancel
Help
Colorize
Preview

Figure 2-4: The anatomy of the dialog box.

Playing Around with Palettes

Elements offers free-floating *palettes* that you can leave on-screen or put away at whim. The palettes, which are basically dialog boxes that can remain on-screen while you work, provide access to options that change the appearance of images and otherwise assist you in your editing adventures. We cover the specifics of using the palettes in chapters to come, but here's a brief introductory tour of how palettes work:

- What may look like just one palette can actually be a collection of palettes sharing the same palette window. For example, in Figure 2-5 the Layers and Layer Styles palettes are housed in the same palette window. To switch to a different palette in a palette window, click its tab.
- When palettes are unwanted, they can often be found sulking in the palette well, that dark gray area on the right side of the Shortcuts bar. You can see their little tabbed heads sticking out of the well. If you find yourself wanting to see one of them again, just click the tab. And if you think you'll need to keep the palette around for a while, drag it out of the well by the tab. You'll make its day.

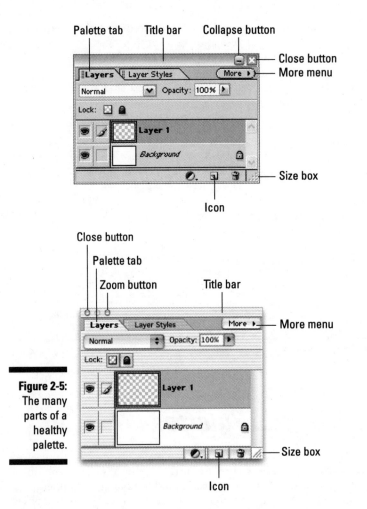

Figure 2-5:
The many
parts of a
healthy
palette.

If you are using Elements with a monitor resolution of 800 by 600 pixels,
you'll probably find that the palette well doesn't work very — um — *well*.
At this screen resolution, the well is very small, causing the palette tabs to
bunch up and therefore making it very hard to click any given tab. For best
results, increase your monitor resolution to 1024 by 768: If this isn't possible,
you'll probably find it easier to bring up palettes by choosing their names
from the Window menu.

✔ You can arrange the order of the palettes within the well to suit your
whim. Click the "thumb grip" at the far-left end of the palette tab and
drag the palette to another location within the well. You can also right-
click (Control-click on the Mac) on a palette tab and choose from a list
of commands to move the palette.

✔ When you're through using a palette for the immediate future, you can click the Close button to make it vamoose. Exactly where it vamooses to depends on how you set the Close Palette to Palette Well option in the palette's More menu. When there's a check mark next to the option, then clicking the Close button sends the palette up to the palette well, where you can bring it forward again simply by clicking its tab. If there is no check mark next to Close Palette to Palette Well, clicking the Close button will make the palette disappear from your screen completely, and it will reappear only when you choose its name from the <u>W</u>indow menu. (Be aware that Close Palette to Palette Well is a toggling command, meaning that you turn it on and turn it off simply by choosing it.) In Windows, the Close button is on the far right of the palette's title bar; on the Mac, it's on the left side of the title bar. To hide and show palettes, you can also use the commands available under the Window menu.

✔ The one exception to the previous point is the File Browser. Clicking the File Browser's Close button always makes it vanish completely; choose Window➪File Browser to bring it back. The reason for this behavior is that the File Browser doesn't have a Close Palette to Palette Well command in its More menu; its command reads Dock Palette to Palette Well, and that's precisely what happens immediately when you choose the command.

✔ Press Tab to hide or display the currently open palettes, the Toolbox, the Shortcuts bar, the Options bar, and (in Windows only) the Status bar, which is covered in Chapter 3. Press Shift+Tab if you want to hide or display just the palettes, but leave the Toolbox, Shortcuts bar, Options bar, and Status bar as is. (Note that this trick doesn't work if the cursor is blinking inside the Layers palette's Opacity option box.)

✔ Some palettes have keyboard shortcuts you can use to hide and display them: F5 for the File Browser, F6 for the How To palette, F7 for the Filters palette, F8 for the Effects palette, F9 for the Layer Styles palette, F10 for the Undo History palette, F11 for the Layers palette, and F12 for the Hints palette.

✔ Some palettes contain icons, just like the Toolbox does. Click an icon to perform a function, such as adding or deleting a layer.

✔ Drag the title bar at the top of the palette to move the palette around on-screen.

✔ Shift+click a title bar to snap the palette to the nearest corner of the screen. For example, if the palette is near the upper-right corner of the screen, Shift+clicking on its title bar moves it all the way into the corner, giving you more space to view your image on-screen.

✔ Every palette except the Info palette has a size box, as labeled in Figure 2-5. Drag the size box to resize the palette.

- ✔ Click the Collapse button (the Zoom button on a Mac) to shrink the palette so that only the most essential options at the top of the palette are visible. It may take one or two clicks to get this to happen, depending on the palette. Click the Collapse button (Zoom button on a Mac) again to bring all the palette options into full view.

- ✔ Alt+click the Collapse button (Option+click the Zoom button on a Mac) to hide all but the title bar and the palette tabs. You can also double-click a palette tab.

- ✔ You can combine multiple palettes into a single palette window by dragging a tab from one palette into another, as shown in Figure 2-6. You can also break any palette into its own window by dragging the palette tab out of the current window.

- ✔ You can also dock palettes vertically. Move the tab of a palette to the bottom of a second palette and you should see a black outline at the bottom of the second palette indicating that you can dock the first palette. You can also dock one palette to the top of another palette in the same manner.

- ✔ Press and hold on the More button on the right side of the palette, just below the title bar, to display the palette menu. Here's yet another hiding place for commands.

- ✔ If you get your palettes in an unbearable muddle, you can always restore things to the way they were when you first launched Elements by choosing Window➪Reset Palette Locations.

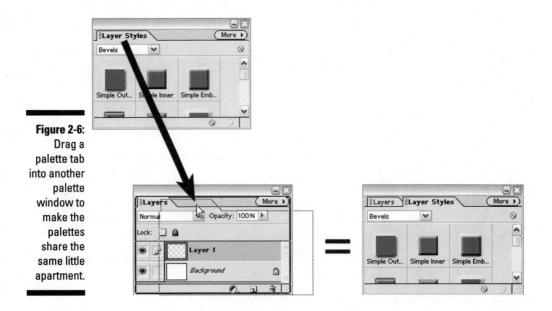

Figure 2-6: Drag a palette tab into another palette window to make the palettes share the same little apartment.

Opening Up Your Toolbox

You're ready to move on to the tempestuous world of the Toolbox. As shown in Figure 2-7, the items in the Toolbox fall into two basic categories — tools and color controls. Future chapters explain in detail how to use the various gizmos in the Toolbox, but here's a basic overview of what's in store:

- ✔ If you click the very top icon in the Toolbox, you bring up the Adobe Online dialog window. If you have access to the Internet, Adobe Online can give you access to tons of great info, such as new Recipes, tips, tech support, upgrades, and news on products and events.

- ✔ The next four sections of the Toolbox (refer to Figure 2-7) are devoted to an assortment of tools that you can use to edit images, just as you might use an assortment of pencils, markers, and scissors in a craft project. To select one of these tools, click its icon. Then use the tool by clicking or dragging it inside your image.

- ✔ A tiny, downward-right-pointing triangle in the bottom-right corner of a tool icon indicates that more tools are hidden behind that icon on a *flyout* menu. To display the flyout menu and reveal the hidden tools, press and hold the mouse button on the icon. Drag over and down the column of tools until your cursor is hovering over the tool you want to use and then release the mouse button.

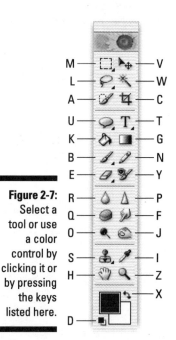

Figure 2-7: Select a tool or use a color control by clicking it or by pressing the keys listed here.

- ✔ You can also Alt+click (Option+click on a Mac) on a tool icon to cycle through all the tools hidden beneath it.

- ✔ The bottom section of the Toolbox contains color selection options. These icons respond immediately when you click them.

- ✔ If you've been clicking away on the Toolbox icons and haven't seen any results, don't panic. Your copy of Elements isn't broken; the icons just don't do anything unless you have an image open. To find out how to open images, see Chapter 3.

- ✔ You can also access all the tools and two of the color controls from the keyboard. For example, to select the Brush tool, you just press the letter B key. To then select the Impressionist Brush tool, which shares the flyout menu with the Brush tool, you press Shift+B. Figure 2-7 shows other keyboard equivalents.

- ✔ If pressing the Shift key with the keyboard letter to access the tools on the flyout menu is just too strenuous, Elements gives you a solution. Choose Edit➪Preferences➪General and deselect the option Use Shift Key for Tool Switch. (In Mac OS X, the Preferences are located under the Photoshop Elements menu.) You can now rotate through the tools by pressing the same letter repeatedly.

- ✔ If you can't remember the keyboard shortcut of a particular tool, pause your cursor over its icon for a second or two. A little label known as a *tool tip* appears, telling you the name of the tool and its keyboard equivalent. If this gets annoying, the feature can be turned off by deselecting the Show Tool Tips option in the General panel of the Preferences.

Chapter 3

"Open!" Says Me

• •

In This Chapter

▶ Opening and closing images

▶ Using the File Browser

▶ Creating a new, blank image

▶ Mastering your image windows

▶ Moving around your image

▶ Zooming in and out

▶ Working with precision in your images

• •

*P*hotoshop Elements presents you with a plethora of tools, menus, and palettes (just check out Chapter 2 if you don't believe us!). However, until you have an image open, those contraptions are intriguing but ultimately worthless — it's like having an easel, a full set of brushes, and a whole paint box full of paints, but no canvas. And with Elements, you can't even climb up on billboards and paint mustaches on the faces in the ads. (Not that we've ever done anything like that.) No, if you want to become a digital Picasso (or Rembrandt, or Monet, or whatever artistic legend you choose), you need an open image.

This chapter explains how to open existing images and also how to create a new, blank canvas for an image you want to paint from scratch. Then we chart a course through the many ways you can navigate around the vast sea of your image. So strap a parrot on your shoulder and hop on board.

Don't Just Sit There — Open Something!

If you're a longtime computer buff, you may expect opening an image to be a relatively straightforward process. You just choose File➪Open or press Ctrl+O (⌘+O on a Mac) and select the image file you want to display, right?

Well, in Elements "O" stands for "options" just as much as it stands for "Open." Scientific studies have shown that if you close your eyes and just click blindly around the Elements interface a dozen times, you'll hit at least three different file-opening features. Elements' main opening tool is the File Browser. As you can see in Figure 3-1, the File Browser is an excellent visual means of browsing through your computer and peeking at the graphics files contained therein.

Image preview

Desktop view   Up one level   Folder path menu   Thumbnail panel

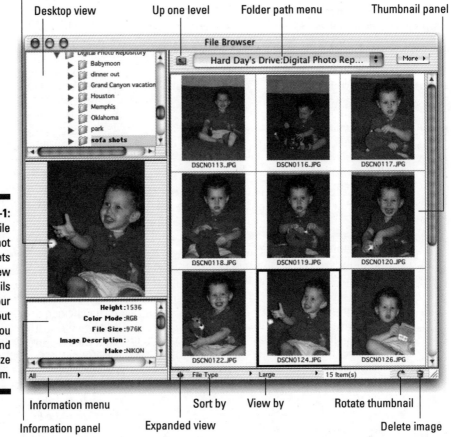

Figure 3-1:
The new File Browser not only lets you view thumbnails of your photos but also lets you rename and organize them.

Information menu   Sort by   View by   Rotate thumbnail

Information panel   Expanded view   Delete image

Opening via the File Browser

You read it here first, folks. In the previous edition of this book, Figure 3-1 had the following caption: "The File Browser is a visual reference that Elements' granddaddy Photoshop would do well to acquire." We'll try not to gloat too much when we tell you that's exactly what happened! With the release of Photoshop 7.0, Adobe did indeed incorporate Elements 1.0's File Browser into the venerable king of image editors. Granted, the File Browser's capabilities were greatly expanded for inclusion into Photoshop, but happily Adobe has let almost all these new features migrate back to Elements 2.0. Perhaps this will be the wave of the future: Elements will introduce a new feature; said feature will be developed and incorporated into Photoshop; the more powerful version of the feature will then be bundled back into the next version of Elements. Stay tuned, and we'll see. Question: When is a palette not a palette? Answer: When it's the File Browser palette. Sure, the File Browser hangs out in the palette well by default, and you can click its tab to access it while it's still docked to the well. But drag it away from the well and you'll see that on its own the File Browser more closely resembles a regular window; the tab goes away, and you can't dock File Browser to the bottom of other palettes. It also interacts with open image windows in a unique way; other palettes always stay on top of image windows, but the File Browser can hide behind image windows if you want. And no other palette has its own button in the Shortcuts bar or its own command under the File menu, but clicking the Browse button or choosing File➪Browse will open the File Browser for you every time.

Anatomy of a browser

Let's examine the architecture of this palette/window hybrid. In the upper-left corner you'll find the Desktop View, which shows you a folder hierarchy of your hard drive with the Desktop at the top. You can navigate and view the contents of folders by clicking the plus icons on Windows or by clicking the twirly arrows on the Mac. Note, however, that you can't see any image files within the Desktop View, just folders. Double-click a folder, however, and the contents of that folder take over the large thumbnail section of the File Browser, showing you a thumbnail image for every image file in the folder. If you make a few changes to the organization of your hard drive while the File Browser is open — things such as adding, moving, and deleting folders — those changes won't show up in the Desktop View until you choose Refresh Desktop View from the File Browser's More menu.

If you find the new features of the File Browser to be a bit overwhelming, you can always click the double-arrow icon at the bottom of the palette to hide the entire left side of the Browser, or, alternatively, deselect the Expanded View option from the More menu. This will make the File Browser very closely resemble the Elements 1.0 version.

The menu at the top of the thumbnail panel shows you the folder path to the currently displayed folder. You can click the menu and choose another folder to navigate backward toward your desktop, or click the Up One Level icon to move backward one folder. In the thumbnail panel, you can double-click an image to open it within Elements, and double-click a folder to see what's inside it. Clicking once on a thumbnail makes it appear in the resizable image preview panel on the left of the palette. Move your cursor to the top, bottom, or right side of the preview area, and then click and drag to expand or shrink the preview.

The area on the left of the palette beneath the image preview shows you a variety of information about the selected image. You can set the menu at the bottom of the palette to All to see all available information, or set it to EXIF to view just the EXIF data.

EXIF stands for Exchangeable Image File, which is a standard format for appending nonpixel information to an image. Many digital cameras use the EXIF format. This information is usually invisible, but the File Browser lets you see it, and it can be quite useful. It typically includes such information as the date and time the photo was taken, the type of camera, the focal length, and other stuff like that. You can also view the EXIF data by choosing the File⇨File Info command and setting the Section menu to EXIF.

Also at the bottom of the palette you'll find a menu with thumbnail sorting options, and another menu, which lets you control the size of the thumbnails and whether you want to include some image information in the thumbnail area. Progressing to the right along the bottom of the palette, you'll see an indicator of how many items are in the currently selected folder and a curved arrow that you can click to rotate the image thumbnail 90 degrees clockwise. Hold down the Alt or Option key as you click to perform a 90-degree rotation counterclockwise.

Clicking this button rotates only the thumbnail, not the actual image itself. However, if you rotate a thumbnail and then double-click it, Elements will open the full image on-screen with the same rotation applied. This is not a permanent change; if you close the image and don't save the changes to the file, the image on disk will not have the rotation applied.

Reorganizing with the File Browser

There's also a trash icon in the bottom-right corner of the File Browser palette. If you select a thumbnail and click the trash icon, or just drag the thumbnail to the icon, Elements actually removes the image from its folder and places it in your computer's Recycle Bin or Trash. This leads us to our next major point about the File Browser: It lets you not only view thumbnails of your files but also actually make changes to the names and organization of your images on your hard drive. For instance, not only can you relocate files to your Recycle

Bin or Trash, you can also drag image thumbnails into the Desktop View panel of the File Browser to move them from the current folder to a new folder. If you want to rename an image, just click the name in the thumbnail panel. Elements highlights the image name and lets you type in a new one.

Although the File Browser's More menu mainly contains commands that correspond to features we've already talked about, there are a couple of other commands worthy of mention. If you want to create a new folder inside the currently active folder, you can choose New Folder. Okay, that one wasn't too exciting, but the next one is great. You can rename an entire folder full of files simultaneously by selecting multiple files and choosing Batch Rename. To select more than one file, you can Shift-click inside the thumbnail panel, or Ctrl- or ⌘-click to select files that aren't next to each other. Or you can choose Select All from the More menu if you want to rename all the images in the current folder. Then choose the Batch Rename command, which will bring up the dialog box pictured in Figure 3-2.

The first choice presented by the Batch Rename dialog box is whether you want to keep the images in the same folder or move them to another one. If you want to move the images, press the Move to a New Folder radio button and click the Choose button to select a new folder.

The File Naming section of the dialog box is where the real action is. You can pick two different variables for creating the names of your files. The three "document name" options retain or change the capitalization of the name currently assigned to the file. Alternatively, you can click and type your own name into one of the option fields. You can also append today's date or sequential strings of numbers and letters.

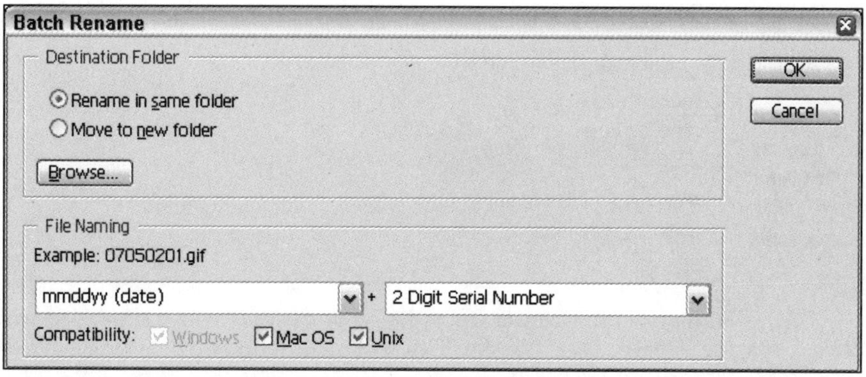

Figure 3-2:
If you don't find default image names like "DSCN0146. JPG" to be very helpful, the Batch Rename dialog box lets you change them to suit your whim.

Batch Rename

Destination Folder

⦿ Rename in same folder
◯ Move to new folder

Browse...

OK

Cancel

File Naming
Example: 07050201.gif

mmddyy (date)   + 2 Digit Serial Number

Compatibility: ☑ Windows ☑ Mac OS ☑ Unix

For instance, let's say that you have a folder containing a couple of dozen photos of your family's vacation in Fiji, and you want the photos to be named "fijivacation01.jpg", "fijivacation02.jpg" and so on. Click and type "fijivacation" in the first field, and then choose 2 Digit Serial Number in the second field. The .jpg extension will be appended automatically. Note that you are required to include a document name, serial number, or serial letter choice when you batch rename your files; otherwise, you'll end up giving all your files exactly the same name — a big impossibility in computer terms.

Go ahead and enable all the check boxes for compatibility with Windows, Mac, and UNIX. You never know where your image files may ultimately end up being viewed!

Opening the ordinary way

The File Browser aside, Elements has several other handy ways to open images. Chapter 1 looked at the Connect to Camera or Scanner options featured on the Welcome screen, including the new Frame From Video option. These same options can be found in the File⇨Import submenu, or by clicking the Import button in the Shortcuts bar. But speaking of the Shortcuts bar, Figure 3-3 shows a convenient one-click Open button also found on the Shortcuts bar; it's the third icon from the left, just past the Adobe.com link and the New file icon. But if you'd rather maneuver through menus, you can choose File⇨Open. Or if clicking icons and choosing menu commands is too much work, just press Ctrl+O (⌘+O on a Mac). The Open dialog box rears its useful head, as shown in Figure 3-4.

Figure 3-3:
If you're the point-and-click type, the Shortcuts bar was made for you.

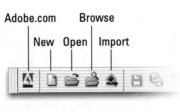

Finding an item in the Open dialog box is somewhat similar to navigating in the File Browser's Desktop View. Just keep looking inside hard drives and folders until you find the folder containing your desired image. If you're not sure whether it's the right one, selecting it with a single click will show you a small preview of the image. When you've found it, double-click it, Press Enter (Win) or Return (Mac), or click the Open button. You're good to go!

Figure 3-4:
This dialog
box lets
you locate
and open
images on
your hard
drive or
some other
disk.

> **Open**
>
> Show: All Readable Documents
>
> From: pix
>
> armsoutstretched.tif
> **cat.psd**
> greatgrin.psd
> inthepark.jpg
> lookdown.psd
> lookup.psd
> whome.gif
>
> Kind: Document
> Size: 6.8 MB
> Created: 4/2/02
> Modified: 4/2/02
>
> Format: Photoshop   6.85M   Find...   Find Again
>
> Go to:
>
> Add to Favorites   Cancel   Open

If you've had an image open fairly recently, you may find it hiding in the File⇨Open Recent submenu. You can set the number of files the Open Recent submenu contains in the Saving Files panel of Elements' Preferences.

Creating a new image

To create a new image instead of opening an existing one, Elements gives you a typically wide range of options. You can use the Welcome screen as mentioned in Chapter 1; use the New icon in the Shortcuts bar (refer to Figure 3-3); choose File⇨New; or press Ctrl+N (on the Mac, press ⌘+N). Whichever method you use, Elements displays the New dialog box.

In the New dialog box, you can name your file; specify the width, height, and resolution (as discussed in Chapter 4); set the color mode (as discussed in Chapter 5); and determine whether you want the file to be filled with white, the current background color, or transparency. Elements 2.0 gives you a new handy shortcut for setting the size and resolution of your file: the Preset Sizes menu. You can choose from a number of standard sizes for print, Web, and digital video work.

In fact, it's a little-known secret, but you can also create your own settings that will show up in the Preset Sizes menu. Located in the Presets folder inside your Adobe Photoshop Elements 2 application folder, the "New Doc Sizes.txt" file is the key. Just open the document and follow the instructions for saving your preset sizes within the document. Although this process isn't for the faint of heart, it's really not that difficult, and if you frequently need to make new images of a specific size and resolution, saving your own preset can be a very useful thing.

Behold the Image Window

After you open up an image, Elements displays the image on-screen inside a new image window. Several new items appear when you open an image, as labeled in Figure 3-5.

The following list explains all:

✔ The title bar lists the title of your image with the file extension (for more on file formats, see Chapter 6). The added bonus is that you can drag the title bar to move the window to a different location on-screen. Easy stuff.

✔ You can choose File➪Close or press Ctrl+W (⌘+W on a Mac) to close an image window. (If you've made some changes to the image, Elements asks you whether you want to save the new and improved image, a process explained in great detail in Chapter 6.)

✔ For PC users: To change the size of the image window, place your cursor over a corner of the window. When a double-headed arrow appears, drag the corner. For Mac users: Place your cursor over the size box in the lower-right corner of the window and drag. On both platforms, the image remains the same; you're just changing the size of the window that holds the image. Give it a try and see what we mean.

✔ On the PC, the Status bar is located at the bottom of the Elements window. On the Mac, it's located at the bottom of the image window. The Status bar gives you information about your image. On the PC, it also provides hints about the tool or command you're using.

PC users, don't see the Status bar on your screen? Choose Window➪Status Bar to display it. Remember that the Status bar disappears when you press Tab to hide the palettes and the Toolbox, as explained in Chapter 2.

✔ The Magnification box lets you zoom in and out on your image, as explained later in this chapter in the section "Zooming in and out on your work."

Title bar   Image area   Scrollbar

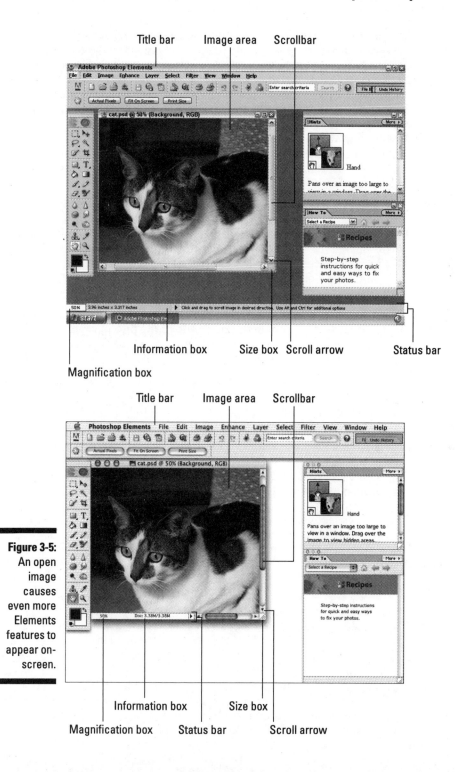

Figure 3-5:
An open
image
causes
even more
Elements
features to
appear on-
screen.

Information box   Size box   Scroll arrow   Status bar

Magnification box

Title bar   Image area   Scrollbar

Information box   Size box

Magnification box   Status bar   Scroll arrow

✔ Next to the Magnification box is the Information box, which shows you by default what the printed size of your document would be. Click the right-pointing arrow, however, and you'll see that this box is a virtual factotum for image information, telling you more than you ever thought there was to know about such matters as image size, resolution, color mode, and so on. Clicking in the Information box itself will always tell you the image's pixel and print dimensions, channel information, and resolution. We cover the most important of these matters later in the book. For the time being, don't worry about the Information box too much. We just didn't want to leave you wondering, "What in the Sam Hill is this thingy here?"

✔ Scrollbars let you navigate around and display hidden portions of the image inside the window. Elements always initially opens an image so that the entire image fits on-screen; no scrollbars are necessary. However, if you enlarge the view of your image sufficiently you will eventually see two scrollbars, one vertical bar along the right side of the image and one horizontal bar along the bottom.

If you click a scroll arrow, you nudge your view of the image slightly in that direction. For example, if you click the right-pointing scroll arrow, an item that was hidden on the right side of the photograph slides into view. Click below or above the scrollbar to scroll the window more dramatically. Drag the scrollbar to manually specify the distance scrolled.

Using the scroll arrows isn't the only way to move around your image; in fact, it's probably the least efficient method. For some better options, check out the techniques presented in the section, "The Screen Is Your Digital Oyster," coming up next.

✔ The area bounded by the title bar and scrollbars is the image area. The image area is where you paint, edit, select details, and, otherwise, have at your image. Obviously, you look at the image area a lot throughout the many pages of this book.

You can open as many images on-screen as your computer's memory and screen size allow. But only one image is active at a time. To make a different window active, just click it or choose its name from the Window⇨Images submenu.

The Screen Is Your Digital Oyster

The Photoshop Elements Toolbox includes two navigation tools: the Hand tool, which lets you scroll the image inside the window with much more ease than the silly scrollbars afford, and the Zoom tool, which has the effect of moving you closer to or farther away from your image. The Hand tool and the Zoom tool are called navigation tools because they don't change the image; they merely alter your view of the image so that you can get a better look-see.

In addition to the above tools, there is another navigational aid, appropriately called the Navigator palette. The palette gives you a super-convenient way to zoom and scroll your image. In fact, after you're familiar with the palette, you may not use the Hand and Zoom tools at all. But in the interest of fair play, we present all the various options for moving around within your image in the upcoming sections.

Using the Hand tool

If you're familiar with other Windows and Macintosh programs, you need to know something about Elements: The scrollbars are relatively useless. Keep away from them. Promise that you'll always use the Hand tool or the Navigator palette (explained shortly) instead. Promise? Good. As for you new users, don't worry — you have no old habits to break.

Consider the following example: The left image in Figure 3-6 shows a young woman displaying a fair amount of attitude. The problem is that the picture is wider than the image window, so you can't see what is motivating her defiant stance.

Hand cursor

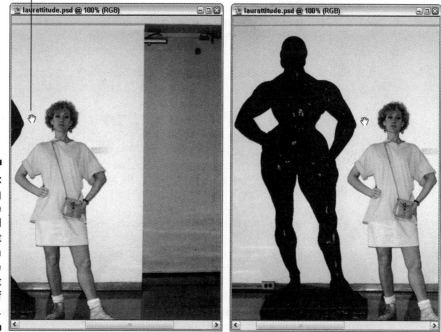

Figure 3-6:
Dragging with the Hand tool reveals that imitation is the sincerest form of flattery.

To view the rest of the scene, select the Hand tool by clicking its icon in the Toolbox. Then position the Hand tool in the image window, as shown in the first example in Figure 3-6, click, and drag to the right. The image moves with the hand cursor, as shown in the second example, and reveals the reason behind the young lady's posturing.

Dragging with the Hand tool is like turning your head to view a new part of your surroundings, except you'll never get a crick in your neck. You can drag at any angle you please — up, down, sideways, or diagonally.

You can also select the Hand tool by pressing the H key. To temporarily access the Hand tool when another tool is selected, press the spacebar. As long as the spacebar is down, the Hand tool is available. Releasing the spacebar returns you to the selected tool.

Using keyboard shortcuts

As in most other programs, you can also use keyboard shortcuts to move about your image. Press Page Up or Page Down to scroll up or down an entire screen. Press Shift+Page Up or Shift+Page Down to scroll in smaller increments. Press Home to go to the upper-left corner of the image, and press End to move to the lower-right corner.

And as if that isn't enough, Elements offers keyboard shortcuts for moving right and left. Press Ctrl+Page Up or Ctrl+Page Down to scroll left or right an entire screen. Press Ctrl+Shift+Page Up or Ctrl+Shift+Page Down to scroll left and right in smaller increments. Mac users, substitute the ⌘ key for the Ctrl key here.

Zooming in and out on your work

When you first open an image, Photoshop Elements displays the entire image so that it fits on-screen. But you may not be seeing the details in the image as clearly as you want. If you want to inspect the image in more detail, you have to move closer. No, don't scoot your chair; read on.

Elements gives you several ways to zoom in and out on your work, as described in these next few sections.

Zooming doesn't change the size of your image in any way — not the size at which it would print, and not the size it would appear on-screen if you e-mailed it to somebody or posted it on the Web. It just temporarily adjusts the size at which you see the image on-screen. Zooming is like looking at some eensey-teensey life form under a microscope. The creature doesn't actually grow and shrink as you vary the degree of magnification, and neither does your image.

The Zoom tool

Using the Zoom tool is one avenue for changing your view of an image. Every time you click your image with the tool, you magnify the image to a larger size. Here's an example of how it works:

1. **Select the Zoom tool.**

   Click the Zoom tool in the Toolbox. It's the one that looks like a magnifying glass. You can also press the Z key to grab the Zoom tool.

2. **Click in the image area.**

   Elements magnifies the image to the next preset zoom size, as demonstrated in the second example of Figure 3-7. The program centers the magnified view about the point at which you click, as much as possible. In Figure 3-7, for example, the boy was zoom-clicked right on the nose.

3. **Repeat.**

   To zoom in farther still, click again with the Zoom tool, as demonstrated in the bottom example of Figure 3-7.

A setting in the Options bar determines whether Elements resizes your image window to match the image when you zoom with the Zoom tool. If you want your image windows to be resized when you zoom, select the Resize Windows To Fit option.

The only hitch comes when the window bumps into a palette. When the window hits a palette that's anchored to the side of the screen (as opposed to floating in the middle of the screen), Elements thinks that it has hit some sort of wall and stops zooming. To get around the problem, simply select the Ignore Palettes option located in the Options bar.

Here's some other Zoom tool stuff to tuck away for future reference:

✔ To zoom out on your image, first switch to the Zoom Out icon in the Options bar (the magnifying glass with the minus sign in it). Holding down the Alt or Option key when you click makes the Zoom tool behave the opposite way from the mode selected in the Options bar.

✔ As you zoom, Elements displays the *zoom factor* in the title bar and the Status bar. A zoom factor of 100 percent shows you one screen pixel for every pixel in your image. (Pixels are explained thoroughly in Chapter 4.)

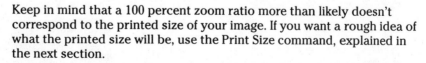

   Keep in mind that a 100 percent zoom ratio more than likely doesn't correspond to the printed size of your image. If you want a rough idea of what the printed size will be, use the Print Size command, explained in the next section.

✔ To magnify just one section of an image, drag with the Zoom tool to surround the area with a dotted outline. Elements fills the image window with the area that you surrounded.

✔ To temporarily access the Zoom tool while another tool is selected, press Ctrl+spacebar (⌘+spacebar on the Mac). Press Ctrl+Alt+spacebar (⌘+Option+spacebar on the Mac) to get the zoom out cursor. In either case, releasing the keys returns you to the previously selected tool.

✔ You can also zoom in and out on your images from the keyboard. Ctrl++ (the plus sign) (⌘++ on the Mac) zooms in; Ctrl+− (the minus sign) (⌘+− on the Mac) zooms out. Although this keyboard shortcut always resizes the window regardless of the settings in the Zoom tool's Options bar, the keyboard shortcut does obey the Zoom tool's Ignore Palettes option, whether you have the Zoom tool selected or not. Note that, technically, the zoom in shortcut is actually Ctrl+= (⌘+= on the Mac); in other words, it's not necessary to also press the Shift key to access the plus sign.

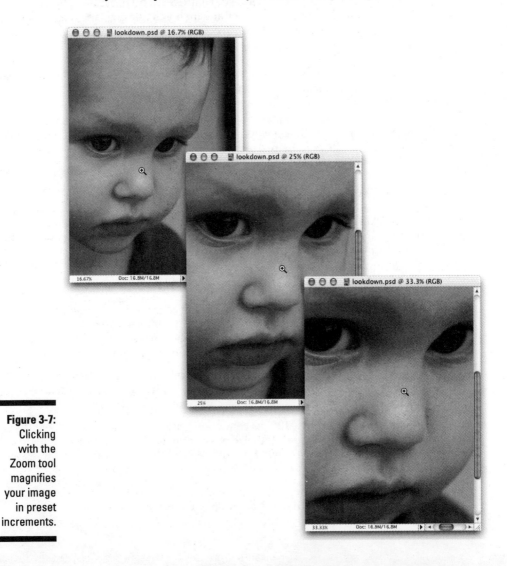

Figure 3-7:
Clicking
with the
Zoom tool
magnifies
your image
in preset
increments.

The View commands

The View menu offers some more ways to change the magnification of your image. The first two zoom commands on the menu, Zoom In and Zoom Out, aren't of much interest; they do the same thing as clicking and Alt+clicking (Option+clicking on a Mac) with the Zoom tool, except that you can't specify the center of the new view as you can with the Zoom tool. But you may find the other View commands helpful at times:

✔ Choose View➪Fit on Screen or press Ctrl+0 (zero) (⌘+0 on the Mac) to display your image at the largest size that allows the entire image to fit on-screen.

✔ Choose View➪Actual Pixels or press Ctrl+Alt+0 (zero) (⌘+Option+0 on the Mac) to return to the 100 percent zoom ratio. This view size shows you one pixel on your monitor for every pixel in the image, which is the most accurate way to view your image.

✔ You can also choose the Fit on Screen view by double-clicking the Hand tool icon in the Toolbox. Double-click the Zoom tool icon to change to the Actual Pixels view.

✔ Choose View➪Print Size to display your image on-screen in a rough approximation of the size at which it will print.

✔ When you have the Hand or Zoom tool selected, you can simply click the Actual Pixels, Fit on Screen, or Print Size buttons in the Options bar.

✔ You can choose View➪New View to create a second view of your image. Don't confuse this with duplicating an image, which creates a new file. New View simply creates a second way of looking at the same file. New View can be useful when you are editing an image in a magnified view, yet want to see the overall results on your entire image without having to continuously zoom in and out.

The Magnification box

Clicking the Zoom tool and choosing the View commands are great when you want to zoom in or out to one of the preset Elements zoom ratios. But what if you want more control over your zooming? The answer awaits in the Magnification box (refer to Figure 3-5).

To enter a zoom ratio, just double-click or click and drag on the Magnification box and type the zoom ratio you want to use. If you know exactly what zoom ratio you want, press Enter (Return on a Mac) to make Elements do your bidding. But if you want to play around with different zoom ratios, press Shift+Enter (Shift+Return on a Mac) instead. That way, Elements zooms your image, but keeps the Magnification box active so that you can quickly enter a new ratio if the first one doesn't work out. When you're satisfied, press Enter (Return on a Mac).

When you use the Magnification box, the image window size doesn't change as you zoom, regardless of whether the Resize Windows to Fit option is selected in the Options bar.

Navigating by palette

The Navigator palette, shown in Figure 3-8, is the best navigational aid in Elements because it actually combines the functions of the Zoom and Hand tools in one location. Choose Window➪Navigator to make the Navigator palette appear on the desktop. To make the palette smaller or larger, drag the size box in the palette's lower-right corner.

View box

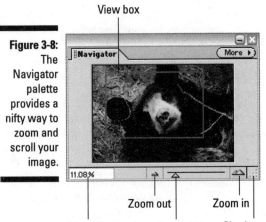

Figure 3-8: The Navigator palette provides a nifty way to zoom and scroll your image.

Zoom out   Zoom in

Magnification box   Zoom slider   Size box

The palette provides a handy, all-in-one tool for scrolling and zooming. It's especially useful when you're working on a large image that doesn't fit entirely on-screen when you're zoomed in for detail work. Here are the how-tos for using the palette:

✔ In the center of the palette, you see a thumbnail view of your image, as shown in Figure 3-8. The palette shows your entire image, even if it's not all visible in the main image window.

✔ See the red box that surrounds a portion of the thumbnail? That's called the view box. The area within the box corresponds to the portion of your image that's visible in the main image window. As you drag the box, Elements scrolls your image in the main image window to display the area that's surrounded by the box. You can also click an area in the thumbnail to move the view box over that portion of the image.

✔ Press and hold Ctrl (⌘ on a Mac), and the cursor in the palette changes to a zoom cursor. If you drag with the cursor while pressing Ctrl (⌘ on a Mac), you resize the view box, which, in turn, zooms the image in the image window.

✔ The palette also contains a Magnification box, as labeled in Figure 3-8. The box works just like the one in the Status bar; just enter a zoom factor and press Enter (Return on a Mac).

✔ To zoom in or out in the preset Elements increments (as with the Zoom tool), click the Zoom In or Zoom Out buttons, labeled in Figure 3-8.

✔ You can also zoom by dragging the Zoom slider — drag left to zoom out, and drag right to zoom in.

If you're having trouble picking out the view box against the colors of your image, you can change the view box's color. Click the More menu and choose the Palette Options command. Then choose a new color from the Color drop-down menu, or click the Swatch to open the Color Picker, where you can choose exactly the shade you want. For more on the Color Picker, see Chapter 5.

Tools for the Terribly Precise

If you've ever used a page layout program such as PageMaker or QuarkXPress, you're no doubt familiar with the concept of *grids*. Shown in Figure 3-9, a grid is an on-screen device that helps you align items in your image. For example, in the figure the grid was used to keep the words spaced both horizontally and vertically in the image.

In addition to grids, Elements offers rulers that run across the top and left sides of the image window. Grids and rulers come in handy when you're feeling the urge to be especially precise with your work. And the Info palette helps you get a bead on exactly what's going on in your image.

Switching on the rulers

To display rulers, choose View➪Rulers or press Ctrl+R (⌘+R on a Mac). To hide the rulers, choose View➪Rulers or press Ctrl+R (⌘+R on a Mac) again.

By default, the rulers use inches as their unit of measurement. But if you want to use some other unit, say pixels instead of inches, go to the Units & Rulers panel of Elements' Preferences, or just double-click a ruler. In the Units section of the dialog box that appears, select a new unit of measurement from the Rulers drop-down menu. You can also right-click (Control-click on a Mac) on either ruler to access a shortcut menu where you can select your desired unit of measurement.

Grid lines   Ruler

Figure 3-9:
Our furry
friend isn't
really
fenced in;
he's just
covered
with grid
lines.

Turning on the grid

The grid positions lines across your image at regular intervals. Although you can't move grid lines, you can turn them on and off, and change the spacing and color of the lines.

To turn on the grid, choose View⇨Grid. To change the spacing and appearance of the grid lines, go to the Grid panel of Elements' Preferences. Elements presents you with a dialog box in which you can choose a color and line style for the grid lines. Specify how far apart you want to space the lines, and choose whether you want to subdivide the grid with secondary grid lines. You can also choose a unit of measurement for the grid.

The lines of a grid have "snapping" capabilities — anything you drag near a grid line automatically snaps into alignment with that line. You turn snapping on and off by choosing View⇨Snap to Grid.

Information, please

The Info palette can be a big help when you need to know precise values related to your image. By default, the Info palette is divided into four parts: The upper two sections give you the exact values for the color of the pixel your cursor happens to be over, the bottom-left section tells you exactly where in the image your cursor is located, and the bottom-right section tells you the dimensions of an active selection.

The units of measurement are changeable in two ways. You can click the tiny little arrows next to the eyedroppers and the crosshair, or you can use the Info palette's More menu.

The bottom-left section works on an x and y coordinate system. Assuming you've set the units of measurement for this section to pixels (usually the most helpful setting, by the way), if you move your cursor into the upper-left corner of the image, you'll notice that the x and y coordinates are both at 0. Move your cursor to the right across the upper edge of the image — along the x-axis — and you'll see the x coordinate grow. Move your cursor down — along the y-axis — and you'll see the y coordinate grow.

The Info palette also gives you different kinds of feedback depending on which tool you're using. If your monitor is large enough — or if you have the luxury of working on a two-monitor system — you may want to keep it open at all times when you're working. In this information age, it's easy to get addicted to watching this palette.

Chapter 4

Pixels: It's Hip to Be Square

. . . .

. . . .

*I*mages that you create and edit in Photoshop Elements — or in any other image-editing application for that matter — are made up of tiny squares called *pixels*. Understanding how pixels work in an image can be enormously confusing to beginning image editors. Unfortunately, managing your pixel population correctly is essential to turning out professional-looking images, so you really do need to come to grips with how pixels work before you can thoroughly master Elements.

This chapter explains everything you need to know to put pixels in perspective, including how the number of pixels in an image affects its quality, printed size, size on-screen, and size on disk. You'll also see how to reduce or enlarge the size of the on-screen canvas on which all your pretty pixels perch. In other words, this chapter proffers pages of particularly provocative pixel paragraphs, partner.

Welcome to Pixeltown

Imagine that you're the victim of a terrifying scientific experiment that has left you 1 millimeter tall. After recovering from the initial shock that such terrifying scientific experiments tend to produce on one's equilibrium, you discover that you're sitting on a square tile that's colored with a uniform shade of blue. Beyond your tile are eight other blue tiles, one to your right and one to your left, one in front and one behind, and four others in diagonal directions. In other words, the tiles are aligned in a perfect grid, just like standard floor tiles but without the grout. You notice upon further inspection that each of the blue tiles differs slightly in shade and tone. As you slowly turn, it becomes evident that you're surrounded by these colored tiles for as far as your infinitesimally tiny, pinprick eyes can see.

You cry out in anguish and fling your dust-speck body about in the way that folks always do when plagued by these terrifying scientific experiments. As though in answer to your pitiful squeals, you start to grow. In a matter of moments, you increase in size to almost 5 centimeters tall. A bug that was considering devouring you has a change of mind and runs away. You can now see that you sit in the midst of a huge auditorium and that all the tiles on its vast and unending floor are colored differently, gradually changing from shades of blue to shades of green, red, and yellow. You continue to grow: 10 centimeters, 20, 50, a full meter tall. The tiles start to blend together to form some kind of pattern. Two meters, 5, 10. Your massive head bursts through the flimsy ceiling of the room. This must be how Alice felt in Wonderland. You've now grown several times beyond your normal height, reaching 20 meters tall.

When you reach the height of a 50-story building, your growth spurt comes to an end. You look down at the ruined auditorium, whose walls have been shredded to rubble by the great edges of your tremendous feet, and you notice a peculiar thing. You stand not on a floor, but on a picture, as rich in color and detail as any you've seen. The tiles, which now appear dot-sized to you, have merged together to create a seamless blend. You would expect the result to have the rough appearance of a mosaic — requiring a heavy dose of imagination to compensate for occasionally choppy transitions — but, in fact, it looks exactly like a continuous tone photograph.

The vision inspires you to claw at your temples, fling your arms about in circles, and shriek, "What's happening to me?!" The answer, of course, is nothing (other than a little overacting, that is). Well, okay, your body may be stretched out of shape, but your eyes are working fine. You see, when you get far enough away from a perfect grid of colored tiles — whether via a terrifying scientific experiment or more conventional means — the tiles disappear, and an overall image takes shape.

What does this little trip down sci-fi lane have to do with Elements? Well, a lot, actually. As is the image on the auditorium floor, your Elements image is made up of a grid of colored squares. In this case, the squares are called *pixels*.

By now, you're probably thinking, "Fine, images are made up of a bunch of itsy-bitsy square pixels. So what? Who cares? Quit wasting my time, darn it." The truth is, these tiniest of image particles are at the heart of what makes Elements and your electronic images tick.

Every single painting and image-editing function in Elements is devoted to changing the quantity, the arrangement, or the color of pixels. That's all Elements does. It sounds so simple that you figure it must be a joke, an exaggeration, or just a plain lie. But it's the absolute truth. Elements is merely an extremely sophisticated pixel counter, colorer, and arranger, nothing more.

Screen Pixels versus Image Pixels

Like the tiles in the preceding story, each pixel in a computer image is perfectly square, arranged on a perfect grid, and colored uniformly — that is, each pixel is one color and one color only. Put these pixels together, and your brain perceives them to be an everyday, average photograph.

The display on your computer's monitor is also made up of pixels. As with image pixels, screen pixels are square and arranged on a grid. For instance, a typical monitor display measures at least 800 screen pixels wide by 600 screen pixels tall. These screen pixels are kind of tiny, so you may not be able to make them out. Each one generally measures around ¹⁄₇₂ inch across.

To understand the relationship between screen and image pixels, open an image. After the image comes up on-screen, double-click the Zoom tool in the Toolbox, or choose View➪Actual Pixels. The Magnification box in the Status bar lists the zoom ratio as 100%, which means that you can see one pixel in your image for every pixel displayed by your monitor.

To view the image pixels more closely, enter a value of **200%** in the Magnification box. A 200% zoom factor magnifies the image pixels to twice their previous size so that one image pixel measures two screen pixels tall and two screen pixels wide. If you change the zoom factor to 400%, Elements gives you a total of 16 screen pixels for every image pixel (4 screen pixels tall by 4 screen pixels wide). Figure 4-1 illustrates how different zoom factors affect the appearance of your image pixels on-screen.

Remember that the zoom factor has nothing to do with the size at which your image would print or display if e-mailed to a friend or posted on the Web — it affects only how your image looks on-screen at that moment. If you want to see on-screen an approximation of your image's print size, choose View➪Print Size. Bear in mind, though, that this is only a very rough approximation.

100%   200%

400%   800%

Figure 4-1:
Increasing
the zoom
factor
makes your
image pixels
temporarily
appear
larger
on-screen
but doesn't
affect the
final image.

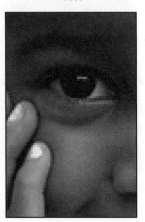
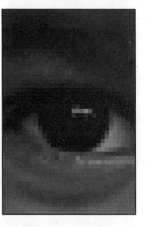

Image Size, Resolution, and Other Tricky Pixel Stuff

An Elements image has three primary attributes related to pixels: *file size,* *resolution,* and *physical dimensions,* as explained in the following list. You control these attributes through the Image Size dialog box, shown in Figure 4-2. To display the dialog box, choose Image➪Resize➪Image Size.

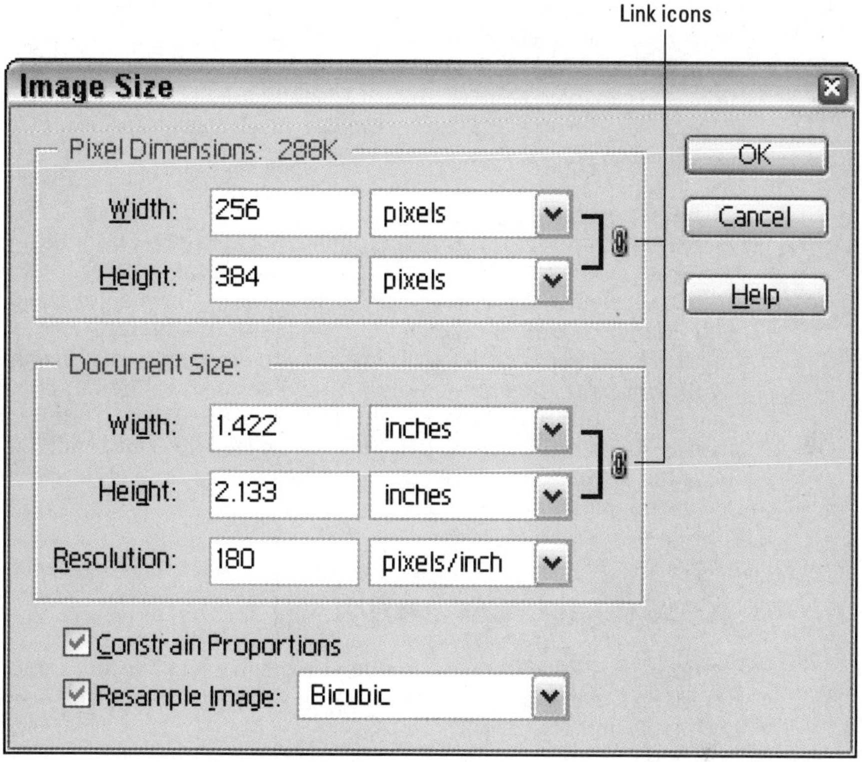

Link icons

Image Size   ☒

┌─ Pixel Dimensions: 288K ──────────────────────┐
│   │   [OK]
│   Width: [256]   [pixels ▼] ┐   │
│   ⫘   │   [Cancel]
│   Height: [384]   [pixels ▼] ┘   │
│   │   [Help]
└───┘

┌─ Document Size: ──────────────────────────────┐
│   │
│   Width: [1.422]   [inches   ▼] ┐   │
│   ⫘   │
│   Height: [2.133]   [inches   ▼] ┘   │
│   │
│   Resolution: [180] [pixels/inch ▼]   │
└───┘

☑ Constrain Proportions
☑ Resample Image: [Bicubic   ▼]

Figure 4-2:
You control
file size,
image
dimensions,
and
resolution
through the
Image Size
dialog box.

If you just want to get a quick look at the dimensions and resolution of an image, click the Information box (next to the Magnification box). Elements displays a little box listing the dimensions, resolution, and other stuff.

- ✔ The *pixel dimensions* of the image is a measure of how many pixels the image contains. The image in Figure 4-1 is 256 pixels wide and 384 pixels tall, for a total of 98,304 pixels. Most of the images you create contain hundreds of thousands or even millions of pixels.

- ✔ The *resolution* of an image refers to the number of pixels that print per inch (or per centimeter, if you're using the metric system). For example, the resolution of the first image in Figure 4-1 is 180 pixels per inch *(ppi)*. That may sound like an awful lot of pixels squished into a small space, but it's actually a little on the low side.

- ✔ Not to be confused with pixel dimensions, the *document size* of an image is its physical width and height when printed, as measured in inches, centimeters, or your unit of choice. You can calculate the document size by dividing the number of pixels by the resolution. For example, the little boy in Figure 4-1 measures 256 pixels ÷ 180 pixels per inch = 1⅜ inches wide and 384 pixels ÷ 180 ppi = 2⅛ inches tall. Measure him with a ruler, and you see that this is indeed the case.

No problem, right? Sure, this stuff is a little technical, but it's not as though it requires an advanced degree in cold fusion to figure out what's going on. And yet, the Image Size dialog box may well be the most confusing Elements dialog box. You can even damage your image if you're not careful. So be extremely careful before you make changes in the Image Size dialog box. (The upcoming sections tell you everything you need to know to stay out of trouble.)

There are other ways to change the print size of your image, chiefly with Elements' Print Preview command (File➪Print Preview). On the Mac, you can also change the print size with the Page Setup command (File➪Page Setup). On either platform, it's also possible that your printer software may give you yet another option for changing the print size. When using any of these methods, Elements scales your image to the new size only during the print cycle. However, the interaction of having up to four different commands telling your printer how large to print an image can be, to put it mildly, confusing. Your best bet is to stick with the Image Size command; it's entirely possible to change the print size with Image Size and yet not permanently affect the quality of your image in any way.

Resolving resolution

Although the Resolution option box seems like just another option in the Image Size dialog box, it's one of the most critical values to consider if you want your images to look good.

The Resolution value determines how tightly the pixels are packed when printed. It's kind of like the population density of one of those ridiculously large urban areas cropping up all over the modern world. Take Lagos, Nigeria, for example, which is a city of approximately 15 million souls. The population density of Lagos is such that there are roughly 267,000 people packed into each square mile.

In order to increase the population density, you have to either increase the number of people in a city or decrease the physical boundaries of the city and scrunch everyone closer together. The same goes for resolution. If you want a higher resolution (more pixels per inch), you can either decrease the document size of the image or increase the pixel dimensions by adding pixels to the image. For example, the two images in Figure 4-3 have the same pixel dimensions, but the top image has a smaller document size, giving it twice the resolution of the larger image — 180 ppi versus 90 ppi.

Conversely, population density goes down as people die, move out, or as the boundaries of the city grow. For example, if we were to mandate that Lagos spread out evenly over the entire 357,000 square miles of Nigeria, the population density would temporarily drop to 42 people per square mile (assuming, of course, that the other residents of Nigeria happened to be on vacation at the time). Likewise, when you increase the document size of an image or delete some of its pixels, the resolution goes down.

Figure 4-3:
Two images
with the
exact same
number of
pixels but
subject
to two
different
resolutions.

Before you get the mistaken idea that this analogy is completely airtight, we should in all fairness mention a few key differences between a typical image and Lagos:

✔ Lagos, as any city does, has its crowded spots and its relatively sparse areas. An image, by contrast, is equally dense at all points. Unlike population density, therefore, resolution is constant across the board.

✔ An image is always rectangular. Lagos can best be described as free form.

✔ Population density is measured in terms of area — you know, so many folks per square mile. Resolution, on the other hand, is measured in a line — pixels per linear inch (or centimeter). So an image with a resolution of 180 pixels per inch contains 32,400 pixels per square inch. (That's 180 squared, in case you're wondering.)

✔ The pixels in an image are absolutely square. The people in Lagos are shaped rather arbitrarily, with undulating arms and legs jutting out at irregular and unpredictable angles.

✔ You have total control over the size and resolution of an image. You can move to Lagos and thereby increase the population by one, but otherwise the population of Lagos is entirely out of your hands.

Changing pixel dimensions

The top two option boxes in the Image Size dialog box enable you to change an image's *pixel dimensions* — the number of pixels wide by the number of pixels tall. Unless you really know what you're doing when it comes to pixels, it might be best to avoid these option boxes.

Lowering the Pixel Dimensions values can be dangerous because what you're really doing is throwing away pixels. And when you delete pixels, you delete detail. Figure 4-4 shows what we mean. The document size of all three images is the same, but the detail drops off from one image to the next. The first image contains 64,000 pixels and is printed at a resolution of 140 ppi; the second contains ¼ as many pixels and is printed at 70 ppi. The third contains only 4,000 pixels and has a resolution of 35 ppi. Notice how details such as the shadows from the girl's eyelashes and the distinction between individual hairs in her eyebrows become less pronounced and more generalized as the pixel population decreases.

Increasing the Pixel Dimensions values isn't such a hot idea either, because Elements can't generate image detail out of thin air. When you raise the Pixel Dimensions values, Elements adds pixels by averaging the preexisting pixels (a process computer nerds call *interpolation*) in a way that may result in image softening and never results in the miraculous reconstruction of detail.

If changing the pixel dimensions is dangerous, you may wonder why Elements gives you the option to do so at all. Well, although we don't recommend ever adding pixels to an image, you may actually need to lower the pixel dimensions. If your file size is really large — that is, your image contains a ton of pixels — you may want to toss some of the pixels overboard.

In an ideal world, you'd want as many pixels as possible because more pixels means greater image detail. But if you're posting your image on the Internet, you may need to reduce your pixel dimensions so that the image will download more quickly and simply so that it can fit on your users' screens. Also, the more pixels you have, the more disk space the image consumes, which can be a problem if you're working with limited computing resources. Large file sizes can also slow down Elements substantially.

Even when you dump pixels from an image, you shouldn't attack the job from the Pixel Dimensions option boxes; you'll discover a better way in the steps in the section "Using the Image Size dialog box safely" later in this chapter.

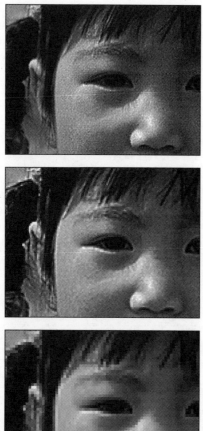

Figure 4-4:
Three
images,
each
containing
fewer pixels
and printed
at a lower
resolution
than the
image
above it.

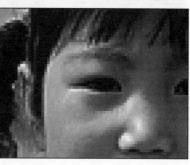

Changing the physical dimensions of the image

The Width and Height boxes in the Document Size portion of the Image Size dialog box reflect the actual printed size of your image. The drop-down menus next to the Width and Height options let you change the unit of measure displayed in the option boxes. For example, if you select picas from the Document Size Width drop-down menu, Elements converts the equivalent Width value from inches to picas. (A *pica* is an obscure typesetting measurement equal to ⅙ inch.) The percent option in the drop-down menu enables you to enter new width and height values as a percentage of the original values. Enter a value higher than 100% to increase the print size; enter a value lower than 100% to reduce the print size.

When you change the document size of the image, the resolution value or the number of pixels in the image automatically changes, too, which can affect the quality of your image. For more information, read the section "Resolving resolution" earlier in this chapter. And for details on how to change the print size without ruining your image, see the section "Using the Image Size dialog box safely" later in this chapter.

Yeah, okay, but what resolution should I use?

There are all kinds of formulas for calculating the optimal resolution for various types of output. But rather than try to explain any of these — what with your head already spinning with Lagos population data — we'll just go ahead and simply list some ideal and acceptable values for certain kinds of print jobs. See whether these work for you.

Type of Job	Ideal Resolution	Acceptable Setting
Full-color image for magazine or professional publication	300 ppi	225 ppi
Full-color slides	300 ppi	200 ppi
Color ink jet printers	300 ppi	200 ppi
Color image for laser printing or overhead projections	180 ppi	120 ppi
Color images for multimedia productions and World Wide Web pages	72 ppi	72 ppi
Black-and-white images for imageset newsletters, flyers, and so on	180 ppi	120 ppi
Black-and-white images for laser printing	120 ppi	90 ppi

Keep in mind that there are no hard-and-fast rules about resolution settings. You can specify virtually any resolution setting between the ideal and acceptable settings and achieve good results. Even if you go with a Resolution value that's lower than the suggested acceptable setting, the worst that can happen is that you'll get fuzzy or slightly jagged results. But there is no wrong setting.

Keeping things proportionate

Both pairs of Width and Height option boxes in the Image Size dialog box list the dimensions of your image. If you enter a different value into an option box and click the OK button, Elements resizes your image to the dimensions you specified. Pretty obvious, eh?

But strangely, when you change the width or height value, by default the other value changes, too. Are these twins that were separated at birth? Is there some new cosmic relationship between width and height that's known only to outer-space aliens and the checkout clerk at your local grocery store? No, it's nothing more than a function of the Constrain Proportions check box, which is turned on by default. Elements is simply maintaining the original proportions of the image.

If you click the Constrain Proportions box and turn it off, Elements permits you to adjust the width and height values independently. Notice that the little link icon (labeled back in Figure 4-2) disappears, showing that the two options are now maverick independents with reckless disregard for one another. You can now create stretchy effects like the ones shown in Figure 4-5. The first example has the width value reduced, with the height value unchanged. In the second example, the height value was reduced, leaving the width value unaltered.

However, in order to deselect the Constrain Proportions check box, you have to select the Resample Image check box. As explained in the highly antici-pated section "Using the Image Size dialog box safely," when you change the width or height of your image with the Resample Image check box selected, Elements either adds or deletes pixels from your image. Obviously, to stretch an image as shown in Figure 4-5, pixels have to be added or deleted. There-fore, if you want to turn off Constrain Proportions, you have to turn on Resample Image.

Using the Image Size dialog box safely

As mentioned earlier in the section "Image Size, Resolution, and Other Tricky Pixel Stuff," you have three image attributes — size, resolution, and dimension — all vying for your attention and all affecting each other. These attributes, in fact, are like three points on a triangle. Change any one of the points, and at least one of the others has to change proportionately. If you decrease the pixel dimensions, for example, either the document size or resolution (number of pixels per inch) must also decrease. If you want to increase the document size, you have to increase the pixel dimensions — add pixels, in other words — or decrease the resolution.

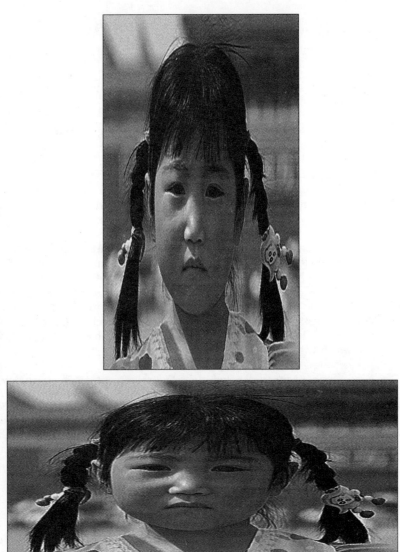

Figure 4-5:
This little
girl was
allowed to
use the
Image Size
dialog box
without
parental
supervision,
providing
clear
examples of
what can
happen
when the
Constrain
Proportions
check box
falls into the
wrong
hands.

Thinking about all the possible permutations can drive you crazy, and besides, they aren't the least bit important. What is important is that you understand what you can accomplish with the Image Size dialog box and that you know how to avoid mistakes. So, now that you have all the background you need, it's finally time for a modicum of fatherly advice:

✔ The first question to ask yourself when using the Image Size command is: "Do I want to change the number of pixels in my image?" If the image is intended for print, the answer is almost certainly "No." In this case, the first thing you should do is deselect the Resample Image check box. Deselecting this box enables you only to change the document size, affecting the size of the image when it is ultimately printed. However, as you adjust the Width or Height values, you must keep an eye on the resolution to make sure that it doesn't fall below an acceptable value (see the "Yeah, okay, but what resolution should I use?" chart for ball-park figures).

✔ If, however, your document is intended for the Web, you may well want to change the number of pixels in your image. Even a one-megapixel digital camera produces images with too many pixels to be seen simultaneously on most computer screens. In this case, make sure that Resample Image is selected. You can totally ignore the Document Size portion of the Image Size dialog box; when preparing images to be seen on a computer screen, the only thing that matters is the pixel dimensions.

Some other things to keep in mind:

✔ When you deselect the Resample Image check box, the Image Size dialog box changes, and the Width and Height options in the Pixel Dimensions portion of the dialog box become unavailable to you. A link icon also connects the Document Size's Width, Height, and Resolution option boxes, showing that changes to one value affect the other two values as well.

✔ Want a surefire way to tell whether you've changed the pixel dimensions? Your image looks different on-screen after you change the Document Size values and exit the Image Size dialog box. As long as the pixel dimensions remain unchanged, you won't see any difference — none, zilch, zippo — on-screen. On-screen, Elements just shows your image pixels with respect to screen pixels; resolution and document size enter into the equation only when you print the image.

✔ If you manage to mess up everything and change one or more settings in the Image Size dialog box to settings that you don't want to apply, you can return to the original settings by Alt+clicking (Option+clicking on a Mac) on the Cancel button. Pressing Alt (Option on a Mac) changes the word Cancel to Reset; clicking resets the options. Now you have your original settings back in place so that you can muck them up again. If you already pressed Enter (Return on a Mac) to exit the Image Size dialog box, click the Step Backward icon in the Shortcuts bar (the down-left pointing arrow) or press Ctrl+Z (⌘+Z on a Mac) to travel backward in time to before you dared to tamper with the image size.

✔ If you performed *another* action after you erroneously resized, you can keep clicking the Step Backward button or keep pressing Ctrl+Z (⌘+Z on a Mac) to keep moving backward in time until the unfortunate image sizing goes away. This does have its limits, which you'll find out more about when we look at the magnificent and powerful Undo History palette in Chapter 7.

✔ Whatever you do, be sure to use the Bicubic setting in the Resample Image drop-down menu. We'd tell you what *bicubic* means, but you don't want to know. Suffice it to say that it keeps things looking smooth.

✔ If you want to change the unit of measure that displays by default in the Image Size dialog box drop-down menus, choose Edit⇨Preferences⇨Units & Rulers and select a different option from the Rulers drop-down menu.

What Does This Canvas Size Command Do?

There's another important command related to the topic of image sizing: Image⇨Resize⇨Canvas Size. Unlike the Image Size command, which in some manner changes the size of the preexisting image, the Canvas Size command changes the size of the page — or canvas — on which the image sits. If you increase the size of the canvas, Elements fills the new area outside the image with the background color, assuming that the image has a background layer (see Chapter 9 for more on layers). If you make the canvas smaller, Elements crops the image. Have you ever written a sign on a piece of poster board and found as you got to the end of a line that you'd been writing too large, giving you no other choice but to scrunch up your letters in an unreadable clump? That's the sort of thing that Canvas Size can fix for you (but only on the computer, needless to say); it can tack on that little bit of extra space to your digital poster board.

When you choose Image⇨Resize⇨Canvas Size, the dialog box, shown in Figure 4-6, pops up from its virtual hole. You can play with the options found in the dialog box as follows:

✔ Enter new values into the Width and Height option boxes as desired. You can also change the unit of measurement by using the drop-down menus, just as in the Image Size dialog box.

✔ You can't constrain the proportions of the canvas the way you can in the Image Size dialog box. Therefore, the width and height values always operate independently.

✔ The Anchor section shows a graphic representation of how the current image sits inside the new canvas. By default, the image is centered in the canvas. But you can click inside any of the other eight squares to move the image to, for example, the upper-right corner. This would mean that the additional canvas would be added to the left and bottom of your original image.

✔ If you reduce either the width or height value and press Enter (Return on a Mac), Elements asks you whether you really want to clip (or crop) the image. If you click the Proceed button and decide you don't like the results, you can always click the Step Backward icon or press Ctrl+Z (⌘+Z on a Mac) to restore the original canvas size.

✔ As with Image Size, if you want to change the unit of measure that displays by default in the Canvas Size dialog box, choose Edit⇨Preferences⇨Units & Rulers and select a different option from the Rulers drop-down menu.

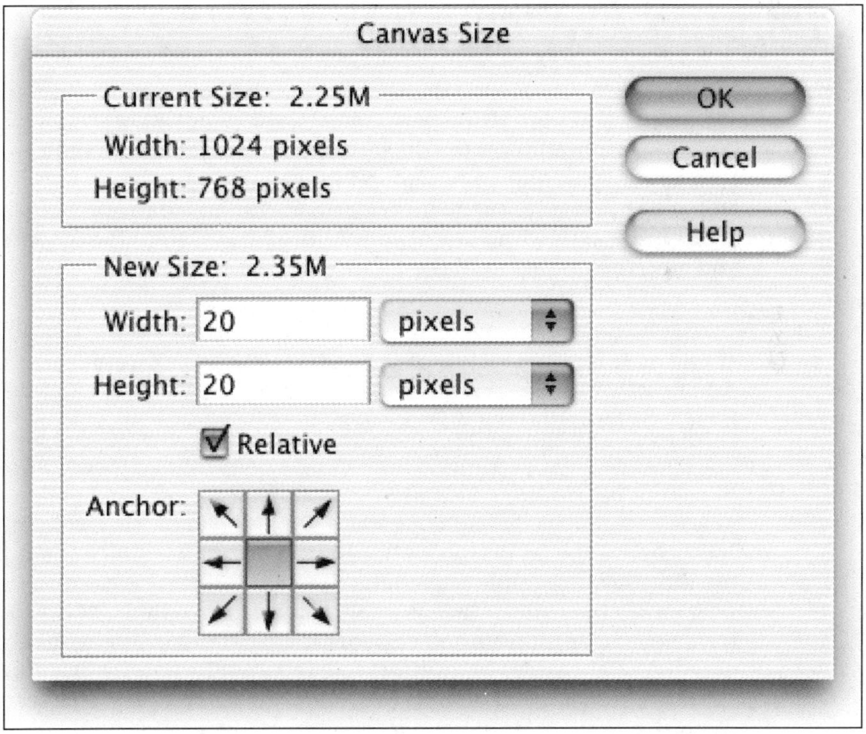

Figure 4-6:
Use the Canvas Size dialog box to change the size of the virtual page on which the image sits.

Canvas Size

Current Size: 2.25M

Width: 1024 pixels

Height: 768 pixels

OK

Cancel

Help

New Size: 2.35M

Width: 20   pixels

Height: 20   pixels

☑ Relative

Anchor:

In the previous version of Elements, using Canvas Size often required a bit of — ick — math. Let's say you had an image that was 256 pixels wide by 128 pixels high, and you wanted to add 75 pixels to both the width and the height. Canvas Side could do this before, of course, but you'd be responsible for doing the addition yourself, adding 75 to both 256 and 128 for a final width of 331 and a height of 203. The new Relative check box in Elements 2.0 makes this a snap; no addition required. In the scenario described above, all you'd have to do is select the Relative check box and type 75 into both the Width and Height fields. When Relative is active, Canvas Size automatically adds the amounts you enter to the current dimensions. This is great for adding, say, a 20-pixel border around an image; just type **20** into both the Width and Height fields, and you're done. Relative works when you're cropping images with Canvas Size too; just select Relative and type in negative numbers, such as *–75*.

Trimming Excess Gunk Off the Edges

Although you can use the Canvas Size command to crop images, it's hardly the best tool at your disposal. Elements, the handy-dandy application that it is, has specialized tools for the job. The Image Size command can definitely turn an 8-x-10 wedding photograph into a nifty wallet-size snapshot without trimming off anyone's vital body parts. But suppose that your spouse up and runs off to Lagos with your next-door neighbor? What do you do then? Why, you crop the cretin out of the picture.

The sharp edges of the Crop tool

Novice photographers have a habit of worrying about getting too much imagery into their pictures. This can be a dangerous concern. In your effort to cut out background flack as you're framing the picture in your camera, you may overcompensate and cut off Grandma's head or the right half of little Joey's body. The fact is, it's better to have too much stuff in your photos than too little, for the simple reason that excess stuff can be cut away, but missing stuff has to be reshot. Since photography was invented, production artists have been taking knives and scissors to just about every image that passes over their light tables in an effort to clip away the extraneous gook around the edges and hone in on the real goods. Called *cropping,* this technique is so pervasive that professional photographers purposely shoot subjects from too far away knowing that someone, somewhere, will slice the image and make it right. As with the Canvas Size command, cropping changes the pixel dimensions and the document size of your image without changing the resolution. (Of course, the content of your image changes, too.)

Inside Elements, you can cut away the unpalatable parts of an image by using the Crop tool. To select the Crop tool without messing with the Toolbox, press C.

Here's how to use the Crop tool:

1. **Drag with the tool around the portion of the image you want to retain.**

   In Figure 4-7, that's the floating spaceman. A dotted rectangle called a *marquee* follows your drag to clearly show the crop boundaries. After you've drawn your marquee, Elements covers the area outside the marquee with a translucent *shield* to better frame the image. You can use the shield controls in the Options bar to specify the color and opacity of the shield or to turn it off entirely. Don't worry if you don't draw the perfect marquee; you get the chance to edit the boundary in the next step.

Handle   Resize cursor   Crop boundary

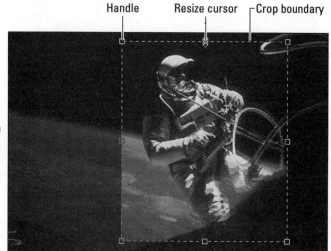

Figure 4-7:
Drag the
square
handles to
change
the crop
boundary.

If you press the spacebar during your initial drag, Elements stops resizing the crop boundary and starts moving the entire boundary. This technique can be helpful when you're trying to position the boundary precisely. (You can also move the boundary, after you create it, without the spacebar.)

2. **Drag the crop boundaries as desired.**

   After you release your mouse button, Elements displays square handles around the edges of the marquee (refer to Figure 4-7). If the marquee isn't the right size, drag a handle to change the crop boundary. Your cursor changes to a double-headed arrow when you place it over a handle, indicating that you have the go-ahead to drag the handle. You can drag as many handles as you please — one at a time, of course — before cropping the image. Holding down the Shift key while dragging from one of the corner handles constrains the proportions of the crop. Holding down the Alt key (the Option key on the Mac) makes the resizing of the crop boundary occur around the visible center point of the crop.

If you move the cursor outside the crop boundary, the cursor changes to a curved, double-headed arrow. Dragging then rotates the crop boundary. Once the crop boundary is rotated, dragging from one of the square handles with the Alt key pressed (the Option key on the Mac) enables you to create a nonrectangular crop, without right angles at the corners. When you accept the crop (see Step 3), Elements does the necessary distortions to convert the nonrectangular crop back into a rectangular image.

3. **After you get the crop boundary the way you want it, double-click inside the boundary to crop the image or click the Commit button in the Options bar.**

   You can also just press Enter (Return on a Mac). Elements throws away all pixels outside the crop boundary. If you rotated the crop boundary in Step 2, Elements rights the rectangular area and thus rotates the image, as shown in Figure 4-8.

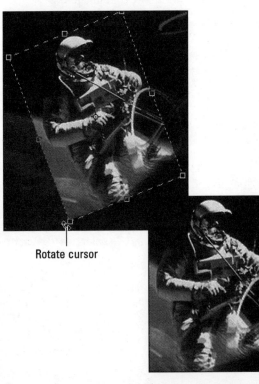

Rotate cursor

Figure 4-8:
If the photograph isn't straight, you can rotate the crop boundary to match (top) while telling Elements to crop and straighten the image at the same time (bottom).

When you rotate an image in this way, Elements *resamples* your image — that is, it rearranges the pixels to come up with the rotated image. As discussed earlier, resampling can damage your image by making the details softer. For best results, don't rotate your image more than once. However, if you rotate your image only in 90-degree increments, Elements doesn't resample your image.

More good news about cropping

Do you think that's all a generous application such as Elements has to offer in terms of cropping images? Ha! Elements has so many terrific cropping techniques that one would be tempted to refer to them as a "bumper crop," if one liked painfully bad puns.

- After you selected the Crop tool, but before you started dragging with it, you may have noticed some other choices in the Options bar. The Width, Height, and Resolution settings are useful for cropping an image to exact dimensions.

  Another option that can be useful is the Front Image option. It enables you to crop one image so that it's the same size as another image. Suppose that you want to make image B the same size as image A. First, open both images. Make sure that image A is the foremost image by clicking its title bar. Select the Crop tool and click the Front Image button in the Options bar. Elements loads the size and resolution settings from image A to the Options bar. Select image B. Drag the Crop tool on the canvas and frame your image; you'll notice that the marquee always stays in the same proportions as image A. When you press Enter (Return on a Mac) to execute the crop, Elements automatically resizes image B to match image A. Note that Elements resamples image B if necessary in order to match the size of image A. Click the Clear button to escape this cropping mode.

- If you've created an active crop boundary and you then change your mind about cropping the image, press Esc or Ctrl+period (⌘+period on a Mac) to get rid of the cropping boundary. Or you can also press the Cancel button in the Options bar.

- To move the cropping boundary in its entirety after you've drawn the marquee, just drag inside the boundary.

- In addition to using the Crop tool, you can crop a *selected area* (see Chapter 8) by choosing Image➪Crop. The selection doesn't even have to be vaguely rectangular; it can be elliptical, polygonal, or even feathered. Elements won't really crop to that shape, but it gets as close to the boundary as it can.

- As mentioned earlier, you can also crop an image by using the Canvas Size command. You may want to consider this method if you need to trim your image on one or more sides by a precise number of pixels to get the image to a certain size. The Canvas Size command can also come in handy if you want to crop a very small area — say three pixels worth — along one or more edges of the image and you have trouble selecting the area with the Crop marquee. You can reduce the size of the canvas using Image⇨Resize⇨Canvas Size to eliminate the offensive pixels; the Relative option can really come in handy here.

The Straighten and Crop Image commands

We interrupt this book for an Elements News Flash: A command known as Straighten Image has arrived on the scene and has taken up residence inside the Image menu. This command, an Elements exclusive, is wanted by Photoshop users everywhere.

Actually, the Straighten Image command has a partner in crime — the Straighten and Crop Image command — and that's why we're dealing with it in this section on cropping. You've probably encountered the dreaded "crooked scan," as seen on the left in Figure 4-9. Sometimes — no matter how meticulous you are about placing a snapshot on the scanning bed of your flatbed scanner, no matter how slowly and gingerly you close the scanner cover — you get a crooked scan. You can raise the scanner cover and try to reposition it manually, or you can go ahead with the scan and attempt to fix it with the Crop tool as shown in Figure 4-8, eyeballing just the perfect angle to correct your crooked scan.

That's where the Straighten Image command comes in. Just go to Image⇨ Rotate⇨Straighten Image, and Elements will attempt to automatically correct the problem. The Straighten and Crop Image command (Image⇨Rotate⇨ Straighten and Crop Image) goes one step further: After it straightens the scan, it crops the background away, ideally resulting in something like the image on the right in Figure 4-9.

You'll find that these commands work much better if you leave a substantial amount of background around your image. In other words, if your scanning software gives you a preview of the image before you actually scan it, and you notice that the photo is skewed in the scanner, go ahead and scan in a large chunk of background (usually the underside of your scanner's cover) surrounding the image. It can also sometimes help to lay a piece of paper between the back of the image and the scanner lid to create a more contrasting background. (Of course you have to raise your scanner cover to do that, so you may as well take another crack at straightening the snapshot manually anyway.)

Elements seems to do a much better job with the automatic straightening than it does with the automatic cropping. Authorities speculate that may be why Straighten Image is available as a standalone command. Details at 11.

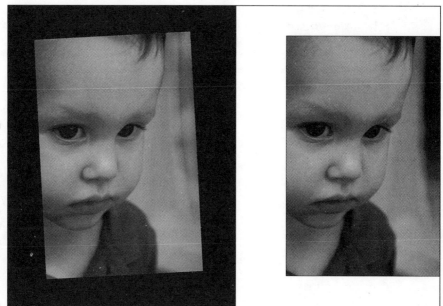

Figure 4-9:
The Straighten and Crop Image command can automatically correct a crooked scan.

Image Gymnastics

If you checked out the Straighten and Crop Image command, you may have noticed your cursor breezing by a whole submenu of Rotate commands under the Image menu. Here's the lowdown on them:

- ✔ **90° Left, 90° Right, and 180°:** These commands rotate the entire canvas. Left is counterclockwise; Right is clockwise. These commands can be useful if your image was scanned on its side or upside down, but it doesn't need cropping or straightening.

- ✔ **Custom:** Allows you to rotate your canvas a specific amount. If you rotate anything other than 90° or 180°, the canvas size will grow in order to accommodate the rotated image.

- ✔ **Flip Horizontal:** Creates a mirror image of your canvas.

- ✔ **Flip Vertical:** Creates a mirror image of your canvas and turns it upside down.

With the exception of Custom, these commands are also available in the new Quick Fix command. For the complete details on Quick Fix, check out Chapter 11.

For the most part, the other commands in the Rotate submenu perform identically to the commands listed here, but they only apply if your image has an active selection (see Chapter 8) or layers (see Chapter 9). The one exception is the Free Rotate Layer command (which becomes Free Rotate Selection when there's an active selection). This command puts you in Free Transform mode, which is discussed freely in Chapter 9.

Chapter 5

Over (and Under) the Rainbow

*A*s you may have guessed from the title, this chapter is all about color — the same kind of color that Dorothy encountered when she passed over the weather-beaten threshold of her old Kansas home onto a path of lemon-yellow bricks in that beloved classic, *Fight Club*. Or was it *The Wizard of Oz*? Maybe so. Anyway, when Dorothy was in Kansas — "under" the rainbow — everything was in black and white. But as soon as she went "over" the rainbow and stepped out of her ramshackle house into the Land of Oz, things were in color. (Yeah, we know that in the movie's original release the "black and white" Kansas scenes were actually shown in sepia tone. What are you trying to do — screw up our otherwise-relevant analogy with trivial facts?)

So what's the lesson here? Kansas seemed pretty dreary and depressing next to Oz, with its helium-voiced midgets, combative trees, and bipedal jungle cats. Color must have it all over black and white, huh?

Well, little Dorothy Gale didn't ultimately think so. And, in truth, the absence of color can offer its own special attractions. It's the mysterious essence of a torch-lit castle on a stormy night. It's the refreshingly personal vision of a 16mm short-subject film you stumble across one evening on Bravo. It's the powerful chiaroscuro of an Ansel Adams photograph. In an age when every screen, page, and billboard screams with color that's more vivid than real life, black and white can beckon the eye like an old friend.

But on the off chance you think all that's a pretentious load of hooey, there's one specific area in which Kansas definitely kicks Oz's keister, and that's in the cost of professional printing. Despite the increasing influence of computers in print houses, color printing can be extremely expensive. Major four-color magazines can spend more on ink than they do on their writers, and that's a sad fact (especially for us magazine writers).

Though by no means free, black-and-white images are generally less expensive to reproduce. Only one ink is involved — black. Other supplies, such as film and plates for the printing press, are kept to a minimum. Black-and-white printing is also incredibly versatile. You can print black-and-white images with any laser printer, you can photocopy black-and-white images using cheap equipment, and you can fax black-and-white images with relatively little loss in quality. And finally, black-and-white images require one-third of the overhead when you're working in Photoshop Elements, meaning that you can edit black-and-white images that contain three times as many pixels as color images without Elements complaining that it's out of memory. Kansas is starting to sound better and better, huh? No surprise, really. The Sunflower State is truly as lovely as its nickname, whereas the Munchkins — to hear Judy Garland tell it — were a bunch of randy booze hounds.

Whether you choose black and white, color, or — like most folks — vacillate between the two, this chapter tells you how it all works. You find out how to use and create colors that you can apply with the painting tools. Not bad for a chapter based on an old MGM musical, eh?

Looking at Color in a Whole New Light

To understand color in Elements, you have to understand a little color theory. If you've had a color image open in Elements, you may have noticed the telltale initials RGB inside parentheses in the image title bar. These initials mean that all colors inside the image are created by blending red, green, and blue light.

Red, green, and blue? That doesn't sound particularly colorful, does it? But, in fact, these colors are the primary colors of light. The red is a vivid scarlet, the green is so bright and tinged with yellow that you may be tempted to call it chartreuse, and the blue is a brilliant Egyptian lapis. It just so happens that these colors correspond to the three kinds of cones inside your eyeball. So, in theory, your monitor projects color in the same way your eyes see color.

Go ahead and turn to Color Plate 1 (but keep a finger here, of course). The colorful photo at the bottom of the plate looks very much like it would on your monitor. But lurking under the surface, as illustrated at the top of the plate, are three different color channels: red, green, and blue. When you see a color image like this on your monitor, you're actually seeing the combination of these three channels. The red image on the left is the one being sent to the red cones in your eyes; the green image in the middle is hitting your green cones, and the blue image goes right to your blue cones.

Pretty nifty, huh? Here's another way to think about it: If you were to take the images you see in the red, green, and blue channels, print them to slides, put each of the slides in a different projector, and shine all three projectors at the same spot on a screen so that the images precisely overlapped, you would see the full-color image in all its splendor.

Yet another way to think about the color channels is as black-and-white images, as shown in Figure 5-1 below. Where areas in the red channel are very light, there will be a lot of red in the corresponding full color image. And where things are dark in the red channel, there won't be much red at all. The same holds true, of course, for the green and blue channels. Compare the boy's blue shirt, red shorts, and the green grass behind.

Every color channel contains light areas and dark areas, just like a black-and-white image. The light and dark pixels from each channel mix together to form other colors. In Elements, this is basically an invisible process; other than a few telltale signs such as those "RGB" initials in a color image's title bar, there's not much evidence that the three color channels exist inside Elements. But it's important to know that they're always there, lurking beneath the surface of your color images.

Figure 5-1:
The black-and-white channels combine to make a full-color image.

The following list explains how corresponding pixels from the different channels mix together to form a single full-color pixel:

✔ A white pixel from one channel mixed with black pixels from the other two channels produces the color from the first channel. For example, if the red is white, and green and blue are black, you get a red pixel.

✔ White pixels from the red and green channels plus a black pixel from the blue channel form yellow. This description may sound weird — two colors, red and green, mixing to form a lighter color — but that's exactly how things work in the world of RGB. Because you're mixing colors projected from a monitor, two colors projected together produce a still lighter color.

Do you follow? No? Well, suppose you had a flashlight with a red bulb and your friend had one with a green bulb. Maybe it's Christmas or something. At any rate, if you were to point your flashlight at a spot on the ground, the spot would turn red. No surprise there. But if you then said, "Look, Nancy, it's the missing key from the old Bigbee place," and Nancy pointed her green flashlight at the same spot, the spot wouldn't get darker, it would get lighter. In fact, it would turn bright yellow. "Gee wizikers, Ned, do you suppose this means Mrs. Welker is innocent after all?" (Unfortunately, we'll never know.)

✔ White pixels from the green and blue channels plus a black pixel from the red channel make a bright turquoise color called cyan. White red and blue pixels plus a black green pixel make magenta.

✔ By a strange coincidence, cyan, magenta, and yellow just happen to be the main ink colors used in the color printing process. Well, actually, it's not a coincidence at all. Color printing is the opposite of color screen display, so the two use complementary collections of primary hues to produce full-color images. The difference is that because cyan, magenta, and yellow are pigments, they become darker as you mix them. Yellow plus cyan, for example, make green.

Your monitor creates white by mixing the lightest amounts of red, green, and blue — the opposite of how things work on the printed page. Color printing exploits the fact that sunlight and man-made light (both referred to as "white light") contain the entire spectrum of visible light, including all shades of red, green, and blue. The primary printing inks — cyan, magenta, and yellow — are actually *color filters*. When white light hits cyan ink printed on a page, the cyan ink filters out all traces of red and reflects only green and blue, which mix to form cyan. Similarly, magenta is a green light filter, and yellow is a blue light filter, as illustrated in detail in Color Plate 2. This and other factors (such as purity of inks, variation of ink tints, whiteness of paper, and lighting conditions) result in the CMYK world. (The "K," incidentally, oddly stands for "blacK." Cyan, magenta, and yellow inks actually combine to make a dark, muddy brown, so black ink is thrown in there as well so that color images can contain pure black.)

✔ White pixels from all three channels mix to form white. Black pixels form black. Equally medium pixels make gray.

Although all this is highly stimulating, it would probably make more sense if you could see it. If you're the visual type, take a look at Color Plate 3. The left side of the figure shows the RGB combinations just discussed. The right side shows RGB mixes that result in other colors, including orange, purple, and so on. Give it the once-over and see if you can't feel your brain grow by leaps and bounds.

Managing Photoshop Elements Color

Now that you have some basic color theory, it's time for basic color management. People want to be able to have a true WYSIWYG (What You See Is What You Get) world. In other words, they want to be able to look at their monitor and see the exact colors they'll get coming out the other end. This "other end" can be in the form of printouts, or just an image on the Web viewed from another monitor.

Gimme good gamma

Getting exact color is next to impossible. Devices can help — expensive hardware and software calibrators that come with high-end monitors deliver very good results — but most of us average Joes and Jos have to manage this dilemma on our own. For Windows users at least, Elements comes with a little help in the form of the Adobe Gamma Control Panel.

1. **In Windows XP, choose Start⇨Control Panel, click Appearance and Themes, and then click Adobe Gamma. For other versions of Windows, choose Start⇨Settings⇨Control Panel and double-click Adobe Gamma.**

2. **Take the deluxe guided tour of the Adobe Gamma Control Panel by choosing Step By Step and letting the wizard show you the way. Click the Next button.**

   If you're supremely confident, pick the Control Panel option. The Control Panel appears, as shown in Figure 5-2, giving you all the necessary setup options in one dialog box. Otherwise, choose Step by Step along with the rest of us Dummies.

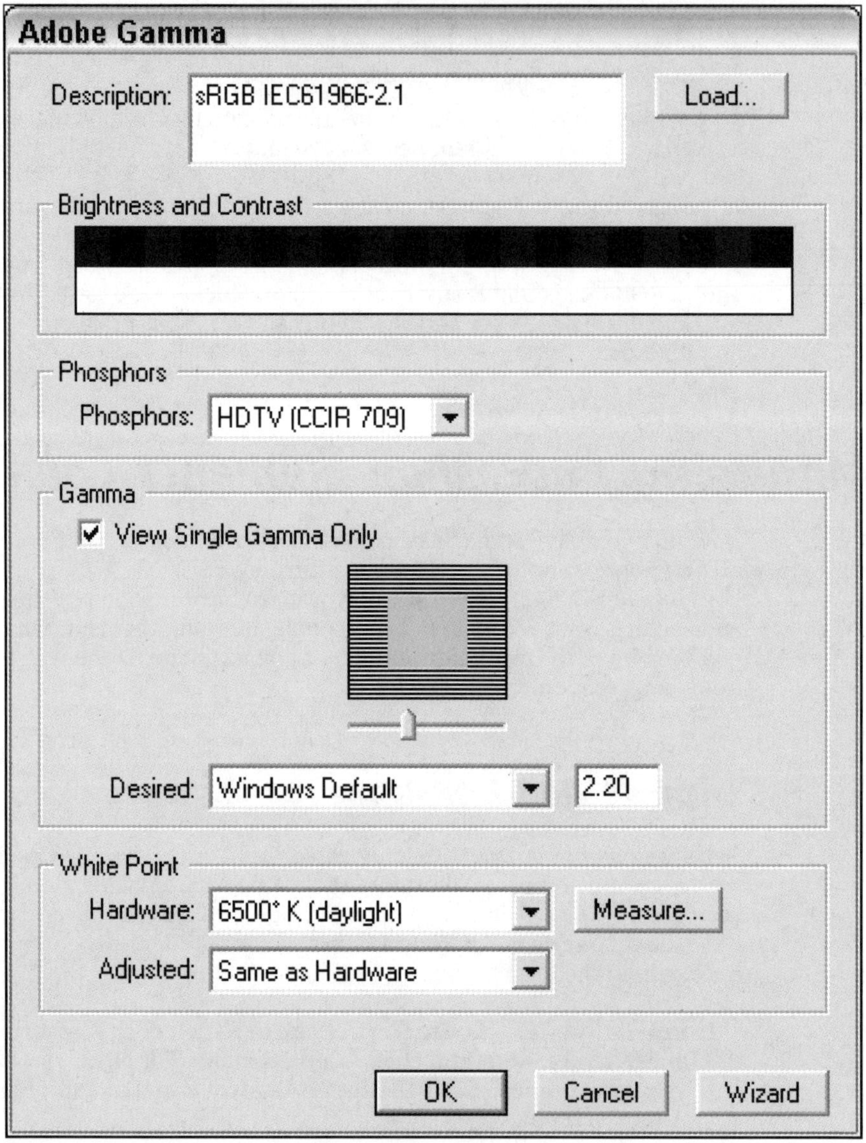

Adobe Gamma

Description: sRGB IEC61966-2.1   Load...

Brightness and Contrast

Phosphors

Phosphors: HDTV (CCIR 709) ▾

Gamma

☑ View Single Gamma Only

Desired: Windows Default ▾ 2.20

White Point

Hardware: 6500° K (daylight) ▾   Measure...

Adjusted: Same as Hardware ▾

OK   Cancel   Wizard

Figure 5-2:
The Adobe Gamma Control Panel is the no-frills method for calibrating your monitor.

3. **Give your monitor profile a distinctive name.**

   What you're doing here is creating a *monitor profile*, a settings file that describes how your monitor displays color. After you've named your profile, click Next.

4. **Adjust the brightness and contrast controls on your monitor.**

   Your monitor most likely has these controls somewhere, probably on the front. Follow the on-screen instructions and click Next.

5. **Choose a setting for your monitor's phosphors.**

   We're guessing you don't know this information right off the top of your head. We'll also surmise that this information may not be contained anywhere in your head whatsoever. If you can't find anything about phosphors in the documentation that came with your monitor, don't sweat it; just accept the default setting and click Next. The really important stuff is coming up next anyway.

6. **Deselect the View Single Gamma Only check box and adjust the three sliders.**

   The idea here is to make the middle rectangles blend in as closely as possible with the outer rectangles. It may help you to move as far away from your monitor as possible, to squint, or to actually look above the rectangles and use your peripheral vision. Sounds weird, we know, but give it a try. Keep the Gamma setting at Windows Default and click Next.

7. **Measure your hardware white point.**

   This defines the general color cast or your screen. Again, you probably don't know this setting by rote. Luckily there's a way to measure this one. Click the Measure button and follow the on-screen instructions. When you're finished, click Next.

8. **Use the same setting as your Adjusted White Point.**

   Just leave this set at Same as Hardware and click Next.

9. **Compare the before and after as desired, then click Finish.**

   Here you can compare how things looked before you went through Adobe Gamma with how they look now.

10. **Save your profile to disc.**

    The default location is perfect; Elements will know just where to find your profile. Click OK, and Elements has the scoop on your monitor.

Mac users don't really need to feel left out in the cold because they don't have Adobe Gamma; there's an excellent monitor-profiling tool built right into the Mac. In OS X, go to your Displays System Preferences and click the Color tab; in OS 9, open the Monitors Control Panel and click the Color button. Then, everyone click the Calibrate button, turn on Expert Mode (who's a dummy here?), and follow along, bearing in mind that not all monitors offer all options:

1. **Adjust your monitor's brightness and contrast settings.**

   Just as in the preceding Step 4 for Adobe Gamma, follow the on-screen instructions.

2. **Drag the three sliders to determine the current gamma.**

   Analogous to the preceding Step 6 for Adobe Gamma, drag the three sliders so that the apples blend in with the surrounding squares. Again, stare, squint, stand on your head; whatever works for you. This is the most important setting, so take your time.

3. **Select your target gamma.**

   We recommend sticking with the Mac Standard, but while you're here, click the PC Standard and see how much darker Windows screens are compared to Mac screens. (This is important to keep in mind when you're creating Web graphics; if a graphic looks dark on your Mac screen, it's going to look *really* dark on a PC screen.) Then click back to Mac Standard and proceed.

4. **Choose your monitor (or a reasonable facsimile thereof) from the list.**

   If you don't see your monitor listed, don't sweat this one. Just accept the default and move on.

5. **Select a target white point.**

   Again, go with the default here, or select No White Point Correction if that looks best to you.

6. **Name your profile.**

   Go with something distinctive and click the Create or Create It button. You should see your new profile in the list on-screen.

Choosing your color settings

Trying to get consistent color is without question the most complex and confusing aspect of working with digital images on the computer. In Elements' granddaddy application, Photoshop, the Color Settings dialog box is an intimidating myriad of options and technical terms designed to make even seasoned pros curl up into a ball on the floor and whimper. Thank your lucky stars, then, that this has all been simplified quite eloquently for Elements. Follow along now, and we promise this won't hurt a bit:

1. **Choose Edit⇨Color Settings. (In Mac OS X, choose Photoshop Elements⇨Color Settings.)**

   You should see a dialog box that bears an uncanny resemblance to the one in Figure 5-3. Only three options to choose from — this doesn't look so bad, does it?

2. **If you're happy with the status quo, leave things at the default setting of "No color management."**

   After all, things have worked pretty well so far, right? If you're happy with the colors you see when you use Elements and print from the application, there's no reason to change a thing.

3. **If you're going to be working with images for the World Wide Web, you can choose "Limited color management."**

   This setting lets you work in a color space called sRGB, which takes into consideration what images look like when displayed on the average PC monitor (which, after all, is what most Web surfers are using). sRGB is a generally agreed-upon standard, endorsed by many hardware and software companies.

4. **If you're working on images for print, you can choose "Full color management."**

   When we're talking about "print" here, we're talking about the world of professional printing — and if you're doing a lot of professional print work, it may behoove you to move up from Elements to the full version of Photoshop anyway. But this setting will help you get by in a pinch. It embeds a hidden profile into the code of your images when you save them. This profile gives the next person to come along an idea of what the image looked like the last time you worked on it.

   The downside to both Limited and Full color management is that not all applications and devices understand sRGB color space or embedded profiles, meaning that things could potentially look worse for your efforts. The safest bet, all things considered, is to use "No color management." But know that the other options are available to you, if you find yourself in a situation where you know they'll come in handy.

5. **Click OK.**

   There now, that wasn't so bad, was it?

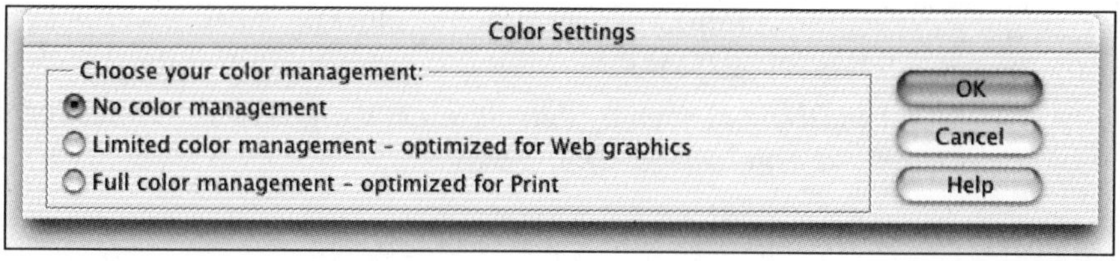

Figure 5-3:
The Color
Settings
dialog box
makes color
manage-
ment a
simple
affair.

Color Settings

Choose your color management:

◉ No color management

○ Limited color management - optimized for Web graphics

○ Full color management - optimized for Print

OK

Cancel

Help

Picking Color the Mix-and-Match Way

We have to say it: You've been very patient. After luring you into this chapter by comparing the subject matter to a beloved classic family movie, we've done nothing but bore you to tears with talk of color theory and color settings. You've really been quite tolerant during the presentation of all this dry, technical mumbo jumbo, and we'd like to take this opportunity to . . . hey — *wake up out there.*

All that sleep-inducing talk about color is important to understand if you're going to get the most out of Elements. But now it's time to turn to more practical color matters. Things such as "How do I choose colors?" and "Where can I keep them once I've chosen them?" Read on, Mac- (or PC) duff.

Juggling foreground and background colors

In Elements' Toolbox, you can work with two colors at a time: a *foreground color* and a *background color*. Most tools and commands paint your image with the foreground color, but a few splash it with the background color.

The Toolbox displays two colors at its bottom. As shown in Figure 5-4, the foreground color is on top and the background color is on the bottom. To get some idea of how these colors work, read the following list:

- ✔ The foreground color is applied by the painting tools, such as the Brush and Pencil.

- ✔ When you use the Eraser tool, you're actually painting with the background color. (Unless you're on a layer, in which case you would erase to transparency. For more on layers see Chapter 9.)

- ✔ When you increase the size of the canvas using Image⇨Resize⇨Canvas Size (as explained in Chapter 4), Elements fills the new empty portion of the canvas with the background color (provided that the image has a background layer).

- ✔ The Gradient tool, by default, creates a gradual shift between the foreground and background colors.

The Toolbox includes icons that enable you to change the foreground and background colors, swap them around, and so on. Here are some guidelines to get you started:

- ✔ Click the foreground color or background color icon to display the all-important Color Picker dialog box. Press Esc or click Cancel to leave that dialog box.

- ✔ Click the Black and White icon (refer to Figure 5-4) to make the foreground color black and the background color white.

- ✔ Click that little two-way arrow icon — childishly labeled Swap 'em in the figure — to swap the foreground and background colors with each other.

- ✔ You can also access the Black and White and Swap 'em icons from the keyboard. Press D to make the foreground black and the background white. Press X to swap the foreground and background colors.

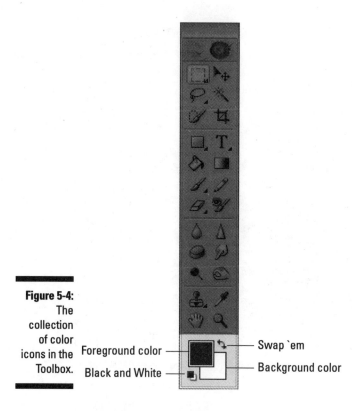

Figure 5-4:
The
collection
of color
icons in the
Toolbox.

Foreground color

Black and White

Swap `em

Background color

Defining colors

You can define the foreground and background colors in Elements in three ways:

- Click the foreground color or background color icon in the Toolbox to summon the Color Picker.
- Use the Eyedropper tool to lift colors from your image.
- Use the Swatches palette.

Using the Color Picker

To access the Color Picker, shown in Figure 5-5, click either the foreground color or background color icon. The first thing you should notice is the enormous square of color on the left of the dialog box; this is known to Elements cognoscenti as the color field. To its immediate right, you'll see a rainbow-colored bar commonly referred to as the color slider. The color rectangle in the upper-right corner of the controls is known, strangely enough, as the color rectangle. And below that you'll see a handful of option boxes and radio buttons. Introduce yourself to all the controls, and get to know their names, because you'll be spending a lot of time in the Color Picker.

Color field   Color slider   Color rectangle
                                    Web safe color alert

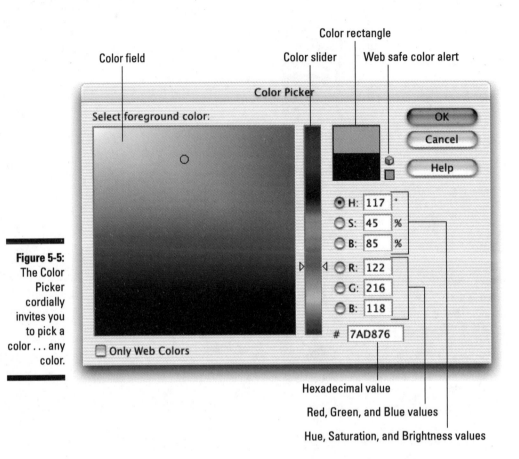

Figure 5-5:
The Color
Picker
cordially
invites you
to pick a
color . . . any
color.

Color Picker

Select foreground color:

○

▷ ◁

☐ Only Web Colors

OK
Cancel
Help

● H: 117 °
○ S: 45 %
○ B: 85 %
○ R: 122
○ G: 216
○ B: 118
7AD876

Hexadecimal value

Red, Green, and Blue values

Hue, Saturation, and Brightness values

Do you want to know the quick and dirty way to select a color using the Color Picker? Okay, here goes:

1. **Click the foreground color or background color icon in the Toolbox, depending on which you want to set.**

2. **Drag in the color slider to set the specific hue you want. (Make sure the radio button next to the H is checked first.)**

3. **Drag around in the color field to set the brightness and saturation for the hue.**

4. **Click OK.**

And that's it. Following these simple steps can reliably get you the color you want every time. There will be times, however, when you'll need to specify certain aspects of colors, and the preceding method won't suffice. It's for times such as these that we now present: The Rest of the Story.

The Color Picker also lets you choose colors numerically by entering values in the option boxes. You can work numerically with three different color modes. The option box at the very bottom is for specifying hexadecimal colors, which is very useful for Web design professionals, but generally classified as *too much information* for our purposes here. The top three option boxes (H, S, and B) let you specify colors according to their Hue, Saturation, and Brightness. We'll skip these for now, and instead turn our attention to the bottom three option boxes. Hopefully those three letters look vaguely familiar to you by now: R, G, and B stand, of course, for Reginald, Gertie, and Bert.

Okay, just seeing if you were paying attention. Here, actually, is more proof that those red, green, and blue color channels we were yammering on about earlier really exist. When using the Color Picker, you can think of red, green, and blue as ingredients in baking the perfect color. You can add 256 levels of each of the primary hues, 0 being the darkest amount of the hue, 255 being the lightest, and 128 being smack dab in the middle. For example, if you set the R value to 255, the G value to 128, and the B value to 0, you get a vibrant orange, just like the one shown in the upper-right corner of Color Plate 3.

If you've never mixed colors using red, green, and blue, it can be a little perplexing at first. For example, folks often have a hard time initially accepting that all yellows and oranges are produced by mixing red and green. We encourage you to experiment. Better yet, we order you to experiment.

If you followed our little orange recipe above, you've probably noticed that the mysterious color rectangle now has a two-toned effect going on. While the top half is sporting that spiffy orange color, the bottom half is modeling the old foreground or background color you started with. That's what the color rectangle is all about: letting you compare your new color against the old one.

The HSB color mode is simply another way of describing color. Rather than break it down into three color channels such as red, green, and blue, the HSB color mode breaks color down according to its Hue (which you can think of as the "color" of the color), Saturation (how rich the color is), and Brightness (how bright or dark the color is).

In truth, using the numeric values in the Color Picker is a very complicated, confusing affair. It works on the principle that the property with the checked radio button gets mapped to the color slider. The color slider then gives you the full range of options for that one property. The other properties are then mapped to the color field, and you can drag around inside the field to hone in on the color you want. Just experiment with this concept for a second, clicking the various radio buttons and dragging around in the color slider and color field. How do you feel? Wait — don't smash your monitor with this book. Just click the H radio button again. There now, isn't that better?

It can't be just sheer luck that the Color Picker defaults to having the Hues mapped to the color slider. The whole dad-gummed dialog box just seems to make sense that way. So keep it that way, we say.

If you're wondering about that almost-omnipresent little 3D cube that pops up next to the color rectangle, it's there to warn you that the color you've chosen isn't Web-safe. The Web-safe palette consists of 216 colors that you can count on to display consistently across the entire World Wide Web, no matter the combination of platform, monitor, or browser. As more and more people upgrade from their old 8-bit, 256-color monitors, this becomes less and less of an issue. But if it concerns you, click the colored square beneath the cube to change your chosen color to the nearest Web-safe color. You can also work in a purely Web-safe world by clicking the Only Web Colors check box beneath the color field.

Lifting colors with the Eyedropper tool

You can also change the foreground or background colors by lifting them from the image. Just select the Eyedropper tool — second from the bottom on the right side of the Toolbox, just above the Zoom tool — and click inside the image on the color you want to use. If you have more than one image open, you can even click inside an image different from the one you're working on.

Here's some stuff to know about this incredibly easy-to-use tool:

- You can press I (for I-dropper) to select the Eyedropper tool instead of clicking its Toolbox icon.
- The Eyedropper by default determines the foreground color. To set the background color, Alt+click (Option+click on a Mac) with the Eyedropper.
- You can temporarily access the Eyedropper tool when using some of the other tools by pressing the Alt key (Option key on a Mac). As long as the key is down, the Eyedropper is available. This trick works when you're using the Paint Bucket, Gradient, Pencil, Brush, Background Eraser, Magic Eraser, Red Eye Brush, and Shape tools.
- If you use the preceding tip, you can change only the foreground color. You need the Alt key (Option on a Mac) to change the background color, so you can't use the key to temporarily access the Eyedropper. You have to select the Eyedropper for real (click its icon or press I) and then Alt+click (Option+click on a Mac). If your keyboard offers two Alt or Option keys, it doesn't help to press both of them!

- Elements 2.0 lets you sample color not just from an open image but from anywhere on-screen. The trick is that you still have to first click the Eyedropper inside an open Elements image. But then, while still holding down the mouse button, drag outside the image and onto your desktop, sampling colors from your desktop image, the menu bar, or whatever you desire.

✔ As you use the Eyedropper, you can keep tabs on the exact R, G, and B values for the colors you're sampling by looking in the upper-left section of the Info palette.

✔ The Sample Size option in the Options bar determines precisely how the Eyedropper tool chooses a color. When set to Point Sample, it chooses the color of the precise pixel it's clicked on. When set to 3 by 3 Average, the Eyedropper looks not only at the pixel it's clicked on but in a 3-pixel by 3-pixel square all around the clicked pixel. It averages together the colors of those nine pixels, and that average color becomes the chosen color. Likewise for 5 by 5 Average, the Eyedropper looks in a 5-pixel by 5-pixel square and averages the color of those 25 pixels. This can be useful if, for example, you want to sample the color of the sky in an image, and you're not as concerned with getting the color of any one pixel as you are with getting the general color of the sky.

Using the Swatches palette

At this point you may be thinking that only being able to keep two colors around — the foreground and the background color — is a trifle, shall we say, limiting. Enter the Swatches palette, as accurately depicted in Figure 5-6. No, it has nothing to do with stylish timepieces; the Swatches palette is nothing less than a repository for color.

Figure 5-6: The Swatches palette. Okay, it loses a little something in black and white.

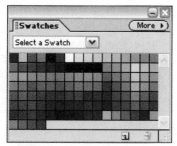

To activate the Swatches palette, choose Window⇨Color Swatches, or click the Swatches tab if it's visible in the palette well. You can then grab the tab and drag the palette out onto the desktop if you want. (It won't hurt it a bit.) As you can see, the Swatches palette already contains a pleasing assortment of colors. If you want a little more information about those colors, click the More button and choose Small List from the menu. You'll see the color swatches along with their descriptive names.

To set one of those colors as the foreground color, all you have to do is move your cursor onto a swatch — like magic, it turns into the Eyedropper tool. Just click, and there you go! If you want to set the background color instead, Ctrl+click (⌘+click on the Mac) on a swatch. Simple, huh?

Elements comes with several preset swatch libraries available from the Select a Swatch menu at the top of the palette, but the real power of the Swatches palette lies in its ability to let you create and save your own customized swatch libraries. To add the current foreground color to the Swatches palette, just move the cursor into the blank, gray area at the bottom of the swatches. The cursor automatically turns into the Paint Bucket tool. Just click, and Elements will ask you to enter a name for your swatch. If you want to dispense with the naming ceremony and just accept the default name, add the Alt key (the Option key on the Mac) as you click. You can also go to the More menu and choose New Swatch, bypassing the Paint Bucket-clicking method altogether.

It's very important to find out how to organize the Swatches palette and to save libraries. If you're like most people, you'll be working along in Elements, mixing colors with the Color Picker, when you happen to come across the perfect color. "Ooh!" you say. "The perfect color! I know what to do: I'll add it to the Swatches palette!" So you hightail your mouse over to the Swatches palette, click to add the perfect color swatch to the default library, and resume work. Now, no matter what you do to the foreground and background colors, you can be sure that your perfect color is always waiting for you.

As your work continues, you discover many more perfect colors and add them to the Swatches palette as well. "Wow," you think. "I sure do love my Swatches palette. Perhaps I should get to know it better." So you decide to investigate it, clicking the Select a Swatch menu. "Hmmm . . . VisiBone2" . . . I wonder what that means?" You select it. . . and BAM! A new set of swatches appears. You quickly switch back to the default set, but the colors you added are gone forever. You sink to the ground, sobbing, "Why, oh why, didn't I read my *Photoshop Elements 2 For Dummies* book thoroughly, from cover to cover? How completely foolhardy of me! I'm going to buy copies for all my friends to ensure that this tragedy never happens to them! In fact, I'm going to buy copies of the book by the truckload and pass them out to total strangers on the street!"

What you should have done (oh sure, *now* we tell you) is save your swatches. All you need to do is go to the More menu, choose Save Swatches, and give your swatch library a distinctive name.

Just as with choosing a different library from the Select a Swatch menu, choosing Replace Swatches wipes out any unsaved changes you've made to the current swatch library. Load Swatches allows you to pick a swatch library and tack it on to the end of the current library. And Save Swatches lets you save the current library for future use.

If you want to check out all the preset swatches, brushes, gradients, and patterns that Elements has to offer, you can always go to Edit➪Preset Manager. All the various categories of presets are accessible via the Preset Type drop-down menu. To the right of each scrolling list of preset icons is a More menu that gives you reset, replace and viewing options, as well as accessibility to the various libraries under each preset category. And, finally, you can also load, save, rename, and delete libraries using the buttons on the right side of the dialog box.

Going Grayscale

Now that we've wasted most of the chapter in the colorful Land of Oz, you may be wondering when we're ever going to decide there's no place like home, click our heels, and head back to good old monochromatic Kansas. Take heart: The heralded hour of black-and-white images has arrived.

The first thing to understand about black-and-white images is that the black-and-white world offers more colors than just black and white. It includes a total of 256 unique shades of gray and is therefore more properly termed *grayscale*. Each one of these shades is a color in its own right, which is why the term "black and white" can inspire fisticuffs among some grayscale devotees.

Second, all the stuff about creating colors in the preceding sections of this chapter holds true for grayscale image editing, as well. You have a foreground and background color. You can define colors in the Color Picker. (No matter what color you choose in the Color Picker, the color will appear as some shade of gray in the foreground color or background color icons.) And you can lift colors from a grayscale image using the Eyedropper tool.

But some aspects of grayscale editing are different than full-color editing, which leads us to the next two sections.

The road to grayscale

Most images that you'll come across will be in color. This means that working in grayscale generally requires a conversion inside Elements.

Unlike a three-channel RGB image, a grayscale image includes only one channel of imagery. If you plan to print in black and white, you should jettison all the extraneous color information, for two reasons. First, it's easier for Elements to keep track of one channel than three. In fact, given the same image size and resolution, Elements performs faster when editing a grayscale image than when editing in color. Second, you can better see what your printed image will look like. When you're designing an image to be printed in black and white, color just gets in the way.

To convert a color image to grayscale, just choose Image⇨Mode⇨Grayscale. Elements asks you whether you want it to discard color information. (The "Don't show again" check box is just Elements' way of asking you if you want it to ask you about this.) You can click OK to convert to grayscale or chicken out and cancel. That's all there is to it. You now have a single-channel grayscale image. If you don't like the results of your conversion to grayscale, you can go back to the full-color original by clicking the Step Backward button in the Shortcuts bar or pressing Ctrl+Z (⌘+Z on a Mac).

Before you change a color image to grayscale, you may want to make a backup copy of the original image, just in case you ever want to have the image available in color in the future. For details on saving images, see Chapter 6.

If you have a layered file and only want to remove color from one layer, choose Enhance⇨Adjust Color⇨Remove Color or press Ctrl+Shift+U (⌘+Shift+U on the Mac). Elements drains the selected layer of all its color. Note that this doesn't convert the image to grayscale; even if the image consists of only one layer and you apply Remove Color, the image will still be RGB. Consequently, the size of the file on disk won't get any smaller either, so you lose the benefits of actually converting to grayscale. (For more information about layers, see Chapter 9.) You can also apply Remove Color to just a selected portion of a layer, including the Background layer. For more on selections, see Chapter 8.

A few more tips in black and white

Here are some final grayscale tidbits:

✔ To add color to a grayscale image, first convert back to RGB by choosing Image⇨Mode⇨RGB Color. Elements won't automatically add a bunch of colors to the image, but it will now let you add colors of your own.

✔ If you use the Image⇨Mode⇨Grayscale conversion method and your color image contains more than one layer (as explained in Chapter 9), Elements asks whether you want to flatten your image. If you want to keep your layers, click the Don't Flatten button.

✔ If you're still using an 8-bit monitor — that is, a monitor that can display only 256 colors — you're better off editing grayscale images. When you edit full-color RGB images, Elements shows only 256 of the 16 million possible colors at a time, resulting in *dithering,* an effect in which a random pattern of pixels is used to emulate lots more colors. When you edit a grayscale image, however, you can see every shade just right. Don't worry that Elements converts your entire screen, including Finder icons on the Mac, and all other background items to grays. This is a normal effect of editing in grayscale on an inexpensive computer system.

Part II
Be Prepared

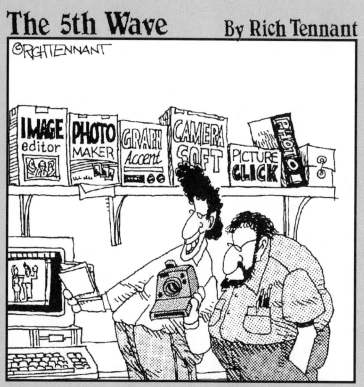

The 5th Wave   By Rich Tennant

"...and here's me with Cindy Crawford. And this is me with Madonna and Celine Dion..."

In this part . . .

Yeah, we know. You want to start doing some image editing. You were very patient through the first part of this book: Jekyll and Hyde, dialog boxes, File Browser, Zoom tool, floor tiles, Image Size, Straighten and Crop, Wizard of Oz, grayscale. All very nice, very interesting, and exceedingly well written (?), but now — if we don't mind too terribly much — you'd really like to get down to doing some image editing. Because you have this picture of yourself from your recent vacation to Maui that you want to e-mail to all your friends, but in the picture you have this unsettling disturbance on your chin that you'd really like to do something about. . . .

Yeah, we know. But here's the cold, hard truth: There are really a few more things you need to know before you start image editing — things like saving files. Photoshop Elements has a truly bewildering array of options for saving files; there are well over a dozen different file formats to choose from. And what if you make a mistake as you're editing that vacation photo, and manage to give yourself a chin of Jay Leno–sized proportions? How can you go back and undo your work? Maybe you know about pressing Ctrl+Z on the PC or ⌘+Z on the Mac, but do you know about Elements' phenomenal time-traveling tool, the Undo History palette? And how much do you really know about printing? For that matter, only when you come to grips with the power of making selections and using layers will you begin to realize the possibilities that Elements contains.

So patience, Gentle Reader. We'll get to the really exciting stuff, we promise. Just make it through this part of the book with us, and it will be nothing but actual image editing from there to the end. Come on, that vacation photo can wait. Chin up!

Chapter 6

Saving with Grace

• •

• •

*I*f you've used a computer before, you may be wondering why we would devote an entire chapter to saving files. After all, you just press Ctrl+S (⌘+S on a Mac) and you're done, right? For that matter, Photoshop Elements lets you click a handy Save icon in the Shortcuts bar — the one that looks like the floppy disk. "What's to know about saving?" you ask. Well, if we were talking about any other program, you'd be right. If this book was about Microsoft Word, for example, we'd say, "Not to worry, Gentle Reader, saving a file is so simple, a newborn lemur could pull it off with the most cursory supervision from a parent or older sibling." If this book was about PageMaker, we'd add, "Saving makes tying your shoes look like a supreme feat of civil engineering."

But this book is about Photoshop Elements. And Elements, as you may or may not be aware, enables you to save images in more flavors than Willy Wonka manages to squeeze into an Everlasting Gobstopper. In the software world, these flavors are called *file formats,* and each one has a different purpose.

This chapter offers a thorough explanation of the saving process, including an exhaustive — well, okay, pretty decent — review of the various file formats you can use. We'll also be taking a look at the two icons to the right of the Save icon in the Shortcuts bar: Save for Web and Save as PDF. With this chapter by your side, saving can be a pretty easy thing to do, after all.

Save an Image, Save a Life

Though we don't know you from Adam — or Eve for that matter — you're probably the kind of person who doesn't like to spend hours editing an image only to see your work vanish in a puff of on-screen smoke as the result of some inexplicable and unforeseen computer malfunction. If you are indeed that kind of person, finding out how to save your image is essential. By saving your image early and often, you improve your chances of weathering any digital storm that may come your way.

Saving for the very first time

If you're working on an image that you created from scratch in Elements by using the File⇨New command, choosing the Save or Save As command brings up the Save As dialog box. If you're working on an image that's already been saved to disk, such as a photograph from a digital camera or scanner, you'll probably want to save another copy of the image containing your changes while leaving the original unaltered. So, before you begin making changes to your image, use the Save As command to save it under a new name and specify where you want to store it on disk. If you do this, the original image remains untouched so that you can return to it at a later date for inclusion in a different project. Here's how to save your image:

1. **Choose File⇨Save As.**

   The dialog box shown in Figure 6-1 appears.

   You can also open the dialog box by pressing Ctrl+Shift+S (⌘+Shift+S on a Mac).

2. **Enter a name into the File Name option box.**

   PC users: Enter a descriptive filename. The filename is followed by a period and a three-character file extension that indicates the file format (explained shortly). To insure maximum compatibility, don't use any spaces or special characters, such as ampersands or brackets, in your filenames; stick with regular letters and numbers to be safe. You don't have to enter the extension because Elements does that for you. Also, make sure there's a check mark in the Use Lower Case Extension box at the bottom of the Save As dialog box, because this aids compatibility as well.

   Mac users: In addition to entering a filename, you also have the option of adding a three-character extension (such as tif) that indicates the file format (explained shortly in "The Elemental Guide to File Formats" section). The Append File Extension option is located in the Preferences command under the Saving Files panel. You can choose Never, Always, or Ask When Saving. You can also choose to save a file with a lowercase extension. If you select the Ask When Saving option, check boxes for Append and Use Lower Case appear in the Save As dialog box.

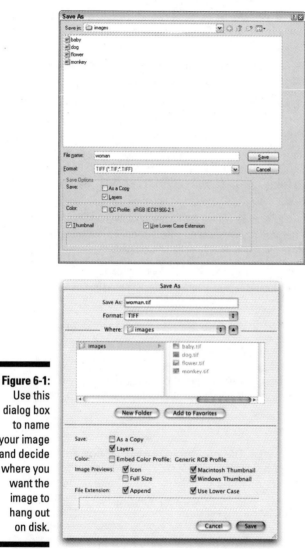

Figure 6-1:
Use this
dialog box
to name
your image
and decide
where you
want the
image to
hang out
on disk.

It's generally best to use the lowercase extension option. This option makes for fewer problems when creating images for the Web.

3. Select a format from the Format drop-down menu.

This is the point at which you have to deal with the image flavors touched on in the introduction to this chapter. The drop-down menu provides all kinds of options, such as TIFF, JPEG, PICT, and others. We'll discuss the ramifications of the important formats later in this chapter.

Some formats are restricted to certain kinds of images. For example, images that contain layers can be saved only in the Photoshop (PSD),

TIFF, or PDF formats. If you try to save a layered image in a format that doesn't accept layers, such as JPEG, the Save As a Copy option will automatically be applied.

4. **Use the Save in (Windows) or Where (Mac) drop-down menu to select the folder in which you want to save the image.**

5. **Select one or more of the next options. Note that option availability is based on the type of image and whether the image has layers (more about layers in Chapter 9).**

   • **As a Copy:** Instead of giving your image a different name, you can check the As a Copy option. This option automatically adds the word "copy" after your file name, thereby ensuring your original remains intact.

   • **Layers:** With this option checked, your image preserves all its layers. If unchecked, your image is flattened into a background. (Repeat after us: More about layers in Chapter 9.)

   • **Color:** Checking this option embeds a color profile into the code of your image (see details in the Color Settings discussion in Chapter 5).

6. **Click the Save button or press Enter (Return on a Mac).**

7. **If another dialog box appears, fill out the options and press Enter (Return on a Mac).**

   Some formats present additional dialog boxes that enable you to modify the way the image is saved. We explain these later where appropriate.

Your image is now saved! Come heck or high water, you're protected.

 The Thumbnail check box(es) at the bottom of the dialog box are visible (Mac) and accessible (PC) only if you've selected Ask When Saving in your Preferences under Saving. If you don't check the Thumbnail options when you save an image, you may not get a preview when you later try to open that image, depending on your operating system.

To make sure that Elements always saves previews, go to the Saving Files panel of Elements' Preferences. When the Preferences dialog box appears, select the Always Save option from the Image Previews drop-down menu. Click OK to exit the dialog box. Now a thumbnail will be saved by default, and you don't have to worry about it anymore.

The only times not to save a preview are when you're saving images for posting on the Web, or you're extremely limited on disk space. Previews make the file size a little bigger, leading to longer download times. The file-saving process also takes a teeny bit longer if you choose to save images with previews. If you're saving images for the Web, however, you'll want to use the Save for Web command discussed later in this chapter.

Joining the frequent-saver program

After you name your new or altered image and save it to disk for the first time, from this point onward press Ctrl+S (⌘+S on a Mac) or choose File⇨Save every time you think of it. Think of it as a nervous twitch you actually want to develop. In either case, Elements updates your image on disk, without any dialog boxes or options popping up and demanding your attention. Then when something goes wrong — notice that we said *when*, not *if* — you won't lose hours of work. A few minutes, maybe, but that comes with the territory.

Creating a backup copy

If creating an image takes longer than a day, you'll want to make backup copies. The reasoning is that if you invest a lot of time in an image, you're that much worse off if you lose it. By creating backup copies — Dog1, Dog2, Dog3, and so on, one for each day that you work on the project — you're that much less likely to lose mass quantities of edits. If some disk error occurs or you accidentally delete one or two of the files, one of the backups will probably survive the disaster, further protecting you from developing an ulcer or having to seek therapy.

So at the end of the day, choose File⇨Save As. The Save As dialog box appears, as when you first saved the image. Change the filename slightly and then click the Save button. Want to be doubly protected? More protection, you say? Save to another disk entirely. If a whole disk goes bad, you've got another copy of the image stashed away safely.

The Elemental Guide to File Formats

Selecting a format in which to save your image is a critical decision. So, you need to pay attention to the sections to come, even if the subject is a rather dry one — which it is. Get a double espresso if you need one, but don't skip this information.

What is a file format, anyway?

Glad you asked. (But do you have to use that bold, italic tone of voice?) A *file format* is a way of saving the electronic bits and pieces that make up a computer file. Different formats structure those bits and pieces differently. In Elements, you can choose from about a zillion file formats when you save your image to disk, which makes things a tad bit confusing.

Luckily, you can ignore most of the file format options. The Raw format, for example, sacrifices colors and other image information, so avoid it. Scitex CT and Targa are very sophisticated formats used by very sophisticated (and well-funded) creative types, so you can forget about those formats, too. Use the Pixar format if you want your toys to come to life and behave in vastly amusing ways, but only when you're not in the room. (Just kidding.)

Actually, you'll probably use only a handful of formats: TIFF, PDF, JPEG, GIF, and perhaps most importantly, the native format, PSD, which Elements inherited from the application that gave it life: Photoshop. The following sections explain the most important file formats and when to use them. (We deal with JPEG, GIF, and PNG in the "Saving for the Web" section coming up in this chapter.)

TIFF: The great communicator

One of the best and most useful formats for saving Elements images is TIFF (pronounced *tiff*), which stands for Tagged Image File Format. TIFF was developed to serve as a platform-independent standard so that both Macintosh and Windows programs could take advantage of it. TIFF is an excellent file format to use for images that are destined to be printed. It can be imported into virtually every page layout and most drawing programs.

When you select the TIFF option from the Save As drop-down menu and click the Save button, Elements displays another dialog box, shown in Figure 6-2. In the area labeled Byte Order, you can tell Elements whether to save the TIFF image for use on a Macintosh or Windows program. Neither option is likely to give you a problem regardless of the platform you're working on, but it's probably a safer bet to go with the flow and select IBM PC. (Why are these options labeled Byte Order? Just to confuse you.)

The TIFF Options dialog box offers several compression methods. If you select one of the methods, Elements compresses your image file so that it takes up less room on disk. LZW compression doesn't sacrifice any data to make your file smaller and is great for compressing images with large sections of a single color. It's known as a *lossless* compression scheme. ZIP compression is also a lossless scheme and works well with images containing large areas of a single color. ZIP compression is common in the Windows world. The last compression method is JPEG, a *lossy* compression scheme, meaning that some of the data that makes up your image will be lost. The term is used with special frequency by Scottish nerds trying to impress women: "Och, ye've got a be-oo-tifully compr-r-ressed image ther-r-r-re, Lossy!" (Sorry, that's a terrible joke. We should be kilt.) There's more on JPEG in the "Saving for the Web" section of this chapter.

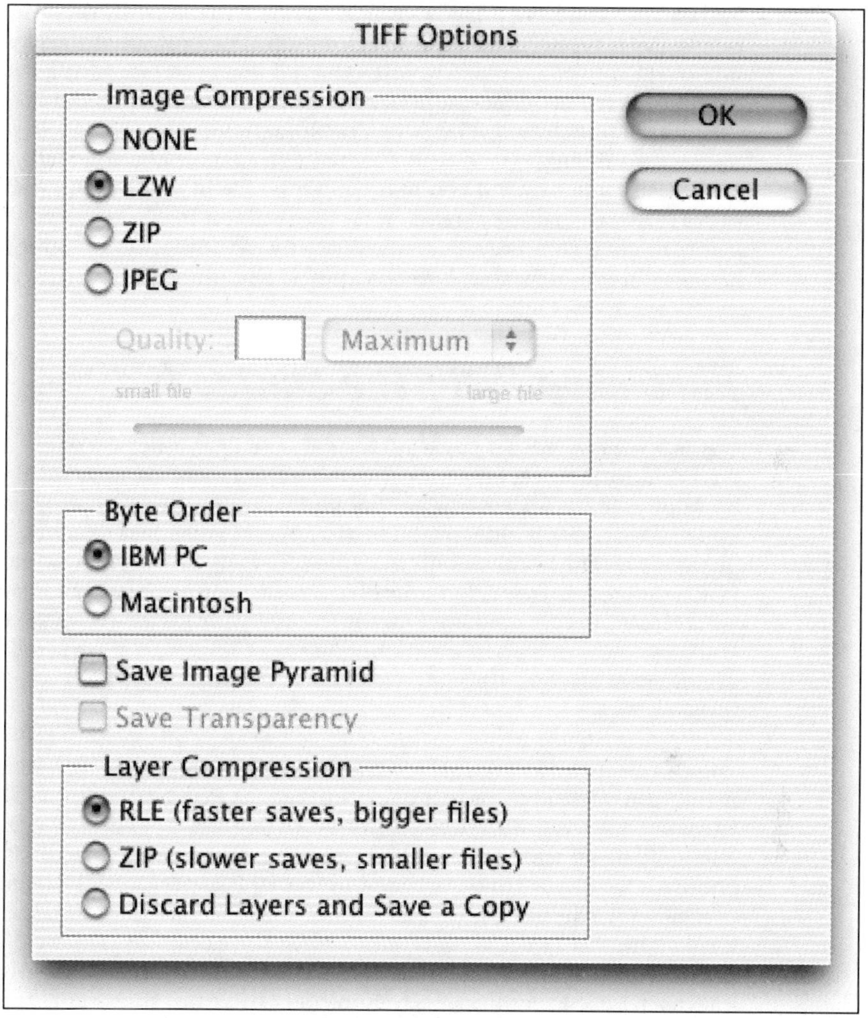

TIFF Options

Image Compression

- ○ NONE
- ● LZW
- ○ ZIP
- ○ JPEG

Quality: [ ] Maximum ▲▼

small file   large file

OK

Cancel

Byte Order

- ● IBM PC
- ○ Macintosh

☐ Save Image Pyramid

☐ Save Transparency

Layer Compression

- ● RLE (faster saves, bigger files)
- ○ ZIP (slower saves, smaller files)
- ○ Discard Layers and Save a Copy

Figure 6-2:
The options
that appear
when you
save a
TIFF file.

Your best bet is to stick with LZW. Most programs that support TIFF also support LZW. For example, you can import a compressed TIFF image into InDesign, PageMaker, or QuarkXPress. Only obscure programs don't support LZW, so there's really no reason not to select this option. LZW compression does make your files open and save a bit more slowly, but the savings in disk space are worth it.

TIFF also supports saving with layers. If the term *layers* is fuzzy to you, check out our upcoming book, *Layers For Dummies*. What the heck — on second thought, we'll just roll that stuff into Chapter 9 of this book. Lucky you.

You can use the Save Image Pyramid option to save multiple versions of an image. Each version has a lower resolution. The bottom of the pyramid is the full image. You can choose to open the full image or one with a lower resolution. Not many programs support pyramid files right now, so it's best to leave this option unchecked. The Save Transparency option has no effect if you're opening your image back up in Elements; transparency will always be preserved. It applies only if you're opening the file in another program that supports PDF transparency (read on for more about PDF). And if you're saving layers in your TIFF, the self-explanatory Layer Compression options give you a choice in the "disk space versus speed" equation.

Photoshop PDF: The can-do kid

PDF is a very versatile, powerful format, and is another excellent choice for cross-platform work. Short for "Portable Document Format," PDF was created by Adobe, so it's little surprise that you'll find it heavily supported by Adobe applications such as Illustrator, InDesign, and PageMaker. In fact, PDF has become an almost universally accepted format; all a person needs to view a PDF document is free Adobe Acrobat Reader software (which is included on your Elements CD). And if you want to save your Elements image with layers (Did you know there's more about layers in Chapter 9? If you've been reading this chapter straight through, we bet you do by now!), PDF is one of only three options.

You can choose Save As, select Photoshop PDF from the Format drop-down menu, and click Save, or just click the Save as PDF button in the Shortcuts bar and click Save. Either way, another dialog box appears. Choose ZIP encoding if you want lossless compression; otherwise select JPEG and choose a Quality setting. As noted in the TIFF section, JPEG is a lossy compression format, but the up side is that the PDF file will be smaller. If your image contains Transparency, you'll have the option of keeping it within your PDF document. The Image Interpolation option means that low-resolution images in your PDF file will be smoothed out rather than appearing pixelated; it's probably best to turn this off, as the interpolation process can't really improve low-resolution images and usually just makes them appear fuzzy.

PICT File: The picture format for Mac OS 9 users

Apple developed *PICT* as the primary format for Macintosh graphics. PICT is based on the QuickDraw screen language. Although Mac OS X has switched to PDF for its major graphics format, just about every Macintosh graphics program still supports PICT.

One nice thing about PICT is that it also offers JPEG compression. Say that you select the PICT File option from the Format drop-down menu in the Save dialog box and press Return. A dialog box with options appears.

If you're saving a grayscale image, the Resolution options are 2, 4, and 8 bits per pixel. Color images offer Resolutions of 16 and 32 bits per pixel. But regardless of which Resolution options you see in the dialog box, don't change them! Doing so deletes colors from your image and prevents you from accessing the PICT format's own built-in JPEG options. Remember that JPEG compression does degrade your image somewhat. If you're using JPEG compression, it's best to always select maximum quality in the PICT File Options dialog box.

Although PICT can use JPEG compression, that doesn't mean that the average Windows user will be able to open a JPEG-compressed PICT file. If you're worried about cross-platform compatibility, make sure you save your image in the actual JPEG format, not as a PICT with JPEG compression.

BMP: The wallpaper glue for PC users

BMP is a popular PC format for saving graphics that you want to make part of your computer's systems resources, such as the wallpaper that you see behind your desktop. Programmers also use BMP to create images that appear in Help files.

When you save a file in the BMP format, the dialog box shown in Figure 6-3 appears. Don't worry about changing any of the options in this box; use the defaults that Elements picks for you. Just make sure that if you're creating wallpaper, you don't select the Compress (RLE) check box; Windows doesn't recognize files saved using this compression scheme. Otherwise, the compression scheme is a lossless (good) one, so select Compress (RLE) if you can.

What about Elements' native Photoshop format?

One strong bit of proof that Photoshop Elements is the offspring of Photoshop (a sterling lineage indeed) is that Elements' native file format is the Photoshop format. The three-letter extension for the Photoshop format is PSD.

PSD, TIFF, and PDF are the only formats that can save the layers in your image; all the others "flatten" (merge) the layers together.

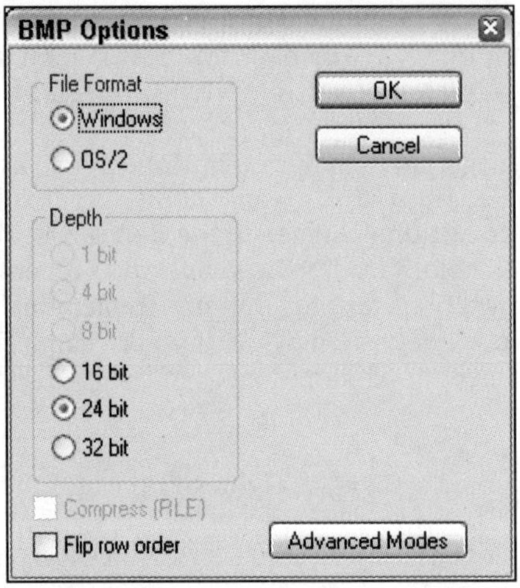

BMP Options

File Format
- ● Windows
- ○ OS/2

OK
Cancel

Depth
- ○ 1 bit
- ○ 4 bit
- ○ 8 bit
- ○ 16 bit
- ● 24 bit
- ○ 32 bit

☐ Compress (RLE)
☐ Flip row order

Advanced Modes

Figure 6-3:
The BMP format is used mostly to create wallpaper for the Windows desktop.

As do TIFF and PDF, the Photoshop format offers a lossless compression scheme. And Elements can open and save images faster in its native format than in any other format. But some other programs don't support the Photoshop format. So, use it when you're sure the program you plan to import the image into supports it and you don't need compression.

What format to use when

Ooh, you cheated, didn't you? You skipped right over the sections on how formats work and why they were invented. Instead of reading all that juicy background information — information that would help you make your own decision about which format to use — you want easy answers.

Okay, fine. You plunked down good money so that understanding Elements would be easy for you, so we'll give you a break just this once. Think of the following list as your study guide to File Formats. But when you're standing around at a cocktail party and the discussion turns to JPEG compression versus LZW, and you don't have an intelligent word to offer, we don't want to hear about it.

✔ If you're just going to use the image in Elements, save the image in Elements' native Photoshop (PSD) format. 'Nuff said.

✔ If your image contains layers ("Layers?" you ask. "Chapter 9!" we answer.) and you want to preserve those layers, you can choose the PSD (Photoshop), TIFF, or PDF formats.

✔ If you want to import your image into another program, TIFF is probably the most compatible choice.

✔ If you want to import your image into another program, saving disk space is a priority, and TIFF's LZW compression isn't doing the job, use JPEG compression.

✔ If you're a Windows user and want to create wallpaper to amuse your co-workers or just yourself, use BMP with RLE compression turned off.

✔ If you're working on a photograph to be sent by e-mail or posted on the Web, use the JPEG file format. For graphics or partially transparent images, use CompuServe GIF. For more on these formats, read the following section.

Saving for the Web

Yes, JPEG and GIF are the two standard file formats to use when saving images for posting on the Web. Yes, you can choose File➪Save As and save your image as a JPEG or GIF. But don't.

Why not? Because (fanfare, please) there is a better way! Using Elements' terrific Save for Web command is, for the most part, vastly superior to using the Save As command to create JPEGs and GIFs. Not only do you get a side-by-side preview of your original image versus the compressed version, but also it's very easy to switch back and forth between JPEG and GIF to determine which is the better format to use in terms of image quality and download time. The Save for Web command gives you almost every option you have when you choose JPEG or GIF from the Save As command; we'll cover the few additional options that Save As provides in the sections to follow.

Hey — what about PNG?

In addition to saving JPEGs and GIFs, the Save for Web command also lets you save images in the PNG file format. PNG stands for *Portable Network Graphics* and was originally designed to replace the popular GIF format. PNG is much more sophisticated than GIF — it supports 24- and 48-bit images, allowing for a broader range of colors, whereas GIF supports only 8-bit images. PNG can support RGB, Grayscale, or Indexed color image modes. You can also have varying levels of transparency in a PNG image, something neither GIF nor JPEG can do. A downside to PNG files is that images are often larger than GIFs or JPEGs because they contain more colors than GIFs and do not have the advantage of JPEG's great compression scheme. This makes the PNG file format good for small images, such as buttons and thumbnails with details. The biggest downside to PNG, however, is that until recently it was not widely supported. The major browsers on major platforms have come around to PNG, but you can hardly count on your users to have the latest versions of those browsers. If you're certain that your image will be viewed using a modern browser, go ahead and try PNG; otherwise, you're still better off choosing between JPEG and GIF.

If you want to go ahead and give PNG a chance, you have two flavors to choose from: PNG-8 and PNG-24. The options for saving a PNG-8 file are virtually identical to saving a GIF, so refer to the GIF section in this chapter for details. Saving a PNG-24 file gives you precious few options, but again, you can refer to the GIF section for more information.

The Save for Web command

To open the Save for Web dialog box, click the Save for Web icon in the Shortcuts bar (the floppy disk in front of the world), choose File⇨Save for Web, or press Ctrl+Shift+Alt+S (⌘+Shift+Option+S on a Mac). You'll see the large window in Figure 6-4. Elements shows the original image on the left along with a copy on the right with compression applied, as it would appear when opened in a Web browser. You can modify the settings along the right side of the window.

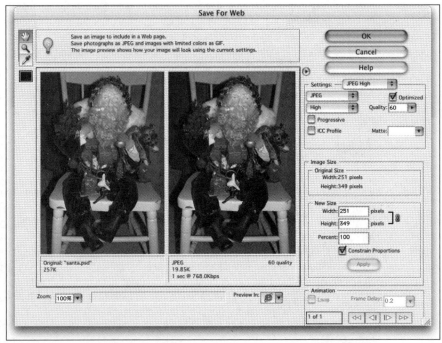

Figure 6-4:
The Save for Web command lets you compare your original image to a Web-compressed version.

To get a closer view, you can zoom and scroll the previews using the Zoom and Hand tools located in the small toolbar in the upper-left corner of the window. You can also change the zoom ratio by changing the Zoom value in the lower-left corner of the window. To preview a set of settings in your favorite Web browser, click the button at the bottom of the window beneath the compressed view of your image. Your image appears in your selected browser window.

If you meant to make your image smaller for posting on the Web using Image⇨Resize⇨Image Size, but you forgot to, Elements 2.0 gives you a convenient way to scale down your image within the Save for Web dialog box. The New Size settings let you do the job by entering pixel dimensions or a new percentage. You'll probably want to keep Constrain Proportions checked, unless you want to squash or stretch your image. After you've made your adjustment, click the Apply button and watch your image shrink!

Aside from that, using Save for Web is just a matter of adjusting the various other options along the right side of the window. The predefined settings appear in the drop-down menu at the head of the Settings section. Some of these may work perfectly for you, or perhaps you'll want to select one as a jumping-off point for creating your own settings with the options below. These options change according to the file format you choose. We'll look at JPEG and GIF in the sections below, and examine the options that the Save for Web dialog box gives you.

JPEG: The best choice for photos

JPEG stands for Joint Photographic Experts Group, but who cares? What's important to remember is that although JPEG can provide very good results with photographs, it does use lossy compression, meaning that some of your image data will be missing.

The good news, however, is that you'll probably never miss what's not around anymore — sort of like when you were a kid and you "lost" your little brother at the park. Depending on the level of compression used, you may notice a slight difference in your on-screen image after you save the file using JPEG. But if the image is saved at High or Maximum quality and then printed, the compression is usually undetectable. As with TIFF's LZW compression, JPEG compression saves you lots of disk space. In fact, a JPEG image takes up less space on disk than an LZW-compressed TIFF file — half as much space, maybe a tenth as much, depending on your settings.

Here are the settings:

✔ **Compression Quality (Low, Medium, High, or Maximum):** Select an option from the drop-down menu immediately below the word JPEG to set the image quality to one of Elements' predefined settings. The

Maximum option is best because it preserves the most image data, but the High option usually produces very good results as well. Note that the Quality slider lets you set the compression to an even higher quality than Maximum's default of 80, and also lower than Low's default of 10. Color Plate 4 shows the results of the four Compression Quality choices.

✔ **Progressive:** This option makes your image download from the Web in incremental stages. A rough "draft" version of the image will appear relatively quickly in your browser, and the image will become clearer in subsequent passes. Although it's nice to quickly give users a hint of what the image will ultimately look like, this option can cause problems in some browsers. For fullest compatibility, leave it unchecked.

Using the "Save As" JPEG Options box instead of the Save for Web command gives you the opportunity to specify the number of passes or "scans" it takes for your image to load fully.

✔ **ICC Profile:** This check box embeds a color profile with the JPEG image. The color profile adds about 3K to the file size, which means an extra second of download time at 28.8Kbps. And thanks to the fact that support for reading ICC Profiles in browsers is pretty sparse, the extra 3K goes wasted. Leave it off.

✔ **Optimized:** Although this option can result in smaller files, it has so little impact on file size — often none whatsoever — it's best to turn it off. This option is unlikely to cause problems with Web browsers, but it may make the image incompatible with other image editors.

✔ **Quality:** This option gives you more incremental control over the quality of compression than the Compression Quality drop-down menu does. Higher values give better image quality but larger file sizes; lower settings give lesser quality but smaller file sizes. You can specify a setting by entering a value into the Quality option box or by using the slider. Where the "Save As" JPEG Options dialog box divides the range of compression into 13 increments, from 0 to 12, the Save for Web value gives you a lot more incremental control, ranging from 0 to 100.

✔ **Matte:** This option applies only when you have transparency in your image. If your image has transparent or translucent pixels — maybe it has an oval, feathered outline that gradually fades to transparency — you must pick a background color to be matted into the image because JPEG doesn't support transparency. For instance, if blue is selected, and the same shade of blue is used as the background for a Web page, then the edges of the image would appear to gradually fade into the Web page. Totally transparent pixels would be filled with the specified blue, and translucent pixels would be mixed with blue.

The Matte menu gives you several options for selecting a color. You can use the Eyedropper tool located in the upper-left corner of the dialog box. You can also choose Other or click the Matte color box to display the Color Picker with three Web-specific options, spotlighted in Figure 6-5. Select the

Only Web Colors check box to select exclusively from the 216-color Web-safe palette. Click the cube icon to the left of the Help button to replace a color with its nearest Web-safe equivalent. And if you're a hexadecimal geek (and proud of it!), you can enter the desired hexadecimal color value into the # option at the bottom of the dialog box.

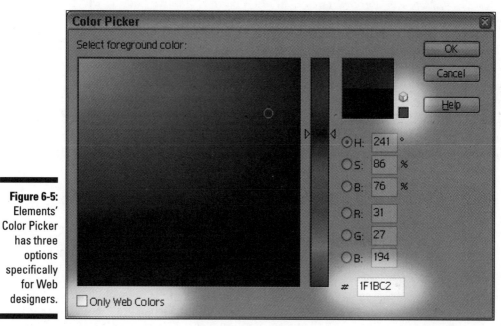

Figure 6-5:
Elements'
Color Picker
has three
options
specifically
for Web
designers.

GIF: The choice of choosy Web designers

Computer hacks are divided on how you pronounce GIF. Some folks swear that the proper pronunciation is with a hard *G* — as in one *t* short of a *gift.* Other experts insist that you say it with a soft *g,* so that the word sounds just like that famous brand of peanut butter. (No, we don't mean Skippy.) Regardless of which camp you decide to join (we're in the peanut butter camp ourselves), GIF is best used for high-contrast images, illustrations created in Elements or imported from a drawing program, screen shots, and text. The biggest drawback to GIF is that it can save images with only 256 colors or less (8-bit color). However, it's the format you want to use for simple — no computer programming skills required — animations, called *animated GIFs.* We'll look at animated GIFs in Chapter 17.

Here are the GIF options:

  ✔ **Color Reduction Algorithm (Perceptual, Selective, Adaptive, Web, Custom):** This drop-down menu controls how the colors are reduced from 16 million to 256 or fewer. The color reduction algorithm creates a palette containing the colors used in the image.

- Adaptive selects the most frequently used colors in your image. If an image contains relatively few colors and you want to keep the colors as exact as possible, apply this palette.

- Perceptual is a variation on the Adaptive palette, which varies the reduced color palette to suit the image. But where Adaptive maintains the most popular colors, Perceptual is more intelligent, sampling colors that produce the best transitions. Use this palette with photographic images (if you don't want to use JPEG), where smooth transitions are more important than actual color values.

- Selective is also a variation on the Adaptive palette, but better preserves Web colors. Use this palette when an image contains bright colors or sharp, graphic transitions.

- Web is a palette of 216 colors and is usually used for graphics that display on ancient 8-bit monitors. There are better palettes to use than Web.

- Custom enables you to load a color look-up table from your hard drive or disk. Not used that often for Web graphics.

✔ **Dithering Algorithm (No Dither, Diffusion, Noise, Pattern):** This option controls how Elements mimics the several million colors that you have asked it to remove from an image. The No Dither option makes no attempt to smooth out color transitions but results in smaller file sizes. Diffusion mixes pixels to soften the transitions between colors. The Noise option mixes pixels throughout the image, not merely in areas of transition. And the Pattern option just plain stinks. Stick with Diffusion.

✔ **Transparency:** If a layered image contains transparent areas, you can keep them transparent by turning on this check box. Bear in mind, however, that transparency in a GIF file is on or off; there are no soft transitions as in an Elements layer.

✔ **Animation:** Applies only when you're creating animated GIFs, covered in Chapter 17.

✔ **Interlaced:** This option results in an interlaced GIF file, in which the image fades into view incrementally as it is downloaded by the Web browser. Although this is a nice option when it works correctly, there can be problems with compatibility. Use with caution.

✔ **Colors:** Here's where you specify the number of colors in an image. You can also select predefined bit depths using the drop-down menu. Start with a low setting (such as 64), and see what happens to your image. Use the lowest number of colors that keeps your image reasonably intact. You may find that photographic images, especially those with a wide range of colors, require a higher setting than nonphotographic images or photos with a limited color range. And JPEG may be a better option for photos anyway.

✔ **Dither:** This wonderful option controls the amount of dithering applied. When, and only when, Diffusion is active, you may modify the amount of dithering by raising or lowering this value. Lower values produce harsher color transitions but lower the file size. It's a trade-off. Keep an eye on the preview to see how low you can go.

✔ **Matte:** This is similar to the JPEG Matte setting. When Transparency is turned off, the Matte color is blended in with translucent pixels, and transparent pixels are completely filled with the Matte color. When Transparency is turned on, the Matte color still blends with translucent pixels, but transparent pixels remain transparent. This setting is useful for making an image blend in with the background color of a Web page.

Choosing CompuServe GIF in the Save As dialog box brings up the Indexed Color dialog box (pictured in Figure 6-6), which gives you a few additional options:

✔ **Palette:** This is the same as the Color Reduction Algorithm option in the Save for Web dialog box. There are a few other choices here:

- Exact: If an image already contains less than 256 colors, the Exact palette appears by default. If this happens, leave it as is.

- System (Mac OS) and System (Windows): Use this palette only if you want to add a graphic to your system (like a desktop pattern or a file icon that will appear on your desktop).

- Uniform: The worst palette of the lot. Consists of a uniform sample of colors of the spectrum. Don't use it.

- Previous: When available, this palette uses the last look-up table created by the Indexed Color command. Usually used when creating a series of high-contrast graphics that need to maintain a consistent look.

Notice that you also have Master versions of the Perceptual, Selective, and Adaptive palettes. Local palettes are based on the colors in the open image, whereas master palettes take into account all currently open images.

✔ **Forced:** Sometimes an adaptive palette can very easily upset extremely important colors. For example, the white background of an image may turn a pale red or blue, even if white was a predominant color. With this option you can lock in important colors so that they don't change. Black and White locks in black and white. Primaries protects eight colors — white, red, green, blue, cyan, magenta, yellow, and black. And Web protects the 216 colors in the Web-safe palette. Very helpful indeed.

✔ **Preserve Exact Colors:** This option preserves areas of flat color when you select Diffusion. It's best to leave this check box turned on. By doing so, colors in your image that are also in the palette aren't dithered; therefore, lines, text, and other small details in your Web images have better on-screen quality.

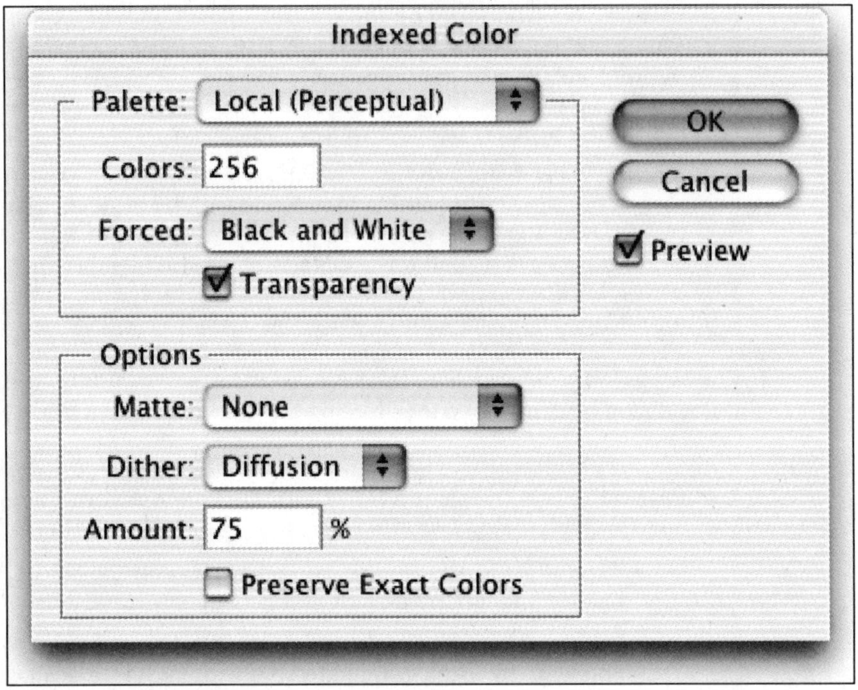

Figure 6-6:
The Indexed
Color
dialog box
controls the
appearance
of GIF
images.

Any GIF file can store transparency information. After saving a GIF file with indexed color, you can make all occurrences of one of those colors transparent using the Color Table command. Choose Image➪Mode➪Color Table to display the dialog box shown in Figure 6-7 and then select the Eyedropper icon below the Preview check box. Now click a color in the palette or in the image itself. Either way, that one color becomes transparent.

The Color Table command suffers one limitation: You can make just one color transparent at a time. To make a second color transparent, you must press Enter (Return on a Mac) to exit the dialog box and then choose Image➪Mode➪ Color Table again.

The Preview menu

Before you exit the Save For Web window, there's one last set of options to explain. At the top of the window, to the right of the compressed image preview, you see an arrowhead in a circle. Click it to reveal the Preview menu, shown in Figure 6-8. The commands in this menu control the appearance and feedback provided by the image previews.

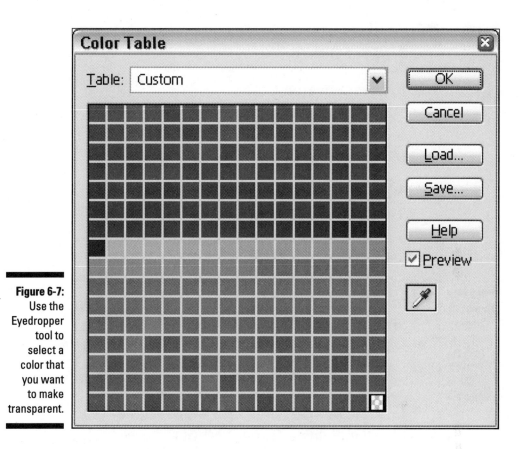

Figure 6-7:
Use the
Eyedropper
tool to
select a
color that
you want
to make
transparent.

The commands are divided into three sections:

- ✔ **Browser Dither:** Select this option to see how a selected preview will look when displayed on an 8-bit monitor. This method is exceedingly useful for determining whether you need to go with a Web-safe palette.

- ✔ **Color Compensation:** Colors shift from one screen to the next and from the Mac to Windows. There's no way to predict exactly how an image will look on another screen, but you can use the four color commands to get a sense. By default, Uncompensated Color is active, so Elements makes no attempt at a prediction. Select Standard Windows Color or Standard Macintosh Color to see how the colors might look on another platform. The final color command, Use Document Color Profile, uses the profile embedded in the document, if one exists.

- ✔ **Size/Download Time:** The final twelve commands change the estimated download times listed below the preview.

122 Part II: Be Prepared

Browser Dither

✓ Uncompensated Color
Standard Windows Color
Standard Macintosh Color
Use Document Color Profile

Size/Download Time (9600 bps Modem)
Size/Download Time (14.4 Kbps Modem)
Size/Download Time (28.8 Kbps Modem)
Size/Download Time (56.6 Kbps Modem/ISDN)
Size/Download Time (128 Kbps Dual ISDN)
Size/Download Time (256 Kbps Cable/DSL)
Size/Download Time (384 Kbps Cable/DSL)
Size/Download Time (512 Kbps Cable/DSL)
✓ Size/Download Time (768 Kbps Cable/DSL)
Size/Download Time (1 Mbps Cable)
Size/Download Time (1.5 Mbps Cable/T1)
Size/Download Time (2 Mbps)

Figure 6-8:
Choose a
command
from the
Preview
menu to
change the
appearance
of the
compressed
preview.

The File Association Manager

If you're a Windows user and you have more than one image-editing program
on your hard drive — particularly if you use both Elements and Photoshop —
it can be a real crap shoot knowing which application is going to open an
image when it's double-clicked. The File Association Manager is just the tool
to settle the matter once and for all. Choose Edit➪File Association, and the
dialog box shown in Figure 6-9 appears. Using the File Association Manager is
a simple affair; just place a check mark in the box corresponding to the type
of file you want to assign to Elements. If you want Elements to open every
possible image format, click the Select All button; if you want it to keep its
mitts off every format, click Deselect All; and if you want to restore things as
they were, click Default.

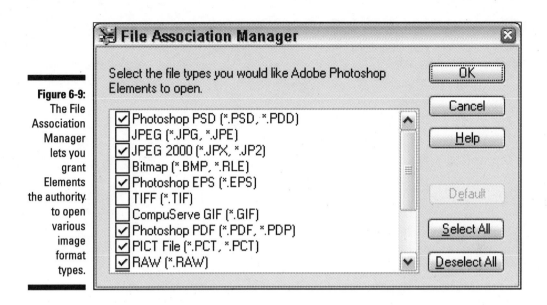

Figure 6-9:
The File
Association
Manager
lets you
grant
Elements
the authority
to open
various
image
format
types.

Although this is a Windows-only feature, Mac OS X users have the same sort of control built into the operating system. While in the Finder, single-click an image file to select it and then choose File⇨Show Info or press ⌘+I. Choose Open With Application from the menu at the top of the Info window and then select an application from the square icon menu below. After you've selected the desired application, click the Change All button and then the Continue button to make the change final. All image files with the same extension will be opened by the application you chose.

Good Night, Image — and Don't Let the Programming Bugs Bite

To put Elements to bed for the night, choose File⇨Exit (File⇨Quit on a Mac) or press Ctrl+Q (⌘+Q on a Mac). Elements may display a message asking you whether you want to save the changes you made to your image. Unless you have some reason for doing otherwise, press Enter (Return on a Mac) to select the Yes button. The program then shuts down.

If you don't want to save your changes, press the N key for "No" (press D for "Don't Save" on the Mac). If you decide that you aren't ready to say good-bye to Elements after all, click the Cancel button or press the Esc key. Sweet dreams.

Chapter 7

It's Perfect. No, Wait! Okay, Print.

• •

In This Chapter

▶ Using the reversing operations

▶ Making sure that your printer is ready to go

▶ Printing with Windows

▶ Printing with a Mac

▶ Getting your image to print out correctly

▶ Sending the image to the printer

• •

*H*ere's how you know that you're a consummate computer nerd: When you snag your favorite sweater, say something highly objectionable to your spouse, or spill a well-known staining agent on your newly installed carpet, your first reaction is not one of panic or regret. You merely think, "Undo."

Unfortunately, the real world provides no Undo command. After a horrible deed is done, it takes an obscenely disproportionate amount of fussing, explaining, or scrubbing to fix the transgression.

Not so in the magical world of personal computing. Photoshop Elements, in fact, gives you access to *multiple undos.* You not only can undo as many as 1,000 actions but also actually *skip* previous steps. In other words, if you have performed five actions and want to return to the way your image looked after your second action, you aren't required to first undo steps five, four, and three. You merely select step two in the digital undo command headquarters — the Undo History palette. As this chapter explains, not only can you turn back the digital clock, you can also truly travel back in time.

And after you're done undoing, then what do you do? Chapter 6 looks at the Save for Web command, a great choice if your final destination is an image you can e-mail to friends or post on the Web. But if you want your image to have a life on the other side of the monitor, then the on-screen image is really just a figment of your computer's imagination. You won't be able to actually *feel* your work until the ink hits the paper. (Even so, try to wait until the ink dries.)

In this chapter you find out how to go from an on-screen, imaginary image to hard copy. But it's hard to explain this process when there are so many unknown variables: what kind of printer you're using, what kind of cabling is installed, and even whether the printer is located in your home or your office. In other words, we're suffering from a terrific deficit of knowledge. So when we start talking about printing, your sympathy and understanding will be appreciated as we explain — very briefly — how to print from Elements using an everyday, generic printer. But first things first: Here's how Elements lets you do the Big Undo.

Time Traveling

The more you work with Elements, the more reflexive your actions become. Certainly, this means that you can work more quickly, but it also means that you are likely to make more mistakes. Reflexive, after all, is a close cousin to thoughtless. And when you don't think, you can wander into some pretty nasty situations.

Exploring the Undo History palette in 11 easy steps

Elements ensures that you aren't punished for working reflexively. To get a sense of just how wonderful this flexibility can be, try out these steps:

1. **Open the Undo History palette.**

2. **Create a new image.**

   The size is unimportant; just make it big enough so that you have room to paint a few brush strokes. Use White for the Contents. After you've created the image, notice that the Undo History palette now has its first *state,* labeled New. A state is a record of exactly what an image looked like at a certain point in time — in this case, the New state shows you what the canvas looked like before you painted anything on it. You can't do anything with this first state; just affirm its existence. That'll make it feel good.

3. **Select the Brush tool and drag across the image.**

   The Brush is the sixth tool down from the left in the Toolbox. It shares a space in the Toolbox with the Impressionist Brush, so make sure that you have the right tool. (The Brush tool icon is the one without the curly line.) Also, tap the D key to set the Foreground color to black. Draw a single brush stroke with the Brush, and no more. Now take a gander at the Undo History palette. You've got a brand new highlighted state labeled Brush Tool under the New state. Again, for now, just notice this.

4. **Take a break.**

   You've worked hard; you deserve it. Watch TV for your daily allowance of 16 hours. Take up macramé. Paint a wall and watch it dry. The point is, no matter how long you're away, Elements remembers the last operation you performed (as long as you don't have a power outage or some similar computing disaster).

5. **Click the Step Backward icon (the curvy downward-left-pointing arrow) in the Shortcuts bar.**

   You should notice two things: Your brush stroke disappears from the image window, and the Brush Tool state becomes grayed out in the Undo History palette.

6. **Click the Step Forward icon (the curvy downward-right-pointing arrow) in the Shortcuts bar.**

   Your brush stroke reappears, and the Brush Tool state in the Undo History palette becomes active again. Are you beginning to see how the Step icons and the Undo History palette are interrelated?

7. **Paint three more strokes.**

   Make sure each stroke is separate from the others. You should now have three more Brush Tool states in the Undo History palette, for a total of four.

8. **This time, rather than clicking the Step Backward icon, use the default keyboard shortcut of Ctrl+Z (⌘+Z on the Mac). Repeat twice.**

   After you've traveled back to your very first brush stroke, try Ctrl+Y (⌘+Y on the Mac) to step forward in time, bypassing the Step Forward icon in the Shortcuts bar. Go ahead and step forward to the last Brush Tool state.

9. **Click the first Brush Tool state in the Undo History palette.**

   This is yet another way to time travel in Elements: By clicking directly on states in the Undo History palette, you can travel backward or forward in leaps without revisiting every state.

10. **Go up to the Edit menu and choose the first command, Undo State Change.**

    The default keyboard shortcut for this command is Ctrl+Alt+Z (⌘+Option+Z on the Mac). You'll notice that this command automatically takes you to the bottom of the Undo History palette.

11. **Choose the command again — but notice that now it's labeled Redo State Change.**

    You're taken back to where you were at the end of Step 9: The first Brush Tool state is active. The Undo/Redo command toggles between the Undo History palette's final state and the state that was active when you chose the command.

Granted, this is all a bit confusing, and in truth there's a measure of redundancy in having both Undo/Redo and Step Forward/Step Backward at your disposal. But remember that Undo/Redo (Ctrl+Alt+Z on the PC, ⌘+Option+Z on the Mac) is a toggling command. It's useful for quickly switching back and forth using the same keyboard shortcut to see whether you like the effect of the last edit you made to your image. Undo/Redo gives you a quick before/after comparison.

Step Backward (Ctrl+Z on the PC, ⌘+Z on the Mac) lets you keep Undoing until you run out of History states. Step Forward (Ctrl+Y on the PC, ⌘+Y on the Mac) lets you do just the opposite, allowing you to keep Redoing until you reach the last action you performed.

If you simply want to reverse the last edit you made to your image, Undoing or Stepping Backward will do the trick. Step Backward has the easier default keyboard shortcut, so it's probably your best choice.

Stepping backward, stepping forward, undoing, and redoing all work whether you have the Undo History palette open or not.

Travel restrictions

Stepping backward, stepping forward, using the Undo History palette, and the Undo/Redo command all combine to give you a great deal of flexibility as you work. However, here are some important things to keep in mind about these tools:

- The only actions you can undo or step through are ones that could actually change the image. For instance, using the Zoom or Hand tools isn't reversible because they affect only temporarily what part of the image you're seeing on-screen.

- The Save, Save As, and Save for Web commands render the Undo command null and void. After the save operation completes, the Undo command appears dimmed, meaning that you can't choose it. You can, however, Step Backward to a state of the image before it was saved, provided that you've kept the image open.

- After you close an image, you wipe the entire slate clean for that image. Elements has no memory of the steps you took to arrive at your current masterpiece.

- You also can't reverse changing a foreground or background color, adjusting a Preference setting, hiding or displaying palettes, changing a setting in the Options bar, or selecting a tool.

The Undo History palette

Let's take a closer look at this powerful palette, depicted in Figure 7-1. The Undo History palette records all your operations and creates a running list of the steps — in other words, the states of your image at those points in history. As you perform each operation, Elements names each state and displays a corresponding icon according to the tool or command used. It records only operations that make a change to the pixels in your image.

Here's a list of the Undo History palette's features and functions and how to take advantage of them:

- ✔ To return to a previous state, click the desired state. Notice that Elements temporarily undoes all steps after that state and that they appear grayed out. Click the Step Backward button in the Shortcuts bar, press Ctrl+Z (⌘+Z on a Mac), or choose Edit⇨Step Backward to return to your last state.

- ✔ The grayed out states are referred to as *undone states.* You can redo an undone state by clicking it. If you perform a new operation when you have undone states in the Undo History palette, the undone states disappear. Choose Edit⇨Undo or Ctrl+Alt+Z (⌘+Option+Z on a Mac) *immediately* to get the undone states back. After you move on to other commands, they're gone for good.

- ✔ To step backward through the palette one state at a time, press Ctrl+Z (⌘ +Z on a Mac). To move forward, press Ctrl+Y (⌘+Y on a Mac). These commands are also accessible via the Undo History palette's More menu.

- ✔ The keyboard equivalents for Stepping Backward and Forward through the Undo History palette and also for Undo/Redo can be customized via the Preferences⇨General command.

- ✔ Drag the history state slider (refer to Figure 7-1) forward and backward to scroll through and see each state rapidly disappear and reappear in order.

- ✔ Elements 2.0 lets you save up to 1,000 history states, a huge increase from 1.0's limit of 100 states. You can establish the maximum number of history states you want to retain in the Preferences⇨General command. If your computer is low on RAM, you may not want to set this value too high. After you exceed your maximum, the oldest step disappears, then the next oldest, and so on.

- ✔ If you're absolutely sure you're happy with your image, and your computer is slowing down or running out of memory, you can delete the history states by choosing the Clear Undo History command from the More menu. If you change your mind, immediately select Edit⇨Undo or press Ctrl+Alt+Z (⌘+Option+Z on a Mac). If you have multiple files open, you can clear all their histories simultaneously by choosing Edit⇨Purge⇨Histories.

✔ If you're working in Elements and you need to manage the number of states in your Undo History palette, you may find it handy to delete the last few states you performed. To do this, select the oldest state you want to delete and choose Delete from the More menu. Elements will delete the selected state and all subsequent states. You can also simply click the trash can icon at the bottom of the palette (refer to Figure 7-1). Alternatively, you can drag and drop the state onto the trash can icon.

✔ Every file has its own history; therefore, you can work on multiple images simultaneously and independently of each other.

✔ After you close your image, its history disappears forever. The states in the Undo History palette aren't saved with the file.

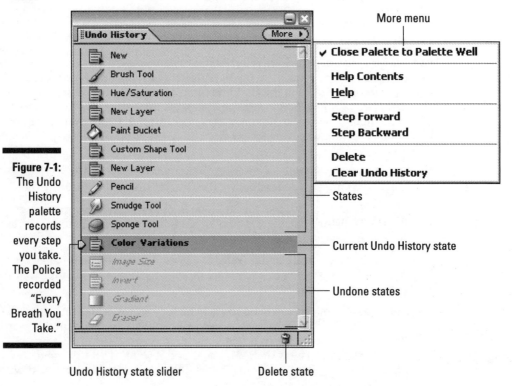

Figure 7-1:
The Undo History palette records every step you take. The Police recorded "Every Breath You Take."

Undo History state slider

Delete state

More menu

States

Current Undo History state

Undone states

Abandoning Edits en Masse

Sometimes you make small mistakes, and sometimes you make big ones. If, after several minutes of messing about, you decide that you hate all your edits and want to return the entire image to its last saved appearance so that you can just start over again, you can possibly do one of two things. First, you may be able to select the top state in the Undo History palette. Selecting the top step theoretically restores the image back to the way it appeared when you first started working on it. However, if you've already exceeded your maximum number of history states as set in the General Preferences dialog box, then the New or Open state has been bumped off the top of the Undo History palette. If this happens, you can choose File⇨Revert. The program reloads the image from disk and throws away all your changes.

Provided that you have a large enough number of Undo History states available, there's an advantage in using the Undo History palette rather than the File⇨Revert command. The Undo History palette can restore the *original* image regardless of whether you saved along the way, whereas File⇨Revert reloads the last saved version, which may include some undesirable changes.

Just in case you change your mind or your fingers slipped, you can reverse File⇨Revert, so breathe easier. The Undo History palette records the Revert command.

The Command Formerly (and Currently) Known as Print

If you've ever wasted an expensive sheet of photo paper on a terrible print, you'll agree that someone really needs to work on being able to undo the act of printing. Imagine if Print appeared as a state in your Undo History palette; clicking the Step Backward icon would feed the paper back into your printer; the ink would be sucked off the paper and back into the cartridges, and then the printer would spit out a pristine white sheet of paper into the feeder tray. Alas, this is not to be. So let's take a close look at printing, and see if we can figure out how to get it right the first time.

For starters, we're going to be totally rash and assume the following:

- ✔ You have a printer.
- ✔ Your printer is plugged in, it's turned on, and it doesn't have a 16-ton weight sitting on top of it. In other words, your printer works.
- ✔ The printer is properly connected to your computer. A cable running out of your computer and into your printer is probably a good sign.
- ✔ The proper printer software is installed on your computer.
- ✔ Your printer is stocked with ribbon, ink, toner, paper, film, pacifiers, little bits of felt, spring-like gizmos that go "ba-zoing," or whatever else is required in the way of raw materials.

If you've used your printer before, everything is probably ready to go. But if something goes wrong, call your local printer wizard and ask for assistance.

This May Be All You Need to Know about Printing

When things are in working order, printing isn't a difficult process. Though it involves slightly more than picking up your mouse and saying "print" into it, printing doesn't require a whole lot of preparation. In fact, a quick perusal of the following steps may be all you need to get up to speed:

1. **Turn on your printer.**

   And don't forget to remove that printer cozy your uncle knitted for you.

2. **Choose File⇨Save or press Ctrl+S (⌘+S on a Mac).**

   Although this step is only a precaution, it's always a good idea to save your image immediately before you print it because the print process is one of those ideal opportunities for your computer to crash. Your computer derives a unique kind of satisfaction by delivering works of art from the printer and then locking up at the last minute, all the while knowing that the image saved on disk is several hours behind the times. If you weren't the brunt of the joke, you'd probably think that it was amusing, too.

3. **Check that the image fits on the page.**

   Click the Print Preview icon in the Shortcuts bar (the one with the printer and the magnifying glass). You can also choose File⇨Print Preview, or press Ctrl+P (⌘+P on the Mac). Elements displays a preview of how your image fits on your chosen paper size. The white area in the Print Preview represents the size of the page. If your image fits entirely inside the white area, it will fit on the printed page. If it exceeds the boundaries of the white area, the image is too big for the page and it needs to be reduced or you need to change the page orientation. To reduce the print size, turn on the Scale to Fit Media check box in the Scaled Print Size section of the dialog box. This should result in your image shrinking in the Print Preview, but it doesn't affect the actual image on disk. To change the page orientation, read on.

Elements 2.0 has swapped the keyboard shortcuts for accessing Print Preview and just plain old Print. Ctrl+P (⌘+P on the Mac) used to bring up the Print dialog box, and Ctrl+Alt+P gave you Print Preview. Now that has been reversed, apparently in the expectation that you'll find Print Preview more regularly useful than Print. However, if this doesn't seem likely to you, you can change it around with the Print Keys setting found in the General panel of the Preferences.

4. **Select a printer, paper size, and page orientation.**

   You accomplish all this inside the Page Setup dialog box, which you can display by clicking the Page Setup button in the Print Preview dialog box. When you've verified your settings, click OK to leave the Page Setup dialog box.

5. **Click the Print button in the Print Preview dialog box.**

   Elements displays the Print dialog box. Here you can specify how many copies of the image you want to print.

6. **Press Enter (Return on a Mac).**

   Experts say that this is the easiest step. Well, one guy got a blister on the end of his finger, but otherwise the vote was unanimous.

Congratulations! You've got hard copy. But on the off chance that you're unclear on how a couple of the preceding steps work or you're simply interested in excavating every possible nugget of information from this book, go forward to probe the depths of the rest of this chapter.

Choosing a Printer in Windows

If you have only one printer hooked up to your computer, you can skip this section entirely. But if you're part of a network or you have more than one printer available to you, you need to tell Elements which printer you want to use.

To select a printer, open the Page Setup dialog box. You can do this by choosing File⇨Page Setup or pressing Ctrl+Shift+P. (In Windows XP, you then press the Printer button at the bottom of the Page Setup dialog box to open yet another Page Setup dialog box.) A dialog box similar to the one shown in Figure 7-2 appears. (Your dialog box may look slightly different depending on your printer and which version of the operating system you're using.)

To select a printer, just choose the printer name from the Name drop-down menu. Click OK or press Enter to exit the dialog box.

Figure 7-2:
You select a
printer in
this dialog
box.

Choosing a Printer on a Mac

The hub of All Things Printing in Mac OS X is the Print Center, located in the Utilities folder inside your Applications folder. Opening the Print Center brings up the Printer List, as shown in Figure 7-3; just click the printer you want to use and you're done.

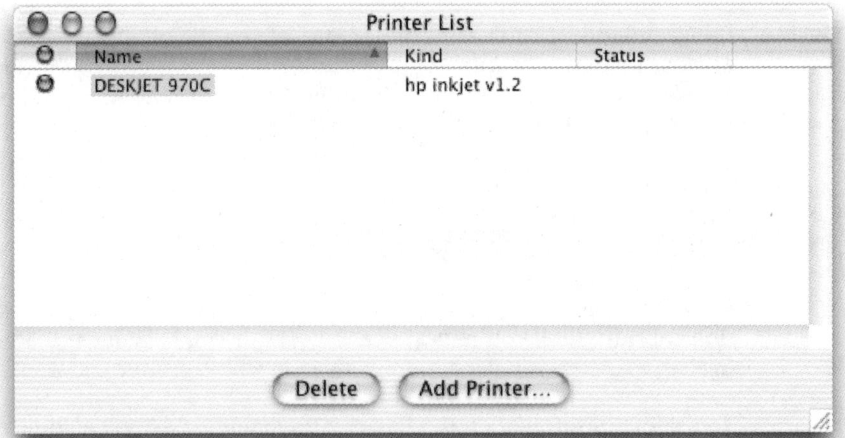

Figure 7-3:
You can
choose your
printer here
in the
Printer List.

If you're using OS 9, you'll need to pay a visit to the Chooser. Provided with every Mac, this little program is designed to let you confirm the connection to your printer. To access the Chooser dialog box, select the Chooser command from the Apple menu. The left side of the dialog box contains a bunch of icons that represent the kinds of printer drivers that are available to your system. Not to be confused with the drivers you use to knock golf balls into uncooperative printers, these drivers serve as a liaison between your computer and your printer.

✔ If you use a PostScript device — meaning a printer that supports the PostScript printer language — select the LaserWriter Driver icon. Nearly every printer over $1,000 supports PostScript, which is, without a doubt, the professional printing standard.

✔ If you see a driver icon that matches your specific model of printer, select it. For example, if you own a Hewlett-Packard DeskJet 970 and you installed the software that came with it, you should see an icon labeled DeskJet 900 Series, which happens to look like your printer. You'd be plum crazy not to select it.

Getting Image and Paper in Sync

The Print Preview dialog box, immortalized in Figure 7-4, offers much more than a preview of your printed image. Here are some of its other wonders:

✔ **Position:** Check the Center Image option to position your image. To enter other position values, deselect Check Image and type values in the Top and Left fields or turn on Show Bounding Box and simply drag your image preview thumbnail to the desired location on the page.

✔ **Scaled Print Size:** This setting enables you to reduce or enlarge the image for printing only. Enter any percentage below 100 percent to reduce the dimensions of the printed image. The printer still prints all the pixels in the image, but the pixels are just smaller. You can also enter a value in the height or width boxes, or turn on Show Bounding Box and resize the image in the preview by dragging from the sides or corners. You'll notice that scale, width, and height are linked, meaning that changing any one affects the other two.

✔ **Scale to Fit Media:** This option makes the image fit exactly on the size of the paper. This is generally a good option only if your image is too large to fit on the page.

✔ **Show Bounding Box:** This option places a box with handles around your image, showing the precise image boundaries and enabling you to reposition and resize the thumbnail image on the page.

✔ **Print Selected Area:** If you select a portion of your image using one of the tools we discuss in Chapter 8, you can print only the selected area by selecting the option that says, surprise, Print Selected Area. If you just want to take a quick look at an isolated area, you can use this option to save time and ink.

✔ **Show More Options:** This brings up the Output and Color Management options (a drop-down menu below Show More Options lets you toggle between the two).

✔ **Output:** This option allows you to add certain items to your print.

   • Clicking Background brings up the Color Picker to let you choose a colored background to print behind your image.

   • Border places a black border around your image, allowing you to specify the thickness.

   • Caption allows you to print a caption under your image. To enter this caption, you first have to Cancel out of the Print Preview box and choose File⇨File Info. Type your desired caption in the Caption field of the General Section, and click OK. When you return to the Print Preview dialog box, you will be able to see where your caption will print under the image preview.

   • Enabling Corner Crop Marks will create printed guides that can help if you plan to cut out your image from the printer paper.

   • The final Output option, Encoding, applies only when printing to a PostScript printer. Check your printer's specifications to determine the appropriate setting.

✔ **Color Management:** This option is based on the idea of *color spaces.* Different devices operate in different color spaces. Monitors, desktop color printers, and high-end offset printers all have their own unique color space. The Color Management options enable you to convert the color space of your image while printing. For example, if you created an RGB Elements document with Full color management turned on in the Color Settings, then your Document Source Profile is Adobe RGB (1998), and you can choose to have your image's color converted to the color space of your Epson printer upon printing. (For more on color management, see Chapter 5.)

In the Print Space section, under Profile, choose Same As Source to print using your Source Space. Your Source Space is determined by the color management (if any) you activated in the Color Settings. If you want to print using the color profile of another device, for example, a Hewlett-Packard or Epson printer, choose that profile from the list.

Choose PostScript Color Management to print to a PostScript printer (PS level 2 or higher). With this option, Elements enables the *printer,* instead of Elements, to manage all the color conversion. Leave Intent set at the default, Relative Colorimetric.

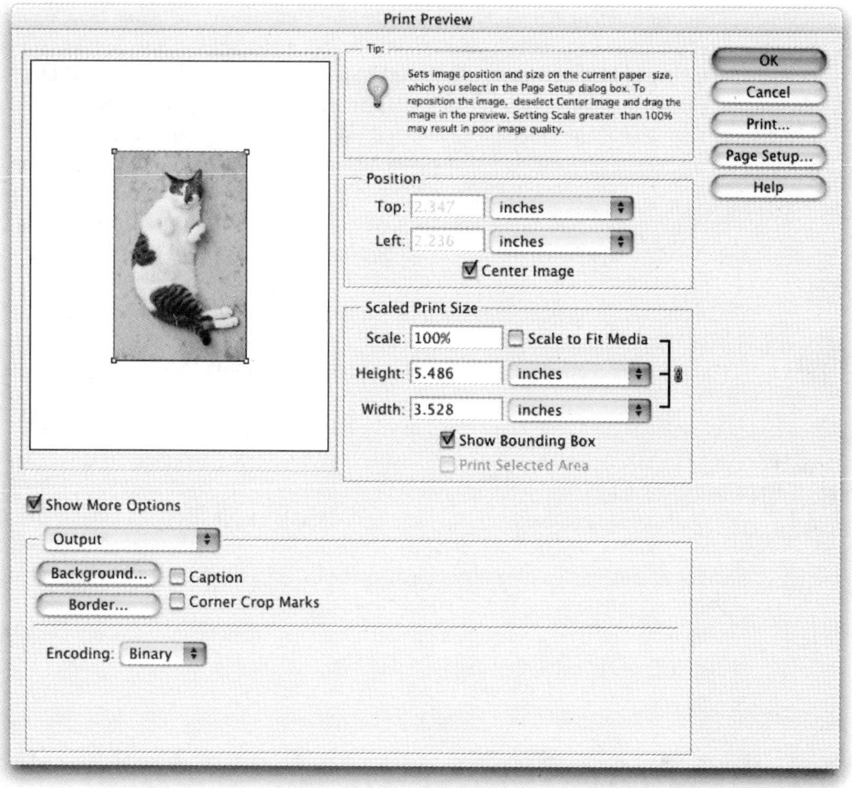

Figure 7-4:
You can
preview
how the
image fits
on the page
by using
the Print
Preview
dialog box.

If all you want to do is print in color from your desktop printer, first choose Same As Source for your Print Space. Then print another copy using your printer's color profile for your Print Space, if you can find the profile in that monstrous list. Compare both copies to see which one looks better. If you have a late model printer, you may also want to check the documentation for the manufacturer's recommendations.

The Page Setup dialog box lets you make additional choices that will affect your final printed output. To open Page Setup, choose File⇨Page Setup, press Ctrl+Shift+P (⌘+Shift+P on the Mac), or simply click the Page Setup button in the Print Preview dialog box.

In addition to scaling and positioning your printed image using the Print Preview, another possibility is to rotate the image on the page. For example, if the image is wider than it is tall, you can print it horizontally by rotating the page 90 degrees. Somewhere in your Page Setup dialog box you should find two choices for Orientation: Portrait and Landscape. (It may be necessary to click the Properties button to access the Orientation options.) If you choose Portrait, your image prints upright on the page; if you choose Landscape, Elements rotates the image so that it prints sideways on the paper.

The specific options found inside the Page Setup dialog box vary depending on the kind of printer you're using. Note that the Page Setup dialog box also offers a scaling option. Scaling options let you reduce or enlarge the image for printing only. Mac users will probably find a Scale option box somewhere within the Page Setup dialog box; Windows users may need to click the Properties button to hunt down this option. When the Properties dialog box appears, click the Graphics tab. If you see a Scaling option, you're in business. As you'll notice, however, you don't have as much flexibility as you do with the Print Preview scaling feature.

The Scaling value remains in effect until you open up the Page Setup dialog box and change it. So, if you don't want to scale future print jobs, be sure to change the setting back to 100% after you print the current image.

As mentioned in Chapter 4, many different factors can determine the size at which your image prints. Although the Image Size command (covered in Chapter 4) is the only one that can potentially damage your image, keeping this from happening is relatively easy (turn off the Resample Image check box). To avoid confusion and unpredictable results (and wasting expensive printer paper) caused by the interaction of so many different influences on the final print size, we recommend using only Image Size to determine the size at which your image prints. Find out how to use Image Size correctly and you'll never be surprised by the results.

Sending the Image to the Printer

After you've made it past the obstacle course of options provided by the Print Preview and Page Setup dialog boxes, you're almost home free. All you need to do is make a few last-minute calls, such as how many copies you want to print. Click the Print button in the Print Preview dialog box to display the Print dialog box, shown in Figure 7-5. You can also click the handy Print icon in the Shortcuts bar (it looks like a printer), choose File➪Print, or press Ctrl+Alt+P (⌘+Option+P on the Mac).As with the Page Setup dialog box, the options available in the Print dialog box may vary depending on your printer.

If the image is still too large for the page, Elements displays an error message to warn you that a portion of your image will be cut off of the page and asks whether you want to proceed. If you say no, the error message disappears, and you can then resize the image to fit the page, as discussed earlier in this chapter. If you say that you want to go ahead and print anyway, the Print dialog box appears.

If you're absolutely confident that your image should fit on your selected paper size, but Elements still barks at you that it won't fit, check the page orientation (portrait or landscape) in your Page Setup dialog box. Even if your image fits on the paper, if it isn't oriented correctly, Elements sometimes thinks it's too large.

That's it. Just click the OK button (Print on the Mac) or press Enter (Return on a Mac), and you're off. Depending on the size of the image, you should have hard copy in a matter of a few minutes.

Chapter 8

Making Selections on the Pixel Prairie

*I*f you're an old ranch hand, you may find it helpful to think of the pixels in your image as a bunch of cows. A pixel may not have any horns, and you don't have to watch where you step when you're around it, but it's a cow all the same. Consider these amazing similarities: Both pixels and cows travel in herds. Come on, when's the last time you saw one pixel out on its own? They're both dumb as dirt. And obstinate to boot. And — here's the absolute clincher — you can round them both up by using a lasso.

The only difference between pixels and cows is in the vernacular. When you lasso a cow or two on the lone prairie, it's called ropin'. When you lasso a mess of pixels, it's called selectin'. And after you select the desired pixels, you can do things to them. You can move them, duplicate them, and apply all kinds of alterations as described in future chapters. Selecting lets you grab hold of some detail or other and edit it independently of other portions of your image. It's a way of isolating pixels to manipulate them.

Granted, there are a few ways to select pixels other than with the lasso: There's a magic wand, a couple of marquee tools, and perhaps best of all a new tool called the Selection Brush. But whichever means you pick, this chapter is all about selecting portions of an image. With a little practice, you can rustle pixels better than most hands rope dogies, and that's no bull.

Learning the Ropes of Selecting

Photoshop Elements provides several selection tools, all labeled in Figure 8-1. These tools include two marquee tools, the Lasso, the Polygonal Lasso, the Magnetic Lasso, an automatic color selector known as the Magic Wand (phoenix feather not included), and the new Selection Brush. Here's how they work:

- ✔ The Rectangular Marquee tool lets you select a rectangular area. Just drag from one corner of the area you want to select to the other. The outline drawn with the tool looks like a border of moving dots — which is how "marquee" managed its way into the tool's name.

- ✔ The Elliptical Marquee, which shares a flyout menu with the Rectangular Marquee, draws oval selections. The word *ellipse*, incidentally, is what mathematicians say when they're talking about ovals. In fact, we could just call it the ovoid marquee tool, but you might forget and think we were talking about some home pregnancy test.

- ✔ Drag inside the image with the Lasso tool to select free-form areas. The shape of the selection conforms to the shape of your drag.

- ✔ Use the Polygonal Lasso tool, which shares a flyout menu with the regular Lasso tool, to select pixels that are married to more than one pixel. Oops, sorry — that's the Polygamal Lasso. The Polygonal Lasso draws selections made up of straight sides.

- ✔ Sharing the flyout with the other two lasso tools is the Magnetic Lasso tool (which sounds like the perfect tool for ropin' a mechanical bull). Click the Magnetic Lasso on the edge of your object and then move the lasso around that edge.

- ✔ The Magic Wand selects areas of continuous color. For example, if you want to select the sky without selecting the clouds, you just click in the sky. At least, that's the way it's supposed to work, but you never know. The Magic Wand isn't always as magical as you may think.

- ✔ The Selection Brush lets you paint over the area you want to select. While in Selection mode, working with the Selection Brush is very similar to the other selection tools, but in Mask mode the real power of the tool becomes apparent.

An active selection in Elements is represented by a line of ever-moving dots, referred to in the digital imaging community as "marching ants." (Just stare at a selection outline for a while and you'll see the resemblance.) Anything enclosed in the outline is selected; anything outside the outline is not selected. Although this is a fairly effective means of indicating an active selection, you may eventually feel that working with these ants is, well, no picnic. The upcoming section "Hiding the Ants," tells how to make the distracting ants turn temporarily invisible, and the Selection Brush tool offers a very effective ant alternative. Read on for details.

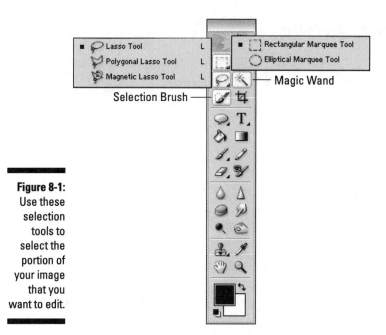

Lasso Tool — L
Polygonal Lasso Tool — L
Magnetic Lasso Tool — L

Rectangular Marquee Tool
Elliptical Marquee Tool

Magic Wand

Selection Brush

Figure 8-1:
Use these
selection
tools to
select the
portion of
your image
that you
want to edit.

Now that you know how the tools work, let's see how to get to the tools.
The arrow in the lower-right corner of the Marquee and Lasso tool icons in
the Toolbox indicates that a flyout menu of hidden tools lurks beneath each
icon (see Chapter 2 for more information).

To switch between the tools on the flyout menus, you can Alt+click
(Option+click on a Mac) on whichever tool icon happens to be visible in the
Toolbox at the time. You can also use the tool buttons available on the far left
of the Options bar. Or, you can select tools using these keyboard shortcuts:

✔ Press the M key to access the active marquee tool. Whichever marquee
tool is active, press Shift+M to get the other one.

✔ Press L to get the lasso tools. As with the marquee tools, a common
shortcut switches you between the three lasso tools: If the regular Lasso
tool is active, pressing Shift+L brings up the Polygonal and the Magnetic
Lassos.

✔ Press W to get the Magic Wand. The tool is more unpredictable than
magical, making W — for Wacky Wand — a logical keyboard equivalent.

✔ Press A to get the Selection Brush. You can remember that A is for *artistic,* and painting on the image is unquestionably the most artistic means
of making a selection.

Throwing lassos

Both the regular Lasso tool and the Polygonal Lasso tool are so easy to use your newborn can master them. If you don't have a newborn, you'll have to muddle through on your own. The Magnetic Lasso is trickier, however, but nothing you can't pick up with a little guidance from a toddler.

Using the regular Lasso tool

Here's a complete set of instructions for using the regular Lasso tool:

1. **Trace around the portion of the image that you want to select with the tool.**

   That's it. In Figure 8-2, for example, the frog was dragged around to select it independently of its surroundings. As the figure shows, Elements displays a dotted outline — those wacky marching ants — around the selected area after you release the mouse button. This outline represents the exact path of your drag. (If you release before completing the shape — that is, before meeting up with the point at which you began dragging — Elements simply connects the beginning and ending points with a straight line.)

Selection outline   Lasso cursor

Figure 8-2:
We selected the frog by dragging around it with the Lasso.

Granted, it's not easy to draw the outline just right, as in Figure 8-2. There's no trick to it; just get plenty of practice. If you have a graphics tablet, such as those made by Wacom, you may find it easier to select with a stylus rather than with the mouse. However, if your outlines aren't perfectly accurate, don't sweat it. There are plenty of ways to modify the outline after you draw it.

Drawing straight-sided selections

Suppose that you want to select a cube sitting in the center of an image. You can try to drag around those straight edges by hand with the Lasso tool, but a better option is to use the Polygonal Lasso, which makes it easy to create selections with straight sides.

To select an object in this manner, click with the Polygonal Lasso to set the beginning of the first line in the selection. Then move the mouse cursor to the point where you want the first line to end and click again. Keep clicking to create new line segments. To complete the selection, you have two options. If you double-click, Elements draws a segment between the spot you double-click and the first point in your selection. You can also move the cursor over the first point in your selection until you see a little circle next to the Polygonal Lasso cursor. Then click to close the selection.

The Polygonal Lasso can also be used for images with both curved and straight segments. You can switch to the regular Lasso in midselection to create a curved segment. Just press and hold down the Alt (Option on a Mac) key and drag to draw your curved line. When you release the Alt (Option on a Mac) key, the tool reverts back to the Polygonal Lasso.

You can also press Alt (Option on a Mac) while drawing a selection with the regular Lasso to access the Polygonal Lasso. Press Alt (Option on a Mac) and click to set the endpoints of your straight-sided segments, as you normally do with the Polygonal Lasso. To start another curved segment, just drag. You can keep the Alt key (Option key on a Mac) down or not — it doesn't matter. But be sure that the mouse button is down any time you press or release the Alt (Option on a Mac) key, or Elements completes the selection outline.

Selecting with the Magnetic Lasso

This lasso tool takes a little getting used to and may not produce a great selection in all cases. But the concept behind it is simple, and if you take some time to understand the method behind its madness, it can be a quick remedy for your selection needs.

The Magnetic Lasso works best with high-contrast images — that is, the object you want to select is a different color than the background. Taking the Options bar settings into account, the Magnetic Lasso analyzes the difference in the color of the pixels between the object you want to select and the background, and snaps to your object's edge. Here's how to use this quirky tool:

1. **Select the Magnetic Lasso tool.**

2. **Click on the edge of the object you want to select.**

3. **Move the cursor around the edge of the object.**

   Don't press the mouse and drag — just move the mouse. Simple! The Magnetic Lasso creates an outline with square anchor points around the edge of the object. If the line is off the mark, back up your mouse and try again. If you need to delete an anchor point as you are moving around the edge, press the Backspace (Delete on a Mac) key. To create your own anchor points, click with the mouse. Adding your own anchor points can be helpful if the Magnetic Lasso seems reluctant to stick to the edge you select.

4. **Continue around the object and click on your starting anchor point to close the outline.**

   You'll see a small circle next to your cursor indicating closure of the outline.

5. **As soon as the outline is closed and you release the mouse, a selection marquee appears.**

6. **Press Esc or Ctrl+period (⌘+period on a Mac) to cancel the Magnetic Lasso in midselection.**

To create a straight segment while using the Magnetic Lasso, press Alt (Option on a Mac) and click with the mouse. You can see that the tool icon of your cursor temporarily changes to the Polygonal Lasso. Release the Alt (Option on a Mac) key and drag for a second to reset the tool back to the Magnetic Lasso. From then on, just move the cursor without clicking or dragging.

Exploring your lasso options

Whether you use the regular Lasso, the Polygonal Lasso, or the Magnetic Lasso, you can modify the performance of the tool via the options common to all three tools in the Options bar (see the next section for options specific to the Magnetic Lasso). Though small in number, the options for the lasso tools are some tough little hombres:

 - Both Feather and Anti-aliased affect future selection outlines drawn with the lasso tools, and not currently active selections. In short, Feather makes the outline fuzzy, and Anti-aliased slightly softens the edge of the outline. If you want to modify an outline that you've already drawn, you have to choose a command under the Select menu (more on this in the section "Automatic selection shifters").

 - Normally, you'll want selections drawn with the lasso tools to have soft, natural-looking edges. This softening is called *anti-aliasing*. If you want to turn off the softening, deselect the Anti-aliased check box in the Options bar. From now on, outlines drawn with the tool will have sharply defined and sometimes jagged edges.

✔ Figure 8-3 shows two lassoed selections moved to reveal the white background in the image. In the left example, the Anti-aliased check box was turned off; in the right example, the option was turned on. The edges of the left example are jagged; the edges of the right example are soft. (Chapter 9 explains all the ways to move selections. But if you want to try moving a selection now, just drag it with the Move tool, which is the top-right tool in the Toolbox.)

✔ Most of the time, you want to leave the Anti-aliased check box turned on. Just turn it off when you want to select precise, hard-edged areas. (Which may be never. Who knows?)

✔ Enter a value into the Feather option box to make the next outline you draw fuzzy. The value determines the radius of the fuzziness in pixels. If you enter a value of 3, for example, Elements extends the fuzzy region 3 pixels up, 3 pixels to the left, 3 pixels down, and 3 pixels to the right. As shown in the first example of Figure 8-4, that's a lot of fuzz. A higher value results in a more fuzzy selection outline, as witnessed in the right example, which sports a Feather value of 10.

Anti-aliasing off; jagged edges   Anti-aliasing on; soft edges

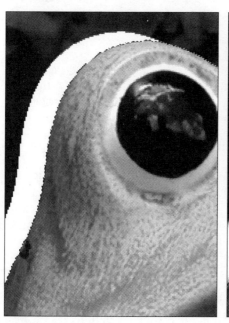 

Figure 8-3: The difference between dragging a jagged (left) and anti-aliased (right) selection.

Feather 3 pixels   Feather 10 pixels

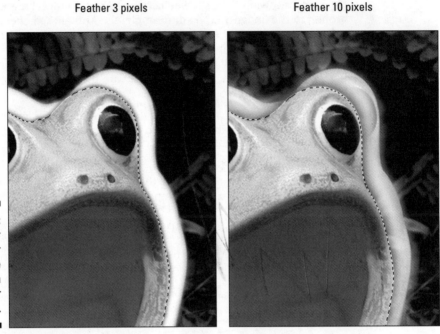

Figure 8-4:
A bigger
Feather
value
means a
fuzzier
froggy.

Looking at the unique Magnetic Lasso options

The Magnetic Lasso has unique options in the bar that are related to the sensitivity of the tool's operation. They are the following:

- **Width:** This option determines how close to an edge you have to move the mouse for Elements to "see" the object. You can set it to a higher number for smooth, high-contrast objects, and it will still hug the edge of the object. Set it to a lower value if the image has a lot of nooks and crannies or the contrast isn't that high. The range of the width option is 1 to 256 pixels. To change it while you are actually using the tool, press the [key to lower the number and the] key to raise the number.

- **Edge Contrast:** This option tells the Magnetic Lasso how much contrast is required between the object and the background before the lasso can be "attracted to" or can hug that edge. The range for the Edge Contrast option is 1% to 100%. If you find a good deal of contrast between the object and the background, put in a higher value in order to get a cleaner selection. If the image is low contrast, lower the value for this option.

- **Frequency:** The number in the Frequency option tells the Magnetic Lasso when to automatically insert anchor points. The range for Frequency is from 0 to 100. If you want more points, insert a higher number; for less points, use a lower value. High values are better for rough, jagged edges, and low values are better for smooth edges. As you move around the edge of your object and create the outline, Elements pins it down with an anchor point.

Start with default settings for the preceding Magnetic Lasso options, carefully make your selection, and see how it works. If your image is low contrast, you may want to lower the Edge Contrast to 5% or so. If edges are jagged or rough, try raising the Frequency to around 70 and lowering the Width to 5 pixels. If all else fails, and the Magnetic Lasso just isn't behaving, you can always go back to the regular Lasso and the Polygonal Lasso. They may not be as high tech, but they're reliable.

Using the Marquee Tools

If you want to create a selection that's rectangular or elliptical, you use — guess what — the Rectangular and Elliptical Marquee tools. The Rectangular and Elliptical Marquee tools are so easy to use that they make the Lasso look complicated. You just drag from one corner to the opposite corner and release the mouse button. (Okay, ovals don't have corners, so you have to use your imagination a little bit.) The dotted marquee follows the movements of your cursor on-screen, keeping you apprised of the selection outline in progress.

But Elements has never been one to provide you with only one way to use a tool — or, in this case, two tools. For example, you can also use these tools to select perfect squares or circles. The program's cup of flexibility forever runneth over, and the marquee tools are no exception.

Grabbing a square or circle

Every so often, you may feel the urge to apply some puritanical constraints to your selection outlines. Enough of this random width and height business — you want perfect squares and circles. Lucky for you, Elements obliges these fussbudget impulses by letting you constrain shapes drawn with the marquee tools:

- ✔ To draw a perfect square, press the Shift key as you drag with the Rectangular Marquee tool. To draw a perfect circle, press Shift as you drag with the Elliptical Marquee tool.

- ✔ Drawing squares and circles is a little trickier than you might expect. For the best results, you should get in the habit to first begin dragging, press and hold Shift, drag to the desired location and release the mouse button, and finally release Shift. In other words, press Shift after you start the drag and hold it until after you complete the drag.

✔ If you press Shift before dragging, you run the risk of adding to the previously selected area, which you may not want to do. Here's the deal: If a portion of your image is already selected, holding down the Shift key first and then dragging will add the new selection to the previous one, rather than constrain the new selection to a square or circle. Befuddling, huh? If this happens to you, deselect everything and start over again. However, if you actually do want to add a square or circular selection to a previously made selection, here's what you do: Hold down Shift, begin to drag, and then keep the mouse button pressed down as you release and press the Shift key again. Weird, but it works.

The marquee tools can come in handy not only for selecting part of your image but they also offer one technique for creating geometric shapes as well. For example, if you want to draw a hollow rectangle, create a selection with the Rectangular Marquee tool. Then choose Edit⇨Stroke to stroke the marquee with a color — in other words, to paint a line along the marquee.

Getting even more control over selections

Are you crazed for control? Do your tyrannical desires know no bounds? If so, you probably aren't appeased by drawing a square or a circle. What you want is to apply even more stringent constraints.

For example, suppose that you're the sort of pixel-oppressor who wants to select a rectangular or oval area that's exactly twice as wide as it is tall. With your marquee tool selected, choose Fixed Aspect Ratio from the Style drop-down menu in the Options bar. The Width and Height option boxes come to life, letting you specify an *aspect ratio,* which is a precise proportion between the width and height of a marquee. To make the marquee twice as wide as it is tall, enter **2** as the Width value. Then press Tab to highlight the Height value and enter **1**. The deed is done.

To constrain the marquee to an exact size, select Fixed Size from the Style drop-down menu, and then enter the exact pixel dimensions of your desired marquee into the Width and Height option boxes.

One last item submitted for your approval: As with the lasso options discussed earlier in this chapter, the marquee options sport Anti-aliased and Feather options, which respectively soften the selection outline and make it blurry. However, the Anti-aliased check box is dimmed when you use the Rectangular Marquee tool. Perpendicular edges never need softening because they can't be jagged. Anti-aliasing, therefore, would be a waste of time.

Drawing from the center out

As mentioned earlier, you draw a rectangle or oval from corner to opposite corner. But you can also draw a marquee from the center outward. To do this, press Alt or Option as you drag with a marquee tool.

If you decide midway into your drag that you don't want to draw the shape from the center outward, just release the Alt (Option on a Mac) key and continue dragging. What was once the center of the marquee now goes back to being a corner.

To draw a square or circle from the center outward, press both Shift and Alt (Option on a Mac) as you drag with the appropriate marquee tool. (If you already have an active selection and you press Shift and Alt — Option on a Mac— before you begin dragging, you end up selecting the intersection of the two selections, as explained later.)

Wielding the wand

The Magic Wand is even easier to use than the marquee tools. (Pretty soon, things get so easy you won't need us at all.) But it's also the most difficult selection tool to understand and predict. To use the tool, you just click inside an image. Elements then selects the color that you clicked on in the image.

'Scuze me while I click the sky

Figure 8-5 shows how the Magic Wand works. In the first image, the Magic Wand tool was clicked in the sky above the fake dinosaur. Elements automatically selected the entire continuous area of sky. In the second example, the selection was made more apparent by pressing Ctrl+Backspace (⌘+Delete on a Mac), which filled the selection with the white background color. The selection outline is gone because the selection was hidden. (Don't worry, hiding selections is explained in full, rich detail in the section "Hiding the Ants.")

Notice that the wand by default selects only uninterrupted areas of color. The patch of sky below the creature's tail, for example, remains intact. Also, the selection seeped slightly into the edges of the dinosaur. Pressing Ctrl+Backspace (⌘+Delete on the Mac) removed very small pieces along the top of the plastic behemoth.

Figure 8-5:
Here's what
happens
when you
click in the
sky above
the T-Rex
with the
Magic
Wand (top)
and fill the
selection
with white.

Teaching the wand tolerance

You can modify the performance of the Magic Wand by accessing the ever-popular Options bar, which offers four basic options — Tolerance, Anti-aliased, Contiguous, and Use All Layers.

We cover Anti-aliased earlier in this chapter, in the section "Exploring your lasso options," so we're not going to beat that poor horse anymore. The Use All Layers option comes into play only when your image contains more than one layer (see Chapter 9). When Use All Layers is turned off, the Magic Wand selects colors only on the active layer. If you want the Magic Wand to select colors from all visible layers, turn the option on.

When Contiguous is active, the Magic Wand selects only pixels that are adjacent to each other. If it is not active, the Magic Wand looks throughout the entire image for any pixels that fall within the Tolerance range.

This brings us to Tolerance, which has the most sway over the performance of the Magic Wand. It tells Elements which colors to select and which not to select. A lower Tolerance value instructs the wand to select fewer colors; a higher value instructs it to select more colors.

Figure 8-6 shows what we mean. Each row of images demonstrates the effect of a different Tolerance value, starting with the default value of 32 at the top and working up to 180 at the bottom. In each case, the Magic Wand was clicked at the same location, just to the right of the big giraffe's schnoz. The left image in each row shows the selection outline created when we clicked the Magic Wand; the right image shows the selection filled with white and then hidden.

The problem is that finding the best Tolerance setting is a completely random exercise in the frustrating art of trial and error. As with changes to any tool setting, changes to the Tolerance value have no effect on the current selection. You have to click with the Magic Wand to try out each and every new value. In fact, here's the typical approach:

1. **Click with the Magic Wand tool.**

   The point at which you click marks the base color — the one Elements uses to judge which other colors it should select.

2. **Express displeasure with the results.**

   Gnash your teeth for good measure.

3. **Enter a new Tolerance value in the Options bar.**

   Enter a higher value to select more colors next time around; enter a lower value to select fewer colors.

4. **Choose Select⇨Deselect or press Ctrl+D (⌘+D on a Mac).**

   Elements deselects the previous selection.

5. **Repeat Steps 1 through 4 until you get it right.**

   There's no foolproof approach or magic formula here; just a whole lotta clickin' and tweakin' goin' on. Doesn't really sound so magical, huh?

Tolerance: 32

Tolerance: 90

Figure 8-6:
A Tolerance
value of 32
selected too
little sky; a
value of 180
selected all
the sky but
also got
some huge
chunks of
giraffe face
and rolling
foothill. A
value of 90
appears to
be just right.

Tolerance: 180

There's one more option that affects the performance of the Magic Wand, but it isn't located in the Magic Wand's Options bar. Guess what it is. Come on, give it a try. Give up? We don't blame you, as it's truly weird and very out of place. The missing Magic Wand option is actually located in the Eyedropper tool's Options bar. Click on the Eyedropper tool and check it out. The Sample Size setting determines how many pixels the Eyedropper looks at when it samples a color. The default setting, Point Sample, means that the Eyedropper will sample only the precise pixel it's clicked upon — just that one single pixel and no others. The color of that pixel becomes the foreground color. However, set Sample Size to 3 by 3 Average, and the Eyedropper looks at not only the pixel it's clicked upon, but also one pixel in every direction — making for a 3-pixel square, or 9 pixels in all. The Eyedropper averages the colors of those 9 pixels, and that average color becomes the foreground color. Likewise, setting Sample Size to 5 by 5 Average makes the Eyedropper look in a 5-pixel square, and it averages the colors of those 25 pixels.

And here comes The Weirdest Thing About Photoshop Elements: That Sample Size option in the Eyedropper's Options bar *affects the behavior of the Magic Wand.* If you set Sample Size to 3 by 3 Average and then switch to the Magic Wand and click, the Wand's selection will be based not just on the pixel it's clicked upon, but on the 3-pixel square of surrounding pixels. And likewise for 5 by 5 Average. Why? We don't know. It's spooky. It's weird. But it's true. And we thought you should know.

Greatness with a brush

New to Elements 2.0, the Selection Brush is a very welcome addition to the Toolbox. The premise of the tool is very simple: You paint in the image with the Selection Brush to create a selection. With the Mode menu in the Options bar set to Selection, the Selection Brush uses the now-familiar marching ants to show where the selection occurs. However, switch to Mask mode and things are different. Now the Selection Brush paints in a strange red overlay on the image. Areas covered with the red overlay are unselected; clear areas are selected. Therefore, when in Mask mode the Selection Brush becomes in effect a *De*-Selection Brush, masking off areas of the image that you want to protect from change.

Follow along, and we'll show you what's so darned great about Mask mode.

1. **Select the Elliptical Marquee tool.**

2. **Set a high Feather value in the Options bar.**

   Maybe something like 30 or so.

3. **Draw a selection.**

   Doesn't look very feathered, does it? The problem is that those marching ants have no way of demonstrating to you that a selection is feathered. They're brilliant at marching around in a one-pixel-wide circle, but lousy at conveying the soft gradual transition of a feathered edge.

4. **Select the Selection Brush tool.**

   Don't deselect your marquee selection; keep it active.

5. **In the Options bar, switch to Mask mode and view the selection.**

   Aha! Now *there's* a feathered selection! The overlay is red where the image is totally unselected, clear where the image is totally selected, and in between there's a gradual fade between red and clear. So when soft edges are important, the Selection Brush is clearly the way to go. Color Plate 5 illustrates.

Let's take a look at the settings in the Selection Brush's Options bar:

- ✔ **Brush menu:** You can select the type of brush you want to use for your selection from this menu. For much more about brushes, see Chapter 14.

- ✔ **Size:** You can select the size of your brush here, type in a pixel value, or click the arrow and drag the slider. However, it will probably be more convenient for you to use the [and] keys to lower and raise the size of the brush, respectively.

- ✔ **Mode:** Switch between Selection (marching ant) mode and Mask (red overlay) mode.

- ✔ **Hardness:** This setting determines how feathered the brush selection will be. Low settings create a very soft edge; high settings create a hard edge. Experiment in Mask mode and you'll get the idea.

- ✔ **Overlay Opacity (Mask mode only):** This setting determines how transparent the overlay will be. A setting of 100 percent totally obscures the underlying image and is probably best avoided; likewise, a setting of 0 percent makes the overlay disappear completely and is useless.

- ✔ **Overlay Color (Mask mode only):** If there's a great deal of red in your underlying image, then it's quite possible that a red overlay isn't the wisest choice. Click the swatch to access the Color Picker and choose a more contrasting color.

One other thing you should know about the Selection Brush: Holding down the Alt or Option key makes the tool behave in the opposite manner. So, holding down Alt or Option in Selection mode makes the tool deselect selected areas; holding down Alt or Option in Mask mode makes the Selection Brush paint in "clear," erasing the overlay and thereby selecting areas of the image.

Selecting everything

When no part of an image is selected, the entire image is up for grabs. You can edit any part of it by using the paint or edit tools or any of about a billion commands. But you can also make the entire image available for edits by choosing Select➪All or Ctrl+A (⌘+A on a Mac) to select everything.

Beginning to see the mystery here? If you can edit any part of the image by deselecting it, why choose Select➪All, which also lets you edit everything? Because some operations require a selection, that's why. For instance, if you want to copy an entire image and paste it into another image (more on copying and pasting in Chapter 9), you need to select the entire image first. Sure, you can carefully drag around its perimeter with the Rectangular Marquee tool, but why bother when you can just Select All?

Deselecting everything

Before we plow into all that whiz-bang, awesome stuff that Elements lets you do to a selection outline, let's first touch on selection's exact opposite, deselection. Though this may seem at face value to be a ridiculously boneheaded topic — one that hardly merits space in a scholarly tome such as *Photoshop Elements 2 For Dummies* — deselecting is actually an integral step in the selection process.

Suppose, for example, that you select one part of your image. Then you change your mind and decide to select a different portion instead. Before you can select that new area, you have to deselect the old one. You can deselect an existing selection outline in several ways:

- Click anywhere in the image with the lasso or the marquee tools.

- To get rid of an existing selection and create a new one at the same time, just drag or click to create the new selection as you normally would. Elements automatically deselects the old selection when you create a new one. Note that the Selection Brush is an exception to this rule; using the Selection Brush always preserves an already active selection.

- Click inside the selection with the Magic Wand. (If you click outside the selection, you not only deselect the selection, you create a new selection.)

- Choose Select➪Deselect or press Ctrl+D (⌘+D on a Mac). Choosing Select➪Reselect or Ctrl+Shift+D (⌘+Shift+D on a Mac) regains your most recent selection. You can do this even after you have performed numerous actions.

- Click the state preceding the final state in the Undo History palette.

Saving and Loading Selections

To deselect, or not to deselect: In Elements 1.0, that was the question. You might have worked for many minutes perfecting a selection, and then used it to good effect. You wanted to move on to editing another area of your image, but in the back of your mind you knew that there was a good chance you might want to work with that selection again — maybe even in the days or weeks to come.

Elements 2.0 solves this dilemma once and for all by actually letting you save selections. The information for the selection is embedded into the code of the image, so if you close and reopen the image, you can still load the selection.

To give this command a try, make a selection and choose Select⇨Save Selection. The only option available to you will be to give your selection a name; once you've done this, click OK. Go ahead and deselect your selection — heck, go ahead and close the image entirely, saving changes. Reopen the image, and now choose Select⇨Load Selection. The name of your saved selection will be visible in the Selection menu; go ahead and click OK, and voila! There's your old selection. Pretty neat, huh?

The other Save Selection options, shown in Figure 8-7, come into play when you are dealing with multiple selections. If you choose Save Selection when you already have a selection saved, choosing the name of a selection in the Selection menu (rather than choosing New) means that you want to overwrite that selection. The Operation radio buttons give you four options for combining your new selection with the old one. You can completely replace the old selection, add the new and old selections together, subtract the new selection from the old one, or keep only the intersection of the two selections.

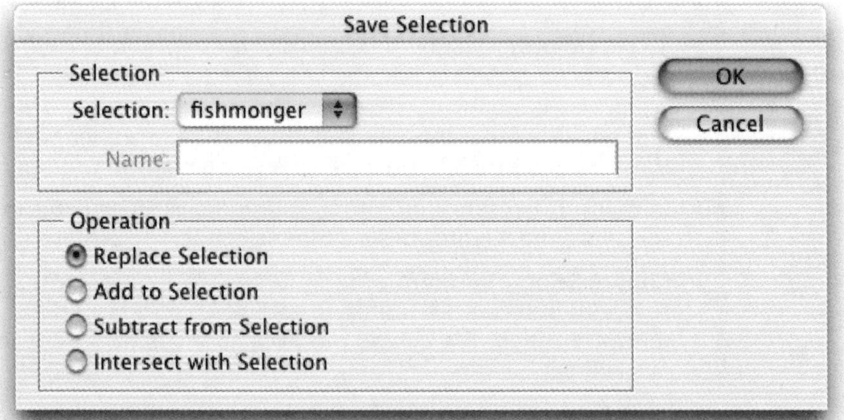

Figure 8-7:
The Save
Selection
dialog box
lets you
store
difficult
selections
for later use.

Save Selection

Selection

Selection: fishmonger

Name:

OK

Cancel

Operation
⦿ Replace Selection
◯ Add to Selection
◯ Subtract from Selection
◯ Intersect with Selection

When you loaded your selection a couple of paragraphs ago, you probably noticed the Invert check box. Selecting this check box inverts the selection before it has loaded, just like pressing Ctrl+Shift+I (⌘+Shift+I on the Mac). Load Selection also lets you use the Selection menu to choose the saved selection you want to load. The Operation radio buttons function just like the ones in the Save Selection dialog box, letting you determine how the loaded selection should interact with any other currently active selections in the document.

And finally, selecting Select⟹Delete Selection lets you select a selection to delete from the Selection menu. Whew.

Hiding the Ants

Here's a vital thing to know about selection outlines when working in Elements. Under the View menu, you'll find the Selection command. The Selection command hides the "marching ants" of the active selection outline. This makes it much easier to see what you're doing as you work, particularly around the edges of the selection; those distracting ants turn invisible. Note, however, that this is not the same thing as deselecting the selection. When you choose View⟹Selection, the selection is still active; the visible evidence of the active selection (the marching ants) has just become invisible.

As with this current edition, the final chapter of the first edition of *Photoshop Elements For Dummies* was entitled "Ten Reasons You Might Possibly Want to Upgrade to Photoshop One Day." And the number one reason we gave? The keyboard shortcut Ctrl+H (⌘+H on the Mac). This is a longstanding keyboard shortcut for hiding the marching ants inside Photoshop, but Elements 1.0 was bereft of this beloved shortcut. No more! Adobe has clearly buckled under to our hard-hitting demands and has given Elements 2.0 the Ctrl/⌘+H shortcut. Little did we know our own power. Seriously, though, commit this keyboard shortcut to memory right away, folks. It's a vital part of making selections.

Although hiding selection outlines is a crucial tool, it also leads to the number one most common mistake while working with Elements. You'll make a selection, press Ctrl/⌘+H to hide the selection, work inside your selection without distraction, and then move to working outside the selection — and nothing will happen. You won't be able to edit your image where you want. You'll get annoyed, start to fume, decide that the problem is that you're just not pressing on your mouse **HARD ENOUGH** — and then become convinced that Elements and your computer are plotting against you. Just take a deep breath, calmly ask yourself, "Did I hide my selection outline?"; answer yourself, "Yes, as a matter of fact, I did"; and then hit Ctrl+D (⌘+D on the Mac). All is well. Phew.

Editing Selections

The first selection outline you create is almost never perfect. Whether you use a lasso, a marquee tool, the Magic Wand, or the Selection Brush, there's almost always some problem with the selection. You didn't get the hair selected right, or a finger is clipped off. Whatever the problem, you can remedy it by adding to the selection outline or by subtracting from it.

Adding and subtracting from a selection

When you've made a selection with a lasso, marquee tool, or the Magic Wand and you then want to add onto it or take away from it with the Selection Brush, it's a no-brainer. The Selection Brush always respects previous selections and doesn't automatically wipe them out when you use it. And regardless of your Mode setting, you can always switch the behavior of the Selection Brush by holding down the Alt or Option key.

However, if you want to use a lasso, marquee tool, or the Magic Wand to add onto or take away from a previous selection, it's a different matter. The four selection modifier buttons in the Options bar, as pictured in Figure 8-8, enable you to make a new selection, add to a selection, subtract from a selection, or intersect a selection. Simply click on your desired selection modifier button and then drag. For instance, if you've made a rectangular selection with the Rectangular Marquee tool and you also need to make a circular selection, first switch to the Elliptical Marquee. Click on the second selection modifier button, "Add to selection." Now when you drag out your circular selection, the rectangular selection won't disappear; instead, the circular selection will be added to it.

Figure 8-8:
The four selection modifier buttons in the Options bar let you modify your existing selection.

New selection

Subtract from selection

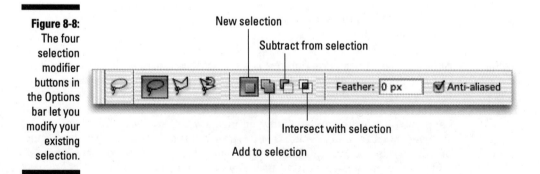

Intersect with selection

Add to selection

It's also possible — and once you get up to speed with Elements, you'll probably find it more convenient — to modify selections using the keyboard. Even if you do use the keyboard, the selection modifier buttons automatically become active when you press the appropriate keys anyway.

To add an area to the current selection, Shift+drag with a lasso or marquee tool, or Shift+click with the Magic Wand. It doesn't matter which tool you used to select the image previously, nor does it matter whether you Shift+click inside or outside the selection.

For example, if you want to select the sky in a photo similar to the one in Figure 8-9, first select the top part of the sky by clicking it with the Magic Wand, as shown in the top example. To add the other areas to the selection, press the Shift key and click those with the Lasso as well, creating the selection outlines shown in the bottom example. To remove an area from a selection, Alt+drag (Option+drag on a Mac) with a lasso or marquee tool or Alt+click (Option+click on a Mac) with the Magic Wand.

When you're adding to a selection, a little plus sign appears next to your cursor. When you're subtracting from the selection, a little minus sign appears. And when you're selecting the intersection of two existing selections (as explained next), a little multiply sign appears. See, your math teacher was right — knowing arithmetic comes in handy in all kinds of situations.

Intersecting a selection with a selection

If you press the Shift and Alt (Option on a Mac) keys together while clicking with the Magic Wand or dragging with a lasso or marquee tool, you select the intersection of the previous selection and the newest one. Confused? Let's see if a picture can be worth at least those 39 words. Take a look at Figure 8-10. If you first drag around the black rectangle, then Shift+Alt+drag (Shift+Option+drag on a Mac) around the gray rectangle, you get the intersection of the two rectangles. Elements selects all portions of the second marquee that fall inside the first marquee and deselects everything else, leaving the selection shown in the right half of the figure. That's an *intersection*.

You can also use the Intersect selection modifier button (the last in the grouping of four buttons in Figure 8-8) in the Options bar to obtain an intersection.

Try selecting an area with the Lasso or one of the marquee tools and then Shift+Alt+clicking (Shift+Option+clicking on a Mac) inside the selection with the Magic Wand. Or click with the Magic Wand and then Shift+Alt+drag (Shift+Option+drag on a Mac) with one of the other selection tools. Either technique creates an intersection.

Figure 8-9:
To select all
areas of the
sky, you can
first select
just the top
(first image),
and then
press the
Shift key
and click
the other
areas with
the Magic
Wand to
select them,
too (bottom).

Figure 8-10: To get the intersection of these two rectangles, first marquee the black rectangle and then Shift+Alt+ marquee (Shift+ Option+ marquee on a Mac) around the gray rectangle (left). The right figure shows the intersection.

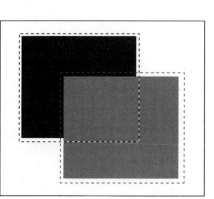 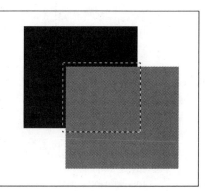

Avoiding keyboard collisions

There are a variety of ways to use the lasso and marquee tools while pressing keys. Pressing Alt (Option on a Mac) while using one of the lasso tools, you may recall, temporarily accesses one of the other lasso tools. Pressing Shift while using a marquee tool results in perfect squares and circles.

But what happens when you start combining those shortcut keys with all the add, subtract, and intersect shortcut keys we've just talked about? We touched on this topic briefly earlier, but the following list should answer your most burning questions:

✔ As previously noted, to add a square or circular area to an existing selection, start by Shift+dragging with the appropriate marquee tool. You get an unconstrained rectangle or oval, just as though the Shift key weren't down. Then midway into the drag — here's the catch — release the Shift key and then press it again, all the while keeping the mouse button down. The shape snaps to a square or circle with the second press of Shift. Keep the Shift key down until after you release the mouse button.

- ✔ Pressing Alt (Option on a Mac) to temporarily access the Polygonal Lasso when the regular Lasso is active causes trouble when you have an existing selection. This is because pressing Alt (Option on a Mac) in that scenario sets you up to subtract from the selection. So, if you want to add or subtract a straight-sided selection, use the Polygonal Lasso — don't try to Alt+click (Option+click on a Mac) with the regular Lasso.

- ✔ The same advice goes if you want to find the intersection of a selection and a straight-sided shape.

Automatic selection shifters

Shift+dragging, Alt+dragging (Option+dragging on a Mac), and all those other wondrous techniques are wildly helpful when it comes to selecting complex details. But they aren't the only selection modifications you can make. Elements offers a handful of automatic functions that reshape selection outlines, blur them, and otherwise mess them up. All the commands discussed in the next few sections reside under the Select menu.

Extending the Magic Wand

Two commands, Grow and Similar, are extensions of the Magic Wand tool (for details on the Magic Wand, see "Wielding the wand," in this chapter). The Grow command expands the size of the selection to include still more continuous colors. For example, if clicking with the Magic Wand doesn't select all the colors you want it to, you can either increase the Tolerance value inside the Options bar and reclick with the tool, or just choose Select⇨Grow to incorporate even more colors. It's kind of a clunky method, especially because the Grow command doesn't have a keyboard shortcut. You'll usually get better results if you Shift+click with the Wand tool, but every once in a while, the Grow command works as you'd expect. (You can use the Grow command with selections made with tools other than the Magic Wand, by the way.)

The Similar command selects all colors that are similar to the selected colors, regardless of whether they're interrupted by other colors. In other words, Similar selects all the contiguous colors that Grow selects, as well as all similarly colored pixels throughout the image.

Both Grow and Similar judge color similarity exactly as the Magic Wand tool does — that is, according to the Tolerance value in the Options bar. So, if you increase the Tolerance value, the commands select more colors; if you decrease the value, the commands select fewer colors. For example, if you want to select all colors throughout the image that are exactly identical to the ones you've selected so far, enter **0** into the Tolerance option box, and choose Select⇨Similar.

Swapping what's selected for what's not

Sometimes it's easier to select the stuff you don't want to select and then tell Elements to select the deselected stuff and deselect what's selected. (It's certainly easier to *do* this than to *write* it.) This technique is called *inversing a selection,* and you do it by choosing Select➪Inverse or pressing Ctrl+Shift+I (⌘+Shift+I on a Mac).

For example, suppose that you want to select the clock tower shown on the left side of Figure 8-11. A typical work of baroque madness, this building has more spikes and little twisty bits than a porcupine. Therefore, selecting it would prove a nightmare.

Selecting the sky, on the other hand, is quite easy. By clicking and Shift+clicking a couple of times with the Magic Wand tool (set here to the default Tolerance of 32), you can select the entire sky in a matter of two or three seconds. Then choose Select➪Inverse to "inverse" the selection so that the building is selected and the sky is deselected. To better show off the selection, it's filled with white in the example on the right, and the selection is hidden. The second example of Figure 8-9 is primed for this technique as well; if we inversed that selection, the arch would be selected, the sky deselected.

Making the selection fuzzy around the edges

You can blur the edges of a selection you are going to create with the lasso or marquee tools by increasing the Feather value in the corresponding Options bar. But more often than not, you want to leave the Feather value set to 0 and apply your feathering after you finish drawing the outline.

To feather an existing selection, choose Select➪Feather or press Ctrl+Alt+D (⌘+Option+D on a Mac). A dinky dialog box with a single option appears on-screen. Enter the amount of fuzziness, in pixels, that you want to apply to the selection and press Enter (Return on a Mac). The selection outline probably won't change very much — as we noted before, marching ants are useless for demonstrating a feathered selection — but you can always pop over to the Selection Brush and take a gander at the selection in Mask mode to see the results.

You can use feathering to make an image appear to fade into view. For example, take a look at the winsome example on the right side of Figure 8-12. If you want to pull off the same effect, first encircle the little charmer with the Elliptical Marquee tool. Then use Select➪Inverse to select the background instead and apply Select➪Feather; we used a value of 15 pixels here. Finally, use Ctrl+Backspace (⌘+Delete on a Mac) to fill the selection with white. The result should look something like a locket photo with fuzzy edges, as shown on the right side of Figure 8-12. This effect is also possible using the Vignette Frame from the Effects palette (see Chapter 17 for more information on Effects).

Figure 8-11:
This building (left) is too darned ornate to select easily, but it's a snap to select the sky and then inverse the selection. Filling the selection with white shows how accurate the selection is (right).

Figure 8-12:
A well-dressed lad (left) receives a classic vignette treatment (right).

Using Border, Smooth, and the rest

The remaining selection outline modifiers, found in the Select⇨Modify submenu, aren't quite as useful, but they do come in handy every now and then:

- ✔ The Border command selects an area around the edge of the selection. You tell Elements the width, in pixels, of the border you want to select. This command is probably the least useful command of the bunch. If you want to color the outline of a selection, it's easier to use stroking. (See the section "Grabbing a square or circle," earlier in this chapter for more on stroking.)

- ✔ Select⇨Modify⇨Smooth rounds off the corners of a selection outline. If the selection is very irregular and you want to straighten the twists and turns, use the Smooth command. You can enter a value from 1 to 100 to tell Elements how far it can move any point in the outline. Start with 2 or 3 to be safe.

- ✔ If you want to increase the size of a selection a few pixels outward, choose Select⇨Modify⇨Expand and enter the number of pixels. The maximum value is 100 pixels; if you want to expand the outline farther, you have to choose Expand a second time.

- ✔ Select⇨Modify⇨Contract is the opposite of the Expand command. This command shrinks the selected area by 1 to 100 pixels all the way around.

Moving selection outlines

To move a selection outline without moving the image inside it, select a tool other than the Move or Crop tool and nudge the selection outline with the arrow keys. You can also drag the selection outline if you choose one of the selection tools and position it within the outline. This is a great way to reposition a selection outline without disturbing so much as a single pixel in the image.

Chapter 9

Layer Layer

• •

• •

*I*nsofar as "high art" is concerned, the heyday for surrealism was 70 to 80 years ago. But the problem with guys like Max Ernst, René Magritte, and even Salvador Dalí was that they never got around to learning how to use Photoshop Elements. Oh, sure, they were long dead by the time Elements debuted. But still, think of what they could have done with Elements' layers. A paintbrush is great, but it pales when compared to Elements as a means for merging photo-realistic images to create flat-out impossible visual scenarios.

Color Plate 6 provides ample evidence. No matter how hard you worked at it, you could never assemble these subjects in a photo shoot. If you had talent streaming like fire-hydrant jets out your ears, you might be able to paint the image, but most of us would have thrown in the towel before we even began.

But we live in a sparkling modern age, filled with more dazzling masterworks of automation than we know what to do with. Thanks to one such masterwork — we speak here of Elements, naturally — it's possible to throw together Color Plate 6 in a couple of hours. Altogether, the composition comprises eight separate layers; however, it required not so much as a single stroke of a painting or editing tool. The images were simply selected, combined, blended together, and finally a few stray pixels were erased that weren't doing the final study in surrealism a lick of good.

Because it may be difficult to distinguish every one of the eight images, Color Plate 7 shows each one individually. The arrows indicate the order in which the images are stacked on top of each other. For example, the grinning gremlin in the lower-right corner of Color Plate 7 lies at the bottom of the composition in Color Plate 6; the butterfly in the upper-left corner of the Color Plate 7 rests at the top of Color Plate 6. The image appears as if you cut out and pasted a picture of the gremlin onto a page, pasted the boat on the gremlin, pasted the tops of the two guys' heads in front of the boat, and so on.

This is the point at which you ask, "Yeah, yeah, yeah, but how in the world do I begin to pull off something like this?" Well, wouldn't you know it — that's what this chapter is all about. And, remarkably, it's all a lot easier than you may think.

Pasting Images Together

Let's use another couple of fishy images as an example. Suppose that you want to paste the fish image on the left of Figure 9-1 into the neighboring kelp image. How do you go about it? Here's one approach:

1. **Open the fish image and select the fish. (To learn about selections, refer to Chapter 8.)**

2. **Choose Edit⇨Copy or press Ctrl+C (⌘+C on a Mac).**

   Copying places a copy of your selection onto the clipboard. The *clipboard* is a temporary storage area for image data. The fish displaces any previous occupant of the clipboard (sent there via Edit⇨Copy or its close cousin, Edit⇨Cut).

3. **Open the kelp image.**

4. **Choose Edit⇨Paste or press Ctrl+V (⌘+V on the Mac).**

   Pasting dumps the current contents of the clipboard into your image. The original fish image remains intact because the fish you pasted into the kelp was merely a copy.

Figure 9-1: A fish (left) and some kelp (right), ready to rendezvous the Layers palette.

But these steps aren't the only way to combine images. You also have these options at your disposal:

✔ To cut a selection from one image and paste it into another, choose Edit⇨Cut or press Ctrl+X (⌘+X on the Mac). Then switch to the other image and choose Edit⇨Paste. The selection is removed entirely from the first image and planted in the second.

✔ You can clone a selection between images by dragging it with the Move tool or Ctrl+dragging (⌘+dragging on a Mac) it with any tool except the Hand or the Shape tools.

This method of cloning between images is known in the computer world as *dragging and dropping,* by the way.

✔ The Copy command copies the contents of the selection from the currently selected layer only. To copy from all layers in the image, select Edit⇨Copy Merged.

✔ To transfer an entire image to another image window, choose Select⇨All or Ctrl+A (⌘+A on a Mac) before dragging or using the Cut or Copy commands.

✔ For a weird but occasionally useful trick, use Edit⇨Paste Into to paste an image inside an existing selection, as described in the upcoming section "Filling a selection with a selection."

Whether you use the Paste command or drag and drop a selection from one image to another, Elements places the pasted image on a new layer. For more on working with layers, turn to the section "Excuse Me, but What's a Layer?"

Filling a selection with a selection

The Edit⇨Paste Into command lets you insert an image into an existing selection outline. For example, suppose you wanted to paste the fish behind some of the vegetation in the neighboring kelp image so that the fish would appear to be intertwined with its environment. As shown in the first example of Figure 9-2, select an area inside the kelp stalks and feather the selection by choosing Select⇨Feather. Then choose Paste Into or Ctrl+Shift+V (⌘+Shift+V on a Mac) to create the fish-inside-the-kelp shown in the second example. (Note that the selection has been deselected in the second example so that you can better see the transitions between fish and stalks.) Elements pastes the selection into the currently selected layer.

You can also paste into the unselected area of an image by pressing the Alt key (Option key on a Mac) as you choose Edit⇨Paste Into. If this had been done with the image in Figure 9-2, for example, the fish would show only where there's unselected kelp.

Figure 9-2:
After
selecting
an area of
kelp (left),
use the
Paste Into
command to
introduce
the fish to
his new
kelpy home
(right).

Resizing an image to match its new home

When you bring two images together, you always have to deal with the issue of relative size. Say, for example, the fish image is much larger than the kelp image. Here's how to ensure that the two images you want to combine are sized correctly:

1. **Magnify the two images to exactly the same zoom factor.**

   To see them side by side, a zoom ratio of 50% or smaller may be necessary.

2. **If either of the two images appears disproportionately large, scale it down (bad pun, we know) by using Image⇨Resize⇨Image Size.**

   In this case, you don't care at all about the document size or resolution of the image; all you care about is the pixel dimensions — that is, the number of pixels comprising the image. If the image you want to copy or drag (fish) is too large, scale it down just enough to fit inside the destination image. If the destination image (kelp) is too large, reduce it as desired. Don't forget about Ctrl+Z (⌘+Z on a Mac) in case you accidentally go too far. (See Chapter 4 for more information about the Image Size command.)

Color Plate 1: The red, green, and blue color channels lurking behind the scenes in Photoshop Elements act like slides in separate projectors pointed at the same spot on a screen. You may find it hard to believe that three primary hues could mix together to produce a full range of colors, but it's true.

Background texture: Sandpaper Effect

Color Plate 2: Pure white light from the sun (or a man-made light source) is made up of red, green, and blue light. When light passes through the cyan, magenta, or yellow printing ink, the ink filters out the red, green, or blue light and lets the other two pass through.

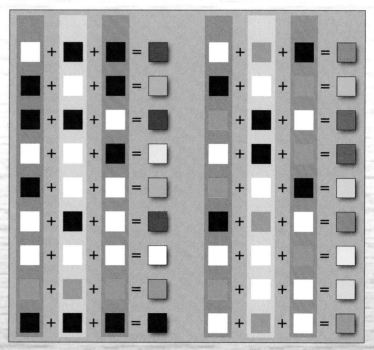

Color Plate 3: This figure shows the way light, dark, and medium pixels in the red, green, and blue channels mix to form various sample colors. Altogether, you can create more than 16 million color variations.

Background texture: Brushed Metal Layer Style

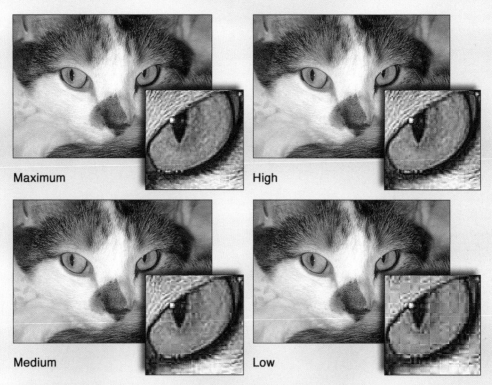

Maximum

High

Medium

Low

Color Plate 4: The Save for Web dialog box gives you four default compression-quality settings for JPEG files. Even the Low setting can provide decent results, but the magnified and sharpened inset eyes show that the image data has definitely been compromised.

Color Plate 5: Cute subject; terrible background. The Selection Brush gives you two modes for making selections: Selection mode (left) surrounds the selected area with a moving dotted line, whereas Mask mode (right) uses a translucent red overlay, letting you actually see the feathered edge of the selection.

Background texture: Tie-Dyed Silk Layer Style

Color Plate 6: This homage to an anchovy pizza bedtime snack was constructed from a multitude of different layers, organized and manipulated using the Layers palette. The Soft Light blending mode gives the heads peering over the edge of the boat their ghostly appearance.

Background texture: Angled Spectrum Layer Style

Color Plate 7: The eight layers that comprise "Dyspepsia." The grinning gremlin at lower right had Image ➪ Adjustments ➪ Invert applied. The "DYSPEPSIA" text layer at top right was first simplified before the metallic border was added to it.

Color Plate 8: The ancient photo at left not only had nicks and tears but also corners that had been cut to fit a round frame. A workout with the Clone Stamp tool created the image at right; the insets show how the Clone Stamp was able to delicately remove the gash across the subjects' faces.

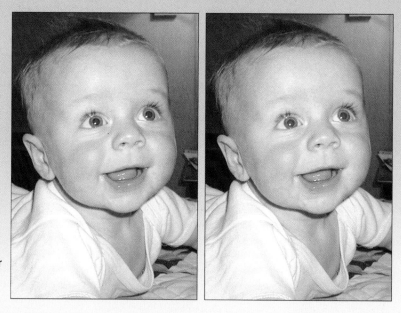

Color Plate 9: The Red Eye Brush tool was used to quickly remove that familiar eerie red glow (left) from the eyes of an innocent youth (right).

Background texture: Sunset Effect

Color Plate 10: The photo on the left of the figure offers a rather pallid view of the world beyond. The Sponge tool in Saturate mode was used to give the landscape a vibrant, painterly appearance (right); we enhanced the contrast by switching to Desaturate mode and draining the color from the inside walls.

Color Plate 11: Although the spider web on the left doesn't look particularly blurry, the Unsharp Mask filter is still able to bring it into much sharper focus (right). The Unsharp Mask settings used here are Amount: 100 percent; Radius: 2.0 pixels; and Threshold: 0 levels.

Background texture: Batik Layer Style

Original   Auto Levels   Auto Contrast

Auto Color Correction   Fill Flash (Lighten: 12)   Levels

Color Plate 12: The original scanned slide seen at the upper left is very dark and suffers from a severe violet color cast. Auto Levels and Auto Color Correction corrected the image fairly well but seemed to introduce a bluish cast of their own. Auto Contrast simply brightened the discolored image, and Fill Flash created a dull, washed-out variation on the original. Although using the Levels command is definitely a lot more work, by applying it to each color channel individually, we were able to both correct the brightness and eliminate any hint of a color cast.

Background texture: Rusted Metal Effect

Color Plate 13: Photoshop Elements' Fill Flash command can take an image in desperate need of a little artificial illumination (left) and bring out details hiding in the shadows (right).

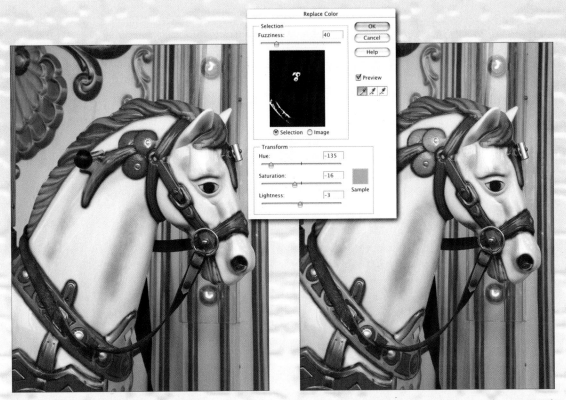

Color Plate 14: The Replace Color command was used to select the pink decorations on the carousel horse (left) and convert them to a brilliant blue (right).

Background texture: Ancient Stone Layer Style

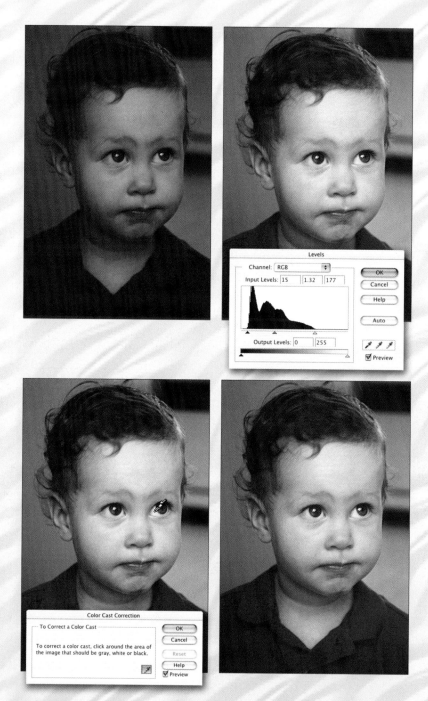

Color Plate 15: Starting with a dark, violet-tinged scan of a slide (upper left), we used the Levels command on the RGB composite to lighten the image (upper right). And although Elements' Color Cast command is far from a sure thing, clicking it here on the white of the young tyke's eye (lower left) did a highly respectable job of correcting the colors in the image (lower right).

Background texture: Waves Layer Style

Lighten

Darken

Increase Red

Decrease Red

Less Saturation

More Saturation

Increase Green

Decrease Green

Increase Blue

Decrease Blue

Color Plate 16: The Color Variations command is another effective way to fix an image. Shown here are the results of various changes to the original image's midtones, using the default intensity.

Background texture: Satin Sheets Layer Style

Original

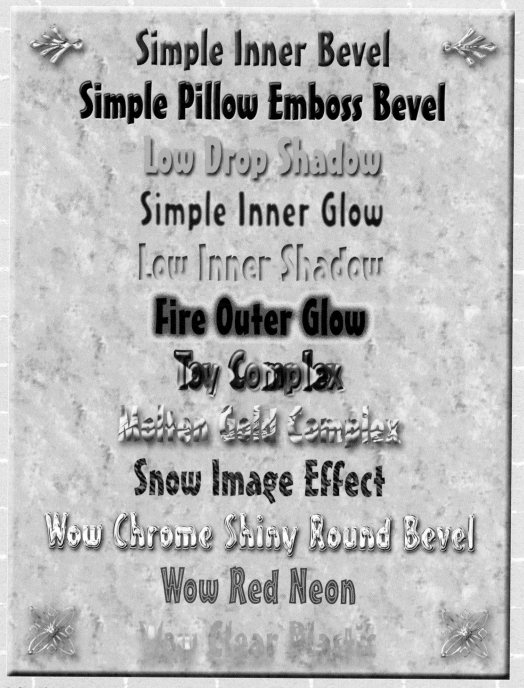

Color Plate 17: Layer styles can work wonders on ordinary text with a single click. The texture behind the text is the Yellow and Orange Complex layer style; the ornaments in the corners were drawn with the Custom Shape tool and given the Wow-Blue/Gray Swirl Chrome layer style.

Background texture: Bricks Effect

Original

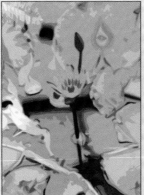
Artistic—Cutout

Artistic—Poster Edges

Artistic—Sponge

Artistic—Watercolor

Brush Strokes—
Accented Edges

Brush Strokes—
Crosshatch

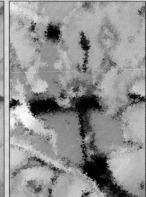
Brush Strokes—Spatter

Sketch—Bas Relief

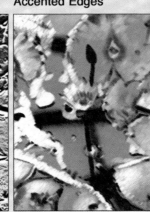
Sketch—
Chalk & Charcoal

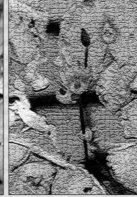
Texture—Craquelure

Texture—Patchwork

Color Plate 18: The filters found in the Artistic, Brush Strokes, Sketch, and Texture categories of the Filters palette can add interesting, "handmade" touches to your photographic images.

Background texture: Denim Layer Style

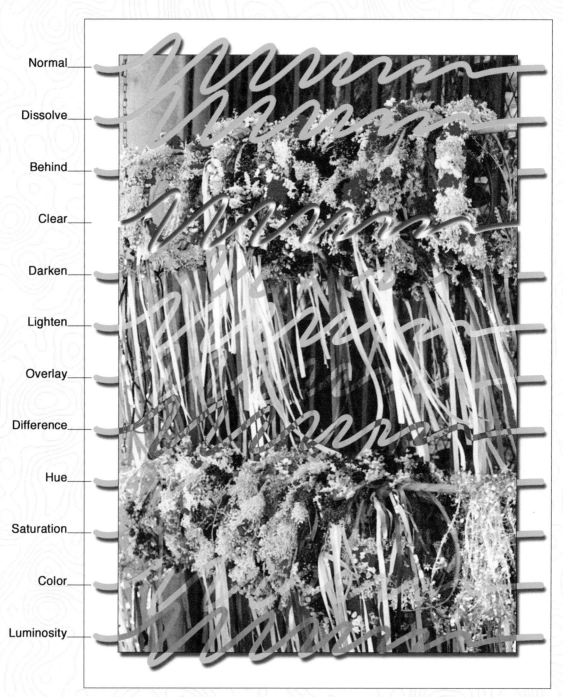

Normal

Dissolve

Behind

Clear

Darken

Lighten

Overlay

Difference

Hue

Saturation

Color

Luminosity

Color Plate 19: The Brush tool's different painting modes can mix the foreground color with the image's colors in interesting and dynamic ways. This plate shows a dozen representative painting modes applied to an image of beribboned wreaths. A Drop Shadow layer style has been added to the wreath image to give a dimensional effect; note that the Clear painting mode basically acts as an eraser, completely wiping out the image and revealing the white layer underneath.

Background texture: Psychedelic Strings Effect

Color Plate 20: In this plate, various style settings for the Impressionist Brush were used to give a hand-painted effect to the original image (inset).

Color Plate 21: The area behind the jar was filled with custom gradients created by using the Gradient Editor.

Background texture: Wood — Rosewood Effect

Color Plate 22: Photoshop Elements' Create Web Photo Gallery command can instantly assemble a Web page out of a folder of your images. Shown here is the Spot Light style, one of 14 presets available.

Background texture: Green Slime Effect

Be careful not to overreduce! Remember that you're throwing away pixels and, therefore, sacrificing detail. Err on the side of keeping the image still a little bit too big. If you go too far, you can always restore the original by choosing File➪Revert, or undoing your steps using the Undo History palette, as discussed in Chapter 7.

3. **Combine the two images.**

   Copy and paste or drag and drop — it's your call.

4. **Position the image more or less where you want it.**

5. **Choose Image➪Resize➪Scale.**

   This command lets you fine-tune the relative size of the imported image with respect to its new home. A marquee with four corner handles surrounds the image. (More on this command at the end of the chapter, in the section "Using the Transform tool.")

6. **Drag a corner handle to scale the image.**

   Shift+drag a handle to scale the image proportionally, as the first example in Figure 9-3 illustrates. After you release the handle, Elements previews how the resized image will look. Don't worry if the preview is a little choppy; the scaled image will be smooth.

   For best results, don't scale the image up; only scale it down. Otherwise, Elements has to make up pixels, which is most assuredly not one of the program's better capabilities.

7. **Move your cursor inside the transform box and double-click.**

   After you resize the image as desired — you can drag the corner handles all you want — move your cursor inside the box. Double-click or press Enter (Return on a Mac) to accept the image's new size and tell Elements to work its magic. You can also click the Commit button (the check mark icon) at the end of the Options bar. The resized image will appear perfectly smooth.

If you decide that you don't want to scale the image before you double-click or press Enter (Return on Mac), press Esc or Ctrl+period (⌘+period on a Mac) to get rid of the box. You can also click the Cancel button (the circle-with-a-slash "no" icon) in the Options bar. If you've already double-clicked or pressed Enter (Return on Mac), you can restore the image to its original size by pressing Ctrl+Z (⌘+Z on a Mac).

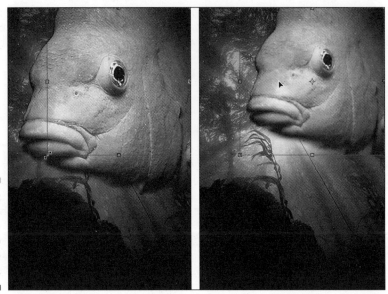

Figure 9-3:
Use the
Scale
command to
refine the
image size.

Excuse Me, but What's a Layer?

Here's a little analogy to get things rolling. Imagine that you have three sheets of acetate — you know, what folks used to slide into overhead projectors to bore audiences before they started using multimedia presentations to bore them. Anyway, on one sheet you draw a picture of a fish. On a second sheet, you draw a fishbowl. And on a third sheet, you draw the table on which the fishbowl sits. When you stack all the sheets on top of each other, the images blend together to create a seamless view of a fish in his happy home. (This is the way cel animation works, if that means anything to you.)

Layers in Elements work just like that. You can keep different parts of your image on separate layers and then combine the layers to create a composite image. You can rearrange layers, add and delete layers, blend them together using different opacity values and blend modes, and do all sorts of other impressive things. And as we mentioned earlier, when you drag and drop between images or use the Paste command, you're creating a new layer.

Another advantage of using layers is that you can edit or paint on one layer without affecting the other layers. That means you can safely apply commands or painting tools to one portion of your image without worrying about messing up the rest of the image — or without bothering to first select the part you want to edit.

You aren't restricted to the layers that Elements creates automatically, however. You can create as many new layers as your computer's memory allows, up to a theoretical 8,000. In the case of the image shown in Color Plate 6, the gremlin head, boat, two guys, rooster, fish, cat, text with border, and butterfly were kept on separate layers. Though they may appear to blend together along the edges, they are, in fact, as distinct as peas in a pod.

Finding your way around the Layers palette

The Layers palette, shown in Figure 9-4, is Grand Central Station for managing layers. Here's what you need to know to navigate the Layers palette:

- The Background is the bottom layer in the image. Every image has a Background (unless the Background has been deleted or turned into a regular layer — read on to see how).

- The order of the layers in the Layers palette represents their order in the image. The top layer in the palette is the top layer in your image, and so on.

- You can edit only one layer at a time — the *active layer*. The active layer is the one that's highlighted in the Layers palette and that has a little Brush icon to the left of its layer name. To make another layer active, just click its name.

- Press Alt+] (right bracket) — Option+] on a Mac — to move up one layer; press Alt+[(left bracket) — Option+[on a Mac — to activate the next layer down. Press Shift+Alt+] (Shift+Option+] on a Mac) to move to the top layer; press Shift+Alt+[(Shift+Option+[on a Mac) to move to the Background or bottom layer.

- An eyeball icon next to a layer name means that the layer is visible. To hide the layer, click the eyeball. To display the layer, click where the eyeball was to bring it back.

- To hide all layers but one, Alt+click (Option+click on a Mac) on the eyeball in front of the name of the layer you want to see. Alt+click (Option+click on a Mac) again to redisplay all the layers.

- If you hide the Background layer, you see a checkerboard pattern anywhere the Background showed through. The checkerboard represents the transparent areas of the visible layers.

- This gray and white checkerboard can be customized in the Transparency section of the Preferences; you can specify the size and color of the squares Elements uses to represent transparency.

- To find out how to use the blending mode pop-up menu and the Opacity setting at the top of the palette, refer to Chapter 13.

- To create a new, blank layer, click the Create New Layer icon at the bottom of the palette (refer to Figure 9-4). To create a duplicate of an existing layer, drag the layer to the Create New Layer icon.

When you create a layer in the manner mentioned in the preceding paragraph, Elements gives the layer a generic name like Layer 1 or Layer 1 copy, and so on. If you want to name the layer, double-click the layer name in the Layers palette and type a new name into the highlighted field. You can also select the layer and choose Rename Layer from the Layer menu or from the Layers palette's More menu.

✔ Alternatively, you can create layers by choosing the New Layer or Duplicate Layer command from the More menu, or by choosing Layer⇨ New ⇨Layer or Layer⇨Duplicate Layer. If you use this method to create a layer, Elements prompts you to give the layer a name.

✔ To delete a layer, select it and click the Trash icon, or just drag the layer to the Trash icon. Be aware that you're throwing away the layer along with the image on it. Layers can also be deleted via Layer⇨Delete Layer or by choosing Delete Layer from the More menu.

✔ If you ever want to create a selection outline around the objects on a layer, Elements gives you an easy way to do it. Just Ctrl+click (⌘+click on a Mac) on the layer in the Layers palette. For more on selections, see Chapter 8.

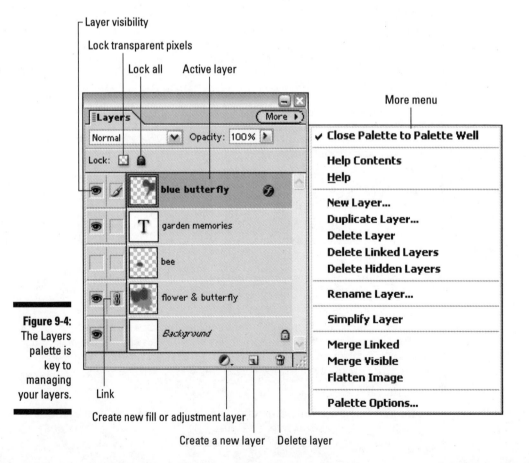

Figure 9-4: The Layers palette is key to managing your layers.

Moving and manipulating layers

Layers are flexible things — you can move them, shuffle their order, and rearrange them as though they were a deck of playing cards. Here's a look at some of the more common layer manipulation moves you may need to make:

✔ To move a layer, drag it with the Move tool. To move the layer in 1-pixel increments, select the Move tool and tap an arrow key. To move the layer in 10-pixel increments, press Shift as you tap the arrow key. Holding down the Ctrl key (the ⌘ key on the Mac) temporarily gives you the Move tool when almost any other tool is selected. So, you can Ctrl+drag (⌘+drag on a Mac) to move a layer, press Ctrl (⌘ on a Mac) plus an arrow key to move a layer in 1-pixel increments, and add the Shift key for 10-pixel increments. Note, however, that this Ctrl/⌘ trick doesn't work when the Hand tool or any of the Shape tools is selected.

✔ Check the Auto Select Layer in the Options bar to switch to a layer when you click with the Move tool on any nontransparent part of that layer.

The Auto Select Layer option has a drawback, in that it makes it very easy to switch layers when you don't want to.

✔ The Show Bounding Box option, which also appears in the Options bar when the Move tool is active and is switched on by default, surrounds the contents of the layer (or the selection) with a box with handles. This box lets you transform a layer without choosing a command. (For more on transformations, see "Transforming Layers and Selections" in this chapter.)

✔ To link an active layer to another layer, click the second column of the Layers palette — just to the right of the Eyeball icon — next to the layer that's not active. A Link icon appears in the column. Now you can move, scale, and rotate both layers simultaneously. To remove the link, click the Link icon.

✔ To delete linked layers in one fell swoop, select one of the layers in the group, and Ctrl+click (⌘+click on a Mac) the Trash icon in the Layers palette.

✔ If you right-click (Control+click on the Mac) an object in the image with the Move tool selected, Elements presents you with a little pop-up menu, which lists every layer that contains pixels at the precise point where you clicked. From the menu, you can select the layer you want to make active. You can also activate the Auto Select Layer option on the fly if you want. With the Move tool selected, Alt+right-click (Control+Option+click on the Mac); Elements automatically activates the appropriate layer. Again, throw the Control key (the ⌘ key on the Mac) into the mix when you have a tool other than the Move tool selected (excepting the Hand and Shape tools).

✔ After you have a few layers in your image, you can move one in front of or behind another by dragging it up or down in the list of layers in the Layers palette. A black line shows where the layer will be inserted. You can't reorder the Background or move any layer below the Background until you convert it to a layer. To convert, choose Layer➪New➪Layer from Background. Or just double-click the Background in the Layers palette, enter a name for the layer, and press Enter (Return on a Mac). Or you can leave the default name of Layer 0 and press Enter (Return on a Mac).

✔ When there's no Background layer and you want to convert an active layer into the Background layer, choose Layer➪New➪Background From Layer. Elements will make the conversion, moving the selected layer to the bottom of the stack if it wasn't already there.

✔ Another way to rearrange layers is to use the commands in the Layer➪Arrange submenu. Click the layer that you want to move in the Layers palette. Then:

1. Choose Layer➪Arrange➪Bring to Front (Shift+Ctrl+]/Shift+⌘+]) to make the layer the topmost layer.

2. Select Bring Forward (Ctrl+]/⌘+]) to move the layer up one level.

3. Select Send Backward (Ctrl+[/⌘+[) to move the layer down one level.

4. Select Send to Back (Shift+Ctrl+[/Shift+⌘+[) to move the layer to just above the Background layer.

✔ You can copy an entire layer to a new image by selecting the layer in the Layers palette and dragging and dropping the layer to the new image. The layer drops at the spot where you release the mouse button and resides one layer above the formerly active layer in the new image.

Flattening and merging layers

Sadly, layers aren't all fun and games. To put it bluntly, they come at a price and require some concerted management skills. First, if an image contains layers, saving it in any format other than Elements' native Photoshop format, PDF, or TIFF merges all the layers into one (refer to Chapter 6 for more about saving). The Photoshop, TIFF, and PDF formats are the only formats that preserve layers. Second, every layer you add also makes your file size grow. And third, layers can slow down Elements. If your computer is perhaps getting a little long in the tooth and you want to keep it running at peak efficiency, it's best to juggle as few layers at a time as possible.

If you want to save your image for use in a different program that cannot utilize Photoshop, PDF, or TIFF formats, but you think you may need to revisit the layered version of the image at some point in the future, you can save the composition to a different file and flatten it — that is, smush all the layers together. To do this, choose File➪Save As. The Save As dialog box appears on-screen. Select your desired file format from the Format pop-up menu. If you select a format other than Photoshop, Photoshop PDF, or TIFF, the Layers option is grayed out, meaning that Elements will automatically flatten the image for you upon saving.

Name the image and press Enter (Return on a Mac). Elements saves the flattened image to a different file.

But useful as that is, you're still going to want to merge layers every so often to keep your image manageable. When things get really out of control, operations can slow to a snail's pace, and that's an insult to the snail. Here are your merging options:

- ✔ To merge several layers into one, hide all layers except the ones you want to merge. In other words, in the Layers palette an eyeball icon should appear next to the names of each layer you want to merge. Hide the eyeball if you don't want to merge the layer. Then choose Merge Visible from the More menu or from the Layer menu at the top of the screen. Or, even simpler, press Shift+Ctrl+E (Shift+⌘+E on a Mac).

  You can merge one layer with other layers to which it has been linked. Choose Merge Linked from the More menu or from the Layer menu. Easier yet, press Ctrl+E (⌘+E on a Mac). Note that the Merge Linked command changes to the Merge Down command if you have no linked layers selected. Merge Down will merge your selected layer with the layer residing below it.

- ✔ If you want to flatten the entire image and get rid of all the layers, choose the Flatten Image command from the More menu or from the Layer menu.

Locking Layers

The last chapter talked about creating selections to limit the active working area — for instance, you can paint inside a selection outline to make sure you leave the surrounding areas untouched. But when you send a selection to a layer, the selection outline disappears. So how do you paint only inside the image on a layer? For example, maybe you want to paint stripes on an object on a layer without going outside the lines.

The solution is to click the Lock Transparent Pixels button near the top of the Layers palette, as shown in Figure 9-4. The transparent areas around the object stay transparent, letting you paint only inside the opaque and translucent pixels. For a quick way to turn the Lock Transparent Pixels check box on and off, press the forward slash key (/).

Clicking the lock icon activates the Lock All option. This prevents you from painting, editing, moving, or transforming your layer. (But you can still make selections.)

Moving and Cloning Selections

Chapter 8 looks at moving a selection outline without moving the contents of the selection. Now that we have a working knowledge of layers, let's look at ways of moving selections along with the pixels they contain:

✔ To move a selection, grab the Move tool (press V to select the tool from the keyboard) and drag. A bounding box appears around the selection to show that you're about to move it from its current home. When you move a selection on the Background layer, the area where the selection used to be is filled with the Background color, as illustrated in Figure 9-5.

✔ You can temporarily access the Move tool by pressing Ctrl (⌘ on a Mac) when any tool but the Hand or one of the Shape tools is selected.

✔ Moving a selection with the keyboard is just like moving the entire contents of a layer, as described earlier. To nudge a selection 1 pixel, press one of the arrow keys while the Move tool is selected. Or press Ctrl (⌘ on a Mac) and an arrow key when any tool other than the Hand or Shape tools is selected. The up arrow nudges the selection 1 pixel up; the right arrow nudges it to the right, and so on, just as you'd think. To nudge a selection 10 pixels, press Shift along with an arrow key while the Move tool is selected.

✔ To clone and move a selection, Alt+drag (Option+drag on a Mac) with the Move tool or Ctrl+Alt+drag (⌘+Option+drag on a Mac) with any tool other than the Hand or Shape tools.

✔ To clone and nudge, select the Move tool and then press Alt (Option on a Mac) and one of the arrow keys. Or, when any tool other than the Hand or Shape tools is selected, press Ctrl+Alt (⌘+Option on a Mac) as you press the arrow keys. Add Shift to clone the selection and move it 10 pixels.

✔ You can move and clone selections between two different images as well. Just drag the selection from its current window into the other image window.

Figure 9-5:
After selecting the Washington Monument (top), it's dragged to a more convenient location (bottom).

Transforming Layers and Selections

The end of Chapter 4 looks at commands that can flip and rotate the entire canvas. Now let's take a look at the related subject of *transforming*. In Elements' parlance, transforming means spinning, stretching, and generally distorting. Technically, even moving is transforming. You can transform a layer or selection when there's a bounding box around it, such as the bounding box that appears by default when you select the Move tool. You can drag from the square handles of the bounding box to transform the layer or selection.

Using the Image menu's commands

The Image menu has three submenus that contain transforming commands: Rotate, Transform, and Resize. The Rotate submenu has the Free Rotate Layer/Free Rotate Selection command (along with other commands that mirror the ones covered in Chapter 4). The Transform submenu has four different transforming commands, and the bottom of the Resize submenu has the Scale command.

These commands work with or without selections. If there is no selection, the commands work on the entire layer. If there is an active selection, the commands affect only the selected area. The only exception to this is the Background layer, which must have an active selection in order to be transformed. If you try to transform the entire Background layer, you'll get a message asking you whether you first want to change the Background into a full-fledged, first-class layer.

Using the Transform tool

There's a secret tool hiding inside Elements that is nowhere to be found in the Toolbox: the Transform tool. Just choose one of the transforming commands or drag a handle of the Move tool's bounding box, and you'll see the Transform tool's mysterious icon appear on the far left of the Options bar (see Figure 9-6), exactly where you'd see, say, the Zoom tool's icon if you had the Zoom tool selected. This implementation in Elements is somewhat confusing; you can manipulate your transformation using the Options bar, or you can freely choose from among the six transforming commands under the Image menu. The latter option is by far the easiest, so let's take a closer look at the commands:

Figure 9-6:
The Options
bar for the
stealthy
Transform
tool.

✔ **Free Rotate Layer/Free Rotate Selection:** This is a scaled-back version of the Free Transform tool, which only allows you to rotate and move the selection. Move the cursor toward the edges or outside of the selection to rotate; move the cursor toward the center to move the selection.

✔ **Free Transform:** This option allows you to scale, move, and rotate the selection. Free Transform can be invoked from the keyboard by pressing Ctrl+T (⌘+T on the Mac).

✔ **Skew:** Skew permits distortion on a given axis.

✔ **Distort:** Distort enables handles to move independently with no axis restrictions.

✔ **Perspective:** When you drag a corner handle, the opposite corner handle on the same side moves as well.

✔ **Scale:** Drag any handle to scale your selection. Press Shift+drag to maintain proportions. Press Alt+drag (Option+drag on a Mac) to scale from the center point outward. (This behavior is similar to that of the Crop tool, as covered in Chapter 4.)

The most useful control found in the Options bar is the "Reference point location" option (the first option on the left). This sets the point around which the transformation happens and is especially useful when rotating the selection.

Ending your transformation

After you finish transforming, press Enter (Return on a Mac), double-click inside the transform box or click the Commit button (the check icon) in the Options bar. To cancel, press Esc or Ctrl+period (⌘+period on a Mac), or click the Cancel button (the "no" icon).

You have many more options available in the Layers palette — blend modes, text layers, adjustment layers, shape layers, fill layers — but we thought it was important to give you a basic introduction to the Layers palette relatively early on in the book. Don't worry: We'll peel away the many layers of the Layers palette as we proceed.

Part III
Realer Than Life

The 5th Wave   By Rich Tennant

"I'VE GOT SOME IMAGE EDITING SOFTWARE, SO I TOOK THE LIBERTY OF ERASING SOME OF THE SMUDGES THAT KEPT SHOWING UP AROUND THE CLOUDS. NO NEED TO THANK ME."

In this part . . .

Photographs are supposed to be little records of a moment in time, right? Sure, it can be a drag to stop whatever fun you're having and smile for the camera. But in the back of your mind you know it's going to be worth it down the road. You can just imagine yourself in the twilight of your years, reflecting on those halcyon days of yore (whatever that means). Was the sky really that blue? Was your face really that wrinkle-free? Was life ever really that brilliantly in focus?

If now, in the prime of your youth (did we lose anyone there?), you give your photos a working over with Photoshop Elements, the answers to those questions will be no, no, and no. You see, Elements has a phalanx of tools designed to make your images look better than they ever did in real life. And we're not just talking about cleaning the dust off a scanned photo or eliminating a case of flash-induced red eye — although Elements can certainly do those things. Elements can dig deep within the shadows and find hidden details, take a gray sky and make it blue, and soften up those wrinkles with no surgery required.

The three chapters in this part tell you how to use Elements to make your images look better — "realer" than life, if you will. Although doing this to your photos now might give you a glorified sense of the past in your later years, there will be an easy remedy. Just take your 54 megapixel digital camera, snap a photo, import it into your 5 googolhertz computer, give it a workout using Photoshop Elements Version 36.0, and compare with your old photos. With all the advancements in technology, you'll be able to make the new reality look much better than the old reality ever could.

Chapter 10

Dusting Off Images (Without the Lemony Scent)

In This Chapter

▶ Applying filters

▶ Using the Dust & Scratches filter

▶ Cleaning up an image with the Clone Stamp tool

▶ Using the Red Eye Brush tool

*I*f you've ever scanned an image, you know the story. You start with a lovely photograph that you've cherished all your life, gingerly place it in your scanner, and the scan ends up looking as though someone stuck it inside a dryer lint trap. Big, gnarly hairs wiggle across the image. Little dust flecks seem to have reproduced like rabbits. And if you really hit the jackpot, you may even spy a few fingerprints on your image. It's enough to make you clean the house, shave the cats, and have your fingerprints sanded off.

Ultimately, that won't get you anywhere. But the dust-busting tools discussed in this chapter can. With a keen eye and a little bit of elbow grease, you can scrub away those imperfections and make your image appear absolutely spotless.

Photoshop Elements offers two methods for dusting away the specks:

✔ The Dust & Scratches filter automates the removal of image imperfections, but it can do more harm than good by getting rid of important detail as well.

✔ The Clone Stamp tool lets you copy portions of an image to cover up blotches. This tool takes more time to use than the Dust & Scratches command and requires a considerable amount of clicking and dragging, but it also results in a better-looking picture.

And as soon as we've gotten the dust out of our eyes, we'll also take a clear gaze at the Red Eye Brush tool, Elements' dedicated tool for exorcising that flash-induced demonic glowing look from the subjects in your images.

Introducing Filters

Before we look at the Dust & Scratches filter, we'd better back up and address the topic of filters in general. If you're a photographer or if you've at least taken a photography course or two, you know how photographic filters work. They refine or refract light to modify the image as it comes into the camera. A daylight filter strains some of the blue out of the image; a polarization lens eliminates reflected light; a fish-eye lens refracts peripheral imagery into the photo.

But real-life filters present some problems. They take up a ton of room in your camera bag, they generally bang around and get scratched, and you never know when you're going to contract a sudden case of butterfingers and drop a lens onto a marble floor. Also, you have to decide which filter you want to use while shooting the photo. Not only is it difficult to experiment through a viewfinder, but also whatever decision you ultimately make is permanent. If you go with a fish-eye lens, you can't go back and "undistort" the image later.

The Photoshop Elements filters are another story:

- ✔ All filters reside in a single palette (surprisingly called the Filters palette).
- ✔ You can undo a filter if you don't like the results.
- ✔ You can preview the outcome of almost every filter.
- ✔ You can apply several filters in a row and even go back and revisit a single filter multiple times.
- ✔ Most Elements filters have no real-world counterparts, which means that you can modify images in ways that aren't possible inside a camera.

If you're a professional photographer, you may want to forgo a few of your camera's filters and take up Elements' filters instead. Granted, you may still want to use corrective lenses to adjust color and keep out reflected light, but avoid a special-effects filter that makes the image look like more than what your eyes can see. Such filters merely limit the range of effects you can apply later inside Elements.

And if you aren't a photographer, filters open up a whole new range of opportunities that no other Elements function quite matches. Filters can make changes automatically, so there's no need to be an artist (although an artistic vision certainly comes in handy). Filters can make poor images look better and good images look fantastic. And you can use them to introduce special effects, such as camera movement and relief textures. Frankly, filters turn Elements into a lean, mean, photo-munching machine.

Applying filters

You have two basic ways to apply Elements filters: the Filter menu and the Filters palette. In the Filter menu, all filters are grouped into submenus; in the Filters palette, filters are grouped into categories. Most filters, when applied using the Filter menu, present a dialog box that lets you tweak various aspects of the filter.

In the Filters palette, you can switch between categories by using the drop-down menu at the top of the palette, or just set the menu to All if you like having your filters organized strictly by alphabetization. Each filter has a thumbnail showing the effects of the filter applied to a sample image. To apply a filter from the Filters palette, click the filter and then click the Apply button at the top of the palette, double-click the filter in the palette, or just drag the filter from the Filters palette into the image window. Heck, you can even choose the Apply command from the Filters palette's More menu if you want. The filter will be applied to the active layer or selection.

If the Filter Options check box is checked at the top of the palette, you'll then be presented with the filter's dialog box (when applicable). If Filter Options is unchecked, Elements will (in almost every case) bypass the dialog box and just apply the default values for that filter. It's strongly recommended that you keep the Filter Options check box checked at all times in order to have the most control over your filters.

A few fast filter facts

Here are some important things to know about using filters:

- The Filters palette has two different viewing modes: List view and Thumbnail view. You'll probably find List view to be more helpful in the long run. One of the List view's best features is that it lets you view the thumbnail of your selected filter right beneath the Original view of the thumbnail image, making it easier to compare the before and after states of the thumbnail.

- If you select some portion of your image, the filter affects the selection and leaves the rest of the image unmodified. If you don't select a portion of the image, the filter affects the entire layer.

- To create smooth transitions between filtered and unfiltered areas in an image, blur the selection outline by choosing Select➪Feather (see Chapter 8).

- After you apply a filter, you can reapply it with the same settings by choosing the first command in the Filter menu or by pressing Ctrl+F (⌘+F on a Mac).

✔ Most filters display a dialog box so that you can control how the filter is applied. If the last filter was one of these, press Ctrl+Alt+F (⌘+Option+F on a Mac) to redisplay the dialog box and apply the filter again using different settings.

✔ To undo the last filter, press Ctrl+Z (⌘+Z on a Mac) or click the Step Backward button in the Shortcuts bar. Unlike a canceled filter, an "undone" filter remains at the top of the Filter menu, so you can later apply it by pressing Ctrl+F (⌘+F on a Mac).

✔ Some filters take a few seconds or possibly even minutes to apply, depending on the size of your image and the power of your computer. You can cancel such a filter in progress by pressing Esc or clicking the Cancel button. The name of the previous filter remains at the top of the Filter menu, so you can't press Ctrl+F (⌘+F on a Mac) to reapply a canceled filter.

Using the Dust & Scratches Filter

With that whirlwind tour of filters out of the way, let's see exactly how to use the Dust & Scratches filter. Automobile aficionados know that the only way to clean a car is to tenderly rub its surface with specially treated pieces of felt dipped in no-tears baby shampoo. They would never take their cars through one of those drive-through wash joints where big floppy pieces of blue plastic flog your car and take little bits of your paint job along with them. That's the main problem with the Dust & Scratches filter — it's akin to sending your image through a car wash. But just because we may not approve of the Dust & Scratches filter, that's no reason for you not to take a crack at it. Maybe you need to clean up an image in a hurry for that last-minute space in the company newsletter, and the car wash solution is the only one you have time to try. And besides, we cover lots of important basic filtering principles as we look at Dust & Scratches, so even if it isn't the pick of the litter, it may behoove you to follow along anyway.

The lab rat for today's outing is Figure 10-1. This figure demonstrates another variety of splatter that can plague images — old photo gunk. The lines, scratches, and dots in this image weren't introduced in the scanning process; they were a part of the original photo. Shot near the beginning of this century, this picture of Halley's comet has held up amazingly well over the years. We should all hope to look half as good when we're its age.

To tidy up an image that presents similar symptoms, go to the Filters palette and scroll down to Dust & Scratches. You can also set the pop-up menu at the top of the palette to Noise, which will narrow your search down to just four filters, or even go up to the Filter menu and choose Noise⇨Dust & Scratches. Elements displays the strange and mysterious Dust & Scratches dialog box, shown in all its glory in Figure 10-2 and explained in the next two sections.

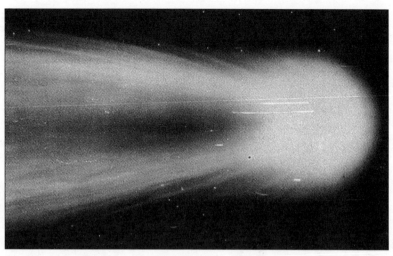

Figure 10-1:
Halley's
comet as it
appeared in
1910, replete
with old
photo gunk.

If you select a portion of your image before you choose Dust & Scratches or any filter, the command affects just the selected area.

Previewing the filter effects

The makers of the Dust & Scratches dialog box knew that at first glance it wouldn't make a lick of sense, so they thoughtfully provided some preview options (shown in Figure 10-2) to enable you to see what happens when you make some otherwise-meaningless adjustment. Here's how these preview options work:

- The preview box shows how your modifications look when applied to a portion of the image.
- If you move the cursor outside the dialog box, it changes to a hollow square. Click an area in the image to capture it inside the preview box.
- You can also scroll the contents of the preview box by dragging inside the box. Your cursor changes to a little hand.
- To magnify or reduce the contents of the preview box, click the plus or minus Zoom button.

- You can also access the standard magnifying glass cursor inside the preview box by pressing the Ctrl (⌘ on a Mac) key to zoom in or the Alt (Option on a Mac) key to zoom out.
- As long as the Preview check box is selected, Elements previews your settings in the image window as well as in the preview box.

✔ You can even use the standard Hand and Zoom cursors inside the image window while the Dust & Scratches dialog box is open. Just press the spacebar to get the hand cursor or Ctrl or Alt (⌘ or Option on a Mac) to get the Zoom cursors. This technique is a great way to preview a filter at two different zoom ratios; one inside the dialog box and one outside.

✔ If Elements seems to be slowing down too much as it tries to preview a filter in the image window, just click the Preview check box to turn off the function.

Preview cursor   Preview box

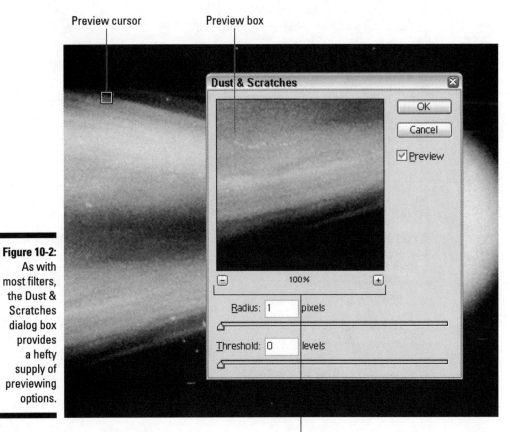

Figure 10-2:
As with most filters, the Dust & Scratches dialog box provides a hefty supply of previewing options.

Zoom buttons

Specifying the size of the speck

The Dust & Scratches dialog box offers just two options that affect the performance of the filter: the Radius and Threshold sliders. The sliders work as follows:

- ✔ Change the Radius value to indicate the size of the dust specks and the thickness of the hairs that you want to eliminate. In geometry, radius means half the width of a circle, so the Radius value is half the width of a dust speck. The minimum value is 1, meaning that the filter wipes out all specks and hairs up to 2 pixels thick.

 "Ah, ha," you may think, "If I just crank up the Radius value as far as it goes (100 pixels), that should be enough to eliminate entire warrens of dust bunnies." Well, no. The Dust & Scratches filter doesn't really know a speck from a tiny bit of detail. So, if you have it rub out 100-pixel radius dust globs, it also rubs out 100-pixel details, such as Uncle Ralph's head. Figure 10-3 shows the effects of setting the Radius value to 1 on the left and 3 on the right. Notice how fuzzy the image becomes with a 3-pixel radius? A general rule of thumb: Never set the radius value higher than 2.

- ✔ The Threshold value tells Elements how different the color of a dust speck has to be from the color of the surrounding image to be considered a bad seed.

 The default Threshold value of 0 tells Elements that dust and image need only be 0 color levels different from each other. Because all colors are at least 0 levels different, Elements ignores the Threshold value and considers only the Radius value. Both images in Figure 10-3 were filtered with a Threshold value of 0.

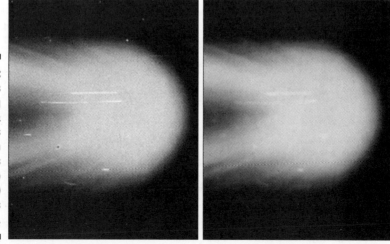

Figure 10-3:
The results of applying the Dust & Scratches filter with the Radius slider set to 1 pixel (left) and 3 pixels (right).

By raising the Threshold value, you tell Elements to be more selective. If you set the value to 10, speck and image colors must vary by at least 10 levels before Elements covers up the speck, as in the first example of Figure 10-4. If you raise the Threshold to 20 — as in the second example — Elements disregards still more potential impurities. Notice that the two horizontal streaks in the second image remain intact, having been ruled out by the Threshold setting. (By the way, the Radius value was set to 3 in Figure 10-4 — something you were warned against doing earlier — in order to make the effects of the Threshold setting more noticeable.)

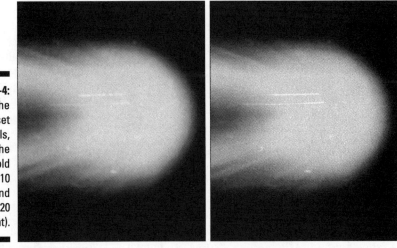

Figure 10-4: With the Radius set to 3 pixels, here's the Threshold set to 10 (left) and then to 20 (right).

Even though the Dust & Scratches filter variously obliterated the detail in Figures 10-3 and 10-4, none of the images are completely free of spots and streaks. Admittedly, this old, moldy picture is a lot worse off than most of your images are likely to be, but the fact remains that the Dust & Scratches filter is an imperfect solution. Just like a cheap car wash, it gets rid of most of the dirt — but not all of it — and it takes away some of the paint and detailing along with it. Even if you go to the trouble of selecting each tiny dust speck individually and running Dust & Scratches on it, you may as well be expending that effort with a superior tool: the Clone Stamp tool.

Experimenting with the Highly Ethical Clone Stamp Tool

If you're willing to expend a little extra energy and you can stand up to your friends when they call you compulsive, the tool of choice for cleaning up images is the Clone Stamp tool. The second tool from the bottom on the left side of the Toolbox, the Clone Stamp tool lets you take a good portion of an image and paint it onto a bad portion. This miraculous process is called, quite naturally, *cloning*.

Stamping out splatters

Want to see how the Clone Stamp tool works? Try out these steps:

1. **Select the Clone Stamp tool from the Toolbox (see Figure 10-5).**

   To select the Clone Stamp tool from the keyboard, press the S key.

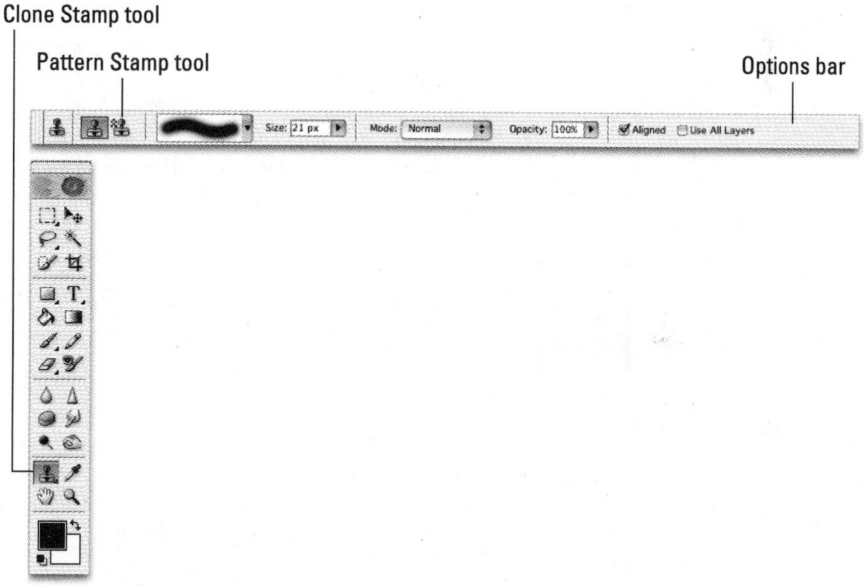

Clone Stamp tool

Pattern Stamp tool

Options bar

Figure 10-5:
The Clone
Stamp tool
and its
trusty
Options bar,
partners in
cloning.

2. **Make sure that the Aligned box is checked in the Clone Stamp tool Options bar.**

   This option lets you clone from relative points in your image. You'll see how it works in a second.

3. **Start dragging randomly inside your image.**

   Whoops, you got an error message, didn't you? As the friendly error message tells you, to use the Clone Stamp tool, you have to tell Elements which portion of your image you want to clone before you begin cloning it. Elements isn't a mind reader, you know.

TIP

Now that you've grasped this valuable lesson, grab a pen and put a big X through Step 3 so that you never make the same mistake again.

4. **Alt+click (Option+click on a Mac) on the portion of the image that you want to clone.**

   For example, to fix that big goober near the beginning of the lower tail of Halley's comet, Alt+click (Option+click on a Mac) at a location that appears to contain similar gray values to the comet stuff that surrounds the goober, as shown in Figure 10-6. The point is to pick a portion of your image that blends in with areas around the blemish you want to eliminate.

5. **Now click or drag on the offending blemish.**

   To apply the digital zit cream, just click directly on said goober. No muss, no fuss; the glitch is gone.

When you click or drag with the Clone Stamp tool, Elements displays a cross cursor along with the stamp cursor, as shown in Figure 10-7. (For clarity's sake in this figure, the painting cursors are set to Standard in the Display & Cursors section of the Preferences.) This cross represents the clone source, or the area that you're cloning from. As you move the mouse, the cross cursor also moves, providing a continual reference to the portion of your image that you're cloning. The distance between the clone source (cross) and destination (stamp cursor) is set by the first two clicks you make: the Alt+click (Option+click on a Mac) to set the source and the click when you begin cloning. (Things work differently when you have the Aligned option unchecked in the Options bar, however, as explained in the next section.)

The dreaded cosmic goober

Alt+click with rubber stamp

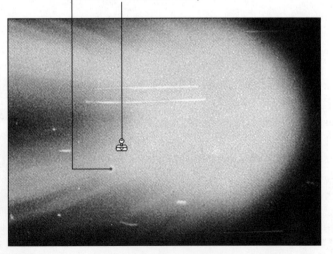

Figure 10-6:
Alt+click (Option+click on a Mac) on a good portion of an image to establish the cloning source.

Clone source   Rubber stamp cursor

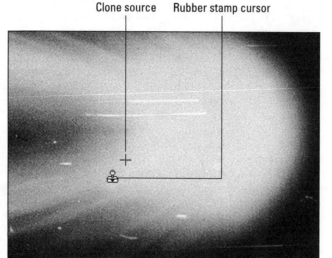

Figure 10-7:
When you
use the
Clone Stamp
tool, a small
cross
follows to
show you
what part of
the image
you're
cloning.

If the cloned area doesn't blend in well, just click the Step Backward button in the Shortcuts bar or press Ctrl+Z (⌘+Z on Mac) and then Alt+click (Option+click on a Mac) in the image with the Clone Stamp tool to specify a better source for your cloning. Click or drag with the tool to test out a different clone. You may have to do this several times to get it just right.

Just for the sheer heck of it, Figure 10-8 shows the comet after a 15-minute workout with the Clone Stamp Tool. Now, isn't that way better than anything from Figures 10-3 and 10-4?

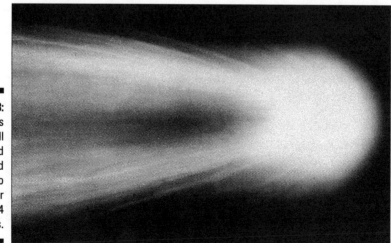

Figure 10-8:
Halley's
comet, all
dressed
up and
nowhere to
go for
another 74
years.

Performing more magic with the Clone Stamp tool

If you never find out another thing about the Clone Stamp tool, you'll be able to clean images quite easily after reading the preceding section. But the Clone Stamp tool is an amazing tool with more facets and capabilities than most Elements tools:

✔ To change the size or shape of the cloning area, change the brush with the palette on the far left of the Options bar. Click the downward-pointing arrow and choose a brush. You'll probably want to stay away from the more exotic brushes when using the Clone Stamp tool. You can also use the Size control in the Options bar, or better yet change the size of the brush on the fly by tapping the [and] keys. For much more on brushes, see Chapter 14.

✔ To make the cloning more translucent or less translucent, use the Opacity slider in the Options bar. Access the slider by pressing the black arrow to the right of the numeric setting. A setting of 100 makes your clone opaque. You can change the opacity by tapping the number keys; tap 5, for instance, to get 50 percent opacity, or 5 twice in quick succession to get 55 percent opacity.

✔ To clean up a straight hair or scratch, Alt+click (Option+click on a Mac) with the tool to specify the source for the cloning as you normally would. Then click at one end of the scratch and Shift+click at the other.

✔ If the first clone doesn't look exactly right but is pretty close, you may want to modify the clone slightly rather than redo it. Lower the Opacity setting in the Options bar and then clone from a different position by again Alt+clicking (Option+click on a Mac) and dragging. This enables you to mix multiple portions of an image together to get a more seamless blend.

✔ Normally, the Clone Stamp tool clones from a relative location. If you move your cursor to a different location, the clone source moves with you. But what if you want to clone multiple times from a single location? In this case, deselect the Aligned box in the Options bar. Now, you can Alt+click (Option+click on a Mac) once to set the source and click multiple times to duplicate that source.

✔ The Pattern Stamp tool, which shares a flyout menu with the Clone Stamp tool in the Toolbox, clones an area with a repeating pattern. The Pattern palette in the Options bar gives you access to Elements' large library of preset patterns; you can also define your own pattern by selecting a rectangular area and choosing Edit⇨Define Pattern. Give it a name, and then select your custom pattern from the bottom of the Pattern drop-down palette in the Options bar. Drag with the Pattern Stamp tool, and you'll see the pattern appear. It's cool but generally not useful.

✔ Speaking of cool but not generally useful, there's a new Impressionist option in the Pattern Stamp tool's Options bar, which makes the Pattern Stamp tool do . . . well . . . an *impression* of the Impressionist Brush. If you want to obliterate your image with whirling, swirling pattern effects, this tool was made to order. And it's fun to experiment with, anyway. You can switch to the Pattern Stamp when the Clone Stamp is active by clicking the Pattern Stamp button on the left side of the Options bar.

✔ You can clone between images with the Clone Stamp tool. If you have two images open, you can Alt+click (Option+click on a Mac) inside one image to specify the source and drag in the other image to clone. It's like painting one image onto another.

✔ Figure 10-9 shows an example Deke created of cloning between images. Starting with the two images on the left side of the figure (which he scaled to the same file size by using Image⇨Resize⇨Image Size, as discussed in Chapter 4), he Alt+clicked (Option+click on a Mac) inside the top image and then dragged with the Clone Stamp tool inside the bottom image. He cloned the woman's face and blouse using a large fuzzy brush and then switched to a smaller brush for the touch ups. To match the skin tones in the forehead and the base of the nose, he cloned from the woman's cheeks at an Opacity setting of 50%. Pretty amazing, huh? Color Plate 8 shows an example of the Clone Stamp tool's terrific work on an old, torn photograph.

Figure 10-9:
By cloning from the top-left image onto the bottom-left image with the Clone Stamp tool, Deke was able to merge the two images to create the strange but nonetheless believable specimen on the right.

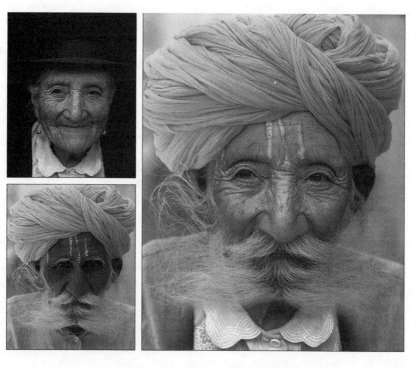

- ✔ If your image contains layers (as discussed in Chapter 9), remember that the Clone Stamp tool normally clones only from the active layer. If you select the Use All Layers check box in the Options bar, the Clone Stamp tool reads the pixels in all visible layers as the clone source. When you then click or drag with the Clone Stamp tool, Elements paints the clone onto the active layer.

- ✔ The Clone Stamp tool also lets you clone using effect modes, which can create special effects by blending the colors of pixels. Effect modes are basically the same thing as blending modes, which are discussed at length in Chapter 13. In the meanwhile, if you have half an hour to waste, play with the different modes and see what you can do. Or spend the time with a loved one instead. Nah, check out those effect modes.

The Clone Stamp tool is unquestionably one of Elements' two or three most useful tools. Take the time to get to know it well.

Getting the Red Out

If you've been on the business end of a modern camera recently, you've probably witnessed a startling display of light just before the picture snapped, something akin to a laser light show at your local planetarium. The multiple strobes that many camera flashes emit nowadays are all about shrinking your pupils to keep out red eye, the longtime scourge of photographers everywhere. If the flash on a camera is too close to the lens, the light from the flash enters the eye, hits the retina, and bounces back into the lens, creating the glowing effect. The modern strobe flashes are indeed quite effective at stopping red eye before it happens.

And that's a very good thing, because red eye is very difficult to correct digitally. The reflected light often blasts away detail, and there's usually no way to know even what color the person's irises are supposed to be. Elements' solution for this problem is the Red Eye Brush tool: If the red eye problem in an image isn't too severe — and especially if the glow is confined to the pupil, and doesn't bleed out into the iris — it can do the trick. The proof — as the popular saying goes — is in Color Plate 9.

The Red Eye Brush tool is located on the right side of the Toolbox, the seventh tool from the top. Here are the controls available to you inside the Red Eye Brush tool's Options bar:

- ✔ **Brush:** Select a brush here. For more information, see the earlier section "Performing more magic with the Clone Stamp tool," or better yet turn to Chapter 14. As with the Clone Stamp, you'll probably want to stick with a rather ordinary default brush.

- ✔ **Size:** Choose a size for the Red Eye Brush tool here. You can also tap the [and] keys to change the size on the fly.

✔ **Current:** This is the color that will be replaced when you use the Red Eye Brush tool. When the Sampling pop-up menu is set to First Click, the Current color becomes the color of the pixel that the Red Eye Brush is currently over. With Sampling set to Current Color, you can click the Default Colors button to automatically set the Current color to a service-able reddish-brown, or click the Current color box to select a different color from the Color Picker.

✔ **Replacement:** This is the color that will replace the Current color in the image when the Red Eye Brush tool is used. The actual color used to replace the Current color is usually a somewhat muted version of the chosen Replacement color.

✔ **Default Colors:** This sets the Replacement color to black. When the Sampling option is set to Current Color, the Default Colors button also sets the Current color to a reddish-brown.

✔ **Sampling:** When set to First Click, the Red Eye Brush will replace the color of the pixel it is clicked upon with the Replacement color. When set to Current Color, the Red Eye Brush will only function if it is clicked on a pixel within the Tolerance range of the Current color.

✔ **Tolerance:** This specifies how close a pixel has to be to the Current color before it is affected. A low setting means that the Red Eye Brush will only affect colors that are very close to the Current color; a higher setting means that the Red Eye Brush is more tolerant of different colored pixels, and will therefore affect them as well.

Although the Red Eye Brush tool is certainly worth giving a spin, Elements actually has another tool that can frequently eliminate red eye with more precision. We're speaking of the Replace Color command, which we'll get to in Chapter 12.

Chapter 11

What Kind of Tool Am I?

*B*ack in the old days, retouching a photograph was a formidable task. If you wanted to remove the reflection from someone's glasses, sharpen the focus of a detail, or tidy up a wrinkle or two, you had to paint or airbrush the photo and hope for the best. Anyone short of a trained professional would more often than not make a complete mess of the project and wish to heck it had never been started. Even the pros found it difficult to match flat colors on a palette to the ever-changing landscape of a photograph.

The beauty of Photoshop Elements is that you can paint not only with specific colors (as explained in Chapter 14) but also with colors and details already found in the image. Using the editing tools — Smudge, Blur, Sharpen, Dodge, Burn, and Sponge — you can subtly adjust the appearance of pixels by shifting them around, boosting contrast between them, or lightening and darkening them. And where the Blur and Sharpen tools leave off, the Blur and Sharpen filters pick up and go the extra mile. The results are edits that blend in with their surroundings.

Retouching images with Elements lets you work in ways that traditional photographers simply can't and also offers a built-in safety net. You can undo any change you make or simply revert to your original image if you don't like how your retouched image turns out. After you finish this chapter, you'll be so inspired to enhance and modify photographic details that you'll welcome problem images with open arms.

Touching Base with Retouching Tools

When push comes to shove, the editing tools are more like than unlike the painting tools. But the editing tools are sufficiently different from their painting cousins to confuse and perplex the unsuspecting neophyte. And unlike the Pencil and Brush, the editing tools don't have any common real-world counterparts. We can't say, "Elements' Smudge tool works just like the conventional Smudge tool that's hanging out in your garage right next to the leaf rake," because recent surveys have shown that almost no one has a Smudge tool hanging in the garage (or anywhere else).

Editing tools would be extremely useful in real life if only someone would get around to inventing them. Take the task of touching up the walls in your rec room. (Come on, everyone has a rec room! Where else would you do your reccing?) Using paintbrushes and rollers alone, this job can be a nightmare. The paint on the walls and the paint in the can may no longer exactly match. If you have to scrape away any dry paint, you'll have a heck of a time matching the texture. And, knowing you, you may very well trip over something and spill paint all over the carpet.

But scan the walls of the rec room into Elements and your problems are solved. Even if you have to retouch both paint and wallpaper, the editing tools, shown in Figure 11-1, can handle the job without incident:

- ✔ Use the Smudge tool to smear colors from a pristine area of the wall to the bare spots and the stains. You can smear the paint as far as you want, just as though it were still wet and in infinite supply. (The section "Smudging Away Imperfections," later in this chapter, discusses the Smudge tool further.)

- ✔ If the transitions between objects in the wallpaper are a little ragged — for example, if the pixels in the little polka-dot mushrooms don't seem to blend naturally with those in the cute little frogs sitting beneath them — you can smooth the pixels out with the Blur tool, which looks like a water drop. This tool blurs the edges between colors so that the colors blend together.

- ✔ To rebuild textures, drag with the Sharpen tool — which looks as though someone took the water-drop-shaped Blur tool and, well, sharpened it. (Must be very hard water.) The Sharpen tool increases the amount of contrast between colors and builds up edges.

- ✔ Together, the Blur and Sharpen tools are known as *focus tools*. The former downplays focus; the latter enhances it. Both tools are eloquently explained later in this chapter in the section "Focusing from the hip."

✔ To lighten a dark area in the wallpaper, drag with the Dodge tool, which looks like a lollipop. This tool lightens up the area evenly.

✔ If an area on the wall has become faded over the years, you can darken it by using the Burn tool, which looks like a hand making the shape of an O.

✔ Are the colors just too darn garish? Or has the color been drained right out? Okay, so these aren't common rec room problems, but if they do occur, you can take up the Sponge tool to remedy them.

✔ The Dodge, Burn, and Sponge tools are called *toning tools,* meaning that they change the colors in an image.

See, don't you wish you had a crack at using these tools in real life? Seems to me that Bob Vila or Tim Allen should get to work on them. There are millions to be made.

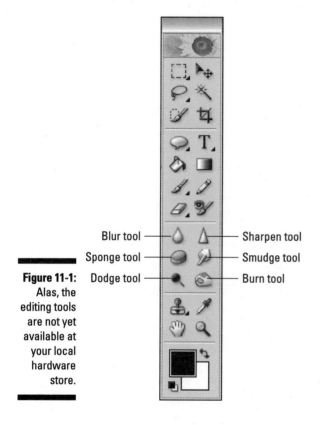

Figure 11-1:
Alas, the editing tools are not yet available at your local hardware store.

Blur tool — Sharpen tool
Sponge tool — Smudge tool
Dodge tool — Burn tool

Smudging Away Imperfections

The shark image shown in Figure 11-2 provides an ideal subject for demonstrating the powers of the Smudge tool. Like so many rough-and-tumble sharks that occupy the inner cities of our oceans, this guy is no stranger to the occasional toothy brawl. Frankly, his face is a mess. He looks like he had a bad time shaving this morning, except he doesn't have little bloodstained bits of tissue paper stuck all over his face. But when you're a shark, you're a shark all the way, and the marks on his face are probably the result of a violent rumble.

But whatever caused his scars, they can be fixed with the help of the Smudge tool. As you may recall from the earlier rec-room analogy, the Smudge tool pushes color from one portion of your image into another. When you drag with this tool, Elements "grabs" the color that's underneath your cursor at the start of your drag and smears it in the direction of your drag.

Figure 11-2:
This shark is on the road to ruin.

The Smudge tool is a great contraption for smearing away scars, wrinkles, overly large noses, droopy ears, and all the other things that plastic surgeons keep their eyes out for. Figure 11-3 shows a magnified view of the shark receiving a thorough makeover with the Smudge tool. (For the sake of clarity, the cursor has been set to Standard mode in the Display & Cursors panel of the Preferences.) The various sharkish defects are smoothed away to the point that the guy looks like he's made out of porcelain.

Light on the smudge, please

Notice that in Figure 11-3, the Smudge tool is being rubbed *with* the grain of the detail. It's tracing along the shark's gills, rubbing along the length of the shark's fins, and dragging up the shark's snout, all in short, discreet strokes. (It's very bad to rub a shark the wrong way.) You get more natural-looking results if you carefully trace along the details of your subject and don't simply drag haphazardly all over the place.

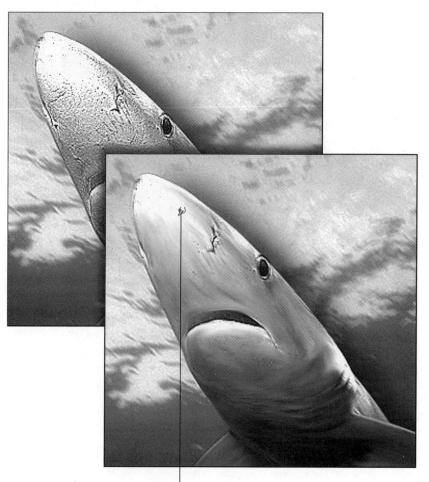

Figure 11-3: As these before (top) and after (bottom) photos prove, the Smudge tool can take years off a shark's face.

Smudge cursor

Retouching with the Smudge tool requires a certain amount of discretion. If you really go nuts and drag over every single surface, you get an oil-painting effect, like the one shown in Figure 11-4. You can create some cool stuff this way, but excessive smudging is not the same as retouching.

Figure 11-4:
You can
convert a
photo into
an oil
painting by
artfully
dragging the
Smudge tool
all over the
place.

Smudge-specific controls

You can modify the performance of the Smudge tool by using the Smudge options (see Figure 11-5):

- ✔ Click and Shift+click to smudge in a straight line. You can also Shift+drag to smudge horizontally or vertically. These Shift+click and Shift+drag techniques work for all the edit tools, by the way.

- ✔ Select another brush in the brushes palette and change the Size option to enlarge or reduce the size of the smudge brush. You can likewise change the brush size for all the edit tools. To display the brushes palette, click the downward-pointing arrow next to the brushstroke icon in the Options bar. (For much more on changing brushes, see Chapter 14.)

- ✔ There are various smudge options in the Options bar. For example, you can adjust the Strength slider by clicking the black arrow to the right of the default setting of 50% and lowering it to create more subtle retouching effects. Increase the Strength setting to make the effect more pronounced.

✔ Remember that you can change the brush size from the keyboard by pressing the bracket keys and change the Strength setting by pressing the number keys.

✔ The Mode drop-down menu gives you two options, Darken and Lighten, which let you smear only those colors that are darker or lighter than the original colors in the image. You also have the Color effect mode, which lets you smear the colors in an RGB image without harming the detail. Pretty nifty. The other effect modes — Hue, Saturation, and Luminosity — range from nearly useless to completely useless. Don't worry about them. And for general purposes, you won't really need to worry about the Mode menu at all when using the Smudge tool. For much more on brush and effect (or blending) modes, see Chapter 13.

✔ Depending on your computer system, Elements may slow down dramatically when you increase the Strength setting above 80% or 90%, select a large brush size, or change the effect mode. And if you do all three at the same time, the program may run so lethargically that you'll think you've crashed. Just go get a cup of coffee, and Elements should be finished when you get back.

✔ Select the Finger Painting check box to dip your brush into the foreground color before smudging. Elements applies a little dab of foreground color at the beginning of your drag and then begins to smear into the existing colors in the image as usual.

✔ The Use All Layers check box doesn't make any difference unless you're editing an image with layers. It enables you to pierce through and pick up the colors from all your layers.

✔ Although the Smudge tool can be fun, there are probably better options at your disposal. If you want to push around pixels to create distortions in your image, the Liquify filter is sort of like the Smudge tool on steroids. Most of Smudge's capabilities are available there, as well as a host of other tools for smearing around your image in useful and amusing ways. To check out the Liquify filter, head on over to Chapter 13. And if your wish is to repair your image, getting rid of imperfections and such, then the Clone Stamp tool may well give you better results. Chapter 10 has the skinny on the Clone Stamp tool.

Figure 11-5:
The options that affect the Smudge tool.

Dodge? Burn? Those Are Opposites?

Wondering why the Dodge and Burn tool icons look the way they do? It's because they have their roots in traditional stat camera techniques in which you shoot a photograph of another photograph to correct exposure problems. The Dodge tool is supposed to look like a little paddle that you wave around to block off light, and the Burn tool is a hand focusing the light. It may seem, therefore, that dodging would make the image darker and burning would make it lighter. But Elements is thinking in terms of negative film, where black is white, up is down, right is left, and Goofus is, of course, a Cornish game hen.

Here's a handy key for remembering which tool does what:

- ✔ The Dodge tool lightens images, just as a dodge ball lightens your body by about ten pounds when it knocks off your head.
- ✔ The Burn tool darkens images, just as a sunburn darkens your body and eventually turns it a kind of charbroiled color.

Or you could remember it this way: The D in Dodge stands for darken; the B in Burn stands for brighten. Except that that is totally incorrect.

Glad we could clear things up.

Generally, you adjust the performance of the Dodge and Burn tools just like the other edit tools and the paint tools. You can find all the tool options, including brush sizes, in the Options bar:

- ✔ The Exposure slider bar, accessed by pressing the black arrow to the right of the default setting of 50%, indicates how much an area will be lightened or darkened. As always, lower the value to lessen the impact of the tool and raise the value to increase the impact.
- ✔ The Range drop-down menu contains just three options: Highlights, Midtones, and Shadows. The default setting is Midtones, which lightens or darkens medium colors in an image and leaves the very light and dark colors alone. Figure 11-6 shows the result of dragging all over the shark with the Dodge tool while Midtones was the active range.

✔ The Shadows range ensures that the darkest colors are affected, whereas Highlights impacts the lightest colors. In Figure 11-7, the Dodge tool was scribbled with while the range was set to Shadows. The payoff is a shark that looks like it ate a tanker full of glowworms. Even the darkest shadows radiate, making the image uniformly light.

✔ To darken an image with similar uniformity, select the Burn tool and set the brush mode to Highlights.

You can use a variation of the Dodge and Burn tools in the form of the Color Dodge and Color Burn blending modes (explained in Chapter 13). When you use the regular Dodge and Burn tools, you simply lighten or darken your image. But if you use one of the painting tools with the Color Dodge or Color Burn blending modes, you can both lighten or darken and infuse the image with color. For example, if you want to lighten an image and give it a yellowish glow, paint with yellow and the Color Dodge blending mode.

Figure 11-6:
By setting the Range to Midtones and dragging indiscriminately with the Dodge tool, the shark was lightened without eliminating contrast.

Figure 11-7:
Using the Dodge tool in combination with the Range set to Shadows makes the shark's darkest shadows tingle with light.

Playing with the Color Knob

The Sponge tool is designed for use on full-color images. Don't try using it on grayscale images because it doesn't do you any good. It's not that it doesn't work — it does — it just doesn't work correctly. On a grayscale image, the Sponge tool either lightens or darkens pixels like a shoddy version of the Dodge or Burn tool.

When you work on a color image, the Sponge tool increases or decreases saturation. Ever used the Color knob on an old television? Turn the knob up, and the color leaps off the screen; turn it down, and the colors look gray. What you're doing is adjusting the TV's saturation. Increasing saturation makes the colors more vibrant; decreasing saturation makes the colors more drab. The Sponge tool works in much the same way.

Here's how you use the Sponge tool:

1. **Select the Sponge tool.**

   Press the Q key (for "quench," maybe?). Elements then displays the appropriate Options bar.

2. **Select the desired Mode option from the drop-down menu in the Options bar.**

   Select Saturate to make the colors vibrant; select Desaturate to make the colors drab.

3. **Press a number key to change the Flow value.**

   You can also drag the slider bar in the Options bar, which you access by clicking the black arrow next to the numeric setting. Either way, the setting affects the impact of the Sponge tool.

4. **Drag with the tool inside a color image.**

   Watch those colors change.

One good use for the Sponge tool is to provide a focal point for your image. Suppose that you have a color photo of a group of people and want to have one person stand out among the others. Select your person (see Chapter 8 for selection methods) and then choose Select⇨Inverse. Now, carefully take the Sponge tool, set the Mode to Desaturate in the Options bar, and drag over the image. You see the colors in the group wash out while your deselected person remains bright and stands out among the crowd. You can also set the option to Saturate to make your chosen person brighter than the rest; just make sure you select Inverse again to deselect the crowd and select the chosen person first. A variation on this idea can be found in Color Plate 10.

Focusing from the Hip

From what we've discovered about the Smudge tool, it's clear that it can be a handy device. But it's not always the right tool for the job. For example, suppose you have a harsh transition between two colors. Maybe one of our shark's teeth looks a little jagged, or you want to soften the edge of a fin. Which of the following methods would you use to fix this problem?

   ✔ Smear the colors a bit with the Smudge tool.

   ✔ Soften the transition between the colors by using the Blur tool.

Okay, you were tipped off by the preceding paragraph saying that the Smudge tool is "not always the right tool for the job," so naturally you chose the second answer. (You did choose the second answer, didn't you?) But a time will come when you run into this exact situation and your first reflex will be to reach for the Smudge tool.

So let's try to drive home the point a bit with the aid of Figure 11-8. The figure starts off with the harshest of all possible color transitions — that is, between white and its archenemy, black. You want to smear the colors together so that they blend a little more harmoniously, so naturally you reach for the Smudge tool. The problem with this method (as shown in the second example in the figure) is that you can't get a nice, smooth transition between the two colors no matter how hard you try. Even if you Shift+drag with the Smudge tool, you get some inconsistent smudging. You might also run the risk of smearing surrounding detail. All this happens because the Smudge tool is designed as a free-form smearing device, not as an edge softener.

Meanwhile, an edge softener is sitting nearby waiting for you to snatch it up. If you drag the Blur tool between the white and black shapes — whether you drag perfectly straight or wobble the cursor back and forth a bit — you get a softened edge like the one shown in the final example of Figure 11-8.

Here are a few other items about the focus tools:

- Just as the Blur tool softens transitions, the Sharpen tool firms the transitions back up.

- At least, that's what the Sharpen tool is supposed to do. In practice, it tends to make an image overly grainy. Use this tool sparingly.

- You can adjust the impact of the Blur and Sharpen tools by changing the Strength settings in the Options bar. As a jumping-off point, try working with the strength set to about 60% for the Blur tool and 30% for the Sharpen tool.

- When you work with the focus tools, you have access to the same effect modes as you do when using the Smudge tool. Again, the important ones are Darken, Lighten, and Color. Any of the three can help downplay the effects of the Sharpen tool and make it more usable. For more on effect (or blending) modes, see Chapter 13.

If you want to adjust the focus of large areas of an image — or an entire image — your best bet by far is to go with the Blur and Sharpen filters. These commands work much more uniformly than the focus tools, and with better results.

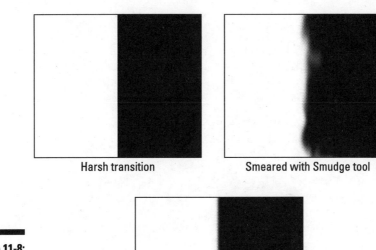

Harsh transition   Smeared with Smudge tool

Softened with Blur tool

Figure 11-8:
The parable
of the harsh
transition,
the Smudge
tool, and the
Blur tool.

Sharpening Those Wishy-Washy Details

No matter how good an image looked before you scanned it, chances are that it appears a little out of focus on-screen. The image in Figure 11-9 is an exaggerated example. Snapped around the time Stonehenge was built, this photo has suffered the cruel scourges of time. It probably wasn't that sharply focused in the first place, but all these many years later, it looks so soft you'd swear that it was sculpted out of gelatin.

The solutions to softness are the four filters found under the Sharpen category of the Filters palette. The following sections explain how these filters work and when — if ever — to apply them.

Figure 11-9:
Antique
images
such as this
one are
notoriously
soft on
focus.

The single-shot sharpeners

The first three sharpening filters — Sharpen, Sharpen Edges, and Sharpen More — are *single-shot filters*. You choose them, and they do their work without complex dialog boxes or other means of digital interrogation. These filters, with their straightforward names, are a breeze to use.

Unfortunately, when it comes to Elements, you get back what you put in — mentally, that is. In other words, if you don't have to work at it, it's liable to deliver rather mediocre results. As demonstrated in Figure 11-10, all three of these Sharpen filters sharpen, but none satisfactorily remedies the image's focus problems.

Figure 11-10 shows the results of applying each of the three single-shot sharpeners to a detail from the original image (shown in the top row). In each case, the filter was applied once (as shown in the middle row) and then a second time (as shown in the last row). For the record, here's what each of the filters does:

✔ Sharpen, as shown in the first column, enhances the focus of the image very slightly. If the photo is already well focused but needs a little extra fortification to make it perfect, the Sharpen filter can do the trick. Otherwise, forget it.

✔ The Sharpen More filter, shown in the second column, enhances focus more dramatically. Although it's easily the most useful of the three single-shooters, it's still fairly crude. For example, the center image in Figure 11-10 isn't sharp enough, whereas the bottom image is so sharp that little flecks — called *artifacts* — are starting to form in the woman's dress. Boo, hiss.

✔ The Sharpen Edges filter, as seen in the third column, is a complete waste of time. It sharpens the so-called edges of an image without sharpening any of the neutral areas in between. In the figure, for example, the filter sharpens the outline of the guy's face but ignores the interior of his jacket. The result is an inconsistent effect that eventually frays the edges and leaves nonedges looking goopy by comparison.

Figure 11-10:
The effects of applying each of the single-shot sharpeners are shockingly shabby.

As you may have gathered by now, we don't wholeheartedly recommend the single-shot sharpening filters. Still, you may want to go ahead and apply Sharpen or Sharpen More to an image to see whether it does the trick. If a single-shot sharpener turns out to be all you need, great. But it probably won't be. Even if you use the Auto Focus feature of Elements' handy new Quick Fix command (seen in Figure 11-11), located under the Enhance menu, you're really just applying the Unsharp Mask filter with its default settings. And as the built-in Quick Fix dialog box Tip recommends, you should apply the actual Unsharp Mask filter to more precisely sharpen details.

You can also summon the Quick Fix dialog box by clicking the handy button in the Shortcuts bar; it's the one that looks like a lightning bolt striking an image.

Figure 11-11:
The Quick Fix dialog box is your one-stop shopping center for many of Elements' one-click commands.

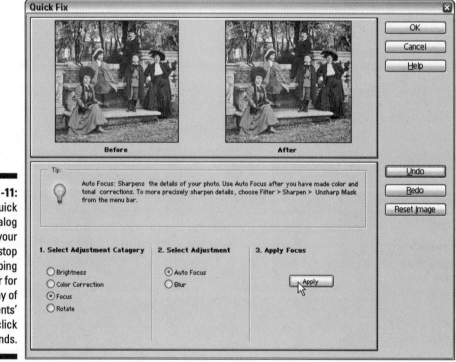

Unsharp Mask: The filter with a weird name

If the Adobe programmers had been in charge of naming Superman, they would have called him "Average Guy from Krypton." Rather than describing what the guy does, the programmers describe his origins. That's exactly what they did with the Unsharp Mask filter. Rather than calling the filter "Supersharpen," which would have made a modicum of sense and may have even encouraged a few novices to give it a try, they named it after an ancient stat camera technique that a few professionals in lab coats pretend to understand in order to impress each other.

So forget Unsharp Mask and just think "Supersharpen." To use the "Supersharpen" command, choose Unsharp Mask. The "Supersharpen" dialog box appears, as shown in Figure 11-12.

Like the Dust & Scratches dialog box (see Chapter 10), the Unsharp Mask dialog box, shown in Figure 11-12, enables you to preview what happens when you change the values in the three option boxes. You can preview the filter inside the dialog box and in the main image window. If you can't quite remember how these previewing functions work, check out Chapter 10. To sharpen an image, use the three slider bars like so:

- ✔ Change the Amount value from 1% to 500% to change the amount of sharpening. Higher Amount values produce more sharpening — but you were probably sharp enough yourself to figure that out.

- ✔ Adjust the Radius value to specify the width of the edges you want to sharpen. If the image is generally in good shape, use a Radius of 0.5. If the edges are soft and syrupy, like the ones in Figure 11-9, use a Radius of 1.0. And if the edges are almost nonexistent, go with 2.0. Although the resolution of your image factors into the equation, you generally don't want to go any lower than 0.5 or any higher than 2.0 (though 250 is the maximum).

- ✔ If you're using a whole number, you don't have to painstakingly type 1.0 or 2.0 into the Radius option box. A simple 1 or 2 will suffice.

- ✔ As with the Threshold option in the Dust & Scratches dialog box, the Unsharp Mask Threshold option determines how different two neighboring pixels must be to be considered an edge. (See Chapter 10 for a review of this concept.) The default value of 0 tells Elements to sharpen everything. By raising the value, you tell Elements not to sharpen low-contrast pixels.

The idea behind Threshold is great, but the implementation in Elements leaves something to be desired. The filter creates an abrupt transition between sharpened and ignored pixels, resulting in an unrealistic effect. Therefore, it's usually a good idea to leave Threshold set to 0.

Supersharpen!!!

Unsharp Mask

OK

Cancel

☑ Preview

100%

Amount: 50 %

Figure 11-12:
Experts
agree that
the Unsharp
Mask dialog
box really
should be
called the
Supershar-
pen dialog
box.

Radius: 1.0 pixels

Threshold: 0 levels

Some sharpening scenarios

Figure 11-13 demonstrates the effects of several different Amount and Radius values on the same detail to which the piddly little Sharpen More command was applied in Figure 11-10. Throughout Figure 11-13, the Threshold value is 0.

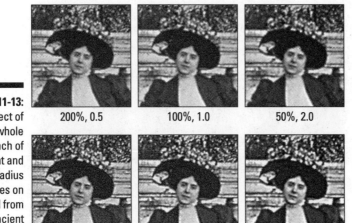

Figure 11-13: The effect of a whole bunch of Amount and Radius values on detail from an ancient photo.

200%, 0.5	100%, 1.0	50%, 2.0
500%, 0.5	250%, 1.0	125%, 2.0

Figure 11-13 is organized into two rows. In the first image in the top row, the Amount value is 200% and the Radius is 0.5. Then the Amount value was halved and the Radius value was doubled in each of the next two images. Though the effect is similar from one image to the next, you can see that the right image has thicker edges than the left image. The differences are subtle; you may have to look closely. Put on your glasses (where applicable).

The bottom row of the figure features more pronounced sharpening effects. The first image in the bottom row has Amount and Radius values of 500% and 0.5. Then the Amount value was progressively halved, and the Radius value was progressively doubled. Notice that the edges in the right image are thicker, and the left image contains more artifacts (those little flecks in the jacket and hat).

After experimenting with a few different settings, the best setting seems to be an Amount of 250% and a Radius of 1.0. Figure 11-14 shows the final image sharpened with these settings.

Blurring Adds Depth

If you want to make a portion of your image blurry instead of sharp, you can apply one of the commands from the Blur category of the Filters palette. Right off the bat, you quick thinkers are thinking, "Blurry? Why would I want my image to be blurry?" This is a classic problem. You're thinking of blurry as the enemy of sharp. But blurry and sharp can go hand in hand inside the same image. The sharp details are in the foreground, and the blurry stuff goes in the background.

Take Figure 11-15, for example. In this image, the background was selected and blurred. The scene becomes a little more intimate, as though the background were far, far away. It also has the effect of making the foreground characters seem more in focus than ever.

To make the effect complete, the lower-right corner of the image was selected, feathered, and blurred. The result is a gradual blurring effect, as though the ground were becoming progressively out of focus as it extends beyond our field of vision.

For the most part, then, blurring is a special effect. Unlike sharpening, which has the effect of correcting the focus, blurring heightens reality by exaggerating the depth of an image. In other words, you never have to blur an image — and you probably won't do it nearly as frequently as you sharpen — but blurring the background can really enhance the sharpness of foreground objects.

The first two commands in the Blur category — Blur and Blur More — are the Dumb and Dumber of the blur filters. Like their Sharpen and Sharpen More counterparts, they produce predefined effects that never seem to be quite what you're looking for.

Choosing Enhance⇨Quick Fix, selecting the Focus Adjustment Category, then selecting Blur, and finally clicking Apply has the same effect as applying the Blur filter.

The "Superblur" command — the filter that offers the powers you need to get the job done right — is Gaussian Blur. The filter is named after Karl Friedrich Gauss, a dusty old German mathematician who's even older than the photograph from Figure 11-9. But just think "Superblur" — or, as Mr. Gauss would have put it, *Überblur.*

Figure 11-15:
Blurring the background as well as a small tip of the foreground (bottom right) brings the family up close and personal.

When you choose Gaussian Blur, Elements displays the dialog box shown in Figure 11-16. The Radius value determines the number of pixels that get mixed together at a time. You can go as high as 250.0, but generally any value over 10.0 enters the realm of the legally blind. In Figure 11-15, the background was blurred with a Radius value of 4.0 and the lower-right patch of ground with a Radius of 2.0.

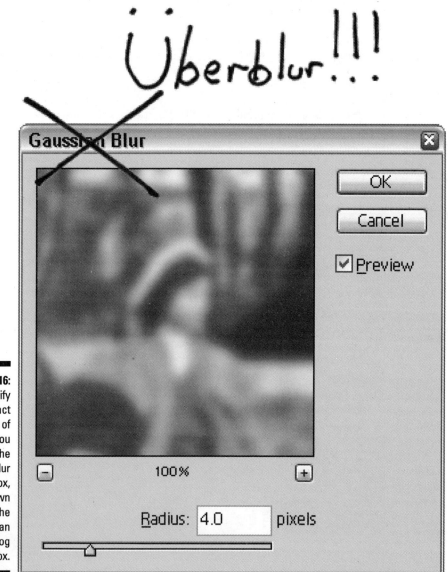

Figure 11-16: Specify the exact amount of blur you want in the Überblur dialog box, also known as the Gaussian Blur dialog box.

Of all the tools and filters we looked at in this chapter, the most valuable to you will be the Unsharp Mask filter. It's not a miracle worker — you can't take an image that's blurred beyond recognition and expect Unsharp Mask to pull details from it. But on soft-to-slightly blurry photos, it's the deal. Odd name and not exactly user-friendly controls aside, Unsharp Mask is without question one of the top ten most important tools that Elements puts at your disposal. In fact, let's really go out on a limb: There's probably not a digital image out there that wouldn't benefit (or that hasn't already benefited) from being given a working over with Unsharp Mask. Color Plate 11 backs us up.

So the next time you're in a movie theater and the screen goes all blurry because the projectionist is making out with his girlfriend and not paying attention to his job, lean your head back and scream at the top of your lungs: "Unsharp Mask! Unsharp Mask!" You'll feel better, and you'll suddenly find you have a lot of empty seats around you in the theater. Isn't digital imaging a wonderful thing?

Chapter 12

The Rainbow Correction

*H*ere's a common scenario for you: You get some pictures or slides back from the photo developer — we're talking regular photos here, not the digital kind — and one of them catches your eye. The color is great, the composition is fantastic, everyone's smiling; it ranks among the best pictures you've ever shot. It's not 100 percent perfect, but you figure you can fix the few glitches with Photoshop Elements.

So you scan the image, open it up, and your heart sinks to the pit of your stomach. The image is dark, colorless, and generally a big, fat disappointment. The snapshot from the photo developer looks far better than this murky mess on-screen.

In a perfect world, this would never happen. But scanning is an imperfect process, and even if your scanner isn't one of those $50 "bargains," seeing a scanned photo on-screen for the first time can be discouraging.

Take Color Plate 12, for example. When viewed in a slide projector, the original slide looked something like the example in the bottom right, but when it was scanned and opened in Elements, the image appeared as shown in the upper left. If you run into a similar problem, never fear — you have cause to be optimistic. The colors may not look like much now, but chances are good that you have enough colors to get by. Though it may be hard to believe, your image very likely contains a few million colors; it's just that they're all squished toward the dark end of the spectrum. Your job is to bring these colors back to life.

We accomplished that very feat in the bottom-right image of Color Plate 12 with one Elements command — Levels. In fact, Levels and the Color Variations command are just about all you need when it comes to fixing up bad scans. You don't need painting or editing tools, selection outlines, or adding colors to the image. Color-correction commands merely stretch the existing colors in the image across the spectrum.

Elements offers many such commands, but you need only a few of these to get the job done. In this chapter, you'll see how these miracle commands work. You'll also find out how to use adjustment layers, which let you do some of your color correcting on an independent layer, thereby providing you with extra flexibility and safety.

Color-Correcting Quickly

Photoshop Elements has a handful of fast color-correction commands designed to improve your image without any fuss on your part. These commands can be found under the Enhance menu, and they're also available in the Quick Fix dialog box, discussed in Chapter 11. These "instant" color-correction commands are definitely worth a try; sometimes they do a great job, and if they actually make your image worse, they're easy enough to undo. Color Plate 12 shows what happens when four of these commands are applied to a dark, discolored scan of a slide.

Granted, not all images are in such bad shape, and different images will respond better to one command than another. As the lower left image in Color Plate 12 shows, Auto Color Correction did better than Auto Levels, Auto Contrast, or Fill Flash at lightening up the image and removing the color cast. However, we were still able to do a better job "by hand" using the more complex Levels command, as shown in the lower-right image. We'll fully explore Levels later in this chapter, but first let's take a look at Levels' not-so-trusty sidekick, Auto Levels.

Auto Levels

Auto Levels is sort of like that weird uncle you basically like, but you're not quite sure you can trust. Choose Enhance➪Auto Levels or press Ctrl+Shift+L (⌘+Shift+L on the Mac) to automatically correct the contrast of an image. (You'll also find Auto Levels in the Brightness category of the Enhance➪Quick Fix command.) For example, Figure 12-1 shows a typical low-contrast image composed entirely of cheerless grays. The inset squares show the lightest and darkest colors in the image as well as some sample shades in between. With the Auto Levels command, Elements automatically makes the lightest gray white and the darkest gray black and stretches out the colors in between. Figure 12-2 shows the result.

Figure 12-1: What a dismal scene: Come to this gas station and get your tank filled with depression. The Grim Reaper will change your oil.

Figure 12-2: The Auto Levels command brings out some strong blacks and whites, but the grays remain dark and dreary. (And the autos don't look any more level than they did already.)

Unfortunately, Auto Levels doesn't always do the trick. Figure 12-2, for example, contains strong blacks and whites, but the grays appear overly dark (as witnessed by the shades in the inset squares). Furthermore, although it's not an issue in a black and white image like this one, Auto Levels has been known to introduce color casts to images. Auto Levels works its preset routine on each color channel individually, and this can potentially tint the entire image an off color, known in the biz as a *color cast*.

Compare this to Enhance⇨Adjust Brightness/Contrast⇨Levels, which you can access from the keyboard by pressing Ctrl+L (⌘+L on a Mac). The Levels command takes some getting used to, but it lets you adjust the medium grays as well as the darkest and lightest pixels. (We cover the command in detail later in this chapter, in the section "Leveling the Contrast Field.") Figure 12-3 shows the Gulf station running in tip-top condition, thanks to the Levels command. See how much clearer the details in the cars now appear?

Figure 12-3:
A nice, even transition of grays makes a day at the gas station seem like a walk through the park.

Further image enhancements

The Enhance menu has a few other "fast and easy" color-correction commands, and also some that skirt along the edges of "slow and difficult." We'll look at Levels and Color Variations at length later in the chapter; for now let's concentrate on the others.

Auto Contrast

Avoid using Auto Contrast (Enhance⇨Auto Contrast). Stick with correcting contrast in an image by using the Auto Levels command — or better yet, Levels, which gives you control.

Auto Color Correction

Based on the new Auto Color command in Photoshop 7, Auto Color Correction is a very welcome addition to Elements 2.0. This command takes an image's midtones into consideration as it corrects the image. More often than not, Auto Color Correction gives more satisfactory results than any of the other one-shot commands. Definitely give it a shot; if you don't like the results, simply undo and try Levels and Color Variations.

Adjust Backlighting and Fill Flash

These commands, both located in the Adjust Lighting submenu, are designed to easily compensate for common photographic lighting problems. You probably have more than a few photos where the subjects in the foreground are in the shadows, yet the background behind them is extremely bright. (You guessed it: The flash didn't go off.) Fill Flash can help bring out details in the foreground, whereas Adjust Backlighting can increase the contrast of the background. (Bear in mind that Elements has no idea what the "foreground" and "background" of the image are; it just looks at the brightness values of the pixels.)

What's so special about these commands is that they perform a correction that you can't pull off just by applying the Levels command to your image. Adjust Backlighting brings out details in bright areas without wiping out details in dark areas as much as Levels would. And likewise, Fill Flash brings out details in dark areas without wiping out details in light areas as much as Levels would. Fill Flash is the more useful of the two; that's probably why Adobe has given it a keyboard shortcut: Ctrl+Shift+F (⌘+Shift+F on the Mac). Adjust Backlighting has a Darker slider, and Fill Flash has a Lighter slider; to use one of these commands, just drag the slider until the image looks better. Color Plate 13 shows Fill Flash brightening up the foreground of an image.

If Fill Flash seems to exaggerate or drain away the colors in your image, the new Saturation slider can come to the rescue. Drag to the left to decrease the intensity of the color; drag to the right to increase the intensity.

Color Cast

Using the Color Cast command (Enhance⇨Adjust Color⇨Color Cast) is a breeze. Just select the command and use the Eyedropper tool to click in your image on an area that should be devoid of color — white, black, or gray. Color Cast will perform the necessary correction to drain the clicked area of color, adjusting the entire image accordingly. This command either works, as in Color Plate 15, or it doesn't, and whether or not it works depends entirely on your image. It's certainly possible that your image may not contain any areas that ought to be white or black; in that case, move on to Color Variations as a color cast correction tool.

While experimenting with Color Cast, make sure you click the Reset button after every unsatisfactory click in the image. The effects of Color Cast are cumulative, and things can get ugly quickly.

Hue/Saturation

This command (Enhance⇨Adjust Color⇨Hue/Saturation) is powerful for changing color and color intensity. The Hue slider rotates the color in your image around the color spectrum. Small adjustments can correct color casts, whereas large adjustments can create very strange effects. Keep an eye on the rainbow-colored bars at the bottom of the dialog box; the top bar represents the colors of your image, and the bottom bar represents the hue shift.

For example, crank the slider until the yellow in the bottom bar is beneath the red in the top bar, and you'll see that red objects in your image have taken on a yellow color. The Saturation slider increases or decreases the intensity of colors, and the Lightness slider changes the overall brightness. Selecting the Colorize check box gives your image one overall tone, useful for creating sepia effects.

One of the most useful functions of Hue/Saturation is to desaturate only certain colors in an image; for instance, photos taken with some digital cameras tend to have oversaturated reds. That's where the Edit menu at the top of the dialog box comes into play. If you choose Reds from the Edit menu, changes you make with the Hue/Saturation controls will affect only the red pixels in your image.

You can also adjust the range of affected colors with the Eyedroppers and Range controls, labeled in Figure 12-4. You can click the left eyedropper in your image to isolate a color, click the middle eyedropper to add a color to the range, and click the right eyedropper to subtract colors from the range. As you do so, you'll see the Range and Fuzziness controls move between the two rainbow bars. You can also drag these around to alter the range of affected colors. The area between the two range controls represents the color range you're isolating. The areas on either side of the range, bracketed by the triangular sliders, represent the "fuzziness," affecting how far outside the range of isolated colors you want your changes to spread.

If that previous paragraph has you scratching your head, don't worry about it. You'll probably never have to use these controls; if you need to isolate a range of colors, one of the six choices under the Edit menu should suffice.

 Although Hue/Saturation is a powerful, useful tool, you should never choose the Hue/Saturation command. "Why?" we hope you're asking. "Well, because," we answer, "Hue/Saturation is available as an adjustment layer!" And for the straight dope on adjustment layers, see the section "Fiddling with Adjustment Layers," later in this chapter.

Remove Color

This command (Enhance➪Adjust Color➪Remove Color) is just the thing for draining the color from a layer or selected area and leaving it black and white. But if you want to convert an entire image to grayscale, see Chapter 5.

Replace Color

Up to now, this chapter has dealt with color-correction commands that are designed to make your images look more like real life. But the Replace Color command approaches the concept of color "correction" from a slightly different angle — more like "That red ribbon I won really *should* have been blue!" Replace Color excels at isolating a single color in an image and turning it into a different color; at its core, it's a close cousin to Hue/Saturation.

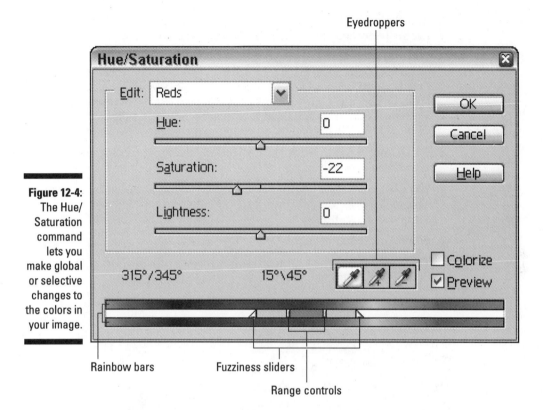

Eyedroppers

Figure 12-4:
The Hue/
Saturation
command
lets you
make global
or selective
changes to
the colors in
your image.

Rainbow bars   Fuzziness sliders

Range controls

To apply Replace Color, choose Enhance⇨Adjust Color⇨Replace Color. The
Replace Color dialog box appears, as nobly depicted in Figure 12-5. The dialog
box is divided into two parts: Selection and Transform.

To use the Replace Color command, do the following:

1. **Apply Replace Color to your entire image, or to a selection.**

   If there are areas of color in your image similar to the one you want to
   replace, it may be a good idea to draw a rough selection around your
   target area. For more on selections, see Chapter 8.

2. **Click the Image radio button.**

   The image or the selected portion appears in the preview.

3. **With the Eyedropper tool, click in your target area within the preview
   or within the image window.**

4. **Switch to the Selection radio button.**

   You should see the results of your selection in the preview window in
   white. Black areas in the Selection preview are totally unselected, white
   areas are completely selected, and gray areas are partially selected.

5. **Adjust your selection with the Add Eyedropper, the Subtract Eyedropper, and the Fuzziness slider.**

   The Add and Subtract Eyedroppers add to and take away from the targeted color area. The Fuzziness slider expands or contracts your selection. Higher Fuzziness values select more colors, and lower values select fewer colors. If you make an arbitrary change to the color using the Transform sliders, you'll be able to see the selection within the image window as well. This can help you judge the quality of your selection.

6. **When you're happy with your selection, change the color using the Transform sliders.**

   You can adjust the Hue (the "color" of the color), Saturation (the richness of the color), and Lightness (how light or dark the color is). The Sample swatch shows you the resultant color of the Transform sliders.

7. **When you're happy, click OK.**

   The color of the selected area has been replaced with your new color. Color Plate 14 fittingly provides an example in living color.

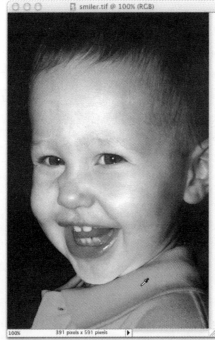
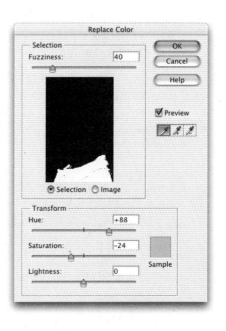

Figure 12-5:
The Replace Color command can isolate and replace an area of color within your image.

Replace Color uses a very sophisticated selection method, which yields results that equal or surpass those of any of the standard selection tools. It's also a very versatile command; as noted in Chapter 10, Replace Color can be a more powerful alternative to the Red Eye Brush tool. Just draw a selection around your subject's eyes, apply Replace Color, select the red glow, and change its Saturation and Lightness.

Brightness/Contrast

The Brightness/Contrast command (Enhance➪Adjust Brightness/Contrast➪ Brightness/Contrast) is utterly and completely worthless. Seriously. If you've never used it, don't start. If you have used it, stop — you're hurting your images. There are plenty of better ways to improve brightness and contrast, the Levels command being foremost among them.

The only nice thing we can say about Brightness/Contrast is that it's available as an adjustment layer, and adjustment layers are really great. Although you shouldn't use Brightness/Contrast as an adjustment layer either; we just brought it up to provide ourselves with a good segue into the next section.

Fiddling with Adjustment Layers

Adjustment layers are really great. They operate just like the layers discussed in Chapter 9, except that you use them expressly to apply color-correction commands. By default, an adjustment layer applies the chosen color correction to every layer beneath it. However, you can always turn off the visibility of an adjustment layer or just delete it entirely, either way restoring your image to its original condition. Adjustment layers are often referred to as *nondestructive*, meaning that they don't permanently change the pixels in your original image; they just float above the pixels, making them look better. It's like having your cake and eating it too.

It's a shame, then, that Elements gives you only two truly useful commands that are available as adjustment layers: Levels and Hue/Saturation. The other choices include Brightness/Contrast (boo, hiss) and a handful of commands also available in the Image➪Adjustments submenu which are handy when you need them, but that probably won't be too often.

Sharing space with adjustment layers are fill layers. You can use fill layers to add a layer of solid color, a gradient, or a pattern. Other than the masking abilities that fill layers share with adjustment layers (see the Technical Stuff icon below), there's really nothing you can do with fill layers that you can't do just by selecting an ordinary layer and filling it with color. Fill layers really have nothing to do with color correction, but for convenience's sake we take a look at them here, too.

As touched on earlier, adjustment and fill layers offer several advantages over ordinary layers:

- ✔ By default, the color correction of adjustment layers affects all the layers that lie beneath it in the Layers palette. Applying an ordinary color-correction command affects only the active layer.

- ✔ You can create as many different adjustment layers as you want. So, if you want a few layers to use just one color correction and the rest of the image to use another as well, you just create two different adjustment layers. You can also create as many fill layers as you desire.

- ✔ Because the color correction "exists" on its own layer, you can experiment freely without fear of damaging the image. If, at some point, you decide that you don't like the effects of the color correction, you can edit the adjustment layer or just delete it entirely and start fresh. You can also edit or delete fill layers.

- ✔ You can blend adjustment and fill layers with the other layers using the Opacity and blending mode settings in the Layers palette, just as you can with any layer. (More on blending modes in Chapter 13.) These features give you even more control over how your image appears.

To create an adjustment layer, do the following:

1. **In the Layers palette, click the layer that you want to color correct.**

   When you create an adjustment layer, Elements places it directly on top of the active layer in the Layers palette. This adjustment affects the layer or layers underneath, depending on whether you turn on the Group with Previous Layer check box as mentioned in Step 2.

   If you select a portion of your image before creating the adjustment layer, the color correction affects only the selected area across all underlying layers.

2. **Choose Layer➪New Adjustment Layer and then select your desired adjustment from the submenu. For this example, let's choose Levels.**

   The New Layer dialog box appears. Here's a field guide to your options: If you want to give your adjustment layer a specific name, enter the name into the top option box.

Skip the Mode and Opacity drop-down menus; if you want, you can change these settings later in the Layers palette. For now, skip the Group with Previous Layer check box. We'll look at this a little later in the chapter.

3. **Press Enter (Return on a Mac).**

   Elements adds the adjustment layer to the Layers palette and displays the Levels dialog box, which is explained in the next section.

Creating a fill layer is just as easy. Simply choose Layer➪New Fill Layer and select solid color, gradient, or pattern from the submenu.

You can also click the "Create new fill or adjustment layer" icon at the bottom of the Layers palette and select an option from the drop-down menu. This bypasses the New Layer dialog box.

If you are wondering what that extra thumbnail is, shown in Figure 12-6, here's a brief explanation. Elements adds a layer mask to every adjustment or fill layer. In short, layer masks are like pieces of clear acetate that hover over the layer. You paint on them to selectively hide or display the adjustment or fill effect. Applying black pixels on the layer mask hides, white pixels show, and any gray color in between displays or hides in varying degrees of trans-parency. In other words, to display the full strength adjustment or fill over the image, leave the layer mask white (the default). To remove the adjustment or fill over the image, paint the mask with black. To partially display the adjust-ment, paint the mask with gray. To isolate only one portion of an image, leave it white and paint the rest of the layer mask black. The Brush and Gradient tools work best for layer masks.

The easiest way to paint on the layer mask is by Alt+Shift-clicking (Option+Shift-clicking on the Mac) on the layer mask thumbnail. If you've ever used the Selection Brush in Mask mode, this should now look very familiar to you. As you then start to paint with black or gray in the image window, you'll see a pink overlay appear on the image. Where things are darkest pink, the layer mask is totally blocking the effect of the adjustment layer. Where things look normal, there's little or no blocking going on. You can also Alt-click (Option-click on the Mac) to view just the mask in grayscale without the underlying image. Shift-click the layer mask thumbnail to turn off the effects of the mask temporarily. Performing either of those commands again will set things back to normal.

Remember that an adjustment or fill layer works just like any other layer in the Layers palette. You can vary the effects of the adjustment by playing with the Opacity slider and blending modes; you can move the layer up or down in the Layers palette to affect different layers; and you can merge the layer with an underlying layer to permanently fuse the color correction or fill to the image. (You can't, however, merge an adjustment or fill layer with another adjustment or fill layer.)

Clipping group icon   Fill layer

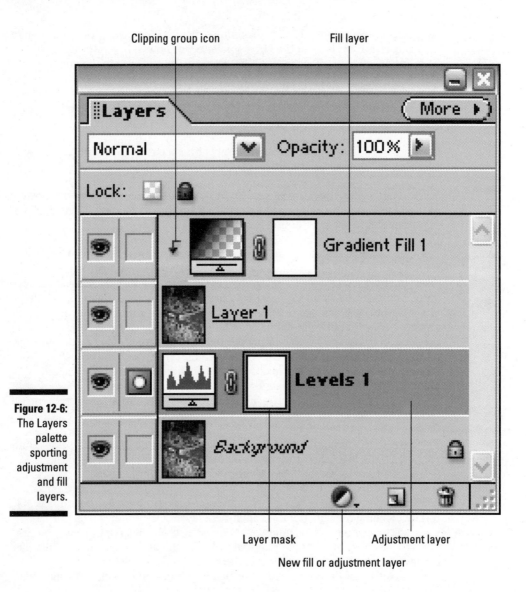

Figure 12-6:
The Layers
palette
sporting
adjustment
and fill
layers.

Layer mask   Adjustment layer

New fill or adjustment layer

If you ever want to change the settings for an adjustment or fill layer, just double-click the adjustment or fill layer icon in the Layers palette. You can also select the adjustment or fill layer and choose Layer➪Layer Content Options. Elements redisplays the appropriate dialog box, where you can modify the settings. To delete the adjustment or fill layer, drag it to the Trash icon in the Layers palette.

To change the type of your adjustment or fill layer, choose Layer➪Change Layer Content and select the new type of adjustment or fill you want.

You can flip back and forth between a view of your corrected image and your uncorrected image by clicking the Eyeball icon next to the adjustment layer name in the Layers palette. When the eyeball is present, the layer is visible, showing you the color-corrected image. When the eyeball is hidden, so is the layer, giving you a "before" view of your image. You can do the same with fill layers.

Before moving on to dissect the Levels command, let's have a brief explanation of the Group with Previous Layer option we told you to skip earlier. If you check this box in the New Layer dialog box, the adjustment or fill layer will affect only the pixels of the immediately underlying layer. Any layers below that will be unaffected. This technique is referred to in Elements' higher circles as a *clipping group*. A clipping group is where you combine multiple layers into a group in which the lowest layer in the group masks the others. You can also create clipping groups with regular layers. In addition to selecting this option in the New Layer dialog box, you can also create a clipping group by selecting the adjustment or fill layer in the Layers palette and choosing Layer⇨Group with Previous or Ctrl+G (⌘+G on a Mac). Or simply press the Alt key (Option key on a Mac) and click the horizontal line between the two layers. Notice that when you hold down the Alt or Option key, your cursor icon changes to an arrow with two circles. After you click, a small down-pointing arrow appears on the top layer (refer to Figure 12-6). To remove the clipping group, simply Alt-click (Option-click on Mac) again or choose Layer⇨Ungroup or Ctrl+Shift+G (⌘+Shift+G on a Mac).

Adjustment layers are so powerful and flexible, we'll crawl out on a limb and say you should absolutely *never* use the Levels and Hue/Saturation commands, but rather apply these commands as adjustment layers. True, most file formats don't support adjustment layers, but if you want to end up with a flat JPEG of an image, it's still a good idea to keep a layered PSD file around as a backup. Why make a permanent change to your original image when you may want to tweak it again later?

Adjustment layers, in a word, rule.

Color-Correcting Correctly

As we mentioned at the beginning of this chapter, Levels and Color Variations are pretty much the only commands you need when color correcting images. Sure, give the others a try. But sooner or later, you'll run into a problem image that just won't respond to the "one shot wonder" commands. That's where Levels and Color Variations come in. Although Color Variations is fairly intuitive, Levels is somewhat intimidating. Don't worry — that's why we're here.

Leveling the Contrast Field

Not one image in this book — except the gloomy-looking Figure 12-1 — has escaped a thorough going-over with the Levels command. This command is one of the most essential functions inside Elements. In fact, if an image displays any of the following symptoms, you can correct it with Levels:

- ✔ The image is murky, without strong lights and darks, like the one in Figure 12-1.
- ✔ The image has a color cast, like the one in Color Plate 12.
- ✔ The image is too light.
- ✔ The image is too dark.
- ✔ The image is gaining weight, losing hair, and developing bags under its eyes.

Whoops, that last item sneaked in by mistake. If an image gains weight, loses hair, and develops baggy eyes, you have to send it on a three-week cruise in the Caribbean. And tell it to stop writing computer books.

Making friends with the Levels dialog box

To apply the Levels command, you can create a new adjustment layer, as recommended in the preceding section, or choose Enhance➪Adjust Brightness/Contrast➪Levels, or press Ctrl+L (⌘+L on a Mac). If you choose the command from the Enhance menu or press the keyboard shortcut, the color correction is applied directly to the image and affects only the active layer.

Either way, the dialog box shown in Figure 12-7 appears. Luckily, you usually don't need to address all the options that inhabit this dialog box. So, before you break into a cold sweat or shriek at the top of your lungs (or do whatever it is you do when you see terrifying sights like Figure 12-7), let's try to distinguish the important options in this dialog box from the stuff you won't use very often:

- ✔ The options in the Channel drop-down menu let you adjust one color channel in a full-color image independently of the other channels. (This is proof-positive that those red, green, and blue color channels we told you about in Chapter 5 are really there.) These options are helpful if you know what you're doing, but they're generally not that important. We did take full advantage of the three color channels to correct the image in Color Plate 12 with Levels, but there are other, easier ways of removing color casts, like with Color Variations.

✔ The three Input Levels option boxes control the settings of the darkest, medium, and lightest pixels in your image, in that order. These options are important, which is why we cover them thoroughly in the next section.

✔ That black birthmark in the middle of the dialog box is called a *histogram*. It shows you how the colors in your image are currently distributed. It also rates the Seal of Importance.

✔ The slider bar directly beneath the histogram provides three triangles, one each for the darkest, medium, and lightest pixels in your image. These triangles are the most important options of all.

✔ The Output Levels option boxes and the accompanying slider bar let you make the darkest colors lighter and the lightest colors darker, which is usually the exact opposite of what you want to do. Mark these options Not Particularly Important on your screen with a grease pencil. (Just kidding.)

✔ The OK and Cancel buttons are as important as always. One applies your changes, the other doesn't. No news here.

✔ Press the Alt key (Option key on a Mac) to change the Cancel button to a Reset button. Click the button while pressing Alt or Option to reset things to the way they were when you entered the dialog box. Very helpful.

✔ Clicking the Auto button is exactly like applying Auto Levels. The only time you might want to use this button is if you should want to apply the Auto Levels command on an adjustment layer.

✔ The three eyedropper icons let you click colors in your image to make them black, medium gray, or white. Steer clear of these icons except to stamp them Not Important, Ditto, and Doubly So.

✔ The Preview check box lets you view the effect of your edits inside the image window. It's very important that you turn this option on.

Figure 12-8 shows the Levels dialog box as it appears after you strip it down to its most important components. (Don't try this at home.) As you can see, the Input Levels options — which include the three option boxes, the histogram, and the slider bar — represent the core of the Levels command. The other options are just icing on the cake.

Histogram

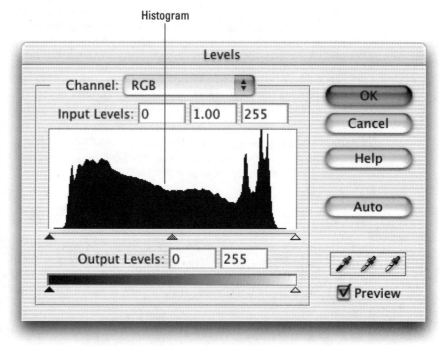

Figure 12-7:
The compli-
cated-
looking
Levels
dialog box
contains
many
options that
you don't
need to
worry about.

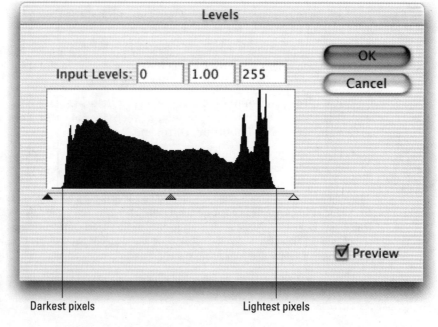

Figure 12-8:
When you
strip the
Levels
dialog box
of its
excessive
regalia, it
becomes
far less
daunting.

Darkest pixels   Lightest pixels

You say you want to be able to admire the quiet beauty of a histogram, but not have any distracting controls in sight that could actually make your image look better? You're in luck! The Histogram command (choose Image⇨Histogram) gives you a view of the histogram for your image, along with a whole bunch of theoretically helpful statistics. But you can't actually *do* anything with this information — not until you close the Histogram, at least. (And this command is so powerless, it doesn't even rate a Cancel button.) Ah well, at least the Histogram command tells you how many pixels you have in your image, in case you were wondering: Although this count may be inaccurate, so perhaps you should count them for yourself. (Oh my, we hope you know that we're kidding.)

Brightness and contrast as they should be

The histogram from the Levels command seen in Figure 12-8 is a graph of the color in the uncorrected image in Figure 12-9. The graph is organized from darkest colors on the left to lightest colors on the right. The peaks and valleys in the histogram show the color distribution. If the darkest colors were black, the histogram would start on the far-left edge of the slider bar. If the lightest colors were white, it would continue to the far-right edge. But as it is, the left and right edges taper off into flatlands. This means that the darkest and lightest pixels in the image are not as dark or light as they could be.

Figure 12-9: This placid scene is simply awaiting an application of Levels.

If some of that information went a little over your head, not to worry. Some folks like graphs, but they make other folks think that they're in a board meeting and start to nod off. Either way, remember that the histogram is provided for your reference only. All that matters is how you adjust the slider triangles underneath the histogram:

✔ To make the darkest pixels black, drag the left slider triangle to the right so that it rests directly under the beginning of the first hill in the histogram. Figure 12-10 shows the dragged triangle and its effect on the image.

✔ To make the lightest pixels white, drag the right-hand triangle to the left so that it lines up directly under the end of the last hill in the histogram, as in Figure 12-11.

✔ The most important triangle is the middle one. Called the *gamma point,* this triangle lets you change the brightness of the medium colors in your image. Drag to the right to make the medium colors darker. But more likely, you want to drag to the left to make the medium colors lighter, as demonstrated in Figure 12-12.

Figure 12-10:
Dragging
the first
triangle
affects the
darkest
pixels in the
image.

Input Levels: 18 | 1.00 | 233

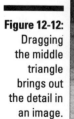

Figure 12-11:
The image
lightens up
when the
white
triangle is
dragged to
the left.

Input Levels: 18 | 1.31 | 233

Figure 12-12:
Dragging
the middle
triangle
brings out
the detail in
an image.

The values in the three option boxes above the histogram update as you drag the slider triangles. The left and right values are measured in color levels. Just like the RGB values in the Color Picker — where you define colors (see Chapter 5) — 0 is black and 255 is white. So if the left value is 18, as it is in Figures 12-10 through 12-12, any pixel that is colored with a level of 18 or darker becomes black. And if that explanation already has your mind reeling, trying to understand how the gamma value — the middle one — works would no doubt make your head explode. The point is, a gamma value of more than 1 lightens the medium colors; a value less than 1 darkens them.

Bear in mind that you can tweak these values for each color channel individually using the Channel menu, just as we did in Color Plate 12. But if you want to see the effect of the Levels command when applied to the combined RGB channels, you need look no further than Color Plate 15. We followed up Levels with the Color Cast command, which in this case worked very well in eliminating the image's color cast.

Take the time to master Levels. It's bound to be good for any image.

If you notice a loss of color in your image after you apply the Levels command, don't worry. You can get that color back by using the Color Variations command, discussed next.

Variations on a Color Scheme

One negative effect of manipulating the brightness levels in an image is that it can weaken some of the colors, particularly if you lighten the medium colors by dragging the gamma point in the Levels dialog box to the left. To bring the colors back to their original intensity, choose Enhance➪Adjust Color➪Color Variations or click the handy Color Variations button in the Shortcuts bar.

Although Elements has a dedicated Color Cast command, the Color Variations command is generally more reliable in curing color casts, in which one color is particularly prominent in the image. A photograph shot outdoors, for example, may be overly blue; one shot in an X-rated motel room may be a shade heavy in the reds. Whatever color predominates your image, the Color Variations command can tone it down with elegance and ease. But first we'll examine how Color Variations can boost the colors in a Levels-corrected image.

Not only has the Variations command from the first version of Elements been rechristened as "Color Variations," but the dialog box contains a bunch of noticeable improvements as well. Undo, Redo, and Reset Image buttons have been added, and the entire box has been reorganized, making it much easier to use.

Turning plain old color into Technicolor

To bolster the intensity of colors in your image — for what it's worth, color intensity is called *saturation* in image-editing vernacular — follow these pleasant steps:

1. **Choose Enhance➪Adjust Color➪Color Variations.**

   The enormous Color Variations dialog box erupts onto your screen, filled with a bunch of small previews of your image.

2. **Select the Saturation radio button in the lower-left corner of the dialog box.**

   Most of the small preview images disappear. Only four remain, as shown in Figure 12-13. The two previews at the bottom of the dialog box represent different color intensities. The top two larger previews show the image as it appeared before you chose the Color Variations command and how it looks now, subject to the changes in the Color Variations dialog box.

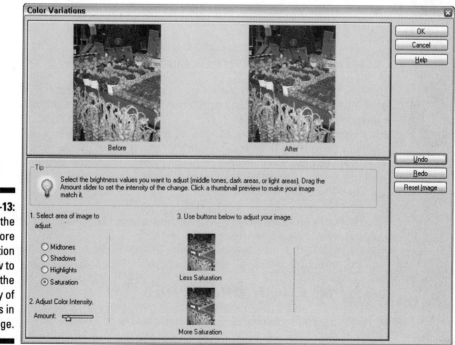

Figure 12-13: Click the More Saturation preview to boost the intensity of the colors in an image.

3. **Drag the slider in the lower-left corner to the left.**

   This slider controls the extent of the changes made inside the Color Variations dialog box. If you drag the triangle to the right, the changes become more drastic; drag it to the left, and they become more gradual. The setting is reflected inside the previews at the bottom of the dialog box. The changes become more subtle as you drag to the left, and therefore the two previews at the bottom begin to resemble each other more and more.

   Because color intensity is a very sensitive function inside Elements, it's best to set the slider pretty far over to the left so that you can make gentle, incremental changes.

4. **To increase color intensity, click the preview labeled More Saturation.**

   Clicking once increases the intensity by a gradual amount, owing to the slider bar setting. To add more intensity, click again. Each time you click, the After preview at the top of the dialog box updates to reflect your latest change.

   If at any time you want to reset the After preview to the original image, click the Reset Image button or just click the Before preview.

5. **When you're satisfied with the increased color intensity, press Enter (Return on a Mac).**

   Elements applies your settings to the original image, just as they were shown in the After preview. No surprises with this dialog box.

Changes you make via the Color Variations dialog box affect only the active layer. Unfortunately, you can't apply the Color Variations command using an adjustment layer as you can the Levels and Hue/Saturation commands. For this reason, Hue/Saturation is arguably a better choice for increasing depleted saturation in an image; you can use it on an adjustment layer, so that your changes won't be permanent. Then again, some people greatly prefer Color Variations' preview-clicking approach. Either way, Elements can satisfy.

Color Plate 16 gives you some idea of the various changes that Color Variations can make to your image.

Casting away bad colors

To remove a color cast using Color Variations, here's what you do:

1. **Choose Enhance⇨Adjust Color⇨Color Variations.**

   The Color Variations dialog box takes over your screen.

2. **Select the Midtones radio button in the lower-left corner of the dialog box.**

   This option lets you edit the medium colors in your image. (You can likewise edit the dark or light colors by selecting Shadows or Highlights, but it's best to start with the Midtones, because that's usually the principal source of the problem.)

   After you select Midtones, the bottom portion of the dialog box fills with eight previews, as shown in Figure 12-14. The six previews on the left let you shift the colors in the image toward or away from the three color channels in Elements — red, green, or blue. The two previews on the right let you lighten and darken the image. But because they're less capable than the gamma point control in the Levels dialog box, you can feel free to ignore them.

   If you're an Elements 1.0 user, you may be wondering what happened to the More Cyan, More Magenta, and More Yellow options. They're still there in Elements 2.0; they've just been renamed. Clicking Decrease Red in 2.0 is the same thing as clicking More Cyan in 1.0; likewise with Decrease Green/More Magenta and Decrease Blue/More Yellow.

3. **Drag the slider in the lower-left corner to the left.**

   As with the saturation earlier, it's best to adjust the colors in small increments.

4. **Click one of the Increase or Decrease previews to shift the colors in the image toward or away from a particular color.**

   Again, Color Plate 16 can give you a good idea of how clicking the previews can affect your image.

5. **If you go too far toward one color, don't panic.**

   You can do one of several things if you think your image is going to pot. If that last click of Increase Red really messed things up, you can click Decrease Red or simply click the Undo button. If you then decide things weren't so bad after all, click Increase Red again or click the Redo button. If you've made a total mess of your image, click the Before preview or click the Reset Image button.

Not only does Elements present you with variations on the colors in your image, it also gives you variations on ways to fix your screw-ups. You've gotta love an application like that.

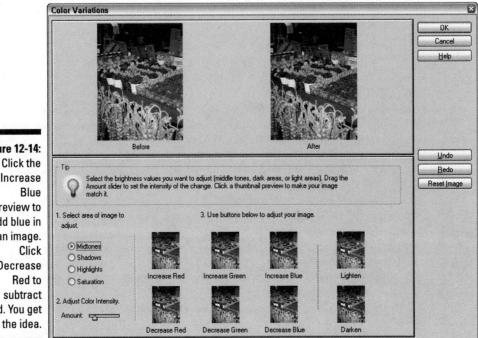

Figure 12-14:
Click the
Increase
Blue
preview to
add blue in
an image.
Click
Decrease
Red to
subtract
red. You get
the idea.

Part IV
The Inspiration/ Perspiration Equation

The 5th Wave   By Rich Tennant

"I THINK YOU'VE MADE A MISTAKE. WE DO PHOTO RETOUCHING, NOT FAMILY PORTRAI... OOOH, WAIT A MINUTE-I THINK I GET IT!"

In this part . . .

Thomas Alva Edison supposedly once said "Genius is 1 percent inspiration and 99 percent perspiration." (Unfortunately there's no record of him actually saying this, as he hadn't invented the phonograph at the time.) While this quote brings to mind visions of sweat dripping down Mr. Edison's neck and into open lightbulb sockets, he does have a point. A brilliant idea is nothing without the hours of back-breaking hard labor necessary to bring it to fruition.

Then again, Edison never used Photoshop Elements. (Recently unearthed evidence shows he never got beyond MacPaint 1.0.) With Elements, it's so easy to get the flashes of genius out of your head and on to the screen that it completely throws Edison's inspiration/perspiration equation out of whack. We're talking 90/10 . . . maybe 85/15 at the *most*. The five chapters in this part of the book deal with the ways Elements lets you express yourself, packing your most inspired, creative, and imaginative thoughts into your images. From painting and drawing to applying drop shadows and bevels, from adding text to stretching faces like Silly Putty — it's all here. We'll also look at some automated features that Elements offers; these amazing commands push the inspiration/perspiration equation to about 99/1, in actuality.

But first, you are going to have to perspire just a teeny bit while we help you learn to master these powerful tools. Feel free to rip the pages from this book one by one as you finish reading them and mop your fevered brow with them. We'll be proud to know that we've provided you with such absorbing literature.

Chapter 13

The Stylish Retouch

Come on, admit it. You're so ready for this chapter, you can taste it. Already, as you were working through the last part of this book, finding out ways to make your images look more like reality, mischievous little ideas began to pop into your head. Maybe you were using the Clone Stamp tool on a scanned image to get rid of some dust specks in the sky, and the thought snuck into your brain: "Gee, you know, this Clone Stamp tool is doing such a good job of cloning bits of sky and obscuring these dust flecks, that I guess — in theory — I could keep using this tool . . . to completely clone away my brother's head!"

Or maybe you were using the Replace Color command to gently tweak the color of your Uncle Waldo's cardigan sweater, and the thought occurred to you: "Well, gee whiz, this Replace Color command is doing such a nice job of changing the color of this sweater, that I guess — in theory — I could instead select Uncle Waldo's skin . . . and turn his head a virulent shade of screaming purple!"

Now if anything like these thoughts occurred to you, don't feel bad. It's perfectly normal to come to the realization that Photoshop Elements' carefully crafted, painstakingly perfected image-correction tools could not only be used, but also abused. Don't feel bad for having those thoughts. (They were just *thoughts*, right?)

In truth, Elements has a host of other tools designed to let you inject your images with your own personal sense of style — no matter how funky, bizarre, or downright perverse that sense of style may be. Some of these tools, such as the layer styles, you'll probably want to use every day. Some of them, such as blending modes, are very useful for special effects. And then there are some — such as the Liquify command — that are more-or-less digital torture devices, letting you vent your aggressions against your foes by pushing around a few pixels.

Add these tools to your Elements arsenal and you'll not only be able to make your images look more real than life, you'll also be able to infuse that life with your personal sense of style.

Using Layer Styles to Shine and Shadow

If you want to create a dimensional-looking Web button or imbue your text with a true sense of depth, this is the place to be. Elements makes the application of effects such as drop shadows, glows, and bevels mere child's play with the Layer Styles palette. Layer styles can be applied to regular layers and type layers (see Chapter 16), but not to the Background layer. Layer Styles are linked to the contents of a layer. If you edit the contents, the styles are updated automatically, which makes using layer styles incredibly flexible.

Here is a step-by-step guide to applying a layer style:

1. **Start with an object on an active layer.**

   With layer styles in the bevel, shadow, and glow categories, you'll see the best results if there's transparency around the edges of the object. Text on a text layer is a great place to start.

2. **Open the Layer Styles palette.**

   By default, it's hiding in the palette well.

3. **Choose a layer styles category from the drop-down menu at the top of the palette.**

   In addition to the old categories (Bevels, Drop Shadows, Inner Glows, Inner Shadows, Outer Glows, Visibility, Complex, and Glass Buttons), Elements 2.0 gives you six new categories: Image Effects, Patterns, Photographic Effects, Wow Chrome, Wow Neon, and Wow Plastic.

4. **Click a layer style within your chosen category.**

   You should see the style immediately applied to your object.

We describe the various types of effects and their settings in the following list, yet a picture is worth a thousand words. See Figure 13-1 and Color Plate 17 for some examples.

- **Bevels:** Create a chiseled 3D effect around the edge of the object.

- **Drop Shadows:** Apply a shadow behind the object, giving the illusion that your layer is floating above the layers beneath it. The Outline, Fill/Outline, and Neon Drop Shadows create strange, unrealistic effects.

- **Inner Glows:** Cast a glow from the edges of the object to within the object.

- **Inner Shadows:** Apply a shadow on the object itself. This creates the effect that the object has been "cut out" from the layer behind it. Try it, and you'll see what we mean.

- **Outer Glows:** Create a glow or halo effect around the object.

- **Visibility:** Make the object itself translucent or invisible, while keeping the layer style visible.

- **Complex:** Just as complex as it sounds, these are premade styles with intricate combinations of layer styles, textures, and colors. Complex layer styles can even be applied one on top of the other for yet more complexity.

- **Glass Buttons:** As simple as it sounds, these are premade styles that can turn your objects into a multitude of different-colored glass buttons.

- **Image Effects:** These layer styles combine the current contents of your object with various effects, such as snow and fog. Probably more useful on photographs than with text or objects drawn with the Shape tools.

- **Patterns:** These fill your object with various interesting textures, such as asphalt, marble, and dry mud.

- **Photographic Effects:** Obviously intended for use on photographs, these are primarily helpful for quickly giving your image a tint, such as sepia.

- **Wow Chrome:** These make your object seem to be made out of shiny chrome.

- **Wow Neon:** If you want a neon glow around the edges of your object, look no further.

- **Wow Plastic:** Similar to Glass Buttons, but often with a drop shadow and/or outer glow added.

In addition to just clicking the style in the Layer Styles palette to apply it to the active layer, there are other ways of applying styles:

- Drag and drop the style from the Layer Styles palette onto the desired layer in the Layers palette.

- Drag and drop the style from the Layer Styles palette onto the desired object within the image window.

Here are some other handy things to know about layer styles:

- To remove all layer styles from a layer, click the Clear Style button in the upper-right corner of the Layer Styles palette, just beneath the More menu. This is very easy to miss. You can also choose Layer⇨Layer Style⇨Clear Layer Style.

Drop Shadow

Inner Shadow

Outer Glow

Inner Glow

Figure 13-1:
The Layer
Styles
palette
makes it
easy to
apply
shadows,
glows, and
other
effects to
images and
type.

- ✔ You can switch between Thumbnail view and List view by clicking the buttons at the bottom of the Layer Styles palette, or by choosing the desired view from the Layer Styles palette's More menu.

- ✔ You can copy and paste layer styles from one layer to another by choosing commands from the Layer⇨Layer Style submenu.

- ✔ You can clear or hide the layer styles for a layer by choosing commands from the Layer⇨Layer Style submenu. If you hide the layer styles for a layer, choose Layer⇨Layer Style⇨Show All Effects to reveal the layer styles again.

- ✔ You can globally scale up or down the layer styles applied to a layer by choosing Layer⇨Layer Style⇨Scale Effects. This can be very helpful if you change the size of the object the layer styles are applied to.

For instance, let's say you have a circular object on a layer with several layer styles applied to it. You decide the circle is too large, so you choose Image⇨Resize⇨Scale, and drag a corner handle of the bounding box to scale down the circle. (You can tell precisely how much you're scaling down the circle by keeping an eye on the Options bar.) You decide that your circle looks good at 50% of its former size, so you hit the Enter key (Return key on a Mac). While your layer style is, of course, still applied to the circle, the style itself hasn't been scaled down. A bevel that looks great on a large circle might be too big for a small one. No problem — just choose Layer⇨Layer Style⇨Scale Effects, enter 50% in the option box, and click OK. The layer style will be scaled down in proportion to the resized object.

It's also possible to edit some layer styles with much greater control after they've been applied, as explained in the next section.

So the High Drop Shadow is too high, and the Low Drop Shadow isn't high enough? Don't despair: Tweak instead! Choose Layer⇨Layer Style⇨Style Settings — or easier still, just double-click the little *f* in a circle on the layer in the Layers palette — to open the Style Settings dialog box, pictured in the rosy blush of its eternal youth in Figure 13-2.

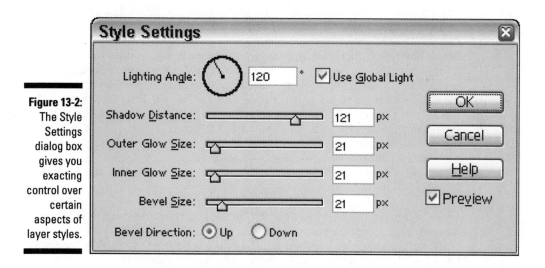

Figure 13-2:
The Style Settings dialog box gives you exacting control over certain aspects of layer styles.

Here's the lowdown on the various controls contained therein:

- ✔ **Lighting Angle:** Determines the direction of the light source for bevels and shadows. Type in a value in degrees — or just drag the little circular dial to set the desired angle.

- ✔ **Use Global Light:** Checking this option keeps the Lighting Angle consistent for all layers in the same image. And this is usually a very good thing, as it makes the various objects in an image seem to exist together in the same "room," so to speak. If this option is checked for all the layers in an image, then making a Lighting Angle adjustment for one layer affects all the layers in the image.

- ✓ **Shadow Distance:** This sets the distance of the drop shadow from the object, and therefore creates the illusion of the object being closer or farther away from the layers beneath it. You can adjust this by dragging the slider, or by dragging the shadow itself within the image window. Notice that dragging the shadow can also affect the Lighting Angle for every layer that has Use Global Light checked.

- ✓ **Outer Glow Size:** Affects the size of the outer glow.

- ✓ **Inner Glow Size:** Affects the size of the inner glow.

- ✓ **Bevel Size:** Affects the size of the bevel. (Boy, writing these books is easy!)

- ✓ **Bevel Direction:** Affects the direction of the . . . oh, okay, perhaps a bit more explanation is in order here. Bevel Direction can be used to make concave surfaces look convex, and vice versa. If the bevel is making your object look as though it's protruding from the image, switching the Bevel Direction to Down will make it look as if it's recessed into the image.

A layer style is *live,* meaning that it updates itself as the contents of the layer change. For instance, the left image in Figure 13-3 shows a circle drawn with the Elliptical Marquee tool and filled, and then finished off with a Simple Sharp Inner Bevel layer style. If you then apply the Ripple filter to the circle, as shown in the middle image of Figure 13-3, the Ripple filter is theoretically applied *before* the layer style, meaning that the bevel applies itself to the rippled edges of the circle. If this isn't what you want — if, instead of a rippled circle with a bevel, you want a beveled circle that's been rippled — you have to simplify the layer first before you apply the filter. Choose Layer⇨Simplify Layer. This will cause Elements to *rasterize,* or render the layer style into just plain pixels. The layer style will look exactly the same, but it will lose its "live," editable status. Then you can apply the filter at will. The right image of Figure 13-3 shows the result.

Layer styles also work splendidly well in conjunction with the Shape tools — so well, in fact, that they can be applied directly from the Shape tools' Options bar. This enables you to quickly create dimensional-looking geometric objects (such as buttons for Web pages), which can be resized at will without any loss in quality. If you resize an object drawn with a Shape tool, it should come as no surprise to you that the layer style changes to accommodate the shape. For more on the Shape tools, see Chapter 14.

Figure 13-3:
A circle with
a layer
style applied
(left); the
same circle
with the
Ripple filter
applied
(middle); the
first circle
after first
being
simplified,
then with
the Ripple
filter applied
(right).

A Few Other Image Adjustments

There is a handful of commands in the Image⇨Adjustments submenu that can do strange things to your image. In truth, you probably won't find them all that useful, but we've gotta talk about them somewhere. So here goes:

- **Equalize:** The Equalize command (Image⇨Adjustments⇨Equalize) takes the brightest and darkest pixels from among the three color channels in the image and maps them to white and black. It then tries to evenly distribute the rest of the pixels between them in terms of brightness. This produces a higher-contrast image but isn't generally as effective as even Auto Levels.

- **Gradient Map:** The Gradient Map command (Image⇨Adjustments⇨ Gradient Map) enables you to map any gradient to the grayscale values in your image. You can produce some interesting special effects with this command.

- **Invert:** The Invert command (Image⇨Adjustments⇨Invert) changes the color of every pixel to its opposite. White becomes black, blue becomes yellow, and so on. The end result resembles a photographic negative, making Invert useful for special effects but not much else.

- **Posterize:** The Posterize command (Image⇨Adjustments⇨Posterize) limits each color channel to a specified number of brightness levels, redrawing your image with fields of solid color. Again, a nice effect, but not useful on a day-to-day basis.

✔ **Threshold:** The Threshold command (Image⇨Adjustments⇨Threshold) turns every pixel in your image either white or black, based on its brightness value according to a threshold you set. If you need it, there it is.

Tending Your Many Splendid Blends

A layer with a layer style applied is a layer proud of its individuality. "Look at me!" it fairly shouts. "I'm not like you other guys milling around in the Layers palette. I've got style, baby! Get a load of that drop shadow. And check out this bevel — am I cut, or what?"

But some layers pride themselves on working as a team, blending together to create an interesting cumulative effect. That's where blending modes can help. At its core, a blending mode is a mathematical formula for combining the pixels in two different layers. It's possible to achieve some bizarre and beautiful effects with modes, but they can be hard to predict. Before we dive into blending modes, let's look at a method of blending layers together that's the oldest trick in the book: changing opacity.

Fooling with layer opacity

One neat trick to try with a layer is to make it partially translucent by using the Opacity slider in the Layers palette. In Figure 13-4, for example, the fish was made partially translucent by setting the Opacity to 70%. In the second example, he was made even more ghostly by lowering the Opacity to 30%. To access the slider bar, click the right-pointing arrow to the right of the Opacity numeric setting.

To change the Opacity setting for a layer from the keyboard, make sure that any tool that doesn't have its own Opacity option in the Options bar is selected and press a number key. Press 9 for 90%, 8 for 80%, and so on, down to 1 for 10%. To return to 100%, press 0. You can also enter more specific Opacity values — such as 72 — by typing the digits quickly.

Keep in mind that the Opacity setting can't be changed for the Background layer because nothing lies behind it. You'd be looking through the Background into the empty void of digital space, a truly scary prospect. The same is true for the blending modes discussed in the next section.

Playing around with blending modes

Many of the options that appear in the blending mode drop-down menu in the upper-left corner of the Layers palette are the same ones we've seen in the Mode menu of Options bar for some of the editing tools (see Chapter 11). You have Darken, Lighten, Hue, and the rest of the gang. Many tools have their own specific name for modes — the Brush uses painting modes, the Smudge tool uses effect modes, the Eraser uses erasing modes — but they all do pretty much the same thing. In the Layers palette, they're referred to as blending modes, and that's as good a name as any. You can also call them overlay modes or blend modes; some high-falutin' folks call them *calculations*. But just plain modes is fine for us regular faluters.

Opacity: 70%   Opacity: 30%

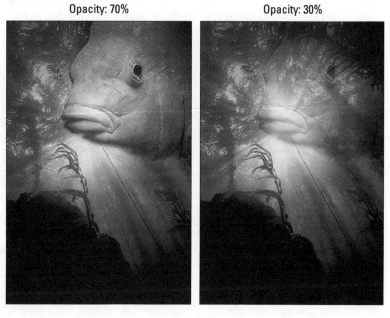

Figure 13-4: Hey, kids, it's Phantom Phish, star of Chapter 9, making a cameo appearance here to show off his translucent super-powers.

Here's a brief description of how the most important ones work:

- **Multiply and Screen:** Multiply burns the layer into the layers behind it, darkening all colors where they mix. Screen does just the opposite, lightening the colors where they mix.

- **Difference:** The Difference mode has no real-world analogy. It creates a photo negative — or inversion — of the blended layers according to their colors. Where one of the layers is black, no inversion takes place. Where the layers are light, you find lots of inversion.

- **Overlay, Soft Light, and Hard Light:** These are similar options; that's why they're grouped together in the blending mode menu. Overlay multiplies the dark colors and screens the light ones. Soft Light produces a more subtle effect. Hard Light is more dramatic than Soft Light or Overlay.

✔ **Color and Luminosity:** As with Multiply and Screen, the Color and Luminosity modes produce exactly opposite effects from each other. The Color mode blends the color of the layer with the detail from the underlying layers. Luminosity keeps the detail from the layer and mixes it with the colors of the underlying layers.

✔ **Color Dodge, Color Burn, and Exclusion:** For some other interesting effects, experiment with the Color Dodge, Color Burn, and Exclusion modes. These are subtly different from the Screen, Multiply, and Difference modes, respectively. Suppose that you have two layers, a Background layer and Layer 1. Color Dodge lightens the pixels in the Background layer and infuses them with colors from Layer 1. Color Burn darkens the pixels and infuses them with color. Exclusion turns all black pixels white, all white pixels black, and all medium colors gray.

✔ **Darken:** Similar to Multiply, this is another mode that can be useful. Say that you want to composite something like a scanned handwritten letter or sheet of music over an image. Obviously, you want only the handwriting or music notes to appear, and not the white paper, which would obscure the underlying pixels. By choosing Darken, only the dark pixels appear; the light area appears transparent. Lighten does just the opposite — displays the light pixels and makes the dark pixels transparent.

✔ **Dissolve, Hue, and Saturation:** These other blending modes range from boring to duller than dull, and they rarely come in handy.

Just so you know, you can mix a translucent Opacity setting with a blending mode, but you can't select more than one blending mode at a time. It would be fun to combine Luminosity with Multiply, for example — you know, to apply detail that only darkens — but you just can't do it. Oh well.

For a look at some of what you can do with blending modes, check out Color Plate 19. Although this plate actually illustrates painting modes, discussed in the next chapter, the effects achieved are the same as with blending modes.

Those Phunky Philters

So far in this book we've looked at filters that can make your images look better, from removing dust and scratches to sharpening and even blurring. But this doesn't even begin to scratch the surface where Elements' filters are concerned. In fact, you'll probably find that there are more filters designed to make your images look weirder than there are to make them look "better." But hey, it's all subjective, isn't it? One man's "freaky" is another man's "normal." Here are a few ideas for imbuing images with your own personal wacked-out style.

Creating motion and puzzle pieces

In addition to Blur, Blur More, and Gaussian Blur, the Blur category in the Filters palette contains three additional filters — Motion Blur, Radial Blur, and Smart Blur — all of which are exclusively special-effects filters. The Motion Blur filter makes an image appear to move in a straight line; the Radial Blur filter can be used to move the selection in a circle or to zoom it outward toward the viewer. The Smart Blur option can find the edges in your image and then blur only between the edges — it's as though Elements is carving your image up into puzzle pieces and then blurring each piece. If you apply the effect in heavy doses, the result is an image that resembles a watercolor painting and isn't too far removed from the effect created by the Artistic category's Watercolor filter (shown in Color Plate 18).

Of the three filters, Motion Blur is the filter you're most likely to use. First, the filter lets you see the preview within the image window, making this filter accessible and predictable. Second, it's much easier to use than the other two. Finally, when compared with Radial Blur, it takes a lot less time to use; Radial Blur is one of the slowest Elements filters.

When you choose Motion Blur, Elements displays the Motion Blur dialog box. The filter smears pixels at a specified angle and over a specified distance. Enter the angle and distance into the appropriately named option boxes. You can also drag the spoke inside the circle to change the Angle value, and drag the slider to change the Distance.

For example, Figure 13-5 shows a couple of discrete applications of the Motion Blur filter. (To see this image without the Motion Blur, take a gander at Figure 11-14 in Chapter 11.) To blur the boy, select him, feather the selection, and apply Motion Blur with an Angle value of 90° — straight up and down — and a Distance of 30 pixels. To blur his sister's arm — the one nearest her beaming brother — use an Angle of 45° and a Distance of 6 pixels. As you can see, Distance values over 20 tend to smear the image into oblivion; smaller Distance values create subtle movement effects.

Giving your images that gritty, streetwise look

Located quite logically in the Noise category is the Add Noise filter. Not to be confused with the as-yet-uncompleted Adenoids filter, Add Noise randomizes the colors of selected pixels. The result is a layer of grit that gives smooth images a textured appearance.

Figure 13-5:
Two unlikely
applications
of the
Motion Blur
filter.

Apply Add Noise to display the Add Noise dialog box, shown in Figure 13-6. Here's how to use the options found therein:

- ✔ Drag the Amount slider triangle or enter a value between 0.10% and 400% to control how noisy the image gets. Low values permit a small amount of noise; high values permit more. Anything over 50% pretty much wipes out the original image.

- ✔ Select a Distribution radio button to control the color of noise. The Uniform option colors pixels with random variations on the shades it finds in the original image; the Gaussian option — which should be labeled High Contrast — colors pixels with more exaggerated light and dark shades. Therefore, Gaussian produces a noisier effect, about twice as noisy as Uniform. For example, an Amount value of 12.5% with Gaussian Distribution produces a similar visual effect to an Amount value of 25% with Uniform Distribution.

- ✔ The Monochromatic check box adds grayscale noise to full-color images. When you turn off the option, Elements adds all colors of noise. (The option has no effect on grayscale images except to shift the pixels around a little.)

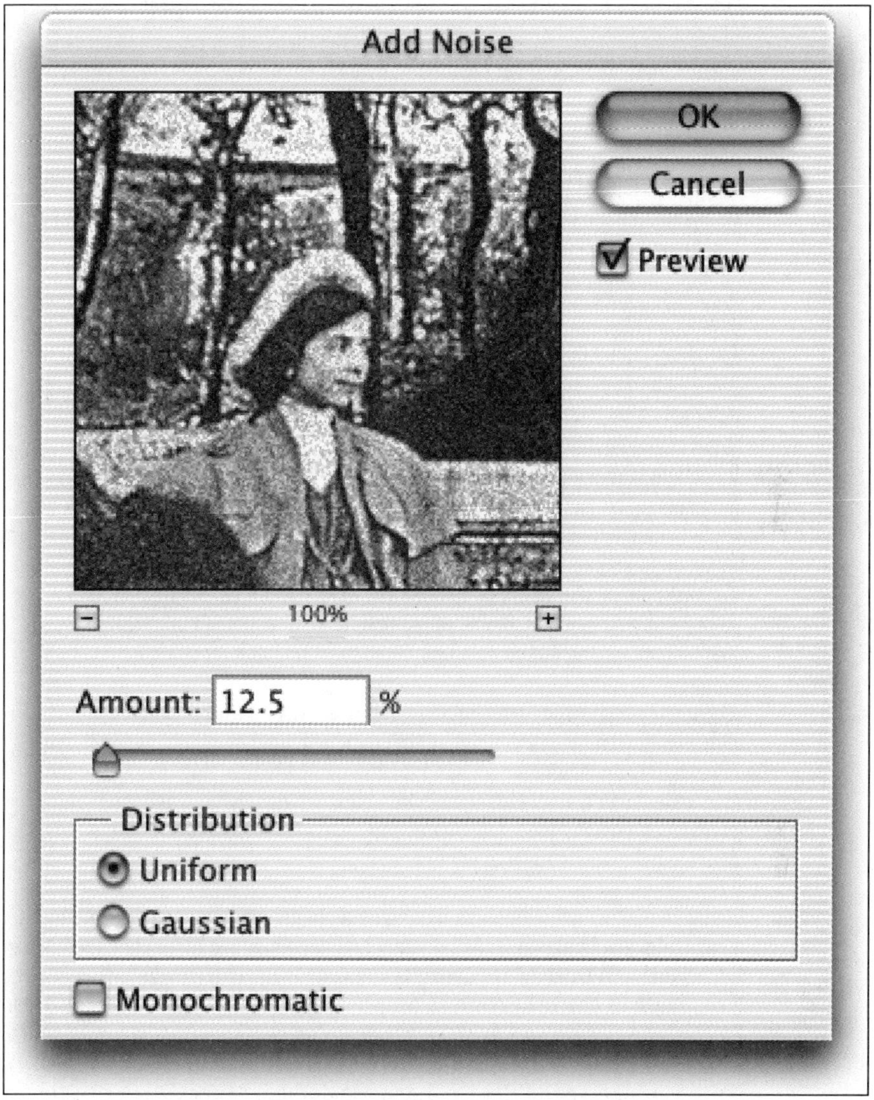

Figure 13-6:
This filter adds "noise" to your image to give it a gritty texture.

Stamping your image in metal

Another intriguing and sometimes useful filter is Emboss, located in the Stylize category. This filter makes your image appear as though it were stamped in metal. The edges in the image appear in relief, and the other areas turn gray.

When you choose Emboss, Elements displays the dialog box shown in Figure 13-7. You enter the angle of the light shining on the metal into the Angle option box. The Height value determines the height of the edges, and the Amount value determines the amount of contrast between blacks and whites.

We're breezing over these options because they aren't the most useful gang in the world. In fact, they can be big time wasters. Here's the important stuff to know:

- ✔ How you set the Angle value doesn't matter. Feel free to drag the spoke on the circle until you get what you want, but don't expect big differences between one angle and another.

- ✔ Set the Height value to 1 or 2. Any value over 2 can impair detail.

- ✔ Okay, the Amount value is useful. Enter 50% for a very subtle effect, 100% for a medium Emboss effect, and 200% for added drama. You can go as high as 500%, but higher values make the contrast between blacks and whites too abrupt for most tastes.

Emboss isn't the kind of filter you go around applying to an entire image. After you've done it once or twice, it gets a little old. Rather, you'll want to apply it to selected areas.

To achieve the thrilling mottled metal effect on the far right of Figure 13-8, first select the dark areas in the mother and son image and apply the Emboss filter with an Angle of 45°, a Height of 2, and an Amount of 200%. Then blur the selection using the Gaussian Blur filter set to a Radius of 2 pixels, as shown in the middle example. Finally, apply Unsharp Mask with an Amount of 500% and a Radius of 2 pixels.

Your reaction may be one of, "Whoa, hold up a minute here. First you blur and then you sharpen? What kind of crazy logic is that?" Well, pretty sound logic, actually. After applying Gaussian Blur, the image turned overly gray, as you can see in the second example in the figure. Luckily, one of the properties of Unsharp Mask is that it increases the amount of contrast between dark and light pixels. So, to bring the blacks and whites back from the dead, the Radius value inside the Unsharp Mask dialog box was set to the exact value used in the Gaussian Blur dialog box — that is, 2.0. Using this value ensured that Unsharp Mask was able to correctly locate the blurred edges and boost their contrast. It's a great technique.

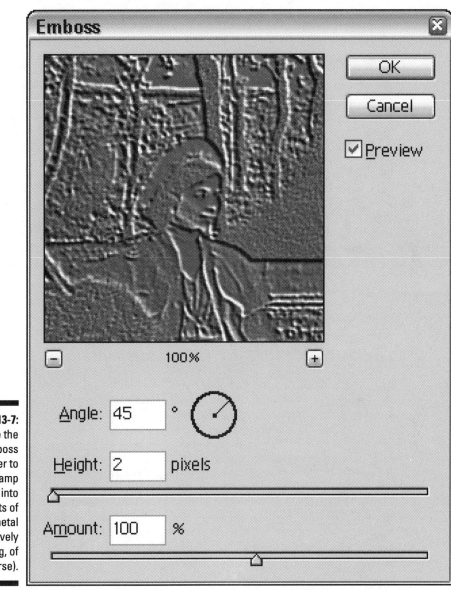

Figure 13-7:
Use the
Emboss
filter to
stamp
images into
sheets of
metal
(figuratively
speaking, of
course).

Figure 13-8:
After selecting the dark portions of the image, the selection was embossed (left), blurred (middle), and sharpened (right), creating a soft relief.

Emboss   Gaussian Blur   Unsharp Mask

Merging colors in flaky images

The next two noteworthy filters — Facet and Median — average the colors of neighboring pixels to create areas of flat color. Both throw away detail, but they're great for smoothing out the imperfections in old, cruddy images such as the one that keeps popping up in this book.

Located in the Pixelate category, Facet is a single-shot filter that roams the image looking for areas of similarly colored pixels and then assigns the entire area a single color. Figure 13-9 shows the elder daughter from way back in Figure 11-9, before she was sharpened. The middle example shows Facet applied. See how the image is now divided into a bunch of globby areas? To make the image clearer, Unsharp Mask was applied to the far-right example, using an Amount value of 250% and a Radius value of 0.5.

Located in the Noise category, Median averages the colors of so many neighboring pixels. To tell Elements the "so many" part, choose Median and enter a value anywhere between 1 and 100 into the Radius option box.

Figure 13-10 shows the result of applying various Radius values to the elder daughter. The top row shows the effects of the Median command; the bottom row shows what happened when Unsharp Mask was applied to each image. Notice how higher values melt away more of the image's detail. A Radius value of 3 makes the image gooey indeed; any higher value is pure silliness.

Figure 13-9:
Starting with the original image (left), the Facet filter was applied (middle) and then the edges were reinforced with Unsharp Mask (right).

Original   Facet   Unsharp Mask

You can use Facet and Median to blur background images, just as we did earlier with Gaussian Blur. Or you can combine them with the Add Noise and Emboss filters to create special effects.

Keep in mind that the real beauty of these more specialized filters is in combining them and applying them to small, selected portions of your image.

Radius: 1   Radius: 2   Radius: 3

Figure 13-10:
The Median filter applied with three different Radius settings (top row) and then sharpened (bottom row).

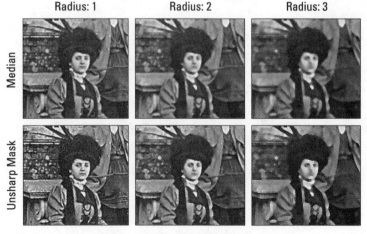

There are a number of filters in the Artistic, Brush Strokes, Sketch, and Texture categories that can make your photographic image seem to be hand painted. Color Plate 18 shows examples of some of the most interesting choices.

Making Taffy with the Liquify Filter

You thought Elements couldn't possibly give you any more ways to take your image out of the realm of reality, right? Well, hold on to your mouse, because the Liquify filter is in the house.

The Liquify filter, among other things, lets you warp, twirl, pucker, and bloat your image. It's enough to make a grown Elements user downright queasy! So take a deep breath and prepare to become "liquified":

1. **Open an image and decide whether you want to distort the whole image or just a portion.**

   You can use an area selected with one of the tools described in Chapter 8. Or you can select a single layer (see Chapter 9). When you select an area, the unselected areas become *frozen* or protected from distortion. In Figure 13-11, the woman's head and a bit of the surrounding background were selected. She looks as if she could use a good warping or two.

2. **Choose Filter➪Distort➪Liquify.**

   You can also find Liquify in the Filters palette. Just open the palette, switch the drop-down menu to "Distort," and you'll see it there. Drag it out of the palette and into the image window, or click the Liquify filter and click the Filters palette's Apply button. A huge dialog box appears, as shown in Figure 13-11. Notice how a pinkish tint covers the nonselected area, similar to the Mask mode of the Selection Brush.

Figure 13-11:
The Liquify dialog box is where you can distort your image into another dimension of reality.

Warp tool
Turbulence tool
Twirl Clockwise tool
Twirl Counter Clockwise tool
Pucker tool
Bloat tool
Shift pixels tool
Reflection tool
Reconstruct tool
Zoom tool
Hand tool

Magnification menu

3. **Select your desired brush size and pressure in the top-right portion of the dialog box.**

   The Brush Size value controls how many pixels are affected at a time and Brush Pressure controls the strength of the stroke. If you're using a graphics tablet, you also can turn on Stylus Pressure to make Elements adjust the Brush Pressure based on the amount of pressure you put on the drawing stylus.

4. **Adjust your view of the image with the new Zoom and Hand tools.**

   And don't forget about the new magnification menu, located in the bottom-left corner of the dialog box.

5. **And now, time for the fun stuff.**

   Use any one of the following tools to wreak havoc on your image. Check out the effects of each in Figure 13-12.

   - **Warp tool:** Pushes the pixels forward under your brush as you drag, creating a stretched effect. This tool gives the most "taffy-like" effect.

   - **Turbulence Tool:** The turbulence tool distorts pixels in random directions as you drag. When you select this tool, you have access to the Turbulent Jitter tool option. Turbulent Jitter specifies the amount of random variation. The minimum value of 1 causes the Turbulence tool to behave much like the Warp tool.

   - **Twirl Clockwise tool:** Rotates the pixels clockwise under your brush as you drag or hold down the mouse.

   - **Twirl Counter Clockwise tool:** Ditto the above, only in a counter-clockwise direction.

   - **Pucker tool:** Moves the pixels toward the center of your brush as you drag or hold down the mouse, giving a kind of pinched look.

   - **Bloat tool:** The opposite of Pucker — moves pixels away from the center, creating a kind of spherical effect.

   - **Shift Pixels tool:** Shifts pixels perpendicular to the direction you move the brush. (In Figure 13-12 the brush was dragged up; ditto for the Reflection tool.)

   - **Reflection tool:** Copies pixels from the area perpendicular to the direction you drag.

   - **Reconstruct tool:** This is a sort of nondistortion tool, letting you restore selected areas of the image back towards the original state by painting over them.

Warp

Turbulence

Twirl Clockwise

Twirl Counter Clockwise

Original

Pucker

Bloat

Shift Pixels

Reflect

Figure 13-12:
The various
effects of
the Liquify
filter can be
downright
terrifying.

6. Click OK and show off your crazed masterpiece.

The best advice there is for understanding the inner workings of the Liquify filter is play, play, play. If you have a few spare moments, open an image and do some freestyle reality altering of your own.

Chapter 14

If a Picture Paints a Thousand Words . . . Then Shut Up and Paint

*N*o, no, the title of this chapter isn't telling *you* to shut up. Heck, we're the ones using up all the words around here. But when it comes to painting, as a novice or casual Photoshop Elements user, you fall into one of two camps: artist or nonartist. Some people are so comfortable with a paint-brush that they feel as though they were born with the device. But a much larger group of Elements users falls into a camp that modern sociologists call "artistically challenged."

Take this quick test to determine where you fall:

✔ After doodling in the phone book, are you so horrified by the results that you rip out the page, pour ketchup on it, and feed it to your dog?

✔ When you're asked by someone to draw a map to your house, do you give them a blank piece of paper and try to assert that you live with a pack of polar bears in a snowstorm in the Arctic?

✔ Do you have recurring dreams in which you suddenly remember that today is the day your final project is due in the art class you've forgotten to attend all year? And as you attempt to quickly paint a lounging model, you notice that the model is fully clothed and you're the one who's naked?

If you answered "Yes" to one of the preceding questions, you can safely assume that you belong to the nonartists camp. If you answered "Yes" to two of the questions, you are so firmly entrenched in the nonartistic tradition that completing a connect-the-dots picture seems like an immense and terrifying project. And if you answered "Yes" to two of the questions and "Oh, wow, I had that exact dream just last night!" to the third, here's one more question: How much does your analyst charge?

Whatever your level of artistic skill, though, a time will probably come when you'll want to rub the Elements painting tools against an image. But don't worry; the Impressionist Brush can make you look like you're an artist even if you aren't, and of course Elements also gives you several tools for erasing your work. For that matter, the shape tools eliminate much of the need for an artistic hand anyway. So take a deep breath, and follow us.

Doodling with the Pencil and Brush

In the last edition of this book, we lamented the fact that Elements 1.0 had only three painting tools: the Pencil, the Paintbrush, and the Airbrush. Adobe has responded to our lamentation by . . . eliminating one of those three tools. Yep, the functionality of the Airbrush has been rolled into the Paintbrush, and that tool is now known as just the Brush tool. Now there's just the Brush and the Pencil. We promise to keep our mouths shut from now on.

Anyway, here's the lowdown on the Pencil and Brush, as shown in Figure 14-1:

  - **Pencil:** The Pencil tool draws hard-edged lines of any thickness.
  - **Brush:** The Brush tool draws soft lines with slightly blurry edges to create more natural transitions.

You can select the painting tools from the keyboard. Press B to select the Brush, and N to select the Pencil.

"But wait," we can practically hear you say. "What about that brushy-looking tool that rooms with the Brush in the Toolbox? Isn't that a painting tool?" Actually, the Impressionist Brush isn't a painting tool for one simple reason: It doesn't apply new color to the canvas. Rather, it swirls the existing colors around in a truly weird fashion. Check it out and see what we mean — or better yet, wait until later in this chapter when we deal with it properly.

When you select the painting tools, Elements, by default, displays a cursor that matches the brush size exactly. If you press the Caps Lock key, however, the cursor changes to a crosshair cursor that can occasionally make it easier to see precisely what you're doing. The crosshair shows you the very center of the brush, regardless of how thick you've made it. (The upcoming section, "Switching the brush size," explains how to change brush sizes.) Press Caps Lock again to return to the brush-sized cursor.

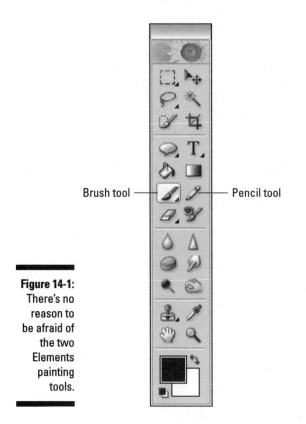

Brush tool ——— | ——— Pencil tool

Figure 14-1:
There's no
reason to
be afraid of
the two
Elements
painting
tools.

If you prefer, you can make your painting tool cursors look like their icons: a little brush or little pencil. To make the cursor reflect the icon, press Ctrl+K (⌘+K on a Mac) to display the Preferences dialog box. Then choose Display & Cursors from the top drop-down menu or press Ctrl+3 (⌘+3 on Mac) to get to the cursor options. The Precise option gives you the Caps Lock crosshair full-time; select Standard from the Painting Cursors radio buttons and press Enter (Return on a Mac). Although they're kind of cute, these so-called "standard" cursors are really the least helpful of all.

The painting tools are small, nonpoisonous, and good with children. So why not take them for a walk and see how you like them? To use the Brush and Pencil tools to create the friendly Mr. Sun image shown in Figure 14-4 (go ahead, flip forward to take a look), just follow these steps:

1. **Click the New icon in the Shortcuts bar, choose File⇨New, or press Ctrl+N (⌘+N on a Mac) to create a new canvas.**

   Elements displays a dialog box that asks what size to make the new canvas. The dialog box offers Width, Height, and Resolution options, as does the Image Size dialog box discussed in Chapter 4.

2. Make the canvas about 400 pixels wide by 400 pixels tall.

That's about 5½ x 5½ inches with a Resolution value of 72 ppi or 4 x 4 inches with a Resolution of 100 ppi. Alternatively, you can select Pixels from the Width and Height drop-down menus, enter **400** into each, and forget about the Resolution value. Also, make sure the Mode drop-down menu is set to RGB Color, and that White is selected in the Contents section.

3. Press Enter (Return on a Mac).

The new empty canvas appears in a new window.

4. Click the Black and White icon at the bottom left of the Toolbox or press the D key to set the foreground color to black.

5. Select the Brush tool.

Click the Brush icon in the Toolbox or press the B key. That's B for "brush"; get it?

6. Draw a circle in the middle of your new canvas.

A rude approximation of a circle is fine. Experts agree that a lumpy circle has more personality.

7. Paint some rays coming off the circle.

Figure 14-2 shows more or less how your image should look so far.

Figure 14-2:
Here comes the sun, drawn exclusively with the Brush tool.

8. Select the Pencil tool.

To access the Pencil from the keyboard, press N. That's N for . . . the third letter of "pencil." Or maybe "nibble"?

9. **Draw a little face inside the sun.**

   Using the Pencil, you get hard-edged lines, as shown in Figure 14-3.

10. **Switch back to the Brush tool.**

    Press B.

Figure 14-3:
A face
drawn with
the Pencil
tool.

11. **Enable the Brush's airbrush capabilities.**

    Click the airbrush icon in the Options bar; it's the one that sort of looks like a knife with a squiggly line behind it.

12. **Change the foreground color to orange.**

    Click the foreground color icon to get the Color Picker. Use the color slider and the color field to get a nice orange, or enter 255 for R, 150 for G, and leave B at 0.

13. **Click and hold — without moving your mouse — inside the sun.**

    Notice that in airbrush mode, the Brush continuously pumps out paint. This is the unique capability of airbrush mode; in normal Brush mode and with the Pencil, the tool only paints when it's in motion.

14. **Paint some shading in the lower-right region of the sun.**

    Figure 14-4 shows a general idea. Airbrush mode is useful for shading images. Of course, the real sun can't possibly have a shadow, but it doesn't have a face either, so we can allow room for some personal expression here.

That's good enough for now. You may want to save this image, because we refer back to it later in this chapter. Then again, if something goes wrong and you don't save the sun, no biggie. You can always re-create it or experiment with a different image.

Remember that at any stage in the previous exercise — or during any other painting mission upon which you may embark — you can always travel backward in time by clicking the Step Backward button in the Shortcuts bar or pressing Ctrl+Z (⌘+Z on a Mac). Everyone makes mistakes, and as we saw in Chapter 7, Elements gives you plenty of ways to correct yours.

Figure 14-4: Use the Brush's airbrush mode to paint a highly unrealistic shadow on the sun.

Performing Special Painting-Tool Tricks

Dragging with a tool inside the image window is obviously the most common way to paint in Elements. But it's not the only way, as the following list makes clear:

✔ To create a straight line, click at one point in the image with the Brush or Pencil, and Shift+click at another. Elements automatically creates a straight line between the two points.

✔ To create a straight-sided polygon, continue to Shift+click at various points in the image. This method is great for creating triangles, five-pointed stars, and all sorts of other geometric shapes.

✔ To create a straight line that's exactly vertical or horizontal, click and hold with the Brush or Pencil, press and hold the Shift key, and then drag with the tool while the Shift key remains down. In other words, press Shift immediately after you begin to drag, and hold Shift throughout the length of the drag. If you release the Shift key while dragging, the line resumes its naturally free-form and wiggly ways.

✔ You may have noticed that there's a Line tool hidden away amongst the shape tools — the "talk bubble"-shaped Custom Shape tool is visible in the Toolbox by default. Although you can draw straight lines with it, too, it's really not a painting tool, but rather a whole different kind of animal. We'll explore the shape tools later in this chapter.

✔ Alt+click (Option+click on a Mac) to get the Eyedropper tool and lift a color from the image. Then drag to start painting with that color.

Choosing Your Brush

If the preceding two sections covered everything about the painting tools, Elements would be a royal dud. But as we all know, Elements is not a dud — far from it — so there must be more to the painting tools than we've seen so far. (This is classic Sherlock Holmes-style deductive reasoning at work here. Element-ary, my dear Watson.)

You can modify the tools to a degree that no mechanical pencil or conventional paintbrush can match. For starters, you can change the size and shape of the tip of the tool, as explained in the next few sections. You can draw thick strokes one moment and then turn around and draw thin strokes the next, all with the same tool. This holds true of any tool that works like a brush, including the editing tools in Chapter 11.

In fact, the whole concept of painting has been greatly improved upon in Elements 2.0. There are new categories of brushes that spew forth eye-popping effects. And brushes are much more customizable than ever, enabling you to tailor the presets to your whim and save the results for later use.

Switching the brush size

To change one brush for a different one, select the Brush tool and click the brushes drop-down menu, which you can reach by clicking the arrow to the right of the long brush stroke icon in the Options bar. Elements displays the brushes palette, shown in Figure 14-5, with the Default Brushes set currently active. Here you can find a total of 65 brushes, and Elements 1.0 users will find some very interesting new brushes toward the bottom of the palette.

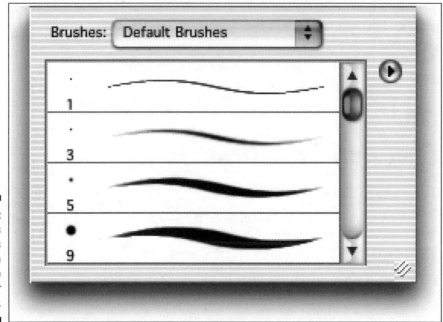

Figure 14-5: The brushes palette lets you switch one size brush for another.

The numbers to the left of the brush stroke icons represent the diameters of the brushes, in pixels. (In case that year of high school geometry has altogether removed itself from your brain, diameter is merely the width of a circle measured from side to opposite side.) To change the brush size, just click a brush stroke icon. Notice that the first six brushes have fairly hard edges, whereas the next twelve have a softer edge. These are followed by nine preset airbrushes, which have the softest edge of all. (Notice that when you select an airbrush preset, the airbrush icon automatically becomes selected in the Options bar.) When you begin using the brush, the brushes palette puts itself back in its hiding place. You can also press Enter (Return on a Mac) or Esc to close the palette.

You can view the brushes palette in six ways — stroke thumbnail (the new default), large and small thumbnails, text only, or a large or small list (a combo of text and thumbnails). Access the brushes palette drop-down menu by clicking the circle with the right-pointing arrow in the upper-right corner of the palette to select any of these viewing options.

Right-click (Control+click on a Mac) on the canvas to display the brushes palette underneath your cursor. Select a different brush and continue painting. The palette then disappears.

As you discovered in Chapter 8, soft edges are said to be *anti-aliased*, whereas blurry edges are *feathered*. Both terms are proof positive that computer professionals actually don't want to be understood by the greater public. They prefer to speak in their own private code.

The Pencil and the editing tools (such as the Smudge and Sponge tools) all provide access to the brushes palette. However, bear in mind that the Pencil tool draws a harsh, jagged line no matter which brush you select. Even the preset airbrushes produce jagged lines when used with the Pencil.

You'll definitely want to check out the other brushes in the Default Brushes set, particularly the grass and leaves brushes. (If you leave your cursor over a brush stroke icon for a second, you'll see a ToolTip, which tells you the name of the brush.) These brushes give you a taste of what can be found in the other brush sets, which we deal with next.

Exploring the other brush sets

There are four new sets of brushes available in Elements 2.0: Dry Media Brushes, Special Effect Brushes, Thick Heavy Brushes, and Wet Media Brushes. All can be useful, but the Special Effect Brushes are downright spectacular. To check them out, click the brushes drop-down menu at the top of the brushes palette, and choose Special Effect Brushes. Click the first one (Azalea), set a nice bright foreground color and a contrasting background color, and drag your brush across an image.

Wow! The brush spits out a variety of different colored, sized, and shaped flowers. This very nicely shows off the fact that there's a new painting engine lurking inside Elements 2.0, letting you achieve effects that were impossible before. We'll look at how to customize these brushes shortly, but for now we bet you'll want to spend a few minutes experimenting with these brushes, and painting masterworks like the one in Figure 14-6.

Making your own brush

There is a total of 287 preset brushes in the combined twelve brush sets that come with Elements. How do we know that? We counted them all for you. You're welcome. Now, you may think that 287 brushes are enough to keep you happy well into your declining years. But rest assured, one day you'll want a brush size that's a little thicker than Option A and a little thinner than Option B. So you'll have to modify one or the other to come up with a custom brush of your own.

Figure 14-6:
This pastoral scene was painted by merely dragging and clicking around with preset brushes from the Default, Assorted, and Special Effect Brushes sets. Okay, maybe butterflies don't usually fly around in snowstorms at night . . . but you get the idea.

Changing the size of the brush is a simple affair; just use the Size control that appears to the right of the brushes palette icon in the Options bar. You can click the arrow to access a slider, or just type in a size. This can be done with any painting or editing tool.

To make other changes, you have to have the Brush tool active. Click the More Options brush icon on the far right of the Options bar. In response to your click, Elements displays the drop-down dialog box, shown in Figure 14-7. Here's how you modify the brush:

✔ To understand the Spacing setting, go to the Default Brushes set and select the sixth one down, the Hard Round 19 pixels brush. Drag it across an open image. Now you would never know it from using a brush like this one, but Elements doesn't really paint a solid line when you drag a brush across an image. Instead, what it does is spit out a succession of shapes. With a basic brush like the one you just used, it spits out little circles, but they're packed so closely together that they look like a solid thick line. Go ahead and open the More Options drop-down dialog box, and increase the Spacing setting all the way up to 1000. Now you'll see that the circle shapes are spaced much farther apart; in fact, the brush stroke icon in the Options bar changes to reflect this. For general purposes, you'll want to leave the spacing option alone, but for brushes such as Azalea in the Special Effects Brushes set, you may well want to control exactly how far apart the flowers or shapes are spit out. That's what the Spacing control does.

✔ The Fade control, similar to the Brush Dynamics available in Elements 1.0, makes a brush stroke gradually fade out over distance. Using Fade is a bit peculiar. The general default of 0# means that a brush stoke will never fade; as long as you keep wiggling the brush, paint will come out. However, one step up from there — 1# — makes the fade happen instantaneously. With a standard round brush, you'll just get one circle, and that's it. As you drag the slider to the right, the fade takes longer and longer, all the way up to 9999# — where we estimate you'd have to keep painting continuously for about five minutes before the stroke entirely faded out. We haven't the patience.

✔ The Color Jitter value makes the color of the brush stroke fluctuate between the current foreground and background colors. Again, the Azalea brush in the Special Effects Brushes set shows this off to full effect.

✔ The Hardness value represents the blurriness of the brush. A value of 100% is hard, like the first six options in the Default Brushes set. Anything else is progressively fuzzier. The 12 feathered options in the Default Brushes set have Hardness values of 0%. The Hardness value isn't available for every brush.

✔ Scatter deals with how far away from the drag of the cursor the brush shapes are spaced. For standard round brushes, you'll probably want to keep this at 0%, but the relatively high Scatter value is one of the things that makes our beloved Azalea brush so special.

✔ Before we talk about the Angle option, which comes next, you need to understand how Roundness works. (You see, the Angle value doesn't have any effect unless you first change the Roundness value.) The Roundness option lets you make the brush oval instead of round. A value of 100% is absolutely circular; anything less results in a shape that is shorter than it is wide.

✔ If you want an oval brush to be taller than it is wide or some other variation on its present state, you can rotate it by changing the Angle value. Ninety degrees is a counterclockwise quarter-turn, 180 degrees is a half-turn, –90 degrees is a clockwise quarter-turn, and so on.

✔ You'll find it much easier to use the diagram in the lower-left corner of the dialog box to change the Angle and Roundness settings. Drag one of the two circular handles on either side of the circle to make the brush oval. To rotate the brush, drag the gray arrowhead or just click at the position where you want the arrow to point. The labels in Figure 14-7 tell the story.

✔ If you're using a graphics tablet, such as the ones made by Wacom, as you paint you can turn on the Pen Pressure option to make the pressure of the drawing stylus affect the Fade and Size of the brush stroke.

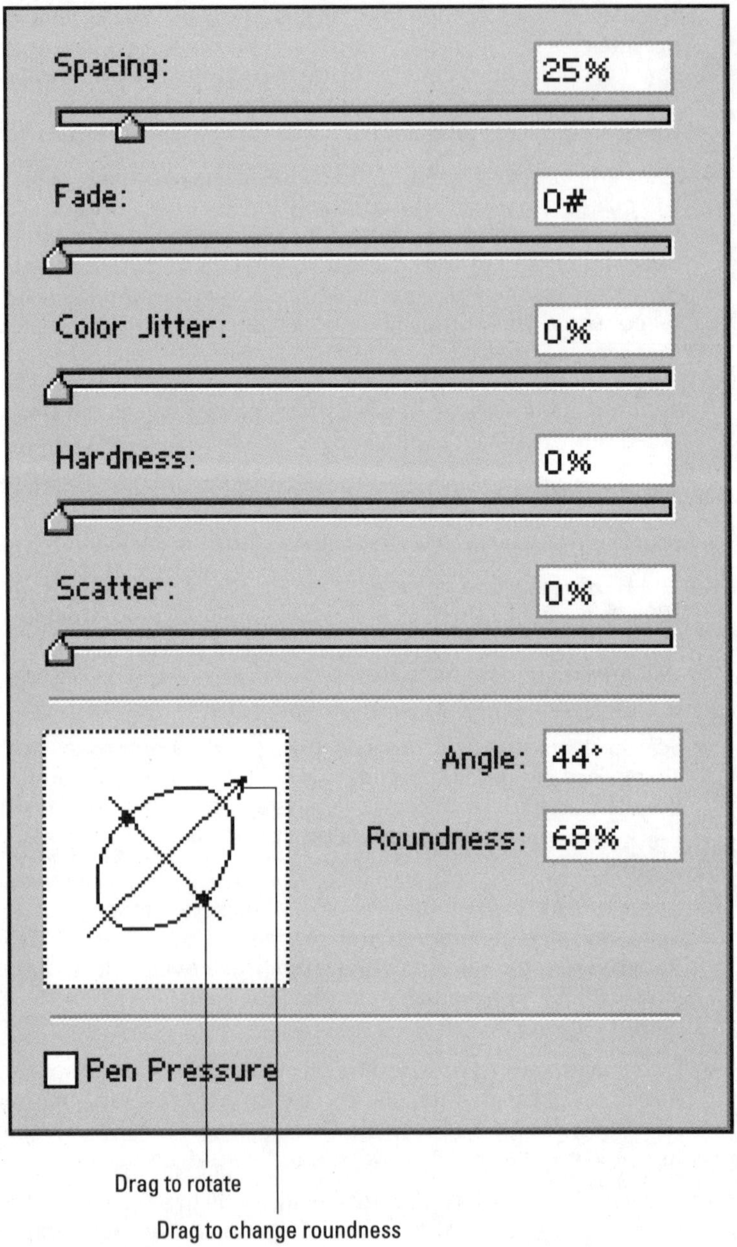

Figure 14-7:
The inner workings of a brush.

Drag to rotate

Drag to change roundness

As you change the settings, the brush stroke icon in the Options bar shows the effect of the modified settings on the brush. After you finish editing the brush, press Enter (Return on a Mac) to accept your changes. Note that this action creates a brush for temporary usage. If you want to keep your brush around for later use, read on.

Saving brushes

After you've edited your brush to perfection, the first step toward saving it is to access the drop-down menu in the brushes palette and to choose New Brush. Here you can give your brush a descriptive name. When you've done so, click OK. And there, at the bottom of the active set of brushes, you'll find your custom-made brush.

You'd think that would be enough to save it forever, wouldn't you? Well, think again. All you have to do is switch to a different set with the Brushes menu at the top of the brushes palette, choose a brush, and then switch back to the previous set where your custom brush was stored. It's gone forever! If this heart-rending situation seems quite similar to the one associated with the Swatches palette as described in Chapter 5, you're right. And there's a similar solution for a happy outcome. After you've saved your custom brush with the New Brush command, you then need to save that set to disk to ensure that your new brush will always be around.

To do this, go once again to the drop-down menu in the brushes palette and choose Save Brushes. Give the set a distinctive name and make sure you save it inside the Brushes folder, which is inside the Presets folder, which is inside your Adobe Photoshop Elements 2 application folder. (Whew.) You can then always access that set from the drop-down menu in the brushes palette. Pick Load Brushes to append your saved set to the currently active one, or pick Replace Brushes to replace the current set with your saved one.

Going nuts with the brushes palette

What we've seen so far would be plenty of brush options for an ordinary program. But Elements is no ordinary program. Elements is never satisfied to supply you with anything short of everything. You have to admire that in a program.

Here's what else Elements offers you, brush-wise:

- ✔ You can quickly change the brush size from the keyboard, without messing about with any controls in the Options bar. Press the right bracket key ( ]) to select a larger brush in varying increments. Increments are as follows: 1 pixel in brushes from 1–10 pixels in size; 10 pixels in brushes from 10–100 pixels in size; 25 pixels in brushes from 100–200 in size; 50 pixels in brushes from 200–300 in size; 100 pixels in brushes from 300 to the maximum of 2500 in size. Press the left bracket key ([ ) to select a smaller brush by the same increments.

- ✔ To raise the hardness of a brush in 25 percent increments, press Shift+]. To lower the hardness, press Shift+[.

✔ To delete a brush size option from the palette, Alt+click (Option+click on a Mac) on it. If you press the Alt or Option key, you get a miniature pair of scissors. That's how Elements tells you that you're ready to clip a brush into oblivion.

✔ To return to the default collection of brushes, choose Reset Brushes from the palette menu. You will lose any brushes you may have created, so make sure you first choose Save Brushes from the brushes palette's drop-down menu.

✔ The Edit⇨Define Brush command gives you yet another way to create a custom brush. Just make a selection in an open image, choose Define Brush, and give your brush a name. Click OK, and it will be added at the bottom of the currently active brush set. Using this technique, you can easily make a brush out of any object in an image, such as a letter of the alphabet or a person's face.

Exploring More Painting Options

Figure 14-8 shows the Options bar that appears when the Brush is active. We've looked at some of these controls, but here's how the other options work:

✔ The first icon on the far left is the tool identifier, which lets you know which tool is active. If you click the icon, you get a drop-down menu where you can reset the default options for the specific tool, or do the same for all the tools.

✔ The next pair of icons lets you switch between the Brush and the Impressionist Brush, because these two tools share the same space in the Toolbox.

✔ The Mode drop-down menu, available with the Brush or Pencil, provides access to a bunch of different painting modes that control how the foreground color applied by the tool mixes with the existing colors in the image. These modes function identically to the blending modes talked about in Chapter 13. There are some fun tricks to perform with some of the modes in the next section.

✔ Available when you use the Pencil or Brush, the Opacity slider bar controls the translucency of the foreground color you're applying. A setting of 100% ensures that the paint is opaque so that you can't see the colors underneath. (When you use a feathered brush, the edges are translucent even at 100%, but the center is opaque.) Any Opacity setting lower than 100% makes the brush translucent.

✔ If you can't quite see your way through to how the Opacity slider works, a visual depiction will make everything clear. Figure 14-9 shows four lines drawn with the Brush, two using a standard brush and two using a feathered brush. In each case, one line is set to 100% Opacity, and the other line is set to 40%.

✔ Just as with a layer's opacity, you can change the Opacity value for tools in 10% increments by pressing a number key. As long as you have one of the painting tools selected, pressing 9 changes the setting to 90%, 8 changes it to 80%, and so on. Press the 0 key to change the setting back to 100%. If you want a more precise setting — say, 75% — just type the value in quickly.

✔ The Auto Erase check box appears when you select the Pencil tool. You can select this option to draw in the background color whenever you click or drag on a pixel painted in the foreground color. It's very useful for making touch ups with the single-pixel brush — click to add the foreground color and click again to change it to the background color.

Figure 14-8:
The Brush Options bar is headquarters for modifying the Brush.

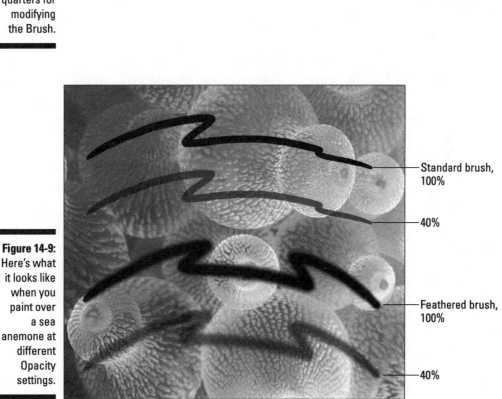

Figure 14-9:
Here's what it looks like when you paint over a sea anemone at different Opacity settings.

Standard brush, 100%

40%

Feathered brush, 100%

40%

Experimenting with painting modes

If you read about blending modes in Chapter 13, you saw how they can be used to combine the colors of pixels in layers. Painting modes work in the same way, except that they combine the painted foreground color with whatever is underneath it. Color Plate 19 illustrates twelve different painting modes, showing how the green foreground color interacts with a colorful background image. Here are a few specific effects you can achieve using painting modes.

For example, consider the sun image shown back in Figure 14-4. Suppose that you want to color in the sun with yellow and the sky with blue.

The problem is, if you try to color in the sun and sky with one of the painting tools, you end up covering the face inside the sun with yellow and the rays outside the sun with blue. You can't fix the problem by lowering the Opacity value, because doing that just results in washed-out colors, and you still obscure some of the sun's detail.

The solution is to select a painting mode. Select Multiply from the Mode drop-down menu in the Options bar. Miraculously, you can now paint both sky and sun without covering up the rays and the face. This is because the Multiply option darkens colors as though you had painted with watercolors. The Multiply option mixes the colors together to create darker colors.

Here are some additional painting modes and other information on this subject that you may find interesting:

- The Screen mode is the exact opposite of Multiply. Multiply mixes colors as though they were pigments, which is why the colors get darker. By contrast, Screen mixes colors as though they were lights, which is why they get lighter.

- The Overlay mode darkens dark colors and lightens light colors, resulting in a heightening of contrast.

- The Difference painting mode is the loopiest mode of them all and the most likely to surprise you. Through a mathematical process too complex to be explained within these humble pages, it creates a photonegative effect.

- You can also have some fun experimenting with Difference's cousin, Exclusion. It sends all blacks to white, all whites to black, and all medium colors to gray.

- Use the Color painting mode to colorize grayscale images or change the color of portions of RGB images.

- The Color Dodge and Color Burn painting modes offer an interesting new twist on the Dodge and Burn tools discussed in Chapter 11. In case you haven't discovered the Dodge and Burn tools yet, you drag with the

Dodge tool to lighten a portion of your image and drag with the Burn tool to darken a portion of your image. If you paint with the Color Dodge mode, you can lighten your image and infuse it with color. Using Color Burn, you can darken and infuse with color. For example, to darken your image and give it a greenish tint, you paint with green using the Color Burn painting mode.

✔ To paint normally again, just select the Normal painting mode.

In addition to adding a few new painting and blending modes, Elements 2.0 has rearranged the order in which the modes appear in the Mode menu. Now similar modes are grouped together, making the results of the modes slightly easier to predict.

Shift+right-click (Shift+Control-click on a Mac) on your canvas with a painting tool to bring up a shortcut menu that provides access to the Edit Brush command and all the painting modes.

Six of the preceding painting modes — Multiply, Screen, Overlay, Difference, Color, and Normal — are superuseful, the kinds of modes you want to get to know on a first-name basis. Exclusion, Color Dodge, and Color Burn are also worth some attention. The others aren't nearly so useful. In fact, they're mostly boring and obscure. But who knows? Maybe you'll feel differently.

"Painting" with the Impressionist Brush

The Impressionist Brush allows you to paint in impressionistic swirls. Although it's not, strictly speaking, a paintbrush, we'll still refer to what the Impressionist Brush does as "painting," for lack of a better word.

Go ahead and open up an image. Select the Impressionist Brush (which shares a flyout menu in the Toolbox with the Brush tool) and just start moving it around on your image. You'll instantly get an idea of what the Impressionist Brush is all about. Figure 14-10 shows an image before and after a grueling workout with the Impressionist Brush. Pretty groovy, huh? Color Plate 20 offers another example of Impressionistic Art.

The performance of the Impressionist Brush depends on the settings in the Options bar, pictured in Figure 14-11. Here are the options:

✔ **Mode:** This drop-down menu assigns a painting mode to the tool. See "Experimenting with painting modes" in this chapter for details.

✔ **Opacity:** Lower this value to create translucent strokes. To lower the Opacity from the keyboard, just press a number key any time the Impressionist Brush is active.

Figure 14-10:
An original image (left) and the same image brought to life with the Impressionist Brush (right).

There are three more options available in the More Options dialog box:

- ✔ **Style:** The Impressionist Brush paints with randomly generated corkscrews of color. You can decide the basic shapes of the corkscrews by selecting an option from the Style drop-down menu. Combine these options with different brush sizes to vary the detail conveyed by the impressionistic image.

- ✔ **Area:** This value defines the area covered by a single dollop of paint. Larger pixel values also mean that the brush lays down more strokes at a time; reduce the value for a sparser look.

- ✔ **Tolerance:** Change this value to give more or less tolerance to where the Impressionist Brush can paint within the image.

If impressionism interests you, experiment with this brush. If not, give this brush a slip. Although it's pretty nifty, it definitely falls under the heading of Whimsical Creative Tools to Play with When You're Not under Deadline.

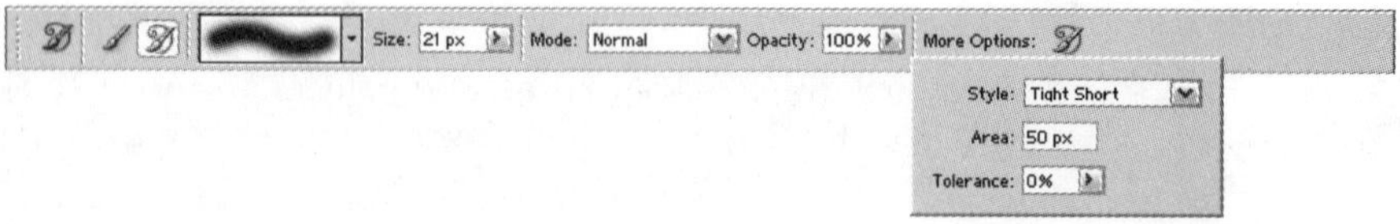

Figure 14-11:
The Options bar offers numerous settings for the Impressionist Brush.

The Powers of the Eraser

What artist's toolbox would be complete without an eraser? Elements' Toolbox wouldn't be complete without three erasers — the Eraser tool, the Background Eraser tool, and the Magic Eraser tool.

To switch between the three eraser tools from the keyboard, press Shift+E.

Working with the regular ol' Eraser tool

The Eraser tool, directly above the Blur tool in the Toolbox, lets you erase in a couple of ways:

- ✔ If you drag with the Eraser in an image that contains only a Background layer, the tool paints in the background color, which is white by default. Technically this may be erasing, but it's really just painting in a different color. Who needs it?

- ✔ If your image contains more than one layer (we discuss layers in Chapter 9), the Eraser works a little differently and becomes a lot more useful. If you drag the Eraser on the Background layer, the Eraser paints in the background color, as usual. But on any other layer, the pixels you scrub with the Eraser become transparent, revealing pixels on underlying layers. (This assumes that the Lock Transparent Pixels button is deselected in the Layers palette. If you click the Lock Transparent Pixels button, the Eraser paints in the Background color.)

The Eraser tool comes in three delicious eraser flavors. To switch flavors, select an option from the Mode drop-down menu in the Options bar.

Two erasers are named after painting tools — Brush and Pencil — and work exactly like these tools. This means that you can change the brush size and adjust the Opacity setting to make pixels only partially transparent in a layered image.

The third option, Block, changes the eraser to the square, hard-edged, fixed-size eraser. All the options in the Options bar then become grayed out. The Block Eraser can be useful when you want to completely erase general areas, but you probably won't take it up very often.

Trying out the somewhat Magic Eraser

Of the Background and Magic erasers, the Magic Eraser is the easier to use and the less capable. If you're familiar with the Magic Wand (see the section on using the Magic Wand in Chapter 8), the Magic Eraser is a cinch to use. The two tools operate virtually identically, except that the Wand **selects** and the Eraser **erases**.

When you click a pixel with the Magic Eraser, Elements identifies a range of similarly colored pixels, just as it does with the Magic Wand. But instead of selecting the pixels, the Magic Eraser makes them transparent, as demonstrated in Figure 14-12. Bear in mind that in Elements, transparency requires a separate layer. So if the image is on the Background layer, Elements automatically floats the image to a separate layer with nothing underneath: hence the checkerboard pattern shown in the second example in the figure — transparency with nothing underneath.

Figure 14-12:
To delete a homogeneously colored background, like the sky at top, click inside it with the Magic Eraser (bottom).

Notice in Figure 14-12 that the Magic Eraser deleted some of the blue sky, but not all of it. This is a function of the Tolerance value in the Options bar. Just like the Magic Wand's Tolerance value, the Magic Eraser's Tolerance value determines how similar a neighboring color has to be to the clicked color to be made transparent. A higher value affects more colors; a lower value affects fewer colors. Therefore, if you want to erase a larger section of the sky in Figure 14-12, you can raise the Tolerance value and click again. (Remember, any change to the Tolerance value affects the next click you make; it does not affect the existing transparent area.)

The other options in the Options bar work as follows:

- **Anti-aliased:** To create a soft fringe around the outline of your transparent area, leave this option turned on. If you prefer a hard edge — as when using a very low Tolerance value, for example — turn this check box off.

- **Contiguous:** When this is turned on, the Magic Eraser deletes contiguous colors only — that is, similar colors that touch each other. If you prefer to delete all pixels of a certain color regardless of their location, turn the Contiguous check box off.

- **Use All Layers:** When turned on, this check box tells Elements to factor in all visible layers when erasing pixels. The tool continues to erase pixels on the active layer only, but it erases them according to colors found across all layers.

- **Opacity:** Lower this value to make the erased pixels translucent instead of transparent. Low values result in more subtle effects than high ones.

For a more detailed description of these options as they affect the Magic Wand tool, read the section on using the Magic Wand in Chapter 8.

Using the more magical Background Eraser

The Magic Eraser is as simple to use as a hammer and every bit as indelicate. It pounds away pixels, but it leaves lots of color fringes and shredded edges in its wake. You may as well select an area with the Magic Wand and press the Backspace or Delete key. The effect is the same.

The more capable, more scrupulous tool is the Background Eraser. As demonstrated in Figure 14-13, the Background Eraser deletes background pixels as you drag over them. (Again, if the image is on the Background layer, Elements floats the image to a new layer to accommodate the transparency.) The tool is intelligent enough to erase background pixels and retain foreground pixels provided — and here's the clincher — that you keep the cross in the center of the eraser cursor squarely centered on a background pixel. Move the cross over a foreground pixel, and the Background Eraser deletes foreground pixels as well. As Figure 14-14 demonstrates, it's the position of the cross that counts.

Like the standard Eraser tool, the Background Eraser responds to the Size setting in the Options bar. You can use the bracket keys [and] to make the brush size smaller or larger.

Figure 14-13: Drag around the edge of an image with the Background Eraser to erase the background but leave the foreground intact.

You can also modify the performance of the Background Eraser using the options in the Options bar. Here are your options:

- ✔ **Limits:** By default, the Background Eraser deletes colors inside the cursor as long as they are contiguous with the color immediately under the cross. To erase all similarly colored pixels, whether contiguous or not, set the drop-down menu to Discontiguous.

- ✔ **Tolerance:** Raise the Tolerance value to erase more colors at a time; lower the value to erase fewer colors. Low Tolerance values are useful for erasing around tight and delicate details, such as hair.

Isn't Elements Just a Paint Program?

Perish the thought. Elements also includes shape tools, which are very handy at drawing geometric objects to be used for things like Web buttons. Shapes are exceptions to the way things generally work inside Elements, because they're not actually pixel-based. The shape tools draw *vector objects,* which can be scaled to any size with no loss in quality. If you painted a circle in Elements on a very small canvas — say, roughly 20 pixels by 20 pixels — and then scaled your canvas up to around 2000 pixels by 2000 pixels using the

Image Size command, the edges of your circle would look very fuzzy. But use the Ellipse shape tool to draw a circle on that 20 by 20 canvas, scale it up to 2000 by 2000 with Image Size, and the Ellipse-drawn circle will look perfect, with razor-sharp edges. Understand the difference?

Figure 14-14: Keep the cross of the Background Eraser cursor over the background you want to erase (top). If you inadvertently move the cross over the foreground, the foreground gets erased (bottom).

The shape drawing tools

There are six different shape tools — the Rectangle, Rounded Rectangle, Ellipse, Polygon, Line, and Custom Shape tools. In addition, there's the Shape

Selection tool, which we'll get to in a minute. To experiment with the shape tools for the first time, do the following:

1. **Select a shape tool from the Toolbox.**

   The "talk bubble"-shaped Custom Shape tool is visible by default. To access one of the other shapes, click and hold your cursor on the visible shape tool, and a flyout menu will appear. Or, just click the visible shape tool in the Toolbox and then choose the specific shape tool you want from the Options bar, as pictured in Figure 14-15. (If you've experimented with the shape tools at all before, go over to the Shape tool icon on the very far left, click it, and choose Reset Tool.)

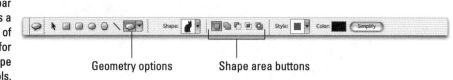

Geometry options   Shape area buttons

2. **Drag with the tool to draw a shape on the canvas.**

   If you have the Layers palette open, you'll see that you just created a new layer. (It really helps to have the Layers palette open while you work with the shape tools.)

   By default, the color of the shape will be the foreground color, but after drawing the shape, you can change the color by clicking the Color box in the Options bar to bring up the Color Picker.

3. **Draw another shape.**

   You'll see that you've created another layer. This happened because the Create New Shape Layer button is selected by default. This button is the left button in the shape area option buttons in the Options bar. Selecting one of the other four buttons will keep the next shape you draw on the same layer, and each of the four buttons has its own options for combining shapes on the same layer. See Figure 14-16 for a visual reference to the effects of the shape area buttons.

4. **Press the Step Backward button in the Shortcuts bar to undo the last shape you drew, click the Add to Shape Area button (the next button over from the Create New Shape Layer button), and draw a shape again.**

   This time make sure your new shape overlaps the old one. Use Step Backward again and experiment with the other three buttons, drawing overlapping shapes. Lather, rinse, repeat.

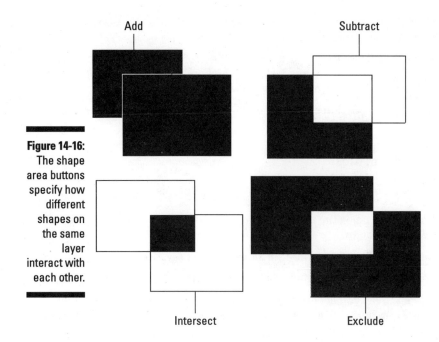

Add

Subtract

Figure 14-16:
The shape
area buttons
specify how
different
shapes on
the same
layer
interact with
each other.

Intersect

Exclude

The drop-down menu in the Options bar at the right end of the row of shape tools gives you access to Geometry options for the tools. The options here vary from tool to tool, but here's a rundown of what they all do:

- ✔ **Unconstrained:** Enables you to draw your shape freely, stretching or squashing it if you want, as you draw.

- ✔ **Square:** Enables you to draw a square with the Rectangle and Rounded Rectangle tools.

- ✔ **Fixed Size:** Enables you to draw a shape with a set width and height.

- ✔ **Proportional:** Lets you draw a shape with a proportional ratio of width and height.

- ✔ **From Center:** This option enables you to draw from the center out, rather than from a corner.

- ✔ **Snap to Pixels:** Aligns the shape perfectly with the "pixel grid" of the image. This ensures that straight lines will always appear crisp.

- ✔ **Radius:** Sets the width of the polygon.

- ✔ **Smooth Corners:** Makes smooth polygon corners.

- ✔ **Star:** Enables the Polygon tool to draw a star.

- ✔ **Indent Sides By:** Creates the spikes of a star when the Polygon tool's Star option is selected. A larger value makes sharper and spikier points.

- ✔ **Smooth Indents:** Curves the sides of a star.

✔ **Circle:** Similar to the Square option, this constrains the Ellipse tool to draw a perfect circle.

✔ **Arrowheads:** Enables you to specify the placement of the arrowhead, the shape of the arrowhead, the width of your line, and the concavity (or curvature) of the arrowhead for the Line tool.

✔ **Defined Proportions:** The opposite of Unconstrained, this keeps you from distorting a Custom Shape as you draw it.

✔ **Defined Size:** Constrains drawing Custom Shapes to the size at which they were created.

Some tools have other options available in the Options bar:

✔ **Radius:** Specifies the amount of curve on the corners of the Rounded Rectangle tool.

✔ **Sides:** Specifies the number of sides for the Polygon tool.

✔ **Weight:** Specifies the thickness of the Line tool.

✔ **Shape:** Gives you access to the Shape palette with the Custom Shape tool. From here you can select a different shape to draw. Click the drop-down menu in the Shape palette to access 16 different libraries of shapes. The drop-down menu also lets you choose from several different viewing options for the Shapes palette.

The Options bar also makes it easy to add layer styles, which we cover in Chapter 13. And the final button in the Options bar is the Simplify button. No, the Simplify button doesn't make all the confusing shape tools disappear. Clicking the Simplify button *rasterizes* your shape layer. Rasterizing is the process of converting your vector shape to pixels, meaning the shape loses its special resizable status. However, simplifying is necessary if you want to add filters and effects to your shape.

The Shape Selection tool

If you're not happy with where you drew a shape, that's when that last shape tool can come in handy. The Shape Selection tool lets you click a shape and drag it to a new location, but it also has a few other tricks up its sleeve:

✔ After you've clicked on a shape, go to Image⇨Transform Shape. This gives you access to four different commands — Free Transform Shape, Skew, Distort, and Perspective — wherein you can distort your shape in any number of interesting ways.

✔ When you have more than one shape on a single layer, selecting the Shape Selection Tool gives you access to the Combine button in the Options bar, which combines various shapes on a single layer into one complex shape.

If all this painting and drawing seems a little daunting at first, don't give up. Just keep on plugging away. Remember, everything's daunting at some time. Heck, feeding yourself once seemed impossible, and yet look how well you do that today. Sure, not as well as some folks, but you're still getting there. Keep your chin up (and wipe it, for good measure).

Chapter 15

The Digital Stencil

● ●

In This Chapter

▶ Painting and editing inside a selection outline

▶ Using the Paint Bucket tool

▶ Using the Fill command

▶ Applying different types of gradients

▶ Stroking a selection

● ●

As the last chapter shows, Photoshop Elements has a whole mess of options for replicating the process of drawing or painting on a canvas. But have you ever spray painted using a stencil? In case you've never engaged in this riveting pastime, here's how it works:

1. Hold the stencil up to the surface you want to paint.

2. Spray recklessly.

When you take the stencil away, you discover a painted image that matches the shape of the stencil. It's the epitome of a no-brainer.

In Elements, you can use a selection outline (see Chapter 8 for more on selections) in the same way. Just as a stencil isolates the area affected by the spray paint, a *selection outline* isolates the area affected by a paint or edit tool. You can also fill a selection outline with color or trace around the selection outline.

In this chapter you're going to discover every nuance of painting, filling, and tracing selections. Chapter 8 explains how to create and manipulate selection outlines; this chapter shows you some of the things you can do with them.

Painting within the Lines

If some portion of an image is selected, Elements treats all deselected areas as protected. You can use any paint or edit tool inside the selection without worrying about harming areas outside the selection.

This chapter utilizes a jar-in-a-nook, which has a certain austere beauty about it. If you want to get an idea of what the jar's contents looked like originally, check out Color Plate 21 (and ignore the rainbow-hued frame for now). The jar is such a lovely object that during the course of this chapter we will, or course, completely muck it up. Specifically, we'll paint the inside of the jar without harming the background. To this end, do the following:

1. **Select the object.**

    This is the only step that takes any work. We started out by selecting the body of the jar with the Elliptical Marquee tool. If you have problems getting the marquee exactly on an object — it's hard to know where to start dragging so that it comes out right — just make sure that the marquee is approximately the right size, and then use the arrow keys to nudge the outline into position. You can also temporarily hold down the spacebar as you're dragging to reposition the selection outline on the image. After we selected the body to our satisfaction, we Shift+dragged with the Lasso tool to incorporate the neck of the jar into the selection as well.

2. **Make any modifications you deem necessary.**

    You may want to blur the selection outline a tad using Select⇨Feather, as explained in Chapter 8. If your selection outline isn't dead on, the Feather command helps to fudge the difference a little.

    You'll probably also want to press Ctrl+H (⌘+H on the Mac) to hide the selection after you've made it. Remember that the selection is still active; pressing this keyboard shortcut or choosing View⇨Selection just turns those distracting marching ants invisible, making it easier to see what you're doing.

3. **Paint and edit away.**

    Feel free to use any tool you want. You can paint with the Brush or Pencil; edit with the Smudge, focus, or toning tools; clone with the Clone Stamp — all with the assurance that the area outside the selection will remain as safeguarded from your changes as the driven snow (or whatever the saying is).

In Figure 15-1, the inside of the jar was painted using a single tool — the BRUSH — with a single brush size and only two colors, black and white. As a result, the jar is transformed into a kind of marble. Looks mighty keen, and there's not so much as a drop of paint outside the lines.

This stenciling feature is so all-fired handy that you'll almost always want to select an area before applying a paint or edit tool. The fact is, the selection tools are easier to control than the painting or editing tools, so you may as well take advantage of them.

Figure 15-1:
Using the
Brush, we
painted the
inside of the
selected jar.

Dribbling Paint from a Bucket

Elements enables you to fill a selection with the foreground color, the background color, a pattern, or a gradual blend of colors called a *gradient*. But before we look at any of these eye-popping options, let's spend a moment kicking around the Paint Bucket tool, which is part selection tool and part fill tool. The Paint Bucket tool (it looks like a tilted bucket of paint) lets you fill an area of continuous color or a selected area by clicking the area.

In Figure 15-2, for example, the Paint Bucket tool was clicked on the row of broccoli in the jar with the foreground color set to white. Elements filled the broccoli with white, turning it into a rough facsimile of cauliflower.

To adjust the performance of the Paint Bucket, access the Options bar, also shown in Figure 15-2. As with the Magic Wand tool, the Tolerance value determines how many pixels in your image the Paint Bucket affects. The only difference is that the Paint Bucket applies color instead of selecting pixels. You can also select the Anti-aliased check box to soften the edges of the filled area. (In Figure 15-2, the Tolerance value is 32, and Anti-aliased is turned on, as it is by default.)

Paint Bucket tool

Figure 15-2:
The Paint
Bucket
fills a
continuous
area of
color with a
different
color.

The problem with the Paint Bucket tool is that it's hard to get the Tolerance value just right. You usually end up stepping backward several times and resetting the Tolerance value until you find the value that colors only the pixels that you want to color. Although it's an okay tool for filling already selected areas, the results you get when you use the Paint Bucket to fill a continuous area of color are just fair-to-middling. It's best to use the selection tools first, and then click with the Paint Bucket; that way you have more alternatives at your disposal.

You can select the Paint Bucket at any time simply by pressing K. (For "kick" — get it?)

Applying Color to Selection Innards

Though filling selection outlines is what the Paint Bucket does best, that doesn't mean it's the best way Elements gives you to fill a selection outline. So what is the best way? Read on:

- To fill a selection with the foreground color, press Alt+Backspace (Option+Delete on a Mac).

- To fill a selection with the background color, press Ctrl+Backspace (⌘+Delete on a Mac).

- When you're working on a layer and want to fill the opaque part of the layer with the foreground color and leave the transparent part transparent, press Shift+Alt+Backspace (Shift+Option+Delete on a Mac). Press Ctrl+Shift+ Backspace (⌘+Shift+Delete on a Mac) to fill the opaque area with the background color. If part of that layer is selected and the selection contains both opaque and transparent pixels, these keyboard shortcuts will fill only the opaque areas of the layer that fall within the selection. (And if all this makes no sense at all, you may want to turn to Chapter 9, which explains layers and transparency.)

✔ Choose Edit➪Fill to display the Fill dialog box, which gives you other options, such as filling the selection with translucent color or a pattern.

✔ Drag with the Gradient tool to create a gradient (a gradual blend) between two or more colors.

Two of these options — Edit➪Fill and the Gradient tool — require more discussion, which is why the rest of this chapter is so filled to the gills with text.

Fill, 1 Command You!

Choose Edit➪Fill to display the Fill dialog box, shown in Figure 15-3. The Use drop-down menu lets you specify the color with which you want to fill the selection, or lets you choose the Pattern option; the Blending options let you mix the filled colors with the colors already inside the selection. We discuss all these options in more detail in this section. Note that filling not only works within a selection, but also on an entire layer. If you don't have an active selection and you apply the Fill command, the entire active layer will be filled.

You can also display the Fill dialog box by pressing Shift+Backspace (Shift+Delete on a Mac).

Selecting your stuffing

The most important part of the Fill dialog box is the Use drop-down menu. Here you select the stuff you want to use to fill the selection or layer. The options are as follows:

✔ The Foreground Color option fills with the foreground color, and the Background Color option fills with the background color. Hopefully you're not surprised by this news.

✔ The next option, Pattern, fills with a repeating pattern. You can define a pattern by selecting a rectangular area and choosing Edit➪Define Pattern. If you don't define a selection, Elements creates the pattern from the entire canvas. You can access the patterns you've created, along with a variety of preset patterns, via the Custom Pattern drop-down menu.

✔ The last three options — Black, 50% Gray, and White — fill with black, medium gray, and white, respectively. What's the point? Well, if the foreground and background colors are set to something like blue and orange, and you don't want to change them, you may find these options useful.

Mixing colors the wrong way

You can enter a value into the Opacity option box of the Fill dialog box to mix the fill color or pattern with the present colors in the selection or layer. You can also mix the fill and the selected color using the options in the Mode drop-down menu, which include Multiply, Screen, Difference, and other wacky blending modes (see Chapter 13).

Notice that we said you *can* do these things, not that you should. The truth is, you don't want to use the Fill dialog box's Blending options to mix fills with selections. Why? Because the Fill dialog box doesn't let you preview the effects of the Blending options. Even seasoned professionals have trouble predicting the exact repercussions of blending modes, and it's likely that you will, too. And, if you don't like what you get, you have to undo the operation and choose Edit⇨Fill all over again.

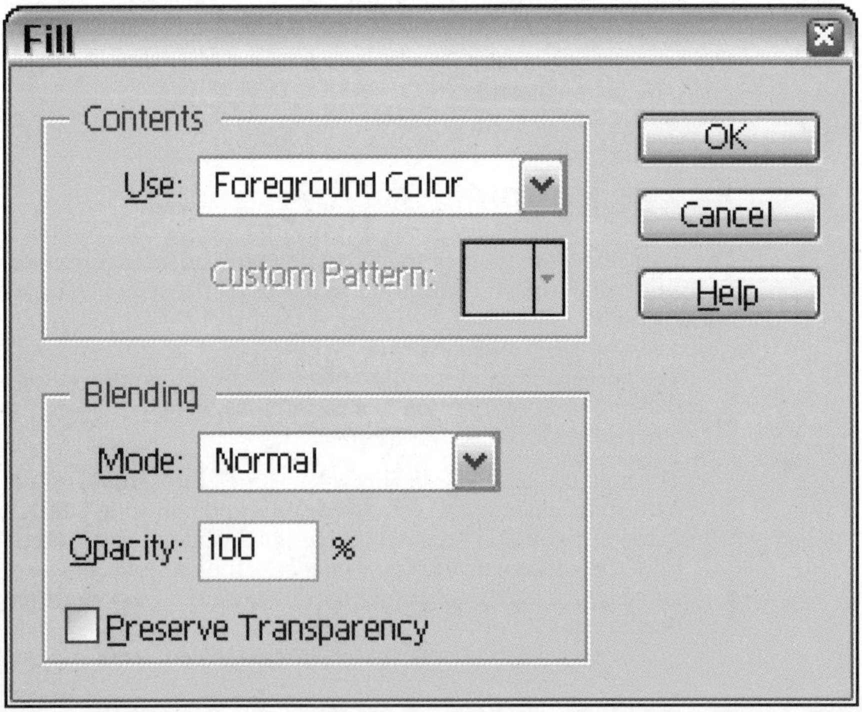

Figure 15-3: Specify how you want to fill a selection or layer by using the options in the Fill dialog box.

The better way to mix fills with selections is to copy the selection to a new layer, fill it, and experiment with the Opacity slider and blending mode options in the Layers palette. Naturally, you have no idea what this means if you haven't read the supremely insightful Chapters 9 and 13. Until you do, take this valuable advice and be content to ignore the Blending portion of the Fill dialog box.

The Preserve Transparency check box comes into play when you're working on a layer other than the Background layer, as discussed in Chapter 9. If the check box is turned on, only the opaque pixels in a selection are filled when you apply the Fill command — the transparent areas remain transparent. If the check box is turned off, the entire selection is filled. The option is dimmed if the Preserve Transparency option in the Layers palette is turned on.

Gradients: The Ever-Changing Color Sea

The Gradient tool lets you fill a selection with a fountain of colors that starts with one specified color and ends with another. By default, the two colors are the foreground color and background color.

But Elements can do more than create simple two-color blends. You can create custom gradients that blend a multitude of colors and vary from opaque to transparent throughout the blend. Elements has five gradient types: Linear, Radial, Angle, Reflected, and Diamond. And the Options bar offers settings that enable you to play with blend modes, opacity, and color reversals.

Checking out the Gradient tool

The following steps provide an insightful, probing introduction to the Gradient tool:

1. **Select some portion of your image.**

   In Figure 15-4, we selected the jar again. Just love that jar. It's so pristine; it just begs to be messed up.

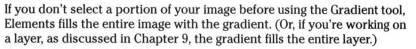

   If you don't select a portion of your image before using the Gradient tool, Elements fills the entire image with the gradient. (Or, if you're working on a layer, as discussed in Chapter 9, the gradient fills the entire layer.)

2. **Select the Gradient tool.**

   To do it quickly, just press the G key.

3. **From the Options bar, select your desired gradient type.**

Figure 15-4:
The
vegetables
inside the
jar have
been
replaced
with a
black-to-
white
gradient.

Gradient picker drop-down palette

4. **If necessary, select the Foreground to Background option, the first swatch, from the gradient picker drop-down palette in your Options bar.**

   It creates a gradient that begins with the foreground color and ends with the background color.

5. **Set the foreground and background colors the way you want them.**

   This step is up to you. You can use black and white or select new colors with the Eyedropper tool or Color Picker. For the purposes of Figure 15-4, the colors are set to black and white.

6. **Begin dragging at the point where you want to set the foreground color.**

   In Figure 15-4, the drag began at the bottom of the jar.

7. **Release where you want to position the background color.**

   In this case, it was the top of the jar. The result is a black-to-white gradation.

If you Shift+drag with the Gradient tool, Elements constrains the direction of your drag to a horizontal, vertical, or 45° diagonal angle.

Changing the way of the gradient

You can mess around with the performance of the Gradient tool by accessing the settings in the Options bar (refer to Figure 15-4).

Like the Opacity settings and Modes available inside the Fill dialog box, the Opacity and Mode options inside the Options bar for each of the gradients are best ignored. If you want to mix a gradation with the existing colors in a selection, create the gradation on a layer and select options inside the Layers palette, as discussed in Chapter 13.

Choosing between the five gradient tools

As stated at the beginning of this section, Elements gives you five gradient tools (see Figure 15-5):

✔ **Linear:** Creates a gradient in which colors blend in a straight line.

✔ **Radial:** The colors blend in concentric circles, from the center outward.

Note: In every example in Figure 15-5, the foreground color is black and the background color is white. You almost always want to set the lighter color to the foreground color when using the Radial option because doing that creates a glowing effect. If the Foreground color is darker than its Background compatriot, the gradation looks like a bottomless pit as you can see from the radial gradient shown in Figure 15-5.

Linear   Radial

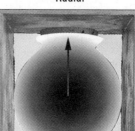

Figure 15-5:
Jar filled with five different gradient types. The arrows indicate the direction that the mouse was dragged.

Angle   Reflected   Diamond

✔ **Angle:** Creates a conical gradation with the colors appearing counter-clockwise.

✔ **Reflected:** If dragged from edge to edge of your selection, a reflected gradient acts like a linear gradient. However, if dragged from the interior to an edge of the selection, the gradient reflects back on itself.

✔ **Diamond:** As does the radial gradient, this tool creates concentric shapes — in this case, diamonds or squares, depending on the angle at which you drag.

Choosing gradient options

You find three check boxes in the Options bar: Reverse, Dither, and Transparency.

✔ **Reverse:** When the Reverse check box is checked, the gradient will start with the background color and end with the foreground color. This option is useful for creating radial gradients while keeping the default colors intact.

✔ **Dither:** The Dither check box is easy. When turned on, it helps eliminate banding. *Banding* is a problem in which you can see distinct bands of color in a printed gradient — that's a bad thing in 9 out of 10 households. Leave the check box turned on unless you're feeling especially contrary and want to create a banding effect.

✔ **Transparency:** The Transparency check box is a little more complicated. Here's the scoop: Gradients can include areas that are partially or fully transparent. In other words, they fade from a solid color to a more transparent color. When the Transparency check box is turned off, Elements creates the gradient by using all opaque colors, ignoring the transparency information.

The best way to get a grip on what the Transparency check box does is to try a little experiment. First, turn on the check box and press D to get the black and white foreground and background colors. Then, choose the Transparent Rainbow option, the next to last swatch, from the gradient picker drop-down palette and draw a gradient. You get a fill pattern that consists of a multicolored rainbow with your background peeking out at the beginning and end of the gradient. Next, draw the gradient with the Transparency check box turned off. You now get a fill of a multicolored rainbow with no background peeking out because Elements is ignoring the transparency at either end of the gradient. In most cases, you don't need to bother with the check box — just leave it turned on.

Selecting your colors

The gradient picker drop-down palette lets you change the way colors blend inside the gradation and select from a variety of prefab gradients. Your choices include:

- **Foreground to Background:** By default, this option is selected. It does just what it sounds as if it does: It blends between the foreground and background colors, as in the examples in Figure 15-5.

- **Foreground to Transparent:** If you select this option, the Gradient tool blends the foreground color into the original colors in the selection. The examples in Figure 15-6 were created with this option selected.

Figure 15-6: Here's the jar filled with a linear and radial gradient and with the Foreground to Transparent option selected.

Linear   Radial

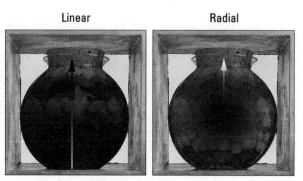

Foreground to Transparent

- **Remaining options:** The rest of the options in the gradient picker drop-down palette create a variety of factory-made gradients, some involving just a few colors and others blending a whole rainbow of colors.

- **Gradient libraries:** You also have at your disposal a vast array of gradient libraries, which have preset gradients that you can easily load for your painting pleasure. Simply click the arrow in the upper-right corner of the gradient picker palette to access the drop-down menu, and scroll down to the bottom where you find the various gradient libraries. Select one and it will replace your current gradient set.

When you select a gradient from the gradient picker palette, Elements displays the gradient in the gradient preview in the Options bar, as labeled earlier in Figure 15-4.

If none of the existing gradients suits your taste, you can create your own custom gradient, as in Color Plate 21. The next section explains the ins and outs of building your own gradients.

In the gradient picker palette's drop-down menu, you can choose between viewing your gradients by thumbnails, text only, or a combination of both text and thumbnails.

Becoming a gradient wizard

It's pretty easy to design your own custom gradient if you just spend a few moments to dissect and understand the various parts of the Gradient Editor dialog box. Start by clicking the Edit button to the right of the gradient preview in the Options bar. The Gradient Editor dialog box, shown in Figure 15-7, appears.

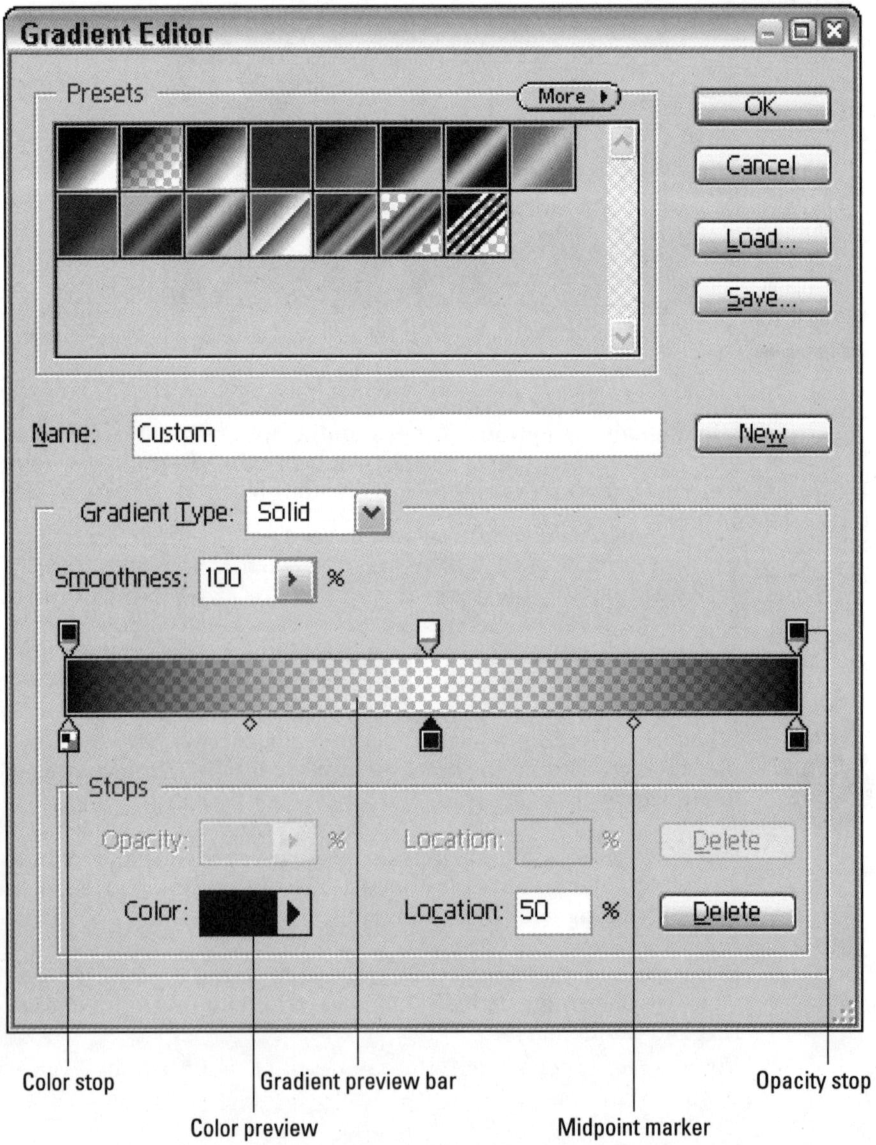

Figure 15-7:
The Gradient Editor gives you complete control over your gradients.

Color stop

Color preview

Gradient preview bar

Midpoint marker

Opacity stop

The Gradient Editor dialog box is a bit complex, and chances are you won't use it much. But the following list gives you a brief introduction to the dialog box and starts you off on creating your own gradient:

- ✔ **Presets:** The palette at the top of the dialog box lists all the preset gradients — the same ones in the gradient picker drop-down palette in the Options bar. Select the gradient you want to use as a starting point for your custom gradient from this palette. It doesn't much matter which you choose; you can change it to your heart's content.

- ✔ **Gradient Type:** You can choose between gradients made with Solid colors or those created with Noise. Noise gradients add noise that randomizes the colors of selected pixels and produces some interesting, yet unpredictable results.

- ✔ **Smoothness:** This option is available only if you choose a Solid gradient. Drag the slider or enter a value to determine how smoothly you blend one color into another color. The Smoothness slider changes to a Roughness slider when you select a Noise gradient type.

- ✔ **Roughness:** This option is available only if you choose a Noise gradient. Roughness affects how roughly or sharply one color transitions into another.

The following options are available only when the Noise gradient type is selected:

- ✔ **Color Model and color sliders:** Enable you to change the color model and or limit the color range by moving the sliders.

- ✔ **Restrict Colors:** Keeps colors from becoming too saturated.

- ✔ **Add Transparency:** Enables you to incorporate transparency in your noise gradient.

- ✔ **Randomize:** Changes the colors in a noise gradient. Remember, it is *random* and every time you click you get a new set of colors. Better than watching reruns on TV.

- ✔ **Stops:** The little house-shaped boxes that appear on either side of the gradient preview bar when the Solid gradient type is selected are called *stops*. There are color stops on the bottom and opacity stops on the top. You use these stops to change the colors, opacity, and location of colors in the gradient, as explained in the upcoming two sections.

Gradients can be managed just as Swatches are, as discussed in Chapter 5. It's important to save your gradient to disk if you want to be able to use it again later.

To remove a gradient from the list, press Alt+Shift (Option+Shift on a Mac) and click the gradient. Note that the scissors icon signifies "delete."

Changing, adding, and deleting colors

To change one of the colors in the gradient, first check to see if the roof on that color's color stop is black. The black *roof* indicates the active color stop — the color that is to be affected by your changes. If the roof isn't black, click the color stop to make it active.

After you activate the color stop, you have one of three choices. You can click the Color preview, which brings up the Color Picker. Or you can access the foreground or background color from the Color pop-up menu. You also have the Eyedropper at your disposal so you can click a color in your image or a color in the Swatches palette.

If you select the color via the Foreground or Background color options, you change the color marked by the color stop to the foreground or background color, respectively. Keep in mind that if you change the foreground or background color, the color in the gradient changes automatically. The change doesn't affect gradients that you've already drawn, but it does affect any future gradients you create. However, you can always select the color stop and choose User Color from the Color pop-up menu, which leaves the foreground or background color but untags it as such so no changes can occur.

Here's some more stuff you need to know about playing with the colors in your gradient:

- ✔ To add a color to the gradient, click just below the gradient preview bar at the point where you want the color to appear. You get a new color stop icon representing the color.

- ✔ To remove a color from the gradient, drag its color stop down and away from the gradient preview bar.

- ✔ If you drag a color stop to the right or left, you can change the position of the color in the gradient. Suppose that you have a gradient that fades from black to white. If you want more black and less white, drag the black color stop toward the white stop.

- ✔ The little diamonds on top of or underneath the gradient preview bar represent the midpoint between two colors or two opacity settings. Using the example of a black-to-white gradient again, the midpoint marks the spot at which the gradient contains equal amounts of black and white. To move a midpoint, just drag the diamond.

- ✔ The Location option box shows the placement of the active color stop or midpoint marker. If you want to be terribly precise, instead of dragging the icons, you can enter a value into the Location box to position a color stop or midpoint marker.

  When a color stop is active, a value of 0% represents the very beginning of the gradient; 100% represents the very end. Midpoint values are always relative to the two color stops on either side of the midpoint. A value of 50% places the midpoint an equal distance from both color stops. The minimum and maximum midpoint values are 5% and 95%.

Changing the transparency

Elements lets you adjust the amount of opacity in a gradient. You can make a portion of the gradient fully opaque, completely transparent, or somewhere in between the two.

Suppose that you want to create a gradient that starts out white, gradually fades to completely transparent, and then becomes completely white again. Here's how to create such a gradient:

1. **Make the foreground color white. Also make sure you have the default set of gradients loaded; choose Reset Gradients from the drop-down menu inside the gradient picker palette in the Options bar.**

2. **Click the Edit button in the Options bar to bring up the Gradient Editor dialog box.**

3. **Inside the Gradient Editor dialog box, choose the Foreground to Transparent (the second swatch) gradient from the Presets palette.**

4. **Take the opacity stop on the right and move it to the center of the gradient preview bar. Leave the Opacity setting at 0% (completely transparent).**

5. **Add another opacity stop at the far right. Change the Opacity setting to 100% (completely opaque).**

   The gradient preview bar now shows your gradient in terms of transparent and opaque areas. Black stops represent opaque areas; white stops represent transparent areas; gray areas represent everything in between. The gradient preview bar also shows you the opaque areas in their actual colors and transparent areas in the gray-and-white checkerboard pattern.

6. **Name your gradient.**

7. **Click New.**

   Your gradient, with its new name, is added to the palette of gradients above. You now have a gradient that fades from fully opaque white to transparent and back to fully opaque white. Apply the gradient to an image to get a better idea of what you just created.

   It's tempting to press Enter (Return on a Mac) after you change the Opacity value, but don't — pressing Enter (Return on a Mac) closes the dialog box. The value you enter into the Opacity setting takes effect without a press of the Enter (Return on a Mac) key. To switch to another option, press Tab.

You can also add as many opacity stops as you want and set different Opacity values for each. To move an opacity stop, just drag it right or left. To delete a stop, drag it off the bar. To move a midpoint, drag it right or left.

The Transparency check box in the Options bar determines whether transparency settings are ignored when you apply a gradient. If the check box is turned off, your gradient is completely opaque. For example, if you turn off the check box when applying the gradient created by the preceding steps, you get a completely white gradient instead of one that fades from white to transparent and back again.

Taking On Borders with the Stroke Command

The last item on this chapter's agenda is Edit⇨Stroke, a command that traces borders around a selection. When you choose this command, Elements displays the Stroke dialog box, shown in Figure 15-8. Enter the thickness of the border you want into the Width option box. This value is measured in pixels, and the range is 1 to 250 pixels.

You can, however, enter units other than pixels. For example, if you type **2 in**, Elements accepts it and converts the value in inches to an equivalent number of pixels.

In Figure 15-9, for example, a 16-pixel wide black stroke was placed around the jar. Then using the same selection, an 8-pixel wide white stroke was placed on top of that. Slick, huh? (Oh, come on, say it is, even if it's just to make us feel better.)

How the border rides the track

The Location options in the Stroke dialog box determine how the border rides the selection outline. The border can cruise around fully inside or fully outside the selection, or it can sit astride (centered on) the selection. Why might you want to change this setting? Well, take another look at Figure 15-9. Suppose that instead of the white border being flanked on either side by black (which was created using the Center option), you want the borders to sit beside each other. If you select the Inside option, the white border appears inside the selection, and the black border inside the white border. If you select Outside, the white border traces the outside of the jar, and the black border extends even farther.

Actually, using the Outside option isn't recommended. It has a nasty habit of flattening the edges of curves. For the best results, stick with Inside or Center.

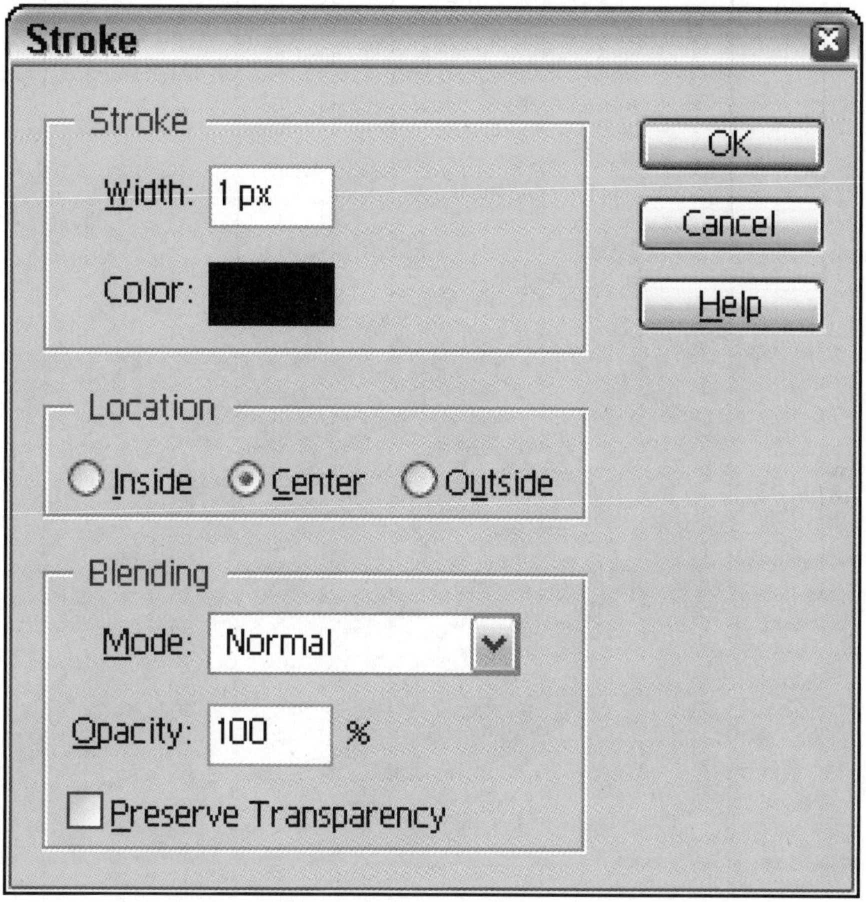

Figure 15-8:
Use the
Stroke
dialog box
to draw a
border
around a
selection.

Mix your stroke after you press Enter (Return)

Like the Blending and Opacity options in other dialog boxes, the ones in the Stroke dialog box don't provide you with a preview of how the effect will look when applied to your image. So, if you want to play with the blending modes or opacity of your stroke, ignore the options in the dialog box. Instead, create a new layer (as explained in Chapter 9) and do your selecting and stroking on that layer. You can then adjust the blending mode and opacity via the Layers palette (as discussed in Chapter 13).

On the off chance that you're curious about the Preserve Transparency check box, it affects only images with layers. If you don't have any layers going, don't worry about it. (Again, we explain layers in Chapter 9.) It just ensures that the transparent portions of layers remain transparent.

We explore the Stroke command more in the next chapter, where we cast a penetrating gaze at the world of type inside Elements. So keep reading if you're curious, or go ahead and take a breather if you need it. We promise not to go ahead without you.

Figure 15-9:
The classic double-border effect, so in demand at today's finer jar emporiums.

Chapter 16

Type Righter

C hapter 8 leads you on a merry tour of the various tools and commands for selecting a part of your image. But that chapter skips one other type of selection outline that you can create in Photoshop Elements, and you'll never guess what it is. Not in a million years. Give up? The answer is *text*. That's right, Elements lets you build a selection outline out of numbers, vowels, consonants, and any other characters you can tap in from your keyboard. Selection outline text is one of the two different kinds of text that Elements lets you create. You can also create regular text, which has the distinct advantage of remaining editable long after you create it.

In general, the Elements approach to text makes it an ideal program for subjecting large letters to special effects. The bigger your text, the better it looks. On the other hand, you shouldn't mistake Elements for a word processor. Even though Elements deals with text admirably, it's still not the best choice for creating large chunks of text; instead, use a word processor such as Microsoft Word or a desktop publishing program such as InDesign, PageMaker, or QuarkXPress.

Working with the Type Tools

Whereas the first version of Elements gave you only two type tools, Elements 2.0 gives you four! Does this mean that you can do twice as much with text now? Well, no. Actually, the two additional type tools don't give you a speck more functionality; Adobe simply moved an option down out of the Options bar and into the Toolbox, thereby creating two additional tools. Both versions of Elements have a Horizontal Type tool and a Vertical Type tool. But if you wanted to create selection outlines out of, say, horizontal text using the previous version of Elements, you selected the Horizontal Type tool and activated the Create Selection option in the Options bar. Now you can choose the Horizontal Type Mask tool from the Toolbox and accomplish the same thing; likewise for the Vertical Type Mask tool.

The Vertical Type and Vertical Type Mask tools are great for Asian fonts, but for Roman letters they probably won't be very valuable to you. Therefore, we're going to pretty much ignore them for the rest of this chapter. It'll make it a lot easier to deal with the similarities and differences between the regular type tools and the type mask tools. So, if you find that you do need vertical type, just remember that the Vertical Type tool behaves almost exactly like the Horizontal Type tool; ditto for the Vertical Type Mask tool and the Horizontal Type Mask tool. And anyway, after creating horizontal letters it's a snap to switch them to vertical letters if you need to; there's a handy button in the type Options bar for just that purpose.

You select the type tools by pressing the T key on your keyboard. (The icon for the tool even looks like the letter T, making this the only tool icon that serves as its own tool tip.) By default, pressing Shift-T will cycle through selecting the various type tools. You can change this by deselecting the Use Shift Key for Tool Switch option in the General pane of the Preferences; if you do so, merely pressing T will cycle through the type tools. Following is a briefing on the difference between the Horizontal Type tool (see Figure 16-1) and the Horizontal Type Mask tool.

✔ **The Horizontal Type tool** creates text on a new text layer (Chapter 9 explains layers in excruciating detail), which enables you to work with the text without worrying about touching the underlying image.

You can come back and edit the text contents and attributes long after you've moved on to another part of the image by simply highlighting the text with the Horizontal Type tool. Although you can't use painting or editing tools on a text layer, you can make the text more or less translucent by adjusting the Opacity percentage in the Layers palette, and you can blend the text with the underlying layers using the blending modes drop-down menu.

✔ **The Horizontal Type Mask tool** enables you to create your text as a selection outline. The minute you click with this tool, the image fills with a pink overlay; for a full explanation of what's up with that, skip ahead to the "Declaring Open Season on Type Selection Outlines" section later in this chapter. Until you decide to "commit" your text, you can work with selection outline text just as you would with regular text. Also, you can manipulate, edit, paint, and otherwise play with a type selection outline as you can with any other selection outline. And because the Horizontal Type Mask tool works like any other selection tool, you can use it to add to or subtract from an existing selection outline (see Chapter 8). Note that once you click the Commit button in the Options bar, you can't edit selection type as you can regular type created with the Horizontal Type tool.

So, which option do you use when? If you want to retain true editability, obviously, use the Horizontal Type tool to create the text on its own layer. Otherwise, it depends on what sort of effect you're trying to create. If you simply want opaque type, choose the Horizontal Type tool. If, on the other hand, you want to create text outlines, such as those shown in Figure 16-3, use the Horizontal type Mask tool and then stroke the selection outline using Edit⇨Stroke.

Just remember that the basic difference between the two type tools is that one creates editable type on a new text layer and the other gives you a selection outline in the shape of your characters. Pick the option that gives you the quickest route to the effect you're trying to achieve.

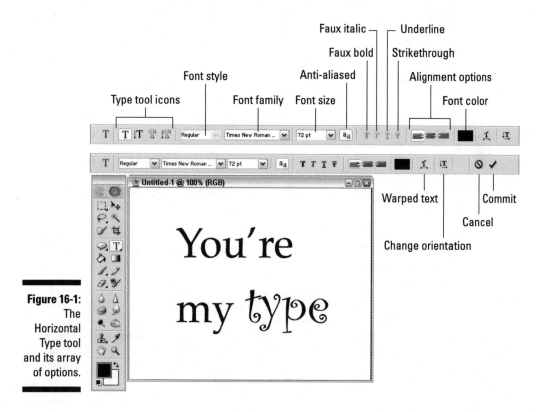

Figure 16-1:
The
Horizontal
Type tool
and its array
of options.

The biggest disadvantage of using the Horizontal Type Mask tool is that when you deselect the text selection, the text becomes permanently fused to the underlying image. But you can get around this problem by waiting to utilize your text selection outlines until you've created a new layer in the Layers palette for just that purpose. Then, any text you create can exist on its own layer so that you can easily move, rotate, paint, and so on. Remember, however, that a regular layer is not the same as a text layer. A text layer provides for editability of contents and attributes. Read on!

Putting Your Words On-Screen

There are many similarities between using the Horizontal Type tool and the Horizontal Type Mask tool. We focus first on the Horizontal Type tool, but if you want to create type selection outlines, you should read this section, too, because we cover all the text formatting options here.

To type a few letters in Elements, select the Horizontal Type tool and click inside the image. It doesn't really matter where you click, by the way. Elements creates a new layer and positions your text at the spot you click, but you can always move the text after you create it. You get a little blinking cursor (called an *insertion marker*) that you may be familiar with from working in other programs. After the insertion marker appears, you're free to enter your text.

Typing what must be typed

Using the Horizontal Type tool creates what is known as a text layer. In the Layers palette you'll notice a new layer with a capital letter T icon indicating that it is indeed a text layer. The name of the text layer corresponds to the text you typed.

Here are a few more things you may need to know while inputting text on your canvas. We'll look at formatting a little later in the section "Changing how the type looks."

 ✔ After entering your text, you may find that you've made a mistake or two. To delete a letter, first make sure the correct layer is active and then click after the letter you want to delete and press the Backspace key (Delete key on a Mac). To add text, click at the point where you want to insert the text and enter the new text from the keyboard. To delete more than one letter, drag to highlight the letters and press the Backspace key (Delete key on a Mac).

> ✔ To replace text, drag over it with the cursor to highlight it and then start whacking those keys.
>
> ✔ Elements places all words on a single line in the image unless you insert a hard return by pressing the Enter key (Return key on a Mac). To achieve the effect shown in Figure 16-1, for example, press the Enter key (Return key on the Mac) between "You're" and "my type."

While typing and editing your text, you can use the Cut, Copy, Paste, and Undo commands under the Edit menu. This enables you to fix mistakes in case you typed some letters or words out of order. For example, to move some letters from one place to another, follow these steps:

1. **Highlight the text you want to move.**

   Drag over the text with the I-beam cursor.

2. **Press Ctrl+X (⌘+X on a Mac).**

   Elements removes the text and puts it in a special location in your computer's memory called the *clipboard.* Ctrl+X (⌘+X on a Mac), by the way, is the shortcut for the Edit⇨Cut command.

3. **Click at the point where you want to move the text.**

   Your click repositions the insertion marker.

4. **Press Ctrl+V (⌘+V on a Mac).**

   Ctrl+V (⌘ +V) is the shortcut for the Edit⇨Paste command. Elements retrieves the text from the clipboard and inserts it at the desired spot.

If you want to duplicate a word, highlight it; then choose Edit⇨Copy or press Ctrl+C (⌘+C on a Mac); reposition the insertion marker; and choose Edit⇨Paste. You can also undo the last edit by choosing Edit⇨Undo or by pressing Ctrl+Alt+Z (⌘+Option+Z on a Mac).

Changing how the type looks

The Options bar provides all the typographic options needed to format your text. These options control the typeface, the type size, the type color, alignment, and all that other rigmarole. When all these characteristics get together in the same room, they're usually called *formatting attributes.* You can, of course, make additional enhancements to the appearance of your text after you return to the image window, but the formatting options let you set up the fundamental stuff.

Here are some things to keep in mind when exploring the type options:

✔ In order to change the attributes of your text, the Horizontal Type tool must be active. If you want to change only a portion of your text, highlight it with the tool. If you want to select all the text, highlight all of it or simply click the Commit button and keep that particular text layer selected in the Layers palette.

✔ If you know what you want, you can always establish your formatting attributes *before* you create your type. Who knows, you may get it exactly right the first time around with no need for further editing.

✔ Select a typeface from the font drop-down menu. Select a style from the font style drop-down menu. Type styles such as bold and italic (sometimes referred to as "oblique") appear in their own submenus.

✔ Enter the size of the text into the font size option box. The Size value is measured in points (one point equals $\frac{1}{72}$ inch), pixels, or millimeters, depending on your Type setting in the Units & Rulers panel of the Preferences dialog box.

✔ If you want to squash or stretch your text, switch over to the Move tool and drag one of the squares on the bounding box. (Note that switching to another tool "commits" the text just as if you'd clicked the Commit button in the Options bar.) You can then switch back to the Horizontal Type tool and, amazingly enough, the text is still editable. It's best, however, to use this option sparingly or else you run the risk of totally destroying the appealing proportions of a typeface. Most typefaces have been designed by trained artists who spend their lives perfecting the shape and form of each letter. Not that you should feel guilty or anything.

✔ In case your font doesn't have a built-in bold or italic state, the type tool Options bar gives you access to Faux Bold and Faux Italic. You can also choose to underline your text, or strike through it for that "pretend you can't read this" look.

✔ By default, the color that first appears in the swatch in the Options bar is the current foreground color. To change the color after you click your type tool but before you create the text, you can use the Swatches palette or the Color Picker, which you can access by clicking on the Foreground swatch in the Toolbox or the color swatch in the Options bar. (If you need a basic color refresher, see Chapter 5.)

✔ Select an alignment option to determine whether multiple lines of text are aligned by their left edges, right edges, or centers.

✔ You can mix most formatting attributes within the same text layer, but alignment is one attribute that cannot be mixed.

There are a couple of options that can be found not only in the Options bar but also in the Type submenu of the Layer menu:

- ✔ **Horizontal/Vertical:** This text orientation option lets you switch horizontal text to vertical text, and vice versa.
- ✔ **Anti-aliasing:** You almost always want Anti-aliasing on because if you don't, your text will have tiny jagged edges, and you probably don't want that.
- ✔ **Warp Text:** This feature is so neat it deserves its own section. So read on.

Warping type into strange and unusual shapes

Warping text in Elements is a little bit like the feature known as path text, found in drawing programs, such as Illustrator, Freehand, and CorelDraw. You can twist, push, and pull to create a variety of cool and crazy effects. Take a glance at Figure 16-2 to see a small sampling of these effects.

Figure 16-2: You can warp type into a variety of both animate and inanimate shapes.

Follow these easy steps to warp your very own text:

1. **Select the text layer in the Layers palette.**

2. **Select a type in the Toolbox and click the Warp Text icon in the Options bar. Or choose Layer⇨Type⇨Warp Text (any tool can be active to choose this).**

3. **In the Warp Text dialog box, select a Style from the drop-down menu.**

4. **Play with the options.**

   Choose Horizontal or Vertical orientation. Adjust the Bend to apply more or less warping. Use the Distortion sliders to apply a perspective effect to the warp.

5. **If you're happy with your warp, click OK.**

   Simple instructions, we know, but in truth the secret to warping text is just playing around with the options. Setting the proper Style is the most important decision; the other options simply give you permutations based on the Style you choose. So pick a Style and start exploring. Luckily, it's such a fun command that you'll enjoy finding out about it (imagine that)!

Editing the Text Layer

If you notice a misspelled word or some other typographical gaffe, select the offending text layer and drag over the text with the Horizontal Type tool to edit it. You can then edit the contents or any of the attributes. When you're through, just switch to a different tool or click the Commit button in the Options bar. Provided you keep your file in the PSD (Photoshop) format, text layers are saved with the image, so you can revise the text at any time as long as you don't simplify the layer (see the section "Simplifying a Text Layer" for more info) or flatten the layers (see Chapter 9 for more on layers).

Here are some things you can do to a text layer and still be able to edit the text:

✔ You can reorder or duplicate the text layer in the Layers palette, just as you can with a regular layer. To move the layer in front of or behind another one, drag it up or down in the list of layers in the Layers palette. A black line shows where the layer will be inserted. To duplicate, drag the layer onto the Create a New Layer icon at the bottom of the Layers palette.

✔ You can lock text layers (see Chapter 9 for more on this feature).

✔ Move or clone the text. Drag with the Move tool to position the text. Alt+drag (Option+drag on a Mac) to clone the text. Note that Alt+dragging (Option+dragging on a Mac) creates another text layer.

✔ Change the orientation of the text layer. Choose Layer⇨Type⇨Horizontal or Vertical to change the orientation, or just click the Change the Text Orientation button in the Options bar.

✔ You can apply any of the blending modes and adjust the opacity of the text layer in the Layers palette.

✔ Perform transformation commands, such as Free Transform and Skew, as found in the Image menu under the Transform submenu. Distort and Perspective transformations aren't available to text layers.

✔ Apply Layer Styles (see details in Chapter 13) to the text layer. Even after you apply the effect, if the type changes in any way (such as a different font or even a different word), the Layer Style magically updates to the changes.

✔ Fill the type with the foreground or background color by using the fill keyboard shortcuts. Press Alt+Backspace (Option+Delete on a Mac) to fill with the foreground color. Press Ctrl+Backspace (⌘+Delete on a Mac) to fill with the background color. Note that the Edit⇨Fill menu command is grayed out — you can utilize only the keyboard shortcuts.

Here are three things you can't do to a text layer, unless you simplify the text layer and convert it to a regular layer (see more about this in the next section):

✔ You can't use any of the painting and editing tools. When you click the painting and editing tools on the text layer, you get an error message saying you must first simplify the type.

✔ You can't apply filters from the Filters palette.

✔ You can't apply effects from the Effects palette.

A text layer can't be created for images in indexed color or bitmap modes because these modes don't support layers of any kind — text or otherwise. Type created in these modes is treated like type created with the Horizontal Type Mask tool; it gets applied to the Background and cannot be edited after it is committed. If you want type included in GIF images you're preparing for the Web, for example, be sure and wait until you finish compositing your layers and editing your type to convert the image to indexed color.

If you decide you don't want the text layer any longer, delete it by dragging the layer to the Trash icon at the bottom of the Layers palette (for help, see Chapter 9). You can also click the layer in the Layers palette and then click the Trash icon.

Simplifying a Text Layer

In order to apply a filter, effect, or paint on a text layer, you must first do what Elements calls *simplifying* the layer. Simplifying is actually just a sort of simpler word for *rasterizing;* it means to convert the text layer into a regular layer containing just pixels. To simplify a type layer, choose Layer⇨Simplify Layer. After simplifying, the type looks the same; however, you can no longer edit the type. (Notice that the T icon isn't there anymore in the Layers palette.) So, a word of advice — be sure the text is exactly the way you want it before you simplify the text layer, because editing capabilities go down the drain. (You could, of course, also just duplicate the text layer by dragging it to the Create a New Layer icon in the Layers palette. Then turn off the visibility for one copy by clicking the visibility eyeball for that layer. That way you have a backup — perfect for when you feel you're not quite ready to make a commitment.)

Declaring Open Season on Type Selection Outlines

As we say earlier, almost all the preceding formatting information applies to type created with the Horizontal Type Mask tool as well. The big difference is that once you click that commit button, hit the Enter key on the numeric keypad, or select another tool, you can't edit your text any longer.

The first thing you may notice when you click with the Horizontal Type Mask tool is the appearance of a funky pink overlay. And as you type, your letters will appear transparent, as if they were cut out of the pink overlay. This is Elements' way of telling you that you are creating a kind of mask, where parts of the layer are masked off and can't be affected by editing. (And when you think about it, that's exactly what you do when you make any kind of selection.) When you click Commit in the Options bar, the overlay disappears and the familiar marching ants of the selection appear. (See Chapter 8 for more on selections.) Now that your newly created selection outline type is there inside your image, you can do all kinds of things with it, including the following:

- ✔ To move a text selection outline, drag with one of the selection tools or press the arrow keys to nudge the selection outline this way or that.

- ✔ To move or clone the text selection, use the same techniques you use to move or clone any other selection (refer to Chapters 8 and 9). Drag with the Move tool to move the text; Alt+drag (Option+drag on a Mac) to clone the text.

In other words, selections that you create with the type selection option work just like any other selection.

✔ You can paint inside the text. After you paint inside the letters, you can use the edit tools to smear the colors, blur them, lighten them, and so on.

✔ You can fill the text with the Foreground color by pressing Alt+Backspace (Option+Delete on a Mac). To fill the text with the Background color, press Ctrl+Backspace (⌘+Delete on a Mac). To fill the text with a blend of colors, just drag across the text with the Gradient tool. It couldn't be easier.

✔ You can apply a border around your type by choosing Edit⇨Stroke.

✔ Before you fill or stroke a selection outline, be sure that your text is positioned where you want it. You can't move the stroked text after you create it without leaving a hole on your layer. Ditto with any other painting or editing commands you apply to a text selection outline. That's why it's a good idea to create a new layer before you create your text selection outline. It enables you to move the text without affecting the underlying image.

✔ If you want to delete text that was created with the Horizontal Type Mask tool — and you didn't create that text on its own layer — you need to undo your steps by using the Undo History palette (see Chapter 7) to bring your image back to its pretext appearance.

The following steps tell you how to create genuine outline type, like the stuff shown in Figure 16-3. You can see through the interiors of the letters, and you can make the borders as thick as you please. What more could you ask from life?

1. **Create a new layer.**

   You don't have to put your text on its own layer, but doing so makes it simpler to edit the text later on if necessary. To create a layer, click the Create a New Layer icon in the Layers palette, as discussed in Chapter 9.

2. **Select the Horizontal Type Mask tool in the Toolbox.**

3. **Set the formatting attributes in the Options bar.**

4. **Click with the tool on your canvas.**

   Type away and then press Enter on the numeric keypad or click the Commit button in the Options bar. Then move the text selection outline into the desired position by dragging it or nudging it with the arrow keys.

5. **Set the Foreground color to white.**

   You can do this quickly by pressing D to get black and white and then X to swap them.

6. **Make sure that the Lock Transparent Pixels check box in the Layers palette is deselected.**

   In the next step, you apply a stroke to the center of your selection outline (that is, with half the stroke appearing on the inside of the outline and half appearing on the outside). If you don't deselect the Lock Transparent Pixels check box, Elements doesn't let you paint on the layer.

7. **Choose Edit⇨Stroke, select the Center radio button, and enter 12 as the Width value.**

   After making your selections in the Stroke dialog box, press Enter (Return on a Mac). You now have a 12-pixel thick, white outline around your type. Depending on the size of your type, you may need to enter a value other than 12.

8. **Make black or some other dark color the Foreground color.**

9. **Choose Edit⇨Stroke and enter 4 as the Width value. Leave the Location at Center.**

   Then press Enter (Return on a Mac). Congratulations! You get the effect shown in Figure 16-3. If you created your text on a layer, as recommended back in Step 1, you can use the Move tool to reposition the text if needed. You can also play with the blending modes and Opacity slider in the Layers palette to change how the text blends with the underlying image.

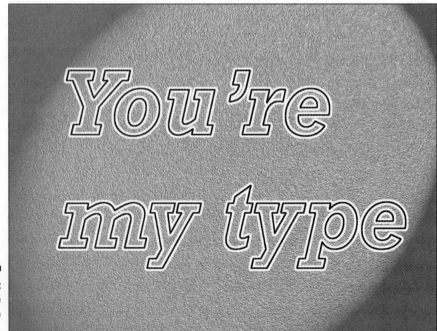

Figure 16-3:
Outline type
created the
correct way.

Although this stroking effect is pretty cool, it pales in comparison to what can be achieved with a text layer created using the Horizontal Type tool and layer styles. Text layers and layer styles go hand in hand. Once you've applied an inner bevel and drop shadow to a text layer, you probably won't ever be satisfied with plain ordinary flat text again. And don't forget that even with a layer style applied, text layers are still completely editable. Although why anyone would need to go back and edit his or her text is a compleet mistery.

Chapter 17

Can Photoshop Elements Do *That*?

. . . .

. . . .

*O*rganizing the many different functions of Photoshop Elements into the chapters of this book was like trying to herd a couple thousand weasels into 16 different pens, making sure they were all correctly sorted by gender, birth weight, IQ, religious persuasion, cholesterol level, and batting average. After a prolonged tussle, a great deal of squirming and wriggling, and much yanking from one pen and plopping down into another, things looked pretty good. Panting, exhausted, we turned around — and saw a few more danged weasels in the corner. These guys seemed to defy any classification. They were rebels. They refused to be pigeonholed — *weaselholed* — by The Man.

And so this, the 17th chapter, contains the weasels that wouldn't go into the 16 other pens.

On reflection though, it became clear that these weasels all had something in common: They all dealt with *automation*. The automation in most of these weasels — okay, these *features* — works just as you'd expect: You tell Elements what to do, say "Go!", and then sit back while Elements does it. And with one feature, animated GIFs, the automation comes after the fact: After the animated GIF is loaded in a Web user's browser, the animation plays back automatically.

Another thing these seven functions have in common: They're probably the most amazing stuff that Elements has to offer. Up to now, Elements has been a hands-on application, and necessarily so. Now it's time to sit back and watch. Prop your feet up. Take off your shoes. And put a pillow on your chest so you won't bruise your chin when your jaw drops open in amazement. This is the stuff that makes you say: "Can Photoshop Elements do *that?*"

Taking on the Effects Palette

An *effect,* in Elements' terminology, is a series of commands — combining filters and layer styles with more mundane stuff such as Filling and Image Sizing — that are prebuilt and prerecorded for your use. As with the Blur More and Sharpen More filters, effects are one-shot wonders — you just apply them, and if you don't like the end result, too bad. There's no tweaking allowed (at least, not until after the fact).

Applying effects from the Effects palette is almost identical to applying filters from the Filters palette. You have three options:

- Click the desired effect to select it, and then click the Apply button at the top of the palette.
- Double-click the desired effect.
- Drag the desired effect from the Effects palette into the image window.

Okay, we lied — there is one other way to apply an effect, and it goes for the Filters palette too. Instead of clicking the Apply button, you can also choose the Apply command from the More menu located in the upper-right corner of the palette. Although why anyone would bypass the Apply button to go for the More menu is completely beyond us.

There are four different categories of effects (or five if you count All):

- **Frames:** As you may expect, these effects can create a frame around your image. Some Frame effects will only operate if a preexisting selection is active. As you saw in Chapter 8, the Vignette effect is quite attractive. Drop Shadow Frame would be a great choice for creating Web images where the Web page's background color was white. And Photo Corners is nice for that retro look.

- **Image Effects:** These are sort of a mixed bag. They perform a variety of different creative processes on your image and work with selected parts of images or entire layers. Fluorescent Chalk and Quadrant Colors perform their magic on the entire layer, regardless of whether there's an active selection. If you want the color in your image to gradually fade out to black and white, Horizontal Color Fade and Vertical Color Fade were made for you. As an alternative, you can also use the Color Fade – Horizontal and Color Fade – Vertical layer styles to achieve the same effect.

✔ **Text Effects:** Probably the most useful of the effects. They require a live text layer in order to work, so first create your text with the Horizontal or Vertical Type tool (see Chapter 16 for more information). While the three Outline effects can be a bit blocky, the other eight options are quite attractive. Use Brushed Metal to give your text a shiny look or Water Reflection to reflect your text in a photo of a body of water, as seen in Figure 17-1. Note that these effects automatically simplify your layer (see Chapter 16), so make sure you're through editing your text before you apply one of the Text Effects.

Figure 17-1: Applying Water Reflection from the Effects palette (left) creates the effect of text reflecting in the water (right).

✔ **Textures:** You can create solid fields of different surfaces, from Bricks to Molten Lead to Sandpaper. The Ink Blots, Marbled Glass, Sunset, and Wood-Pine effects can only work on the entire layer, regardless of whether there's an active selection or not. To see the Textures effects in action, turn back to the color pages in the book. Many of the backgrounds behind the color plates are rendered out Textures.

Batch Processing

If you've got a whole bunch of different images that you need to make conform in terms of file format and image size, the Batch command is just the ticket. All you have to do is tell Elements where the files are, what you want the common file format to be, whether you want it to make changes in image size, and where to save the files. Click OK, and Batch does the rest.

Here's the step-by-step game plan:

1. **Choose File⇨Batch Processing.**

   The Batch dialog box appears, as shown in Figure 17-2.

2. **Use the Files to Convert drop-down list to locate the images that you want to batch process.**

   Choose Folder if the images are already grouped together in a folder somewhere on your hard drive. Then click the Source button, navigate to the correct folder, select it, and click Choose. If you have other folders containing images inside your Source folder and you want to batch process those too, click the Include All Subfolders check box.

   Choose Import if you want to get the pictures from a scanner, a digital camera, or a PDF file. Pick your source on the From pop-up menu. When you click OK after choosing your other settings, Elements will take you to another dialog box, depending on the type of device and plug-ins you have installed. If you've chosen PDF file, you'll be asked to locate the file and then be given a chance to preview the images to be extracted from the PDF.

   Choose Opened Files if you want to batch process all the currently opened files in Elements.

3. **Choose your desired file format from the Convert File Type drop-down menu.**

   You have Elements' usual long list of possibilities.

Batch

Tip:
Converts the file format or image size of several images at once, and lets you automatically rename the converted files. Click the Destination button to select the folder for the converted files.

OK
Cancel
Help

Files to convert: | Folder |

Source...

☑ Include All Subfolders

Conversion Options

Convert file type: | JPEG Max Quality |

Image Size

☑ Convert Image Size

Width (pixels) [   ]   Height (pixels) [   ]

Resolution: | 72 dpi | ☑ Constrain Proportions

File Naming

☑ Rename Files

Example: MyFile001.gif

| Document Name | + | 3 Digit Serial Number |

Compatibility: ☑ Windows ☑ Mac OS 9 ☑ Unix

Output Options

Destination...   Macintosh HD:Users:galen:Pictures:

Figure 17-2:
The Batch dialog box lets you tell Elements everything it needs to know in order to process your files.

The Batch dialog box now gives you four different JPEG compression settings to choose from — a big improvement over the first version of Elements, which gave you only medium-quality JPEGs.

4. **Choose whether you want to change the image size or resolution.**

Once again, Elements 2.0 improves upon Elements 1.0. The new Constrain Proportions check box ensures that images of varying sizes won't get squashed or stretched if you activate Convert Image Size.

5. **Specify a File Naming convention.**

If you want the files you're saving to have different names from the source files, click the Rename Files check box. The options here are very similar to those found in the File Browser's Batch Rename command, as covered in Chapter 3. It's necessary to have at least one of the document name, serial number, or serial letter options chosen, so that Elements doesn't overwrite each file in turn by giving it the same name as the last file. You can choose from the long lists of options, or type a name into one of the two fields. If these images are destined for the Web, it's a good idea to make sure you have all three Compatibility check boxes checked.

6. **Specify where you want the files to be saved.**

   After clicking the Destination button in the Output Options section and navigating to the appropriate place on your hard drive, you may want to take the opportunity to click the New Folder button and save the batch-processed images into their own folder.

7. **Click the OK button, and sit back while Elements automatically processes the images according to your guidelines.**

Attaching a File to E-Mail

So you want to share your Elements masterpiece with the world? Elements would like nothing more! That's why there's a new Attach to E-mail command in Elements 2.0. Just click the button in the Shortcuts bar — it's the one with the paper clip and envelope — or choose File⇨Attach to E-mail.

If your image is already a JPEG and is of sufficiently small file size and pixel dimensions, your e-mail program will automatically fire up, and an unaddressed, outgoing e-mail file will open with your image already attached. Otherwise, a warning message will appear. You can click Send As Is to go ahead and attach your file to an e-mail, or click Auto Convert. If you click Auto Convert, Elements will change the pixel dimensions of your image as necessary so that either the width or height is 1200 pixels, save your image as a JPEG, and then attach that file to an unaddressed, outgoing e-mail. That should make the receiver of the e-mail very happy; the reduced file size means that the image will download faster, and the JPEG file format means that the recipient will definitely be able to open the file after it has downloaded!

Projecting a PDF Slideshow

Here's another thing that PDF, the "can-do kid" (see Chapter 6), can do: make a slide show out of a group of images. If you're making a presentation on a computer and have a series of image files you want to show, this is an elegant, simple solution. Just choose File⇨Automation Tools⇨PDF Slideshow, and the dialog box shown in Figure 17-3 appears.

If the images you want to include in your slide show are already open in Elements, clicking the Add Open Files check box will automatically include them. Otherwise, click the Browse button and locate your files with the resulting Open dialog box. Click the Choose button to specify where you want to save your PDF slide show file, and give it a name.

The Slide Show Options give you control over a few aspects of the presentation. If the Advance Every _ Seconds check box is active, you can enter the number of seconds that you want each image to be displayed before the next image takes over. If the check box is unchecked, each image in your slide show will stay on-screen until you click the mouse. If you want the slide show to endlessly repeat, click the Loop After Last Page check box. And the neatest part of a PDF slide show is the transitions from slide to slide. There are a large number to choose from; set it to Random Transition if you like being pleasantly surprised. If you want to access the standard PDF saving options, click the Advanced button; otherwise, click OK.

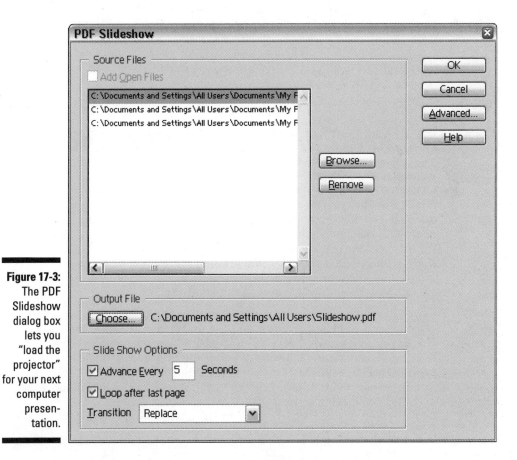

Figure 17-3:
The PDF Slideshow dialog box lets you "load the projector" for your next computer presen-tation.

As long as the computer on which you'll be making the presentation has Adobe Acrobat Reader (a free download from www.adobe.com), you're in good shape. Just double-click the PDF file and enjoy the show!

Converting a Multipage PDF File

Here's one more PDF trick that Elements 2.0 can pull off. If you have a multi-page PDF file and you need to open all the pages within Elements, it can be a drag to repeatedly open the file and choose a single page at a time to open. The File⇨Automation Tools⇨Multi-page PDF to PSD command can convert the PDF file into a folder of individual PSD files, each page in its own individual file.

Select the PDF file you want to convert by clicking the Choose button. The Page Range option lets you convert the entire document or a consecutive group of pages. The Output Options let you choose a resolution, color mode, and whether you want Elements to anti-alias the resulting PSD files (recommended for maximum image smoothness). And finally, the Destination options let you choose a destination folder for your PSD files and choose a Base Name for the files; the files will have names like "document0001.psd," "document0002.psd," and so on. Click OK and let Elements go nuts!

Creating and Printing a Contact Sheet

Elements has the capability of creating a digital version of a traditional contact sheet. This feature takes a folder of images, creates thumbnails, and arranges them on a single page. It's good for record-keeping purposes because it enables you to catalog large quantities of files. It's also useful for merely checking out a big batch of images.

Here are the steps for creating and printing a contact sheet:

1. **Choose File⇨Print Layouts⇨Contact Sheet.**

   In Elements 1.0, this command was called Contact Sheet II. Does that mean that the new version, simply called "Contact Sheet," isn't as advanced as the old version? Not really. There's actually one small improvement for Elements 2.0, so maybe this time it should really be "Contact Sheet III." Or maybe Adobe is taking after George Lucas, who made episodes four, five, and six of the Star Wars saga before he made the first three episodes.

2. **Click on the Choose button in the Contact Sheet dialog box (see Figure 17-4).**

   Locate the folder containing the images you want to print. Count the number of images in your folder.

3. **Specify the size and resolution of the contact sheet.**

   If you are unsure about resolution, see Chapter 4 for details.

   If you deselect the Flatten All Layers check box, your finished file will contain each image on its own individual layer and each caption on its own editable text layer. This can be helpful if you might want to tweak the layout or rename the files, but otherwise it just balloons the file size. However, even if you do check Flatten All Layers, your finished document will have two layers: a Background layer and a layer with all the thumbnails and captions on it.

4. **Specify a color mode — RGB Color or Grayscale.**

   For information on color modes, see Chapter 5.

5. **Specify the order and the number of columns and rows for your layout in the Thumbnails section.**

   Be sure that the number of thumbnails you create can accommodate (or exceeds) the number of images in your folder.

6. **Choose if you want to use the Filename As a Caption for your images.**

Contact Sheet

Source Folder
Browse...
☑ Include All Subfolders

OK
Cancel
Help

Document
Width: 8   inches
Height: 10   inches
Resolution: 72   pixels/inch
Mode: RGB Color
☑ Flatten All Layers

Figure 17-4:
The Contact
Sheet
dialog box
presents
options for
size and
layout
of your
thumbnails.

Thumbnails
Place: across first
Columns: 5   Width: 1.584   inches
Rows: 6   Height: 1.223   inches

☑ Use Filename As Caption
Font: Arial   Font Size: 12 pt

7. **Specify the Font and Font Size.**

8. **Press Enter (Return on a Mac) or click OK.**

   An automated process opens, copies, pastes, resizes, and positions each file. When the process is complete, you should see a file similar to the one in Figure 17-5.

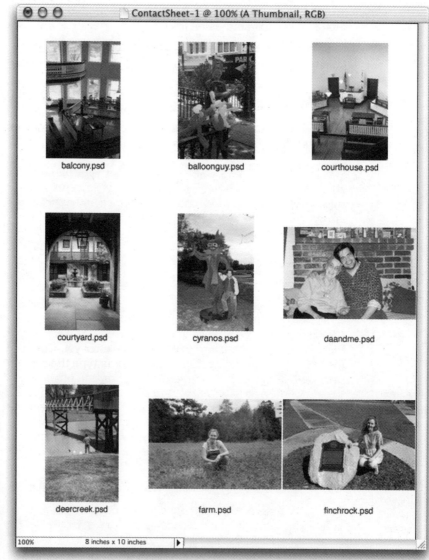

○ ○ ○   ContactSheet-1 @ 100% (A Thumbnail, RGB)

balcony.psd   balloonguy.psd   courthouse.psd

courtyard.psd   cyranos.psd   daandme.psd

deercreek.psd   farm.psd   finchrock.psd

100%   8 inches x 10 inches   ▶

Figure 17-5:
Contact sheets can provide a good method for cataloging a large quantity of images.

Creating and Printing a Picture Package

Another feature that may come in handy is Picture Package. This command has been greatly improved for Elements 2.0: It now lets you fill a page with multiple copies of *multiple* images, whereas you were limited to one image in version 1.0. The images are scaled to common print sizes, such as 5 x 7, 4 x 5, and wallet snapshots. Whether you're a professional photographer or just want to print some pictures of the kids for Grandma, this command does it all.

1. **Choose File➪Print Layouts➪Picture Package.**

2. **Locate the first image you want to include in your layout.**

   Choose Frontmost Document from the Use menu if you want to start your Picture Package layout with the frontmost open document. Otherwise, choose File and then click the Choose button to navigate to the desired file.

3. **Choose your desired Document settings.**

   Start by picking a Page Size appropriate for your paper and printer. Then choose a layout from the Layout menu. The large preview area on the right will give you a good idea of what you'll end up with. Choose an appropriate resolution and color mode (see Chapters 4 and 5 for more on these topics). As with the Contact Sheet feature, deselect Flatten All Layers if you want to be able to tweak your layout by hand after the Picture Package command is through.

4. **Choose a label for each image, if desired.**

   If you've entered a copyright, caption, author, or title for your images in the File➪File Info command, you can utilize that information in the Content menu here. But we'll bet you haven't. You can cancel out of the Picture Package command and do so, or better yet, use the name of the file or some Custom Text as a label. You can type the custom text in the provided field. Select a font, font size, color, and opacity level. Then decide where you want the text to appear within the image. Be warned that Centered does indeed put the text smack in the center of your image; one of the other choices will put it in a corner, which is probably more what you had in mind. You can also rotate the text as needed; a little trial and error will probably be required for you to figure out the appropriate settings.

5. **Select other images for inclusion in your Picture Package.**

   Right now, your layout utilizes only one image. However, you can click any image within that layout and replace it with a different file. Just use the resulting Select an Image File dialog box to locate the file, and it's done!

6. Press Enter (Return on a Mac) or click OK.

An automated process opens, copies, pastes, and positions each file. When the process is complete, you should see a file similar to the one in Figure 17-6.

Figure 17-6: The Picture Package command can give you instant octuplets.

Creating a Web Photo Gallery

The File⇨Create Web Photo Gallery command assembles a folder of images into a Web site, complete with HTML pages and JPEG images. You specify the name of your page, the size of the thumbnails, and the size and compression of the larger gallery images. Elements 2.0 gives you ten new styles from which to choose. Figure 17-7 shows Simple, one of the four remaining old styles, and the new Spot Light style is shown in Color Plate 22.

Here are the various options involved in creating a gallery:

- **Choose a style:** You can display the various styles via the tiny preview thumbnail in the dialog box.

- **Enter an e-mail address:** If you want a clickable e-mail address to appear on your Web page, enter it in the Email field.

- **Choose your preferred extension:** Unless you know you need a specific choice, .htm or .html should work fine for you.

Figure 17-7:
The Simple Web Photo Gallery style assembles your images into an index of thumbnails (rear) and a series of pages for the larger gallery images (front).

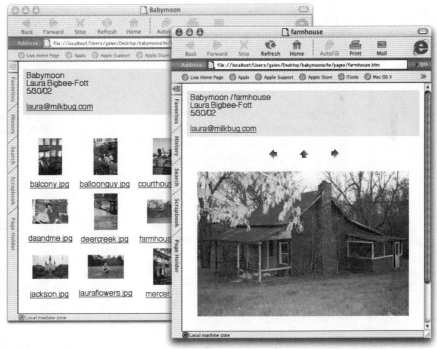

In the Folders section, you can specify the folder that contains the images you want to use in your online gallery, whether to use images in folders within your chosen folder, and a destination for your gallery files. If you're using the Table style, you can also select a background image to display behind your gallery.

Elements 2.0 gives you many more Options from which to choose, although not all gallery styles use all options. Here's a look at the five different categories:

- **Banner:** The Site Name will appear in the browser's title bar, as well as on the page itself. You can also enter the photographer's name, contact info, and a date if you want that information to appear on the site. And finally, you can specify a font and font size for this information.

- **Large Images:** These options establish the settings for the large images (the image that loads when the user clicks on a thumbnail). If you want to resize your images, you can quickly choose from Small, Medium, or Large settings, or enter your own pixel amount. The Constrain option determines how that pixel amount will be used. If you choose Width, all large images will have a width of the specified pixel amount; likewise for Height. Choosing Both makes Elements resize the larger of the height or width to the specified pixel amount for each image. You can set your desired JPEG compression level with the JPEG Quality menu or the File Size slider. Border size lets you specify the size of the border around each image, if you want one. You can specify a title for each image using the filename or information you've entered in the File⇨File Info command. And finally, you can choose a font and font size.

- **Thumbnails:** The options here mirror those found for the Large Images, with one exception. You can specify the number of Columns and Rows in which you want your thumbnails to be displayed. It's important to know the number of images you'll be using in order to determine the appropriate settings here.

- **Custom Colors:** This option enables you to choose colors for all the various components of your Web page. Note that if the Table Style is used, Elements will use an attractive textured background or your specified image for the site, and the Background and Banner color options won't apply.

- **Security:** These options mirror the Label options for the Picture Package command (see "Creating and Printing a Picture Package," earlier in this chapter). They embed text within the pixels of your image, thereby making people less likely to download the images from your site and use them for their own nefarious purposes.

  After you click OK, Elements does a little work on its own and then displays the Web page in your Web browser. Elements saves the HTML file and the JPEG images in your Destination folder.

Creating an Animated GIF

So you're tired of still, static images. You want excitement. Life. Movement. You're in luck, because Elements is not only an amazing tool for creating still images, but it's not too shabby at animation either! Animated GIFs have been enlivening Web pages for quite a few years now, and Elements' Save for Web command makes creating them a breeze.

Chapter 9 mentions that the Layers palette works similarly to traditional cel animation. Indeed, the Layers palette holds the key for creating animated GIFs as well. Elements programs an animated GIF to display the different layers of the Layers palette in sequence, from bottom to top. If you plan your file correctly, so that each layer represents a point in time immediately after the layer below it, it's easy to build an animation in this way.

We're going to explain this feature by walking you through the creation of an actual animated GIF. We're going to create the effect of the word "motion" moving across the document and stopping in the center. While we'll actually move the word across the image — or "frame," as they say in the movie biz — progressively layer by layer, we'll also add the Motion Blur filter to heighten the effect.

1. **Create a new document.**

   We set ours to 600 pixels Width, 100 pixels Height, and Contents White, but the 468 x 60 Web banner preset should work well for you too.

2. **Type the word "motion" in the image with the Horizontal Type tool.**

   Choose a highly contrasting color, such as black.

3. **Simplify the layer.**

   Choose Layer⇨Simplify Layer. This is necessary for when you apply the Motion Blur filter.

4. **Duplicate the layer seven times.**

   We dragged the motion layer onto the Create New Layer icon seven times, as shown in the top-left image in Figure 17-8.

5. **Apply the Motion Blur filter to the bottom motion layer.**

   The Motion Blur filter is in the Blur section of the Filters palette. Keep the Angle set to 0 degrees, and set the Distance to 70 pixels.

6. **Apply the Motion Blur filter to each of the motion layers except the top copy, decreasing the Distance setting as you move up the layer stack.**

   We gave the first copy a Distance setting of 60, the next copy up a Distance of 50, and so on. You can hit Ctrl+Alt+F (⌘+Opt+F on the Mac) to reapply the filter with access to the dialog box. Don't apply the filter to the top copy.

7. **Select the Move tool and move the bottom motion layer to the left until only the very rightmost portion of the blurred text is showing. Move the layer above it to the left, but not quite as far. Keep moving up the stack, moving the layers progressively less far to the left, so that the next-to-the-top layer is barely moved at all. Leave the top layer where it is.**

   After you select the Move tool, you can use the left arrow key to nudge the layer to the left without moving it vertically. You can also add the Shift key to the left arrow key to move the layer in ten-pixel increments. You'll probably need to turn on and off the visibility of layers to better see what you're doing.

8. **Choose File⇨Save for Web.**

   The Save for Web dialog box appears. Adjust your GIF settings as desired (see Chapter 6 for details). To fill the transparent areas in the motion layers with white, set the Matte color to White. Click the Animation check box; this gives you access to the Animation controls at the bottom right of the dialog box.

   If you want the animation to play over and over, click the Loop check box. The Frame Delay setting determines how long in seconds each frame displays on-screen before the next frame replaces it. For this animation, 0.1 or 0.2 is a good setting.

   You can view the frames by clicking the VCR-style buttons in the Animation section of the dialog box (see the bottom-left image in Figure 17-8). The far-left and far-right buttons take you to the beginning and end of the animation, respectively. The second button takes you back one frame, and the third button takes you forward one frame.

   If you want to preview the animation in real time, choose a browser in the Preview In menu to the left of the Animation controls. The browser will open up and play the animation. If you didn't set the animation to loop, you can click the Refresh or Reload button in the browser to watch it again.

9. **Click OK in the Save for Web dialog box.**

   The image on the right in Figure 17-8 shows the nine frames that make up the final animation.

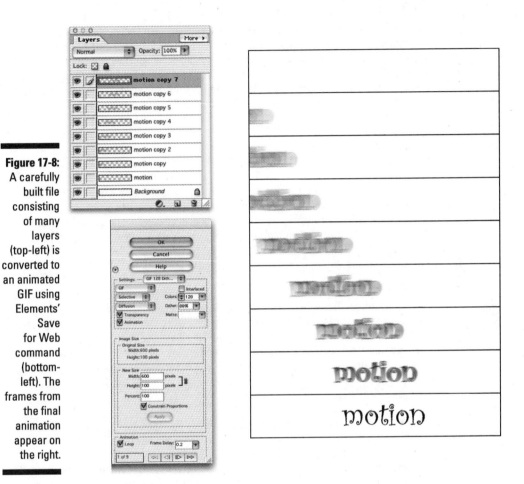

Figure 17-8: A carefully built file consisting of many layers (top-left) is converted to an animated GIF using Elements' Save for Web command (bottom-left). The frames from the final animation appear on the right.

Creating Panoramic Pictures with Photomerge

And last, but certainly not least, we come to the one feature that just might make long-time Photoshop users want to spend their hard-earned money to buy Elements: the Photomerge command. Photomerge is an exclusive feature of Elements. What Photomerge does is simple in premise: If you shoot a group of photos, each capturing a section of a larger scene, Photomerge can automatically stitch them together into one big panoramic shot. And we do mean automatic; if the images are ideally framed, there's almost no work necessary on your part.

The effectiveness of Photomerge depends hugely on the suitability of the photos you're trying to unite. Images need to overlap, but not too much; Adobe recommends an overlap of between 30 to 50 percent. However, too much overlap can cause just as many problems. The best advice is to over-shoot, taking more photos than you'll need, with large areas of overlap, and then removing the unnecessary ones after you're inside the Photomerge dialog box.

While Photomerge can correct for rotational problems between images, photo sequences shot with a tripod yield the best results. If your camera has automatic exposure compensation, your results will improve if you can turn it off. If you're shooting a building with an expanse of sky behind it, the visi-ble parts of the building will appear much darker in shots predominantly filled with sky. Photomerge can somewhat compensate for the difference in exposure, but turning off automatic exposure is still a good idea. And finally, remember that Photomerge compositions don't have to be exclusively hori-zontal in nature; vertical shots of tall objects such as buildings work well too.

It may be a good idea to use Image Size to reduce the pixel dimensions of the photos you'll be using before applying Photomerge. In version 1.0 of Elements, you could actually do this within Photomerge itself, although that capability has been removed for version 2.0. If you're trying to merge six photos taken in a horizontal line, and each image is 2,000 pixels wide, then your final panorama will be somewhere in the neighborhood of 8,000 pixels after the areas of overlap are considered. That's a very big image, and if you don't have enough RAM, Photomerge may not be able to handle it.

If you find this to be the case, choose Image⇨Resize⇨Image Size. Make sure both Constrain Proportions and Resample Image are checked, with Bicubic chosen in the Resample Image menu. Set a Width or Height menu to Percent, and enter a smaller percentage, such as 75 or even 50. Click OK. You may want to choose the Save As command and save the image in a different loca-tion if you want to keep your original higher-resolution image around. Repeat this process for all the images you want to merge, taking care to resize them all by the same percentage value.

Now then. Here's how to use the Photomerge command:

1. **Choose File⇨Create Photomerge.**

   The first Photomerge dialog box appears. Any opened images will already appear in the list.

2. **Click the Browse button to add additional photos you want to merge.**

   You can Shift+click images to select a group. When you've selected all the images you need, click Open. The images are added to the list. If you made any mistakes in selecting images, you can click on an image's name in the list and click the Remove button.

3. **When you've selected your images, click OK.**

The magic begins. You can watch Photomerge opening up each of your images, and then apparently combining them all into a very long document. What's it doing? Who knows? But it's fun to watch.

You may have to wait a few minutes, depending on the number and size of the images involved, but eventually the main Photomerge dialog box opens, as seen in Figure 17-9. You'll see Elements' best effort at assembling the photos in the large window. If it's encountered problems and can't even guess where to place some of the images, those will be in the long horizontal box at the top of the window.

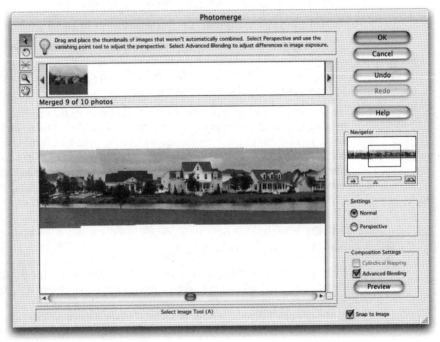

Figure 17-9: The workspace of the Photomerge command gives you lots of ways to tweak the construction of your panoramic shot.

Photomerge has a Navigator window very similar to Elements' Navigator palette, which lets you zoom in and out on your image by clicking the buttons on either side of the slider or by dragging the slider itself. You can also reposition the view box to center in on the portion of the composition you need to see. The Move View tool (in the upper-left grouping of tools) doesn't need to be fingerprinted for us to know that it's our old buddy the Hand tool in disguise; you can even type (H) to switch to it or hold down the spacebar to temporarily access it, and use it to drag the composition within the large window. The Zoom tool (Z) is also available for your zooming pleasure. And don't forget the new Undo and Redo buttons, giving you greater flexibility as you work.

4. **If there are images in the top portion of the dialog box that you want to try to place into the composition, click on them with the default Select Image tool (A) and drag them into the large window.**

   As you drag, the image will turn translucent so that it's easier to see how it might overlap with the other images. The Snap to Image check box can also be deselected if you don't want Photomerge to try to help you place the image by "snapping" it to areas of similar pixel content. You can also rearrange images within the large window with the Select Image tool, in case Photomerge didn't do such a good job of placing them to begin with. If an image you're trying to place needs to be rotated, click the Rotate Image tool (second from the top in the upper-left grouping of tools) or type (R) and drag to rotate the image.

5. **Adjust the perspective of the composition if desired.**

   Adjusting perspective can help solve distortion problems within your composition. The wider your composition is, the more dramatic these problems can be. However, the composition can also be too wide for perspective correction to be effective.

   To adjust the perspective, first select the Perspective radio button in the Settings section of the dialog box. Then select the Set Vanishing Point tool (third from the top in the upper-left grouping of tools) or type (V), and click an image in your composition. You will typically want to click the centermost image. If you're having trouble telling where one image stops and the next one starts, hold down the Alt key (the Option key on the Mac). A red outline will appear around the border of each image as you pass over it with the tool; however, the image containing the vanishing point will have a light blue border instead of a red one.

6. **Adjust the Composition Settings.**

   One problem that Perspective can introduce to your composition is the "bow tie" effect, where the overall composition is stretched tall on the edges and squeezed in the middle. When available, turning on Cylindrical Mapping can help untie the "bow tie" effect. Advanced Blending helps correct problems resulting from different exposures in adjacent images. The effects of the Composition Settings are only visible in Preview mode; click the Preview button to see the Cylindrical Mapping and Advanced Blending. Click Exit Preview to leave the preview.

7. **When you're satisfied with your settings, click OK.**

   Elements will work a little more magic, and then your finished panorama will appear on-screen. You'll probably want to crop the image to eliminate areas where the transparency shows around the stitched photos.

Although it's neat that Elements can automatically construct a panoramic image from a series of individual images, with almost no work on your part whatsoever, why can't it also perform the necessary cropping automatically? Gee, what a slacker.

Part V
The Part of Tens

"Why don't you try blurring the brimstone and then putting a nice glow effect around the hellfire."

In this part . . .

. . . we say goodbye, but not before we take a last, loving look at Photoshop Elements 2.0 from a different angle. You've made it this far with us, as we've painstakingly sifted through the enormous mountain of Elements features and functions. You've gone from "What's a pixel?" to creating animated GIFs to liven up your Web site. Just getting through each tool and command has taken us a few hundred pages (sixteen of them in color), but we've done it. So what's left?

We start this final part with a chapter on ten important techniques to remember, all of them centering on easily forgotten keyboard shortcuts. From there, we wrap up the book with ten things you *can't* do with Elements, but you can do with Elements' almighty ancestor, Adobe Photoshop.

Catch the common thread? Both of the following chapters center around the number ten. Hence the title of this part of the book: The Part of Tens. Why tens? Well, we could tell you tales of Little Indians, fingers and toes, or Woodmen (okay, we guess that last one doesn't really count), but those would be nothing more than tales. The Part of Tens is the Part of Tens because it's a ...*For Dummies* tradition, that's why. And to break with tradition, we'd have to be Dummies indeed.

Chapter 18

Ten Shortcuts to Commit to Long-Term Memory

● ●

In This Chapter

▶ Hiding Selection Outlines

▶ Hiding the Toolbox and palettes

▶ Changing an option box value

▶ Scrolling and zooming

▶ Changing the brush size

▶ Creating straight lines

▶ Adding to, subtracting from, and reselecting selection outlines

▶ Moving, nudging, and cloning

▶ Filling a selection

▶ Stepping through the History palette

● ●

*P*rofessor, politician, and Pulitzer Prize-winning author Odell Shepard once said, "Memory is what makes you wonder what you've forgotten." No doubt Odell — or Odie, as his friends called him — was talking about that feeling you get (usually when you're in bed, trying to sleep, or when you're on the way home from work and it's too late to turn back) that you've forgotten something that's pretty much going to send your life spinning into a state of absolute chaos. This feeling is commonly known as the Odie Syndrome.

Well, we can't help you with every aspect of your life, but we can help you with Photoshop Elements. Suppose, for example, that you wake up at 2 a.m. with the dreaded suspicion that you've forgotten an important Elements shortcut. You'd just have to give up on your technological pursuits and take up beet farming. But thanks to this chapter, people like you can live happy and productive lives again because these pages contain the most important Elements shortcuts. A few minutes of reading will restore order in your life.

The following tips don't begin to address all the many Elements shortcuts. For some additional timesavers, be sure to check out (or rip out) the Cheat Sheet at the front of this book.

Hiding Selection Outlines

Ctrl+H (⌘+H on the Mac)

After you've selected part of your image, this shortcut makes those distracting marching ants turn temporarily invisible, making it much easier to see what's going on in your image. Don't confuse this with deselecting your selection; with the ants hidden, you can still edit only the part of your image that's selected. This is probably the most frequently used shortcut of all; we're elated that Adobe included it in Elements 2.0.

Mac OS X users need to be aware of a setting located in Photoshop Elements⇨Preferences⇨General. When the Use System Shortcut Keys option is active, it actually changes the ant-hiding keyboard shortcut. With the release of OS X, Apple made ⌘+H a system-wide shortcut for hiding the active application, whatever it might be. Trouble is, this conflicts with Adobe's long-standing Photoshop keyboard shortcut for hiding selection outlines. Adobe decided to override Apple on this, and take ⌘+H for its own ant-hiding purposes, assigning ⌘+Control+H to hiding Photoshop and Elements. However, the Use System Shortcut Keys preference reverses this; if you select this preference option, then ⌘+H will hide Elements, and ⌘+Control+H will hide the marching ants.

Displaying and Hiding the Toolbox and Palettes

Tab

Just press the Tab key. The Toolbox, the Options bar, the Shortcuts bar, all the palettes, and the Status bar on the PC disappear, leaving just you and the image. To bring everything back, press Tab again. To make the Toolbox, Options bar, Shortcuts bar, Status bar, and palettes flash crazily on-screen and off, press Tab over and over again until your finger gets numb. It's not clear why you'd want to do this, but we like to spell out all the options.

If you want to hide the palettes but keep everything else visible, by the way, press Shift+Tab. Press Shift+Tab again to bring the palettes back.

If you have a dialog box open or an option in the Options bar active, Tab and Shift+Tab take you to the next option box or move you back one option box, respectively. But after you close the dialog box or deactivate the option, Tab and Shift+Tab control your palettes and Toolbox once again.

The F keys

Press F5 to display File Browser, F6 for the How To palette, F7 for the Filters palette, F8 for the Effects palette, F9 for the Layer Styles palette, F10 for the Undo History palette, F11 for the Layers palette, and F12 for the Hints palette.

Changing an Option Box Value

Up arrow, down arrow

Activate the option box and use the up or down arrow key to raise or lower the value by 1. Press Shift+↑ or Shift+↓ to raise or lower the value by 10, respectively. Then press Enter (Return on a Mac) again to accept the new value.

Scrolling and Zooming

Spacebar

Press the spacebar to temporarily access the Hand tool. As long as the spacebar is down, the Hand tool is available. Spacebar+drag to scroll the image.

Ctrl+spacebar and Alt+spacebar (⌘+spacebar and Option+spacebar on a Mac)

To get to the Zoom In cursor, press Ctrl+spacebar (⌘+spacebar on a Mac). Pressing Alt+spacebar (Option+spacebar on a Mac) gets you the Zoom Out cursor. This means that you can magnify the image at any time by Ctrl+spacebar+clicking (⌘+spacebar+clicking on a Mac). To zoom out, Alt+spacebar+click (Option+spacebar+click on a Mac). You can also Ctrl+spacebar+drag (⌘+spacebar+drag on a Mac) to marquee an area and magnify it so that it takes up the entire image window.

Ctrl++ (plus) and Ctrl+− (minus) (⌘++ and ⌘+− on a Mac)

Another way to magnify or reduce the image is to press Ctrl++ (plus sign) (⌘++ (plus sign) on a Mac) to zoom in or Ctrl+− (minus sign) (⌘+− (minus sign) on a Mac) to zoom out.

Double-click the Hand tool icon

To zoom the image so that you can see the whole thing on your monitor, double-click the Hand tool icon in the Toolbox or press Ctrl+0 (zero) (⌘+0 on a Mac).

Double-click the Zoom tool icon

To restore the image to the 100% (Actual Pixels) zoom factor, double-click the Zoom tool icon or press Ctrl+Alt+0 (zero) (⌘+Option+0 on a Mac).

Shift+Enter (Shift+Return on a Mac)

When you change the zoom factor by using the Magnification box in the Status bar, press Shift+Enter (Shift+Return on a Mac) instead of Enter (Return on a Mac) after you enter a new zoom value. That way, the option box remains active after Elements zooms your image. If you need to further magnify or reduce your image, just enter a new zoom value from the keyboard. When you have the image at the magnification you want, press Enter (Return on a Mac) to finalize things.

This trick also works when you're using the Magnification box in the Navigator palette.

Changing the Brush Size

Left bracket ([)

Press [(left bracket) to reduce the brush size in the following increments: 1 pixel increments to a size 10 pixel brush, 10 pixels increment to a size 100 pixel brush, 25 pixels to a size 200 pixel brush, 50 pixels to a size 300 pixel brush, and 100 pixels to a size 2500 pixel brush.

Right bracket (])

Press] (right bracket) to increase the brush size by the same increments listed in the preceding "Left bracket ([)" section.

Shift+[and Shift+]

For the round and fuzzy round brushes, Shift+[(left bracket) reduces the hardness of a brush in 25 percent increments. Shift+] (right bracket) increases the hardness in 25 percent increments.

Creating Straight Lines

Shift+click

To create a straight line with any of the painting or editing tools, click at one end of the line and Shift+click at the other. Elements connects the two points with a straight line.

Click with Polygonal Lasso and Alt+click (Option+click on a Mac) with regular Lasso and Magnetic Lasso

The Polygonal Lasso creates straight-sided selections; you just click to set the first point in your selection and keep clicking to create additional points.

When working with the regular Lasso tool, you can temporarily switch to the Polygonal Lasso by Alt+clicking (Option+clicking on a Mac). Alt+click (Option+click on a Mac) to set the first point in the selection and keep Alt+clicking (Option+clicking on a Mac) until you finish drawing the desired outline.

When working with the Magnetic Lasso, press Alt (Option on a Mac) and click with the mouse to get the Polygonal Lasso. Release the Alt key (Option key on a Mac) and drag momentarily to reset to the Magnetic Lasso.

However, don't use this approach when you want to add to or subtract from an existing selection. When you have an active selection, pressing Alt (Option on a Mac) subtracts from the selection instead of switching you between lasso tools. So use the actual Polygonal Lasso tool to add or subtract straight-sided areas from a selection.

Adding to, Subtracting from, and Reselecting Selection Outlines

Shift+drag and Shift+click

To select an additional area of your image without deselecting the part that is currently selected, Shift+drag around the new area with a lasso or marquee tool or Shift+click with the Magic Wand.

Alt+drag and Alt+click (Option+drag and Option+click on a Mac)

To deselect an area of the selection, Alt+drag (Option+drag on a Mac) around it with a lasso or marquee tool or Alt+click (Option+click on a Mac) with the Magic Wand.

Shift+Alt+drag and Shift+Alt+click (Shift+Option+drag and Shift+Option+click on a Mac)

To retain the intersection of the existing selection and the new outline you draw with a lasso or marquee tool, Shift+Alt+drag (Shift+Option+drag on a Mac) with the tool. To retain an area of continuous color inside a selection, Shift+Alt+click (Shift+Option+click on a Mac) with the Magic Wand.

Ctrl+Shift+D (⌘+Shift+D on a Mac)

To reselect your last selection, press Ctrl+Shift+D (⌘+Shift+D on a Mac).

Moving, Nudging, and Cloning

Ctrl (⌘ on a Mac)

To move selections and layers, use the Move tool. To temporarily access the Move tool when any tool is active, press and hold Ctrl (⌘ on a Mac). This shortcut doesn't work with the Hand tool or any of the Shape tools.

Arrow

To nudge a selection one pixel, press one of the arrow keys with the Move tool selected or press Ctrl (⌘ on a Mac) and an arrow key with any tool except the Hand or Shape tools.

Shift+arrow

To nudge a selection 10 pixels, select the Move tool and press Shift with an arrow key. Or select any tool but the Hand or Shape tools and press Ctrl+Shift (⌘+Shift on a Mac) with an arrow key.

Alt+drag, Alt+arrow, and Shift+Alt+arrow (Option+drag, Option+arrow, and Shift+Option+arrow on a Mac)

To clone a selection and move the clone, Alt+drag (Option+drag on a Mac) the selection with the Move tool. You can also press Alt (Option on a Mac) with an arrow key to clone a selection and nudge it one pixel. Press Shift+Alt+arrow key (Shift+Option+arrow key on a Mac) to clone and nudge 10 pixels.

With any tool other than — yes, you guessed it — the Hand or Shape tools, you can accomplish the same cloning feats by pressing and holding the Ctrl key (⌘ on a Mac) with the other keys. Pressing Ctrl (⌘ on a Mac) temporarily accesses the Move tool, remember?

Drag with a selection tool

To move a selection outline without moving anything inside the selection, just drag it with a marquee tool, lasso tool, or the Magic Wand. You can also press the arrow key or Shift+arrow key to nudge the selection outline in 1-pixel and 10-pixel increments, respectively. This works with any tool except the Move and Crop tools.

Ctrl (⌘) with a Shape tool

Pressing Ctrl (⌘ on a Mac) with any of the Shape tools brings up the Shape Selection tool, letting you quickly move shapes and lines.

Filling a Selection

Ctrl+Backspace (⌘+Delete on a Mac)

To fill a selection with the background color, press Ctrl+Backspace (⌘+Delete on a Mac). If the selection exists on the background layer, you can also press just Backspace (Delete on a Mac) to accomplish the same thing. However, if the selection is on a layer or is floating on the background layer, pressing Backspace (Delete on a Mac) wipes out the selection instead of filling it. So, pressing Ctrl+Backspace (⌘+Delete on a Mac) instead of Backspace (Delete on a Mac) to fill your selections is a good idea.

Alt+Backspace (Option+Delete on a Mac)

To fill any selection with the foreground color, press Alt+Backspace (Option+Delete on a Mac).

Shift+Backspace (Shift+Delete on a Mac)

Press Shift+Backspace (Shift+Delete on a Mac) to bring up the Fill dialog box, which lets you fill a selection with all kinds of stuff.

Stepping through the History Palette

Ctrl+Z and Ctrl+Y (⌘+Z and ⌘+Y on a Mac)

To step backward one History state at a time, press Ctrl+Z (⌘+Z on a Mac). To step forward one state at a time, press Ctrl+Y (⌘+Y on a Mac). You can change these keyboard equivalents via the General panel of the Preferences.

Chapter 19

Ten Reasons You Might Possibly Want to Upgrade to Photoshop One Day

. . . .

In This Chapter

▶ The Healing Brush

▶ Viewing channels

▶ Using CMYK color mode

▶ The Brushes palette

▶ Drawing paths

▶ Correcting with Curves

▶ Recording Actions

▶ Painting from the History palette

▶ Adding annotations

▶ Jumping over to ImageReady

. . . .

*B*y this late stage in the book, we'd certainly like to think you're so pleased with Photoshop Elements — and your newfound skills in using it — that the thought of all other image editing applications has completely faded from your memory. But there is one image editor that can probably never be driven from your mind by Photoshop Elements — and that's Photoshop itself. We've already told you that, in Elements, you've got the majority of Photoshop's power for a tiny fraction of its price. But still, you could be wondering . . . "What exactly am I missing?"

That's the purpose of this chapter: to give you a good idea of how the power of Elements is extended in Photoshop. This chapter is by no means designed to make you want to spend hundreds of dollars on new software. You've got a great thing in Elements, and unless you plan on making a living creating graphics, Elements is probably the only program you'll ever need. But Photoshop does have some amazing and useful features, and we thought you might be curious about them. So after a good deal of deliberation, we've singled out ten interesting, cool Photoshop features that are missing in Elements.

Now, you'll notice that the word "upgrade" appears in the title of this chapter. It's not a well-known fact, but you can, in fact, upgrade from Elements to Photoshop. The upgrade costs roughly the price of Photoshop minus the price of Elements, and it's available directly from Adobe only. You can call (800) 492-3623 for details if you're interested.

So, without further palaver, here are the Ten Reasons You Might Possibly Want to Upgrade to Photoshop One Day.

The Healing Brush

We'll just bet that one of your favorite Elements tools is the Clone Stamp. When it comes to eradicating bits of gunk that got scanned in along with your image, or erasing wrinkles and zits from your loved ones' faces, nothing can beat that good ol' Clone Stamp, right? Well, until Photoshop 7 came along, we'd answer that with an assertive "Right!" But Photoshop 7 has the new Healing Brush (seen in Figure 19-1), and, frankly, it out-clone-stamps the Clone Stamp.

The technology behind the tool is actually quite different, although the tool operates almost identically to the Clone Stamp. You Alt- or Option-click to set a source point, and then start clicking or dragging away, fixing imperfections. The catch is that you don't really have to worry about finding an exact color match between your cloning source and the spot you want to clone over. The Healing Brush samples the image texture from the source, rather than the exact pixels. The end result is one of the most intuitive tools we've ever encountered. The Healing Brush just seems to *know* what you're trying to do, and does it without a fuss. It's amazing. It's a miracle.

It just *knows*.

Healing Brush tool

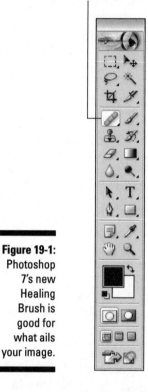

Figure 19-1:
Photoshop
7's new
Healing
Brush is
good for
what ails
your image.

The Channels Palette

We've talked about color channels in this book, but when using Photoshop Elements, you have to more or less take our word that they exist. Channels do pop up in a couple of different commands, such as Levels and Histogram, but by and large they are a phantom presence. Not so in Photoshop; there's actually a Channels palette in Photoshop, which lets you view and edit each color channel individually. You also can directly edit *alpha channels,* which control transparency in images. The fact that channels are a tangible, easily viewable presence in Photoshop makes it much easier to be in complete control of every pixel in your images. Figure 19-2 features the Channels palette showing off another Top Ten Photoshop feature.

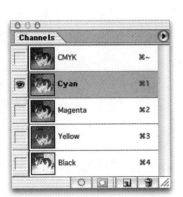

CMYK Color Mode

Just as RGB color mode rules when viewing images on-screen, CMYK color mode rules on paper. As Color Plate 5-2 illustrates, cyan (C), magenta (M), and yellow (Y) inks absorb different portions of the spectrum of light and bounce back other portions to your eyes. Black ink (K) is also added because in the imperfect real world, cyan, magenta, and yellow inks combine to produce a muddy brown, not black. Because Photoshop is a vital tool for preparing images for print, Adobe lets you work directly with your images in CMYK color mode, as shown in Figure 19-2. Combine the CMYK mode with Photoshop's advanced color management capabilities, and it becomes a lot easier to ensure that a fussy client's teal and mauve-colored logo will be the precise shades of teal and mauve when it comes back from the printer.

The Brushes Palette

Brushes also got a major upgrade with Photoshop 7, and although some of that has trickled down into Elements 2.0, Photoshop's Brushes palette gives you incredible control over brushes. As shown in Figure 19-3, the Brushes palette gives you advanced control over features such as Scattering, Texture, Jitter, and Noise. Elements is generous where brushes are concerned, but as is frequently the case, Photoshop gives you more power and control.

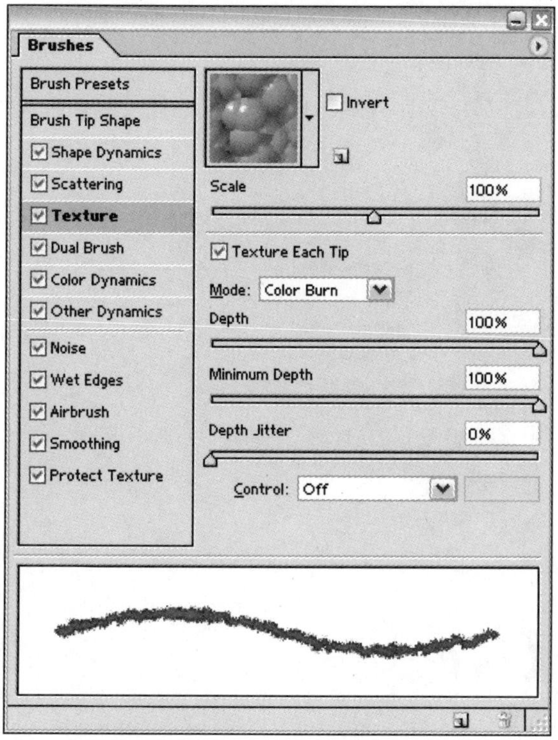

Figure 19-3: The Brushes palette lets you tweak your custom brushes to suit your whim.

Following the Paths

Elements gives you a small sampling of Paths with the Shape tools (see Chapter 14). However, Photoshop gives you a host of tools for drawing your own vector-based paths, as seen in Figure 19-4. Photoshop uses *bezier* tools for drawing paths, which enable you create shapes by clicking anchor points and dragging control handles. It takes a while to master the bezier tools, but after you do, you can draw any shape imaginable. After you've drawn a path, you can then convert it into a selection or manage it with the Paths palette.

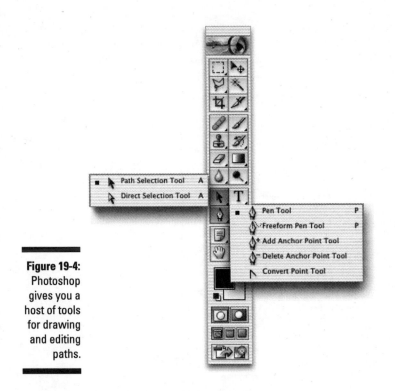

Figure 19-4:
Photoshop
gives you a
host of tools
for drawing
and editing
paths.

Eyeing Those Curves

If you thought Levels was an intimidating command, get a load of Curves! True, the Curves command makes using Levels seem positively intuitive, but it can accomplish things that Levels simply can't. By clicking to add points to a line and dragging the points around the graph shown in Figure 19-5, you create a curve that can be used to give you unparalleled control over the brightness levels in your image.

Par for the course, Elements gives you just a tiny taste of Curves in the Adjust Backlighting and Fill Flash commands. Although these commands are models of simplicity, they do perform Curves-like image correction, letting you bring out details at one end of the brightness spectrum without completely wiping out details at the other end.

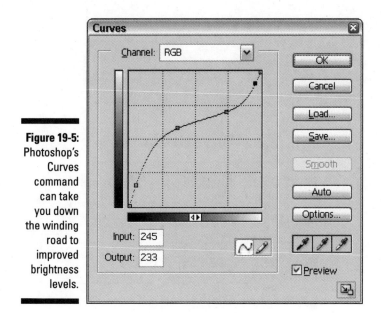

Figure 19-5:
Photoshop's
Curves
command
can take
you down
the winding
road to
improved
brightness
levels.

Lights . . . Camera . . . Actions

If you think Elements' Batch Processing feature (see Chapter 17) is the coolest thing since sliced bread, then Photoshop's Actions are definitely for you. Batch Processing lets you take a bunch of files and automatically convert them so they have the same file type, image size, resolution, and naming convention. Actions let you take a bunch of files and do almost *anything* to them. Just set up a new Action, click the Record button in the Actions palette (see Figure 19-6), and then go to town on your image. You can change the image size, apply filters, make selections and fill them, create text layers — almost any operation you can perform in Photoshop, you can record with the Actions palette. And from there, you can perform that sequence of commands on another image with a click of the Play button.

Photoshop also comes with prerecorded Actions — but that's really no big deal, because Elements has prerecorded Actions too. "How can Elements have prerecorded Actions when it doesn't have an Actions palette?" we hear you ask. Well, Elements' Effects are actually nothing more than a set of prerecorded Actions given a new name and a nice tidy palette to live in. Of course, you can't record your own Effects, but they should give you some idea of the awesome time-saving powers of Actions.

- ▼ 📁 Default Actions.atn
- ▶ Vignette (selection)
- ▶ Frame Channel - 50 pixel
- ▶ Wood Frame - 50 pixel
- ▶ Cast Shadow (type)
- ▶ Water Reflection (type)
- ▶ Custom RGB to Grayscale
- ▶ Molten Lead
- ▶ Make Clip Path (selectio...
- ▶ Sepia Toning (layer)

Figure 19-6:
The VCR-style controls at the bottom of Photoshop's Actions palette let you record and play back a sequence of image-editing operations.

Being an Art Historian

Whereas Elements' History palette lets you travel back in time and reverse mistakes, Photoshop's History palette also gives you the option of sending only *portions* of your image backward in time. The History Brush (see Figure 19-7) lets you paint from a previous History state of your image onto the current state. You could, for instance, apply an artistic filter to your image and then paint from the previous nonfiltered state of your image onto the filtered state, in effect erasing the filter from wherever you paint. Likewise, the Art History Brush (see Figure 19-7) packs the whirlin', twirlin' power of Elements' Impressionist Brush with the History Brush's time-traveling capabilities, making for a truly creative experience.

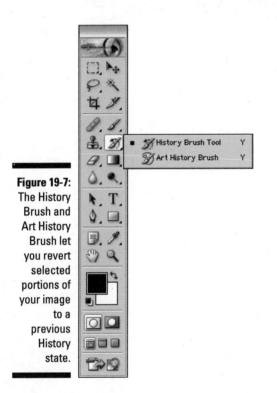

Figure 19-7: The History Brush and Art History Brush let you revert selected portions of your image to a previous History state.

Photoshop Speaks!

Okay, this one is truly weird. But if you're passing an image along to be reviewed by a coworker or client, it's understandable that you might want to also give them a note about the image, saying something like "Do you like this font?" or "Should I heal this zit off the model's nose?" The Notes tool lets you click and add a virtual yellow sticky note to your image. Of course, it doesn't actually meld into the pixels in the image, but it sort of floats above the surface as a little icon viewers can click to see your comments (see Figure 19-8).

But that's nothing compared to the Audio Annotation tool. Click the Audio Annotation tool on your image, and you actually get a chance to record a spoken message that is embedded into the image. The audio message appears on the image as a little speaker icon; you can double-click the icon to play the message back. Although this certainly could be a useful tool for passing comments along with an image, we'd like to propose an alternative use for this multimedia tool: recording mood music to be listened to while your work of art is viewed. Sure, you've done a great job of cleaning up that spaghetti picture for the Italian restaurant's ad campaign — but wouldn't it be even more effective if the restaurant owners could listen to *That's Amore* while they're reviewing your work on-screen? We think so.

Audio Annotation icon

Notes icon

Figure 19-8:
Audio Annotations and Notes mean that your Photoshop work doesn't necessarily have to speak for itself.

A Little Help to Get Your ImageReady

And finally, one last thing you'll get if you upgrade from Elements to Photoshop is . . . an additional application! Adobe ImageReady is installed along with Photoshop on your hard drive. ImageReady bears a very strong resemblance to Photoshop (see Figure 19-9) but is tailored specifically for creating Web graphics. In fact, Elements inherits its animated GIF-making capabilities (see Chapter 17) not from Photoshop, but from ImageReady. Other Web features that ImageReady can handle include roll-over Web buttons that change as a Web surfer's cursor moves over them and image maps that let you assign different Web links to various portions of a graphic.

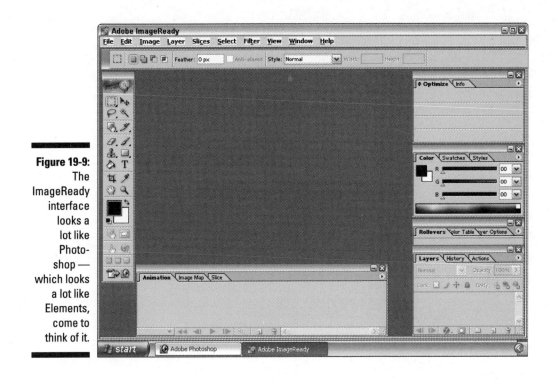

Figure 19-9:
The
ImageReady
interface
looks a
lot like
Photo-
shop —
which looks
a lot like
Elements,
come to
think of it.

Index

• R •

Radial Blur filter, 263
Radial Gradient tool, 309
radio buttons, dialog box element, 33, 35
radius, shape tool option, 297, 298
Radius values, Dust & Scratches filter, 193
RAM (random access memory), 29, 129
rasterize, 258, 328
Raw file format, 108
recipes, How To Palette, 22–23
Reconstruct tool, 271–272
Rectangle tool, 295–298
Rectangular Marquee tool, 142–143,
    149–150
Recycle Bin (Windows PC), thumbnail
    images, 44–45
Red Eye Brush tool, 200–201
Reflected Gradient tool, 310
Reflection tool, 271–272
resampling, 79
resolutions, 36, 65–70
Restore Down button, Windows PC, 29, 30
Return key, hard returns, 323
reversing operations, 125–131
RGB (red-green-blue) channels, 84–87
rotate cursor, crop boundary, 78
Rounded Rectangle tool, 295–298
rulers, 57–58

• S •

Sandpaper effect, 336
saturation, 247–249
Save As dialog box, 104–106
Save Selection dialog box, 158
scaling
  images when printing, 138
  layer styles, 256–257
  pasted images, 172–174
  transformations, 183
scanners, 19–20, 80–81
scars, Smudge tool, 206
Scitex CT file format, 108
Screen mode, 261, 288
screen pixels, versus image pixels, 63–64

scroll arrows, image window, 49, 50
scrollbars, image window, 49, 50
scrolling, shortcuts, 357–358
Search Results palette, 23–24
searches, Shortcuts bar entry, 23–24
Select Import Source window, accessing
    from Welcome screen, 19–20
Select⇨All (Ctrl+A/⌘+A) command, 157
Select⇨Delete Selection command, 159
Select⇨Deselect (Ctrl+D/⌘+D) command,
    157
Select⇨Feather (Ctrl+Alt+D/⌘+
    Option+D) command, 165, 189
Select⇨Grow command, 164
Select⇨Inverse (Ctrl+Shift+I/⌘+Shift+I)
    command, 165, 213
Select⇨Load Selection command, 158
Select⇨Modify command, 167
Select⇨Modify⇨Border command, 167
Select⇨Modify⇨Contract command, 167
Select⇨Modify⇨Expand command, 167
Select⇨Modify⇨Smooth command, 167
Select⇨Reselect (Ctrl+Shift+D/⌘+
    Shift+D) command, 157
Select⇨Save Selection command, 158
Select⇨Similar command, 164
Selection Brush tool, 1, 142–143, 155–156
selection outlines, 356, 359–361
selections
  active (marching ants), 142
  adding/subtracting from, 160–161
  anti-aliasing, 146–147
  aspect ratios, 150
  automatic functions, 164–167
  background fills, 304
  borders, 167
  circles, 149–150
  cloning, 171, 180–181
  constrains, 150
  cutting/pasting, 171
  deleting, 159
  deselecting everything, 157
  edge contrast, 148
  editing, 160–167
  Elliptical Marquee tool, 142–143, 149–151
  expanding/contracting, 167

• T •